Microwave
More from your Microwave

Compiled by Judith Ferguson, Jacqueline Bellefontaine
   and Nina Morgan
Recipes tested and prepared by Jacqueline Bellefontaine
Photographed by Peter Barry
Designed by Philip Clucas MSIAD

CLB 1962
This edition published in the United States 1989 by Gallery Books
An imprint of W.H. Smith Publishers, Inc.
112 Madison Avenue, New York, New York 10010
© 1989 Colour Library Books Ltd, Godalming, Surrey, England
Text filmsetting by Words and Spaces, Hampshire, England
Color separations by Hong Kong Graphic Arts Ltd, Hong Kong
Printed and bound by Graficromo, S.A., Spain
All rights reserved
ISBN 0 8317 6099 0

Acknowledgement
**The publishers wish to thank Samsung (UK) Ltd for the loan
of microwave ovens, Lakeland Plastics of Windermere,
Cumbria for providing cookware and accessories and
Corning Ltd for the supply of Pyrex and microwave
cookware. Thanks also to Peter and Jackie Petts of the
Herbary Prickwillow, Ely, for providing herb produce and
plants for use in the Herbs and Spices section of this book.**

Microwave
MORE FROM YOUR MICROWAVE

GALLERY BOOKS
An Imprint of W. H. Smith Publishers Inc.
112 Madison Avenue
New York City 10016

CONTENTS

INTRODUCTION

People are usually of two minds about microwave ovens: experienced cooks are sceptical while inexperienced cooks are mystified. Most people who don't own one think a microwave oven is an expensive luxury. Those of us who have one, though, would find it difficult to give it up. Great advances have been made in the design and capabilities of microwave ovens since the demand for them first began in the Sixties. But whether you are an advanced cook or just a beginner, it helps to understand what makes a microwave oven work.

The energy that makes fast cooking possible is comprised of electromagnetic waves converted from electricity. Microwaves are a type of high frequency radio wave. The waves are of short length, hence the name microwave.

Inside the oven is a magnetron, which converts ordinary electricity into microwaves. A wave guide channels the microwaves into the oven cavity, and a stirrer fan circulates them evenly. Microwaves are attracted to the particles of moisture that form part of any food. As the microwaves are absorbed, to a depth of about 1½-2 inches, they cause the water molecules in the food to vibrate about 2000 million times a second. This generates the heat that cooks the food. The heat reaches the center of the food by conduction, just as in ordinary cooking. However, this is accomplished much faster than in conventional cooking because no heat is generated until the waves are absorbed by the food. All the energy is concentrated on cooking the food and not on heating the oven itself or the baking dishes. Standing time is often necessary to allow the food to continue cooking after it is removed from the oven.

Most microwave ovens have an ON indicator light and a timer control. Some timer controls look like minute timers, while others are calibrated in seconds up to 50 seconds and minutes up to 30 minutes. This can vary slightly; some models have a 10 minute interval setting. Some ovens have a separate ON-OFF switch, while others switch on with the timer or power setting. Almost all have a bell or buzzer to signal the end of cooking time.

Cooking times will vary according to the wattage of the oven. The terms used for the different settings also vary from oven to oven.

thickest part of the food and the correct temperature set on the attached control. When that internal temperature is reached, the oven automatically turns off, or switches to a low setting to keep the food warm. Special microwave thermometers are also available to test internal temperature and can be used inside the oven. Conventional thermometers must never be used inside a microwave oven.

A cooking guide is a feature on some ovens, either integrated into the control panel or on the top or side of the oven housing. It is really a summary of the information found in the instruction and recipe booklet that accompanies every oven. However, it does act as a quick reference and so can be a time saver.

Power Setting Comparison Chart

	Other Terms and Wattages	Uses
Low	One or two, keep warm, 25%, simmer, defrost, 50-300 watts.	Keeping food warm. Softening butter, cream cheese and chocolate. Heating liquid to dissolve yeast. Gentle cooking.
Medium	Three-six, 40-75% medium low, medium high, stew, braise, roast, reheat, 400-500 watts.	Roasting meat and poultry. Stewing and braising less tender cuts of meat. Baking cakes and custards. Cooking hollandaise sauces.
High	Seven, full, roast, bake, normal, 100%, 550-700 watts	Quick cooking. Meats, fish, vegetables, cookies, pasta, rice, breads, pastry, desserts.

Weights and Measures

LIQUID			DRY	
Metric	Imperial	American	Metric	Imperial
30ml	1 fl oz	2 tbsps	30g	1oz
60ml	2 fl oz	4 tbsps/¼ cup	60g	2oz
90ml	3 fl oz	5 tbsps/⅓ cup	90g	3oz
140ml	¼ pint	½ cup	120g	4oz/¼ lb
280ml	½ pint	1 cup	180g	6oz
430ml	¾ pint	1½ cups	225g	8oz/½ lb
570ml	1 pint	2 cups/16 fl oz	250g	9oz
700ml	1¼ pints	2½ cups	340g	12oz/¾ lb
850ml	1½ pints	3 cups	400g	14oz
1 litre	1¾ pints	3½ cups	450g	1lb
1150ml	2 pints	4 cups	560g	1¼ lbs
			675g	1½ lbs
			790g	1¾ lbs
			900g	2lbs
			1kg	2¼ lbs

Altering Times

If your oven is not 700W, convert timings in the following way:

500W oven – Add 40 seconds for each minute stated in the recipe.

600W oven – Add 20 seconds for each minute stated in the recipe.

650W oven – Only a slight increase in the overall time is necessary.

Some ovens come equipped with a temperature probe which allows you to cook food according to its internal temperature instead of by time. It is most useful for roasting large cuts of meat. The probe needle is inserted into the

Turntables eliminate the need for rotating baking dishes during cooking, although when using a square loaf dish you may need to change its position from time to time anyway. Turntables are usually glass or ceramic and can be removed for easy cleaning. Of all the special features available in microwave ovens, turntables are one of the most useful.

Certain ovens have one or more shelves so that several dishes can be accommodated at once. Microwave energy is higher at the top of the oven than on the floor, and

Facing page: with the availability of so many different browning agents, there is never any need for microwaved food to appear anaemic and appetizing.

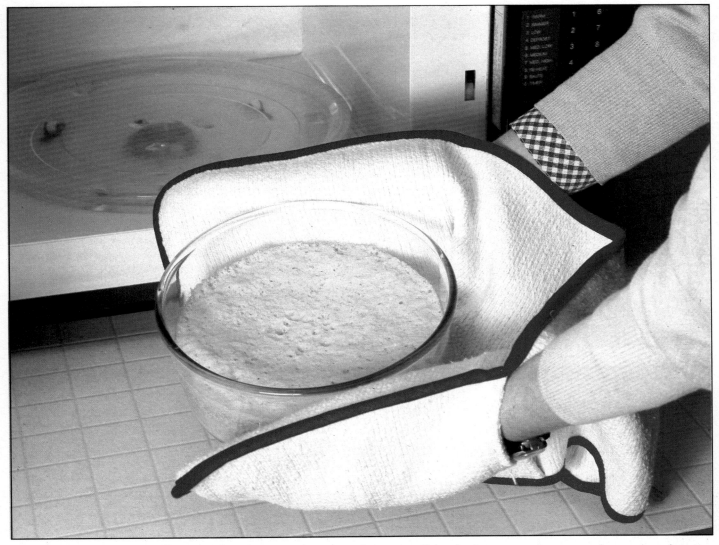

Facing page: a selection of materials suitable for wrapping or covering food, including a handy plastic cover with adjustable steam vent. This page: hot food heats up baking dishes, so always use oven gloves.

the more you cook at once the longer it all takes. However, these ovens accommodate larger baking dishes than those with turntables.

If you do a lot of entertaining, then an oven with a KEEP WARM setting is a good choice. These ovens have a very low power setting that can keep food warm, without further cooking, for up to one hour. If you want to program your oven like a computer, choose one with a memory control that can switch settings automatically during the cooking cycle.

Browning elements are now available in microwave ovens. They look and operate in much the same way as conventional electric broilers, and if you already have a broiler, you probably don't need a browning element. Some ovens allow the browning element to be used at the same time as the microwave setting, which is a plus.

Combination ovens seem to be the answer to the problem of browning in a microwave oven. While the power settings go by different names in different models, generally there is a setting for microwave cooking alone, a convection setting with conventional electric heat and a setting which combines the two for almost the speed of microwave cooking with the browning ability of convection heat. However, the wattage is usually lower than in standard microwave ovens, and so cooking time will be slightly longer.

On combination settings, use recipes developed for microwave ovens, but follow the instructions with your particular oven for times and settings. Some ovens have various temperature settings to choose from. Breads, poultry, meat and pastries brown beautifully in these ovens, and conventional baking dishes, even metal ones, can be used with a special insulating mat. Beware of certain plastics as they can melt in a combination oven.

Safety and Cleaning

One of the questions most commonly asked is "Are microwave ovens safe to use?". They are safe because they have safety features built into them, and they go through rigorous testing by the manufacturers and by independent agencies.

If you look at a number of microwave ovens you will see that the majority of them are lined with metal, and metal will not allow microwaves to pass through. The doors have special seals to keep the microwaves inside the oven and have cut-out devices to cut off microwave energy immediately the door is opened. There are no pans to upset, no open flames or hot elements and the interior of the oven stays cool enough to touch.

Although microwave ovens don't heat baking dishes, the heat generated by the cooking food does, so it is a good idea to use oven gloves or pot holders to remove dishes from the oven.

It is wise periodically to check the door of your oven to make sure it has not been bent. Check latches and hinges, too, to make sure thay are in good working order. Don't use baking dishes that are too large to allow the turntable to rotate freely; this can cause the motor to over-heat or cause dents in the oven sides and door, lowering efficiency and affecting safety of operation.

Microwave ovens **are cleaner and more** hygienic to cook with than conventional **gas and electric** ovens. Foods do not spatter as much and spills **do not burn**, so clean-up is faster. The turntables and shelves **can be** removed for easier cleaning. Use non-abrasive cleansers and scrubbers, and be sure to wipe up any residue so that it does not build up around the door seals. Faster cooking times and lower electricity consumption combine to make microwave ovens cheaper to run than conventional ovens, especially for cooking small amounts of food.

The best guide to how your own oven works and how to get the most from it is the manufacturer's instruction booklet, which you should read and understand before you begin, and refer back to often. There are some basic rules to remember, though, and as in conventional cooking most are common sense:

Quantity

Food quantities affect cooking times. Generally, if you double the quantity of a recipe, you need to increase the cooking time by about half as much again.

Density and Shape

The denser the food, the longer the cooking time. When cooking foods of various densities or shapes at the same time, place the thicker part of the food to the outside of the dish, thinner part toward the middle. Arrange pieces of food in a circle whenever possible, and in a round dish. If neither of these arrangements is possible, cover the thinner or less dense part of the food with foil for part of the cooking time.

Size

The smaller a piece of food the quicker it will cook. Pieces of food of the same kind and size will cook at the same rate. Add smaller or faster-cooking foods further along in the cooking cycle. If you have a choice of cooking heights, put food that is larger and can take more heat above food that is smaller and more delicate.

Covering

Most foods will cook, reheat or defrost better when covered. Use special covers that come with your cookware, or simply cover with plastic wrap. This covering must be pierced to release steam, otherwise it can balloon and possibly burst. Tight coverings can give foods a "steamed" taste. Wax paper or paper towels can also be used to keep in the heat and increase cooking efficiency.

There has been some question as to the safety of plastic wrap for use in microwave ovens. When exposed to heat, some of the plasticisers used in the manufacture of these wraps can transfer into the food. At present, brands of plastic wrap are on the market which are made in a different way, avoiding the use of harmful plasticisers, and which thus circumvent the problem.

Standing Time

Microwave recipes usually advise leaving food to stand for 2-10 minutes after removal from the oven. Slightly undercooking the food allows the residual heat to finish it off, and microwave recipes take this into consideration. In general, foods benefit from being covered during standing time.

Using the Right Equipment

The number of different baking dishes and the range of equipment for microwave cooking is vast. Explore cookware

Facing page: infusing, that is heating liquids almost to boiling point with flavoring ingredients and leaving them to stand before straining, improves flavor.

Equipment

Type	Uses	Special Instructions
Browning Dish	Chops, steaks, sausages, stir-frying, nuts, eggs.	Pre-heat to instructions.
Ceramic	Pies, cakes, quiches, casseroles, vegetables, desserts.	Use plastic wrap if no covers. Cook and serve in same dishes.
China	Reheating.	Plate meals in advance. Avoid china with gold or silver trim. Use cups for tea. Reheat soup.
Cooking Bags	Frozen food, reheating, fish, vegetables.	Pierce bag to release steam cut across top to open after cooking.
Corning Ware	Casseroles, pies, quiches, vegetables, desserts.	See ceramics.
Custard Cups	Poach eggs, bake custards, small cakes.	Do not use metal or painted cups.
Glass Measures	Heat liquids. Make sauces.	Use a large enough size to allow stirring and whisking.
Glass Dishes, Casseroles	See ceramic.	See ceramic. Wine glasses for warming only. Thin glass may crack.
Metal	Combination ovens only.	Use insulating mat according to oven instructions.
Paper Plates, Cups, Containers	Breads, rolls, cakes, beverages, use for defrosting and reheating.	Absorb moisture. Best used on defrost or medium settings.
Paper Towels	Cooking bacon. Defrosting and reheating bread, rolls, cakes, covering defrosting foods.	Absorb moisture and fat. Remove immediately from the food after cooking.
Muffin Pans	Egg poaching. Small cakes, custards.	Line with paper cases for cakes.
Plastic	Various uses – casseroles, freezer to oven. Good for reheating and defrosting.	Remove lids from plastic boxes before heating. Not suitable for some combination ovens. Foam containers only suitable for warming. Fatty or sugary foods can cause melting.
Plastic Wrap	Covering dishes.	Pierce to release steam. Do not stretch too tightly. Lift carefully to avoid steam.
Pottery	Cooking and reheating.	Some painted or glazed finishes unsuitable. Avoid metal trim.
Pyrex	See glass.	
Straw Baskets, Bamboo Steamer	Warm rolls, reheat vegetables.	Use for serving. Use only for warming or reheating.
Tupperware	See plastic.	
Waxed Paper	Covering, lining baking sheets.	Prevents spattering. Holds in heat.
Wood	Warming bread rolls.	Can warp or dry out if heated too long.

departments and find your own favorites. Follow your oven instruction booklet carefully since it will give you good advice on which cookware is best for your particular oven. In general, microwave energy penetrates rounded shapes particularly efficiently, so round dishes, oval dishes and ring molds work very well.

Browning dishes do work, and the results are impressive. There are several different designs, but all are treated with a special material that absorbs microwaves and becomes extremely hot. You can seal the surface of meat just as you would in a frying pan and some dishes have lids, allowing you to stew or braise in the same dish. Use oven gloves or pot holders to remove browning dishes from the oven, and set them on a heat-proof mat to protect work surfaces. The equipment chart lists the most common items and their main uses.

These pages: various stages in caramel making.

Mention should be made of the use of foil in microwave cooking. Some manufacturers do not recommend its use, so you must consult your instruction booklet. If you can use it you will find it helps protect the breast bone of poultry, thin ends of roasting joints, heads and tails of whole fish, tender parts of vegetables, in fact any part of the food that is likely to cook too quickly.

There are a number of basic techniques that, once mastered, can make food preparation faster and easier, with better finished results:

Softening, Melting and Infusing

Butter, margarine and shortening are high in fat so they readily attract microwave energy and soften and melt quickly. To soften, heat on MEDIUM – MEDIUM LOW for 10-50 seconds for ½ cup.

Mix softened butter or margarine with an equal amount of flour to form a thickening paste for sauces – *beurre manie* in French, kneaded butter in English. This can be refrigerated or frozen in small amounts for use whenever you need a thickening agent.

Softened butter can be mixed with herbs, garlic, anchovy paste, tomato paste and cheese, to name but a few ingredients, and used on bread, baked potatoes, vegetables, fish, meat and poultry. Mix butter with honey, jam or fruit purées to spread on bread or scones.

Softened butter, margarine or shortening creams faster and more easily for baking mixtures. It will be easier to incorporate the sugar to get a light fluffy mixture and a lighter result after baking.

Melt butter, margarine or shortening more quickly, with less chance of burning small amounts. 1 tbsp takes just 30-40 seconds to melt on HIGH.

Clarified butter is much easier to make in a microwave oven than by conventional means. 1 cup melts in 1¼-2 minutes on HIGH. The salt in the butter will immediately

Above left: a selection of microwave baking dishes. Above: melting chocolate. Facing page: to dissolve gelatine, soak in liquid and melt until clear.

rise to the surface and can be skimmed off. Allow the butter to stand 2 minutes to let the milk solids settle to the bottom and then carefully spoon off the butter oil. Use on fish, vegetables, to seal a pâté or for conventional sautéeing.

Browned butter, the classic French *beurre noisette*, is easy to make in a microwave oven. Heat 1 cup butter on HIGH for 5-6 minutes, stirring twice. The butter will turn golden brown and have a nutty flavor. Enhance it with lemon juice or a sprinkling of herbs.

Cheese melts and softens rapidly in a microwave oven, but because it has a high protein content, it can toughen and become stringy. A MEDIUM setting is best to melt cheese sprinkled on as a topping. For this purpose, try Emmental, Gruyère, mozzarella or mild Cheddar. Very hard cheeses and mature Cheddar become crisp when melted and will look curdled in a sauce.

When making a cheese sauce, add finely grated cheese to the hot mixture and stir. Cover tightly and set aside. The cheese will melt smoothly in the residual heat. Stir once more and serve.

Facing page: softening cream cheese, butter and honey or jam makes for easier measuring and mixing. This page: softening hard brown sugar with a slice of apple in a loosely sealed plastic bag.

Cream cheese, curd cheese and ricotta often need to be softened before use. 6 tbsps of these cheeses will soften in 30-60 seconds on MEDIUM. Be sure to remove cream cheese from its foil wrapper and gently mash this type of cheese with a fork as it softens.

Cheese tastes best served at room temperature, but if you forget to take it out of the refrigerator there is an instant remedy. Heat hard cheese, such as Cheddar, on MEDIUM LOW for 30-45 seconds and soft cheese, such as Brie, for 15-30 seconds.

Syrups such as molasses, corn syrup and honey are easier to measure when liquefied for a minute or two on HIGH. Some syrups, like pure maple syrup, will crystallize slightly after opening unless used quickly, but when melted on HIGH for 1-2 minutes will become clear again. Certain varieties of honey are naturally thick and crystalline. 2-3 minutes on

HIGH is enough to make them clear and liquid. Stir all syrups and honey while they are melting to ensure even heat.

Soften hard brown sugar by sprinkling lightly with water and adding a slice of apple to the sugar in a plastic bag. Tie loosely and microwave on HIGH for 30-60 seconds. Leave to stand 5 minutes. Check after 15 seconds for amounts under 1 cup.

Chocolate should be melted on a MEDIUM setting and stirred often. High temperatures can cause chocolate to crystallize and harden. There is no need to add water to chocolate when melting it as there is no chance of scorching in a microwave oven.

Combine chocolate and margarine or shortening, ½ tsp fat for every ½ oz chocolate, to melt for drizzling, making dessert or liqueur cups or painting onto leaves to use as decoration. The chocolate will be more liquid when warm, but will still solidify when cool.

To make chocolate curls, soften block chocolate on LOW for 30-60 seconds or until just barely warm. Turn the block over halfway through the time. Draw a swivel vegetable peeler across the surface towards you to form curls. Use to decorate cakes and desserts.

To melt gelatine, sprinkle 1 tbsp onto no less than 3 tbsps liquid in a small dish. Leave to stand 2-5 minutes to soften. Microwave on HIGH for 1-2 minutes or until liquid and clear. If the gelatine in a dessert, such as a cold souffle, sets before you want it to, melt it again in the oven for 30-60 seconds.

Jams and jellies melt on HIGH in about 30 seconds for

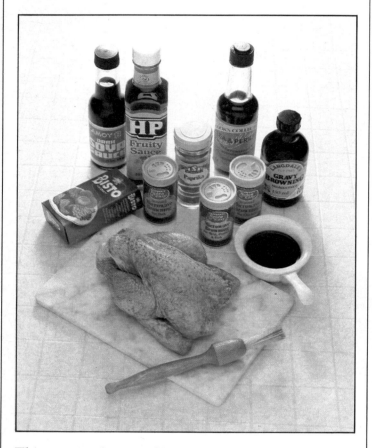

This page: a selection of browning agents that give appetizing color to meat and poultry. Facing page: toppings to give an appealing finish to baked goods.

2 tbsps. 1 cup will melt in 1½-2 minutes. Use as toppings for puddings, cakes or ice cream. Use as glazes for fruit tarts or even meat and poultry. Warm jam is also much easier to spread as a cake filling.

Soften peanut butter to make it easier to add to other ingredients for cake or biscuit recipes or simply to spread on bread.

Heat ice cream for about 30 seconds on MEDIUM to soften and make it easier to scoop to serve. To add flavorings to ice cream, scoop 4 cups into a large bowl and soften 30-60 seconds on MEDIUM, stirring well. Stir in toasted nuts, finely chopped chocolate, chopped fruit or liqueurs and

refreeze. Pack into decorative molds or even mixing bowls in several different layers to make bombes.

Sugar dissolves in water or other liquids easily without crystallizing. Double the quantity of liquid to sugar will make a simple syrup for poaching fruit. Equal measures of water and sugar cooked on HIGH for 10-12 minutes will caramelize. Do not allow the syrup to get too brown, though, as it continues to darken after it is removed from the oven.

Give cooking liquids more flavor by heating them nearly to the boiling point with flavoring ingredients and leaving them to infuse before straining to use.

For Bechamel sauce, use a slice of onion, a bay leaf, and a few black peppercorns in the milk.

Infuse whole coffee beans or vanilla pods in milk or cream for ice creams or mousses and custards.

Add citrus peel to liquids for poaching fish or for fruit and dessert sauces.

Browning, Basting and Topping

Use bastes or glazes that have soy sauce, Worcester sauce or gravy browning to give color to meat and poultry. The addition of marmalade, redcurrant jelly or honey to a glaze will help it cling to the food.

When using dry breadcrumbs or crushed cereals as a coating for meat, fish or poultry, dip or brush food with melted butter to help the coating stick. Toasted ground nuts also make a good coating for meat or poultry. Sprinkle the top of casseroles with breadcrumbs toasted in melted butter, crushed corn flakes or potato chips, grated cheese or simply paprika.

Add ingredients like nuts, cocoa, spices or herbs to pastry, or use whole-wheat flour.

Crushed cookies, bran, oatmeal, browned nuts, and streusel toppings are but a few ideas to give an appetizing appearance to microwave baked goods. Mix brown sugar and spices to sprinkle on as well. Colorful frostings or glazes are also an idea. There are also sprinkle-on microwave seasonings, which react with heat to give flavor as well as color to a whole range of foods.

Preserving and Pickling

Sterilize jars the easy way. Add about 2 tbsps water to clean jars or bottles. Heat on HIGH for 2-3 minutes and drain upside-down on paper towels. Metal lids and rubber seals, however, are best sterilized outside the microwave oven. Paraffin wax for sealing is impervious to microwaves, and so must be melted conventionally.

Whole preserved fruit and pickled vegetables cannot be heated long enough to kill bacteria so they must be stored in the refrigerator.

Should pectin be necessary to help jams set, it can be added at the same time as other ingredients.

Prepare flavored vinegars and oils by sterilizing attractive bottles and adding herbs, spices, garlic, onions, fruit or citrus peel. Pour over a good quality vinegar or oil and heat briefly to help the flavors infuse. Store in a cool place.

Microwave preserving is cleaner, cooler and quicker than by the conventional method, and you will have no sticky pots to wash. You can also make preserves and pickles in smaller quantities for more variety.

This page: cook tender vegetables directly on their serving dishes. Facing page: very little liquid is needed to plump dried fruit.

Fruit and Vegetable Cookery

Vegetables cook quickly in the microwave, and with very little water, so they retain their color, texture and nutrients. Usually, 4-6 tbsps of water is all that is necessary for 1lb. Frozen vegetables usually don't need water.

Cover dishes when cooking vegetables and always snip two steam holes in the plastic wrap. Whole vegetables, such as cauliflower or corn-on-the-cob, can be wrapped

Cooking Vegetables

Type	Quantity	Mins. on High	Mins. Stdg. Time
Artichokes	4	10-20	5
Asparagus	1lb	9-12	5
Eggplant	2 med.	7-10	5
Beans	1lb		
Green		8	3
Lima		10	3
Beets	2	10-12	3
Whole			
Broccoli	1lb	6-10	3
Brussels Sprouts	1lb	7-9	3-5
Cabbage	1lb		
Shredded		7-9	3
Quartered		9-12	5
Carrots	8oz		
Whole		18	6
Sliced		10	5
Cauliflower	1lb		
Whole		11-13	3
Florets		7-10	3
Chicory	4	5	3
Corn-on-the-Cob	2 ears	6-8	3
Zucchini	1lb	5	3
Fennel	1 bulb		
Sliced		2-8	3
Quartered		10-12	
Leeks, sliced	1lb	10-12	3
Mushrooms	8oz	2	3
Okra	8oz	4	3
Onions, small	8oz	7-8	3
Sliced	2	10	3
Parsnips	8oz	8-10	3
Peas, shelled	1lb	10-15	5
Pea pods	8oz	2-3	3
Peppers	2 sliced	3	3
Potatoes			
New	1lb	10-12	5
Baked	2	9-12	5
Boiled	1lb	6-7	5
Spinach	8oz	4-5	3
Turnips	8oz	12	3

completely in plastic wrap and cooked with no water. Vegetables cooked in their skins, such as potatoes, need no covering, but skins should be pierced several times with a fork to release steam.

Cut vegetables to an even size, or choose those of nearly the same size so they cook in the same length of time. Arrange tender portions of vegetables, such as the tips of asparagus spears or flower ends of broccoli, to the center of the dish wherever possible, since the microwave oven will begin cooking at the outer edge of the dish first.

Facing page: rehydrating dried pulses in a microwave oven cuts out the need for overnight soaking. This page: for microwave "stir-frying" use a browning dish.

Rearrange large vegetables or turn them over halfway through cooking time. Stir cut vegetables occasionally to ensure even cooking.

To blanch vegetables for freezing, cook as usual, but put immediately into cold water to stop cooking. Drain and

This page: heating citrus fruit in a microwave makes it possible to extract more juice. Facing page: "blanching" onions, nuts and tomatoes for easier peeling.

spread on paper towels to dry completely. Pack in freezer containers or boiling bags. Alternatively, spread vegetables out on baking trays and freeze, uncovered. Once solid, pack and freeze. This will keep large vegetables in individual pieces and small vegetables free-flowing. You can even blanch vegetables inside the boiling bags. When cooked, chill in cold water, pat the bag dry and freeze in the same bag.

Peel peaches and apricots easily by bringing water to the boil – 4 cups takes about 8-10 minutes – and dropping in a

few pieces of fruit at a time. Leave to stand 1-2 minutes, depending on the ripeness of the fruit. Transfer to cold water. The peel should come off easily.

Peel tomatoes in the same way. Pickling or button onions can be cooked briefly in boiling water – about 1 minute. The

These pages: to defrost frozen foods, microwave in the serving dish and stir to break up lumps and distribute heat evenly.

skins should come off easily, leaving the onions whole.

Get more juice from lemons, limes and oranges by heating 20-30 seconds on HIGH.

Slightly underripe avocados can be softened by the same method.

To plump up dried fruit, sprinkle with water and cover. Microwave on HIGH for 30-60 seconds, stirring occasionally. Leave to stand, covered, for 2-3 minutes. Substitute brandy or rum, lemon or orange juice for the water, if desired, and stir the fruit into ice creams, cake mixtures or sauces.

Eliminate overnight soaking for pulses with the microwave rehydrating method. Place dried peas, beans or lentils, covered with water, in a large bowl or casserole and cover tightly. Microwave for 8-10 minutes on HIGH, or until the water boils. Boil for 2 minutes more and leave to stand, covered, for 1 hour. Pulses will take almost as long to cook in a microwave oven as they do by conventional methods, but they do not become as starchy or mushy. Do make sure pulses are fully cooked; it is dangerous to eat them undercooked.

Rice and Pasta Cookery

Rice and pasta take nearly as long to cook in a microwave oven as they do on the stove top.

However, both pasta and rice cook without sticking together and without the chance of overcooking. This is because most of the actual cooking is accomplished during

Cooking Rice and Pasta

Type	Quantity	Water	Mins. on High	Mins. Stdg. Time
Brown Rice	1 cup	2 cups	20	5
White Rice (long grain)	1 cup	2 cups	10-12	5
Quick Cooking Rice	1 cup	1½ cups	6	5
Macaroni	3 cups	3½ cups	6	10
Quick Cooking Macaroni	3 cups	3½ cups	3	10
Spaghetti	8oz	3½ cups	6-10	10
Tagliatelle/Fettucine	8oz	3½ cups	5-9	10
Pasta Shapes	3 cups	3½ cups	6	10
Lasagne Ravioli Cannelloni	6oz-8oz	3½ cups	6	10

standing time. All kinds of rice and shapes of pasta benefit from being put into hot water with a pinch of salt and 1 tsp oil in a deep bowl. There is no need to cover the bowl during cooking, but, during standing time, a covering of some sort will help retain heat. Soak large pieces of pasta, such as lasagne or long spaghetti, in hot water to soften before cooking. This will ensure that they remain completely submerged throughout the cooking time. Rinse all shapes of pasta thoroughly in hot water to remove most of the starch.

Reheating and Defrosting

Most ovens incorporate an automatic defrosting control in their setting programs. If your oven does not have this facility, use the lowest temperature setting and employ an on/off technique. Turn the oven on for 30 seconds-1 minute and then let the food stand for a minute or two before repeating the process. This procedure allows the food to defrost evenly without starting to cook at the edges.

Above: special plate stands allow two servings to be reheated at the same time.

Always cover the food when defrosting or reheating. Plastic containers, plastic bags and freezer-to-table ware can be used to freeze and defrost food in.

Meals can be placed on paper or plastic trays and frozen. Cover with plastic wrap or wax paper.

Usually, foods are better defrosted first and cooked or reheated second. There are exceptions to this rule so be sure to check instructions on pre-packaged foods before proceeding. Food frozen in blocks should be broken up as it defrosts. Use a fork to tear out small shreds of ground beef from the main block as it defrosts. Remove defrosted pieces and continue with the remainder. Carefully ease pieces of vegetable or fruit out as they defrost.

When reheating foods in a sauce, stir occasionally to distribute heat evenly. Spread food out in an even layer for uniform heating. To tell if reheating is completed, touch the bottom of the plate or container. If it feels hot, then the food is ready. Foods can be arranged on plates in advance and reheated very successfully, an advantage when entertaining.

Give foods new life when reheating. Add Worcestershire or soy sauce to stews and sauces.

Pasta and rice reheat superbly without overcooking. Use this to your advantage to create almost instant meals. Toss pre-cooked pasta or rice in butter and add herbs or garlic and cheese. Pre-cook onions, mushrooms, peppers or other vegetables and add with ham, shrimp or other pre-cooked meat or fish.

Personalize convenience foods by adding other ingredients such as tomato paste, wine, herbs and spices before reheating.

Make stock in your microwave oven and then freeze it for instant use anytime. Stock can be frozen in large blocks for soups, or in ice cube trays to add just a small amount to sauces.

Egg Cookery

In microwave ovens, the yolk of an egg, which contains more fat, cooks before the white. For this reason, standing time is very important as it allows the white to finish cooking without toughening the yolk.

Eggs can be fried in a browning dish. Preheat the dish according to the manufacturer's instructions and melt butter or margarine or fry bacon first and use some of the fat. Break in two eggs and they will fry in about 15-30 seconds, with 2-3 minutes standing time.

Scrambled eggs are even easier and they are much lighter and fluffier than those conventionally cooked. Butter isn't necessary except for flavor, so the calorie conscious can leave it out. Eggs will scramble in about 1½ minutes. They will begin to set around the edge of the dish first, so occasional stirring is necessary for even cooking. Standing time is important to allow the eggs to finish cooking in residual heat. Try additions such as chopped mushrooms, peppers or green onions in your scrambled eggs.

Make a soufflé or puffy omelet in a round pie dish in about 3-5 minutes on a MEDIUM setting. These omelets are

Defrosting

	Mins. on Low/ Defrost Setting per 1lb	Mins. Stdg. Time	Instructions
Pork, Veal, Lamb, Beef for Roasting	8-10	30-40	Pierce covering. Turn frequently.
Ground Beef or Lamb	7-8	5-6	Pierce wrapping. Break up as it defrosts.
Hamburgers	6-8	5	Use shorter time if individually wrapped. Pierce wrapper and separate when starting to defrost. Turn patties over once.
Bacon	6-8	5	Cover in paper towels. Separate as slices defrost.
Sausages	6-8	5	Cover in paper towels. Separate as defrosting.
Whole Chickens, Duck, Game Birds	5-7	30	Pierce wrapper. Remove giblets as soon as possible. Cover leg ends, wings, breast bone with foil part of the time. Turn several times.
Poultry Pieces	6-8	15-20	Pierce wrapper. Turn several times.
Casseroles, filled crêpes (for 4 people)	4-10	10	Defrost in dish, loosely covered. Stir casseroles if possible.

	Mins. on Low/ Defrost Setting per 1lb	Mins. Stdg. Time	Instructions
Vegetables	1-8	3-5	Cover loosely. Break up or stir occasionally.
Fish Fillets and Steaks	6-10	5-10	Pierce wrapper. Separate during defrosting. Use greater time for steaks.
Whole Fish	6-8	10	Pierce wrapper. Turn over during defrosting. Cover tail with foil halfway through.
Shellfish	6-8	6	Pierce wrapper. Stir or break up pieces during defrosting.
Bread Loaf	2-4 (per average loaf)	5-10	Cover with paper towels. Turn over once.
1 Slice Bread	20 seconds	1	Cover in paper towels.
Rolls 6 12	1½-3 2-4	3 5	Cover in paper towels. Turn over once.
Cake	1½-2	2	Place on serving plate. Some frostings not suitable.
Fruit Pie 9″	8-10	6	Use a glass dish. Place on inverted saucer or rack.

Reheating

	Quantity	Setting	Time from room temp. (minutes)	Special Instructions
Spaghetti Sauce	8oz 1lb	Med.	5-6 7-8	Stir several times. Keep loosely covered.
Beef Stew	8oz 1lb	Med.	5-5½ 6-7	Stir occasionally. Cover loosely.
Casseroles	8oz 1lb	Med.	5-7 7-8	Stir occasionally. Cover loosely. Use the shorter time for chicken, fish or vegetables.
Chili	8oz 1lb	Med.	5-5½ 6-7	Stir several times. Keep loosely covered.
Pork Chops	2 4	Med.	5 7½	Turn over halfway through. Cover loosely.
Lamb Chops	2 4	Med.	4-5 6-10	Turn over halfway through. Cover loosely.
Sliced beef, pork, veal	4oz 8oz	Med.	3-5 6-7½	Add gravy or sauce if possible. Cover loosley.
Sliced turkey, chicken, ham	4oz 8oz	Med.	2½-5 4-6	Add gravy or sauce if possible. Cover loosely.

	Quantity	Setting	Time from room temp. (minutes)	Special Instructions
Pasta	4oz 8oz	Med. or High	2-3 5-6	Stir once or twice. Add 1 tsp oil. Use shorter time for High setting.
Rice	4oz 8oz	Med. or High	2-3 4-5	Stir once or twice. Add 1 tsp oil or butter. Use shorter time for High setting.
Potatoes	4oz 8oz 1lb	High	1-2 2-3 3-4	Use the shorter time for mashed potatoes. Do not reheat fried potatoes. Cover loosely.
Corn-on-the-Cob	2 ears 4 ears	High	2-3 4-6	Wrap in plastic wrap.
Carrots	8oz 1lb	High	1-2 2-4	Cover loosely. Stir once.
Turnips	8oz 1lb	High	1-2 2-4	Cover loosely. Stir carefully.
Broccoli Asparagus	4oz 8oz	High	2 2	Cover loosely. Rearrange once.
Peas Beans Zucchini	4oz 8oz	High	1-1½ 1½-2	Cover loosely. Stir occasionally.

Facing page: a few of the many types of container that can be used for defrosting and reheating food in the microwave oven. Right: when poaching eggs, prick the yolk to prevent bursting.

versatile and can be filled with savory ingredients for a appetizer or light meal, or with jam or fruit for a dessert.

Beautifully-shaped poached eggs are easy in a microwave oven. Measure 2 tbsps of water in a custard cup and add ¼ tsp vinegar. Cover and bring to the boil. Break in an egg and pierce the yolk with a skewer to prevent bursting. Arrange cups in a circle on the turntable and cook on MEDIUM for 2-3 minutes for 4 eggs. Cover and leave to stand 2-3 minutes to finish cooking. If chopped hard-cooked eggs are needed, simply poach the eggs 1-2 minutes longer and chop after standing time. *Never* cook an egg in its shell; it will burst due to build up of steam.

To make egg-based sauces such as Hollandaise or custard sauce, use a deep bowl or glass measure to allow room for

Facing page and above left: stir scrambled eggs often during cooking time for a lighter, fluffier result. Allow standing time to finish cooking. Above: cover the thin ends of poultry joints with foil to prevent overcooking. Chicken breasts can be given color by "branding" with a hot skewer.

Meat and Poultry (per 1lb.)

	Mins. on High	Mins. on Medium	Internal Temperature Before Standing	After Standing
Beef: boned and rolled				
rare	6-7	11-13	130°F	140°F
medium	7-8	13-15	150°F	160°F
well-done	8-9	15-17	160°F	170°F
Beef: bone in				
rare	5	10	130°F	140°F
medium	6	11	150°F	160°F
well-done	8	15	160°F	170°F
Leg of Lamb	8-10	11-13	170°F	180°F
Pork	9-11	13-15	180°F	185°F
Ham				
Uncooked, boned	1st 5	15-18	130°F	160°F
Bone in	1st 5	15½-18½	130°F	160°F
Pre-cooked, boned	1st 5	12-15	130°F	
Bone in	1st 5	10-15		
Chicken	6-8	9-11	185°F	190°F
Duck	6-8	9-11	185°F	190°F
Turkey	9-11	12-15	185°F	190°F
Poussins	15-20 total			

whisking and keep a bowl of cold water on hand to dip the base of the cooking bowl in if the sauce starts to curdle. A Hollandaise sauce made with 2 egg yolks will cook in about 1 minute on MEDIUM. The sauce should be whisked every 15 seconds. A 2 egg yolk custard sauce cooks in about 1 minute on LOW if the yolks are added to a hot sauce. Flavor Hollandaise sauce with chopped herbs and a dash of tarragon vinegar to make Bernaise sauce – delicious on steak or fish. Liqueurs, chocolate or coffee make interesting additions to a basic custard sauce.

Meat and Poultry

The leanest and most tender cuts of meat available should be chosen for cooking in the microwave. Braising and stewing

Small Cuts of Meat, Poultry and Game

Type	Mins. on High	Mins. on Medium	Special Instructions
Steaks (1½″ thick) 4-6oz			Use a browning dish pre-heated to manufacturer's instructions. Use timing for rare when cooking kebabs
rare	2-3		
medium rare	3-4		
medium	5-7		
well-done	7-9		
Lamb Chops	7-9		Use a browning dish
		13-15	Cook in liquid
Lamb Fillet		10-12	Brown, then cook in liquid
Pork Chops	7-9		Use a browning dish
		13-15	Cook in liquid
Pork Fillet		15	Brown, then cook in liquid
Veal Chops	7-9		Use a browning dish
		13-15	Cook in liquid
Smoked Pork Chops	4-6		Pre-cooked and browned
Ham Steaks	3		Pre-cooked and browned
Ground Meat (1lb)	5		Break up with a fork as it cooks
Hamburgers	2½-3		Use browning dish
Lamb Patties	2½-3		Use browning dish
Meatballs (1½ lbs)	10-12		
Duck Portions			Use browning dish
1 Breast (boned)	6		
2 Legs		15	Brown each side first
Chicken			
1 Breast		2-3	Brown first if desired
1 Leg		3-4	
2 Pieces		3-6	
3 Pieces		4-7	
4 Pieces		7-9	
Turkey Cutlets		10-15	
Turkey Legs (1lb)	1st 10	13-16	
Bacon		4	On rack or paper towels
		1	Per side on pre-heated browning dish
Sausages		2	Use browning dish

Use MEDIUM settings to cook most meats and whole birds. Hamburgers and smaller cuts of meat such as chops and steaks can be cooked on HIGH.

A browning dish is excellent for cooking these small cuts. They will require no standing time when cooked in this way. Use a browning dish for cubed meats for stews to give a little natural color to the sauce and to seal in the meat juices.

Meatballs can be cooked in a browning dish or arranged in a circle in a casserole and cooked with or without a sauce. Either way, they need to be rearranged several times during cooking.

Sausages must be cooked in a browning dish to give them color, but there is a choice of methods for bacon. Use a microwave roasting rack or place strips between paper towels to absorb fat as the bacon cooks. Prick the skins of sausages to prevent bursting.

Large joints of meat and poultry must be turned several times during cooking and should be covered during standing time.

Drain the drippings at intervals during cooking since this liquid will attract the microwave energy away from the meat or poultry and slow down cooking.

Foil is very effective in protecting the thinner parts of joints and birds. Remove the foil about halfway through cooking time.

Variety meats, such as liver or kidneys should be pricked with a fork several times to prevent bursting.

Fish and Seafood

A fillet of fish cooks in 2-3 minutes, while shellfish take even less time. Cooking should end when the fish or seafood is slightly undercooked so that standing time can finish it off without toughening and drying out.

Arrange fillets in a circle with the thinner ends toward the center of the dish. Cover with paper towels or add liquid and cover with plastic wrap. The liquid can be water and lemon juice or wine, and the addition of a bay leaf, onion slice and a few black peppercorns gives a good flavor. This liquid can then be used to make a sauce for the fish.

To keep the thin ends of salmon or cod steaks in place, secure with wooden picks. Turn steaks over halfway through cooking time.

Whole fish can be "fried" in a browning dish. They can also be poached in bags, shallow, covered dishes or enclosed in wax paper – en papillote. To keep the head or tail of a large, whole fish such as salmon from over-cooking, wrap it in foil. Be sure to check the instruction booklet of your particular oven, though, before using foil. Wrap the foil in several layers of plastic wrap and cover the body with a single layer, if desired. If the fish is too large for your dishes, or will not lie flat on the turntable, curve it to fit and loop string loosely

steak can be used, but there will be no real time saving as these cuts need slow cooking to tenderize them. However, the more expensive cuts will not shrink as much, so they are more economical to use.

Facing page: a whole small fish can be "fried" in a browning dish.

Fish and Shellfish (per 1lb.)

Type	Mins. on high	Type	Mins. on high
Cod Steaks and Fillets	4-5	Salmon (Whole) per 1lb	8-9
Halibut and Turbot Steaks and Fillets	4-5	Salmon Steaks and Tail pieces	2-7
Smoked Fish (poached)	1-2	Sea Bass (Whole) per 1lb	8-9
Sole Fillets	2-3	Shrimp Langoustines	2-5
Mackerel	10-12	Scallops	2-5
Trout	8-10	Mussels	2-3
Herring Fillets	6-8	Oysters	1-2
Tuna Steaks	5	Squid	6
Monkfish Tail Portion Sliced	8-9 2-5		

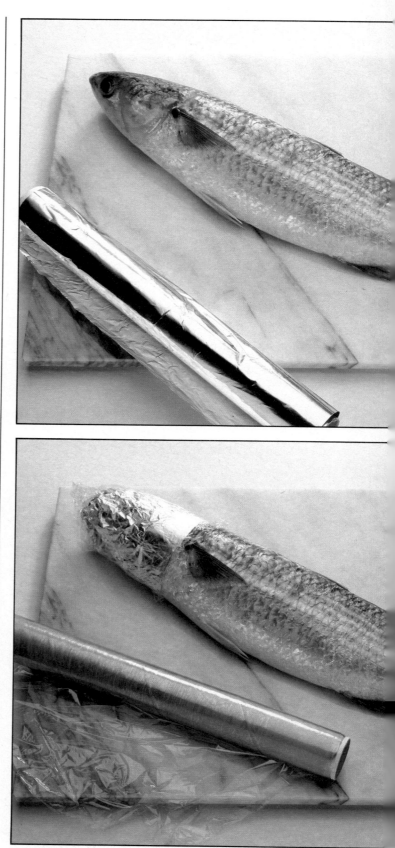

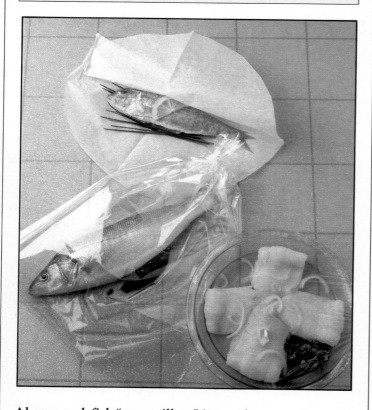

Above: cook fish "en papillote", in parchment or in cooking bags, to keep in moisture and flavor. Wrapping foil around the head and tail of a fish (top far right) will help protect these parts from overcooking, while cling film wrapped around the fish (right) protects the skin and retains the heat. Far right: curve a large fish to fit the oven turntable.

around the head and tail to keep the fish in shape. Make sure that the foil ends do not touch the sides of the oven as the fish turns. Remove foil halfway through cooking time.

Shellfish can toughen if cooked too quickly at too high a temperature. Add them to a hot sauce and leave to stand 5 minutes to cook in residual heat. Alternatively, cook small pieces of shellfish for about 3 minutes on HIGH, or use a lower setting for a slightly longer time. The following chart is a quick guide to cooking times for fish and shellfish but, as with all cooking, the results will vary from oven to oven.

Open oysters by heating them 45 seconds on HIGH. They will prise open much more easily.

Baking

Baking is one of the most surprising things a microwave oven does. Quick breads, those leavened with baking powder or soda and sour milk, rise higher than they do in a conventional oven and they bake more quickly. If using a square or loaf dish, cover the corners with foil for part of the cooking time to keep that part of the bread or cake from drying out before the middle is cooked. Cakes also rise much higher and a single layer will bake in about 6 minutes on a medium setting.

The dough-like microwave meringue mixture (facing page top) will triple in size once cooked (facing page bottom). Above: baking a pastry shell on an inverted saucer allows the base to crisp.

Eliminate salt from cake batters as it tends to make the batter bubble, causing a very coarse texture.

Microwave ovens can cut the rising time for yeast doughs nearly in half, and a loaf of bread will bake in an astonishing 8-10 minutes.

Cookies will not usually crisp in a microwave oven. However, they bake to a moist, chewy texture which is often just as pleasing. A batch of 3 dozen will cook in about 10 minutes, one batch at a time.

Pastry is not as much of a problem as most people believe. Prick the base and sides of the pastry well after lining a pie or flan dish. It is essential to bake the pastry shell "blind" – without filling – in order to dry the base. Pastry will not bake to an even brown, but it will crisp. Alternatives are sweet or savory cookie or cracker crusts.

To let air and heat circulate underneath breads, cakes and

pastry shells, place them on a rack or inverted saucer. This allows the base to cook faster and more evenly. Once baked and cool, keep microwave-baked goods well covered. They seem to dry out faster than those conventionally baked.

Microwave meringues are the real magic trick. The mixture is prepared like thick frosting and must be pliable enough to shape. Cut very small pieces of the mixture and place well apart on a microwave baking sheet; the meringues will triple in size and become light and crisp. The amount of powdered sugar needed will vary with the size and age of the egg white. New eggs tend to have more liquid whites which take up more sugar. Soft meringues for topping pies will rise beautifully but will not brown. Sprinkle lightly with brown sugar or toasted coconut, or broil for a few seconds.

Above: warming the liquid helps dissolve yeast. Top right: foil wrapped around the corners of a rectangular baking dish ensures even cooking. Right: a decorative ring mold for microwave cakes. Facing page: poppadums microwave to perfect crispness if first brushed with a little oil.

Special Tips

Here are several microwave "secrets" that don't seem to fall into any particular category:

* Dry herbs for storage by placing sprigs between paper towels and microwaving until the herbs can be crumbled. Cool and seal tightly.

* Heat grated citrus peel from 1 orange or 2 lemons on a plate for 1-2 minutes on HIGH. Leave to cool completely until dry and store in airtight containers.

* To skin almonds, bring 1 cup water to the boil in about 2-3 minutes on HIGH and add 1 cup nuts. Microwave 1 minute on HIGH and drain. The skins should slip off easily.

* For chestnuts, make a horizontal cut in the rounded side and place in a bowl of water. Cover and bring to the boil. Boil 1 minute on HIGH and leave to stand 5-10 minutes. Peel one chestnut at a time, leaving the others covered in water.

Microwaving is the ideal way of drying herbs (above), citrus peel and crumb toppings (facing page).

* Nuts such as pecans, walnuts or Brazils should be brought to the boil in water in a covered bowl. Leave to stand 1 minute, drain and cool. Open carefully; the shells will fill with water. The nuts should come out whole.

* Toast nuts, sesame seeds and sunflower seeds in melted butter for 3-7 minutes for nuts and 3-4 minutes for seeds on HIGH. Stir often while microwaving, and do not allow them to brown too much. They will darken as they cool.

✳ Coconut needs no fat to toast. Sprinkle in an even layer on a plate and heat on MEDIUM for 3-4 minutes, tossing frequently with a fork. Leave to cool and store in airtight containers.

✳ Crisp cereals and snack foods on paper towels for 15-60 seconds on HIGH. Allow to cool.

✳ Wrap bread, rolls or coffee cake in paper towels and heat 15-30 seconds on HIGH to warm and freshen.

✳ To make croûtons, cut bread into ½ inch cubes and spread in an even layer on a baking dish. Microwave 4-5 minutes on HIGH, stirring every 2 minutes until dry. Leave to cool and store airtight or freeze. For flavored croûtons toss in melted butter and sprinkle with herbs, garlic powder or grated Parmesan cheese before microwaving.

✳ Cut bread in cubes and microwave 4-5 minutes on HIGH. Cool and crush in a blender or food processor to make breadcrumbs for toppings and coatings. Store in airtight containers or freeze.

Facing page: the warm, even temperature required for yogurt-making is easily maintained in a microwave oven. Above left: a few moments in the microwave ensure that cereals and snack foods can be served perfectly crisp. Above: croûtons made the microwave way. Left: when warming bread or freshening a slightly stale loaf, wrap in paper towels to absorb moisture.

∗ Warm brandy 15 seconds on HIGH for drinking, 30 seconds on HIGH in a heatproof container for flaming. Ignite with a match OUTSIDE the oven.

∗ To make yogurt, pour 3½ cups milk into a large bowl. Heat on HIGH until the temperature reaches 190°F. Stir several times while heating. Cool the mixture to 115°F and stir in ⅓ cup natural yogurt. Cover the bowl and reheat on MEDIUM-LOW when the temperature falls below 115°F. Allow to stand 3-4 hours. Check the temperature frequently and reheat as before, at least every 30 minutes. Refrigerate when the mixture sets, and keep no longer than 2 weeks.

∗ Cook poppadums by brushing both sides lightly with oil and cooking 30 seconds on HIGH for one. Wontons can be cooked in the same manner.

∗ Popcorn needs special equipment. *Do not* try to pop it in a paper bag. It will often catch fire!

* Make your own liqueurs using brandy or vodka as a base. Add colorings and flavorings of your choice to a sugar syrup and heat about 5 minutes.

* Specialty coffee- and tea-based drinks are easy to make and take about 5 minutes heating. A warming cup of hot chocolate takes about 2 minutes.

Recipe Conversion

Once you master the art of microwave cooking, the time will come when you want to adapt your favorite recipes. To convert your own recipes, follow these rules:

* Look for similar microwave recipes with the same quantities of solid ingredients, dish size, techniques and times.

Whether toasting nuts and coconut (this page) or making a cup of tea or coffee (facing page), the microwave oven will perform it perfectly.

* Reduce liquid quantities by one quarter. More can always be added later in cooking.

* Fat will attract microwave energy and slow down the cooking of the other ingredients in the recipe. Cut the amount used by at least half.

* Reduce the seasoning in your recipe; microwave cooking intensifies flavors.

* Microwave cooking takes approximately a quarter of the time of conventional cooking. Allow at least 5 minutes standing time before checking to see if the food is cooked. You can always add a bit more time at this point if necessary.

100 MICROWAVE SECRETS

Microwave

100 MICROWAVE SECRETS

SOUPS AND APPETIZERS

Stuffed Avocados

PREPARATION TIME: 10 minutes

MICROWAVE COOKING TIME: 10 minutes

SERVES: 4 people

½ cup milk
2 black peppercorns
1 small bay leaf
1 slice onion
1 small blade mace
1½ tbsps butter or margarine
2 tbsps flour

FILLING
2 tomatoes, skinned, seeded and chopped
3oz cooked, peeled shrimp
½ cup mushrooms, roughly chopped
4 green onions, roughly chopped
1 tbsp chopped parsley
1 tsp chopped marjoram
Dash tabasco
Salt and pepper
2 avocados, halved and stoned
Juice of half a lemon

TOPPING
⅓ cup grated Parmesan cheese
4 tbsps dried breadcrumbs

Pour the milk into a large glass measure and add the bay leaf, peppercorns, blade mace and a slice of onion. Heat on HIGH for 2 minutes and then leave to stand for 5 minutes, loosely covered. Melt the butter or margarine in a small, deep bowl for 30 seconds on HIGH. Stir in the flour and when well mixed strain on the infused milk. Heat for 2 minutes on HIGH until thickened, stirring frequently. Add the tomatoes, shrimp, mushrooms and green onions to the sauce. Add the parsley, marjoram and dash of tabasco and season with salt and pepper. Scoop the flesh out of the avocado, leaving a ¼ inch lining inside each shell. Sprinkle the scooped out flesh and shell with lemon juice. Stir the flesh

This page: Stuffed Avocados (top) and Oeufs en Cocotte (bottom). Facing page: Crab and Tomato Quiche (top) and Country Pâté (bottom).

into the other ingredients in the sauce and spoon the sauce into the avocado shells. Combine the Parmesan cheese and breadcrumbs and sprinkle over the top of each avocado. Cook the avocados for 3 minutes on HIGH, or until the sauce is bubbling slightly. Brown under a broiler if desired and serve immediately. NOTE: this recipe may be prepared with slightly under-ripe avocados, which will soften in the microwave oven.

Tomato Chartreuse

PREPARATION TIME: 15 minutes plus chilling time

MICROWAVE COOKING TIME: 4½-8 minutes

SERVES: 4 people

Juice of half a lemon made up to ½ cup with cold water
1 tbsp gelatine
1½ cups tomato juice
½ tsp tomato paste
1 bay leaf
Salt and pepper

GARNISH
3oz mushrooms, sliced
3 green onions, chopped
3 tbsps olive or vegetable oil
1 tbsp white wine vinegar
Salt and pepper
Chopped mixed herbs

Combine the lemon juice and water in a small glass bowl and sprinkle over the gelatine. Allow to soak for 5 minutes. Combine the tomato juice, tomato paste, salt, pepper and bay leaf in a large glass measure or bowl. Microwave the tomato mixture on HIGH for 2½-5 minutes or until boiling. Allow to stand for 2 minutes and remove the bay leaf. Heat the gelatine mixture for 1-2 minutes on HIGH and pour into the tomato mixture when the gelatine dissolves. Dampen a 2½ cup mold and pour in the tomato mixture. Alternatively, use 4 individual molds. Chill in the refrigerator until set, about 2 hours. To speed up the setting process put

into the freezer for 30 minutes, remove and place in the refrigerator until set. Combine the mushrooms and the olive oil in a small bowl and cook for 1 minute on HIGH, stirring occasionally. Leave to cool and combine with the vinegar, green onions and salt and pepper. Add a pinch of chopped mixed herbs and set aside. When the tomato mixture has set, loosen from the sides of the mold and turn out onto a serving plate. Alternatively, dip the mold into warm water for 30 seconds to help loosen the mixture. Pile the mushroom mixture on top of the mold or each individual mold using a draining spoon to drain away excess dressing. Serve chilled.

Oeufs en Cocotte

PREPARATION TIME: 10 minutes

MICROWAVE COOKING TIME: 9 minutes

SERVES: 4 people

1 tbsp butter or margarine
4oz mushrooms, chopped
2 tbsps flour
4 tbsps dry white wine
2 tbsps milk
2 tsps chopped mixed herbs
1 tbsp capers, chopped
4 eggs
Salt and pepper
4 tbsps heavy cream
Paprika
Nutmeg

Place the butter in a small casserole and melt on HIGH for 30 seconds. Add the chopped mushrooms and cook for 2 minutes on HIGH. Stir in the flour and add the wine and milk. Cook for a further 1-2 minutes on HIGH, or until thickened. Add the capers, mixed herbs and salt and pepper to taste. Divide the mixture into 4 custard cups and make a well in the center of the mixture in each

Right: Tomato Chartreuse.

dish. Break an egg into the center of the mixture in each cup. Pierce the yolk once with a sharp knife. Cook for 3-4 minutes on HIGH or until the white is set and yolk is still soft. Place a spoonful of cream on top of each egg and sprinkle with paprika and nutmeg. Cook for 1 minute on LOW to heat the cream. Serve immediately.

Crab and Tomato Quiche

PREPARATION TIME: 20 minutes

MICROWAVE COOKING TIME: 18 minutes plus 6 minutes standing time

SERVES: 4 people

PASTRY
1 cup whole-wheat flour
4 tbsps margarine
2 tbsps vegetable shortening or lard
Pinch salt
4 tbsps ice cold water
3 eggs
4 tbsps light cream
Salt and pepper
½ cup shredded cheese
½ cup frozen peas
2 green onions, finely chopped
6oz white crabmeat or crab sticks, flaked
4 tomatoes, peeled and sliced

TOPPING
1 tbsp dry, seasoned breadcrumbs
2 tbsps grated Parmesan cheese

Put the flour, salt, margarine and shortening into the bowl of a food processor and work until the mixture resembles fine breadcrumbs. With the machine running, add the water gradually until the dough holds together. It may not be necessary to add all the water. Roll out the pastry on a floured board to ⅛ inch thickness and place in an 7 inch pie dish. Trim the edge and flute the pastry. Refrigerate for 10 minutes. Beat the eggs with the salt, pepper and the cream. Add the cheese, peas, onions and crabmeat. Prick the base of the pastry and cook it on HIGH for 2-3 minutes, or until starting to

crisp. To help crisp the base, place the pastry on an inverted saucer or a microwave oven rack. Pour the filling into the pastry shell and decorate the top with the tomatoes. Cook on MEDIUM for 10 minutes. Mix the topping ingredients together and sprinkle over the top of the quiche 5 minutes before the end of cooking. Serve hot or cold.

Curried Chicken Kebabs with Cucumber Sauce

PREPARATION TIME: 10 minutes

MICROWAVE COOKING TIME: 6 minutes

SERVES: 4 people

3 chicken breasts, skinned and boned

MARINADE
2 tbsps vegetable oil
1 clove garlic, crushed
2 tsps curry powder
¼ tsp cayenne pepper
1 tbsp chopped coriander leaves
Juice and grated rind of 1 lime
Salt and pepper

SAUCE
½ cucumber, grated
1 cup plain yogurt
1 tbsp chopped fresh mint
1 tsp mango chutney
Pinch salt and pepper

Cut the chicken into 1 inch wide strips. Combine the ingredients for the marinade and mix in the chicken to coat each piece. Leave to marinate for 1 hour. Thread the chicken onto wooden skewers and put onto a microwave roasting rack. Cook for 5 minutes on HIGH, turning the kebabs frequently while cooking. Leave to stand, covered, for 1 minute. While the chicken is marinating,

Right: Curried Chicken Kebabs with Cucumber Sauce.

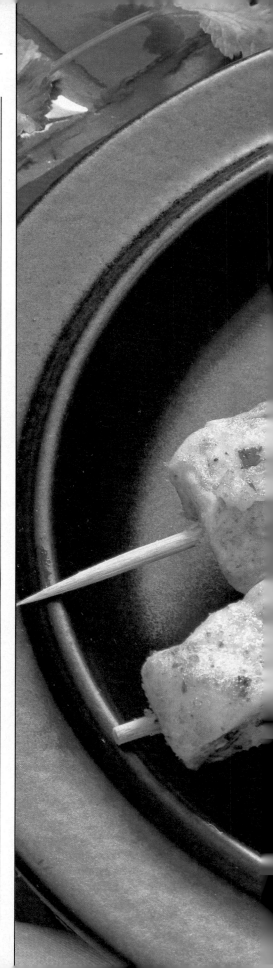

sprinkle the grated cucumber lightly with salt and leave to stand. Rinse thoroughly and pat dry with paper towels. Combine with the remaining sauce ingredients and serve with the chicken kebabs.

Country Pâté

PREPARATION TIME: 10 minutes

MICROWAVE COOKING TIME: 15 minutes

SERVES: 6-8 people

8oz ground pork
8oz ground veal
4oz ham, ground
4oz pork liver
3oz ground pork fat
1 clove garlic, crushed
4 tbsps brandy
Ground allspice
Thyme
1 bay leaf
2 tsps green peppercorns
8 slices bacon, bones and rind removed
Salt and pepper

Place the ground pork, veal and ham in a food processor. Remove the skin and ducts from the liver and add to the meat in the food processor. Add the pork fat, garlic, brandy, allspice, thyme and salt and pepper. Process once or twice to mix thoroughly, but do not over-mix. The mixture should be fairly coarse. Stir in the green peppercorns by hand. Line a glass loaf dish with the bacon and press the meat mixture into the dish on top of it. Place the bay leaf on top of the mixture, fold any overlapping edges of the bacon over the top and cover the dish with a double layer of plastic wrap. Place the dish of pâté in a larger shallow dish with hot water to come halfway up the sides of the pâté dish. Cook on MEDIUM for 6 minutes. Leave to stand for 5 minutes, then cook a further 10 minutes on MEDIUM. Cover with foil, press down and weight. Leave to chill 2-4 hours or overnight. Remove bay leaf and cut mixture into thin slices to serve.

Watercress and Potato Soup

PREPARATION TIME: 10 minutes

MICROWAVE COOKING TIME: 20 minutes

SERVES: 4 people

3 tbsps butter or margarine
1 shallot, finely chopped
1lb potatoes, peeled and diced
1½ cups chicken or vegetable stock
Salt and pepper
1½ cups light cream
1 bunch watercress
Ground mace
Dash lemon juice

Put the butter, shallot and potatoes into a large bowl. Loosely cover and cook for about 2 minutes on HIGH. Add the stock, salt and pepper and re-cover the bowl. Cook for about 15 minutes or until the vegetables are soft. Reserve 4 small sprigs of watercress for garnish and chop the remainder, removing any thick stems. Add the chopped leaves to the other ingredients in the bowl, re-cover and cook for another 2 minutes on HIGH. Allow the soup to cool for a few minutes and pour into a food processor. Purée until smooth. The soup should be lightly flecked with green watercress. Return the soup to the bowl and add the cream. Cook for 3-4 minutes on LOW or MEDIUM until heated through. Do not allow the soup to boil. Stir in a pinch of ground mace and lemon juice to taste. Serve the soup garnished with small sprigs of watercress. May be served hot or cold.

Stilton and Walnut Soup

PREPARATION TIME: 10 minutes

MICROWAVE COOKING TIME: 18 minutes

SERVES: 4 people

3 tbsps butter or margarine
1 large onion, finely chopped
4 tbsps flour
1½ cups chicken stock
1 bay leaf
1 sprig thyme
Salt and pepper
1½ cups milk
2 cups Stilton cheese, crumbled (half Cheddar and half blue cheese may be substituted)
4 tbsps heavy cream
4 tbsps chopped walnuts

Put the butter and the onion into a large bowl and loosely cover with plastic wrap, pierced several times. Cook for 6 minutes on HIGH, stirring occasionally. Stir in the flour, add the stock gradually and mix well. Add the bay leaf, thyme and salt and pepper and cook, uncovered, for 10 minutes on HIGH. Remove the herbs and crumble the cheese into the soup. Add the milk and stir to mix well. Cook for 1 minute on HIGH, uncovered. Stir in the cream and cook a further 1 minute on HIGH. Serve garnished with the chopped walnuts.

Facing page: Stilton and Walnut Soup (top) and Watercress and Potato Soup (bottom).

FISH AND SEAFOOD

Herring Lyonnaise

PREPARATION TIME: 20 minutes

MICROWAVE COOKING TIME: 13-14 minutes

SERVES: 4 people

4 even-sized herrings, gutted, fins trimmed and heads removed, if desired
Seasoned flour for dredging
4 tbsps butter or margarine
2 large onions, peeled and thinly sliced
1 red pepper, seeded and thinly sliced

Cut 2 slits in the skin on the side of each herring and set them aside. Heat a browning dish according to the manufacturer's directions and when hot drop in half the butter. Cook the onions and peppers for 4-5 minutes on HIGH to brown slightly and soften. Set aside and reheat the browning dish. Meanwhile, dredge the herring in flour and when the browning dish is hot, drop in the remaining butter. Cook the herring 2 at a time for 2 minutes per side on HIGH. Repeat with the remaining herring. Place all the herring in a serving dish and top with the onions and the peppers. Reheat for 1 minute on HIGH and serve immediately.

Seafood Kebabs

PREPARATION TIME: 20 minutes

MICROWAVE COOKING TIME: 6-7 minutes plus standing time

SERVES: 4 people

8oz jumbo shrimp
8oz monkfish tails
1 green pepper, seeded and cut into 2 inch pieces

1 red pepper, seeded and cut into 2 inch pieces
8 even-sized mushrooms, stems trimmed

BASTING MIXTURE
2 tbsps soy sauce
1 tsp coarsely ground black pepper

This page: Cod with Crispy Topping (top) and Seafood Kebabs (bottom). Facing page: Herring Lyonnaise (top) and Sardines with Mustard and Herbs (bottom).

½ tsp grated fresh ginger
1 tsp lemon juice
½ tsp honey

Peel the shrimp and cut the monkfish tails into an equal number of 1 inch cubes. Thread onto 4 wooden skewers, alternating with the remaining ingredients. Mix together the basting ingredients and brush over the kebabs. Place on a microwave-proof roasting rack in a shallow dish and cook on MEDIUM for 6-7 minutes, turning and basting frequently until the fish is cooked and the shrimp have turned pink. Allow to stand, covered, for 1-2 minutes before serving. If any basting mixture remains after cooking, pour over the kebabs to serve.

Sweet and Sour Shrimp

PREPARATION TIME: 20 minutes

MICROWAVE COOKING TIME: 7-10 minutes

SERVES: 4 people

SAUCE
1½ tbsps cornstarch mixed with 4 tbsps water
½ cup light brown sugar
8oz can unsweetened pineapple pieces
1 green pepper, seeded and sliced
1 clove garlic, crushed
6 tbsps white wine or cider vinegar
1½ tbsps soy sauce
2 tbsps tomato ketchup
2 tomatoes, peeled and quartered
3 green onions, diagonally sliced
Salt and pepper
1lb cooked, peeled shrimp

Mix the cornstarch and water in a large glass measure or deep bowl and mix in the sugar. Drain the pineapple and add the juice to the bowl. Add the pepper, garlic, vinegar, soy sauce, tomato ketchup and salt and pepper. Cook, uncovered, for 5-7 minutes, stirring after 1 minute, until the sauce clears and thickens. Add the reserved pineapple and the tomatoes and green onions to the sauce. Leave the sauce to stand, covered, for 5 minutes. Stir in the shrimp and heat on MEDIUM for 2-3 minutes until all the ingredients are hot. Serve with rice or crisp chow mein noodles.

Cod with Crispy Topping

PREPARATION TIME: 10 minutes

MICROWAVE COOKING TIME: 9-11 minutes

SERVES: 4 people

TOPPING
4 tbsps butter or margarine
1½ cups seasoned breadcrumbs
2 tbsps paprika
4 tbsps grated Parmesan cheese
2 tbsps sesame seeds
2 tsps chopped parsley
Salt and pepper

FISH AND POACHING LIQUID
4 cod fillets
Juice of 1 lemon
½ cup water
1 bay leaf
4 black peppercorns

GARNISH
Lemon wedges

Heat a browning dish according to the manufacturer's directions. Melt the butter or margarine in the dish and add the breadcrumbs. Stir well and heat for 1 minute on HIGH until lightly brown. Add the remaining ingredients and heat for a further 1 minute on HIGH. Set aside. Put the cod, lemon juice, water, bay leaf and peppercorns into a casserole. Cover loosely with plastic wrap or waxed paper and cook for 5-6 minutes on HIGH. Allow the fillets to stand for 1-2 minutes and then lift out of the poaching liquid with a draining spoon. Place the fish on a serving plate and top each fillet with some of the breadcrumb mixture. Heat through for 30 seconds-1 minute on HIGH and serve with lemon wedges.

Right: Sweet and Sour Shrimp.

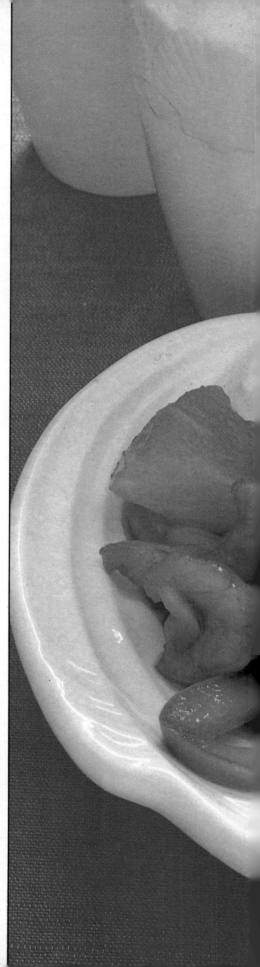

Trout en Papillote

PREPARATION TIME: 20 minutes

MICROWAVE COOKING TIME:
23 minutes plus standing time

SERVES: 4 people

4 10oz trout, gutted and trimmed
2 carrots, peeled and cut into matchsticks
3 sticks celery, cut into matchsticks
2 small leeks, trimmed, washed and
*   shredded*
4 tbsps butter
4 tbsps white wine
2 tsps thyme
2 tsps chopped parsley
Salt and pepper
4 small bay leaves

Place each fish on a sheet of lightly-oiled waxed paper. Place the carrots in a small casserole with 2 tbsps water, cover and cook on HIGH for 2 minutes. Add the celery and cook a further 2 minutes on HIGH. Add the leeks and continue cooking for 1 minute on HIGH. Add salt and pepper. Place an equal portion of the vegetables on top of each trout. Melt the butter for 30 seconds on HIGH and put 1 spoonful on top of each trout along with 1 spoonful of white wine. Place 1 bay leaf on top of each trout and seal the parcel. Cook on HIGH for 9 minutes per 2 fish parcel. Repeat with the remaining 2 fish and allow to stand for 3 minutes before opening to serve.

Sardines with Mustard and Herbs

PREPARATION TIME: 25 minutes

MICROWAVE COOKING TIME:
9 minutes

SERVES: 4 people as a main course or 6 as an appetizer

12-16 sardines, depending upon size
1 tbsp olive oil
1 shallot, finely chopped
4 tbsps whole grain mustard
2 tbsps dry white wine
2 tbsps chopped fresh mixed herbs
Salt and pepper

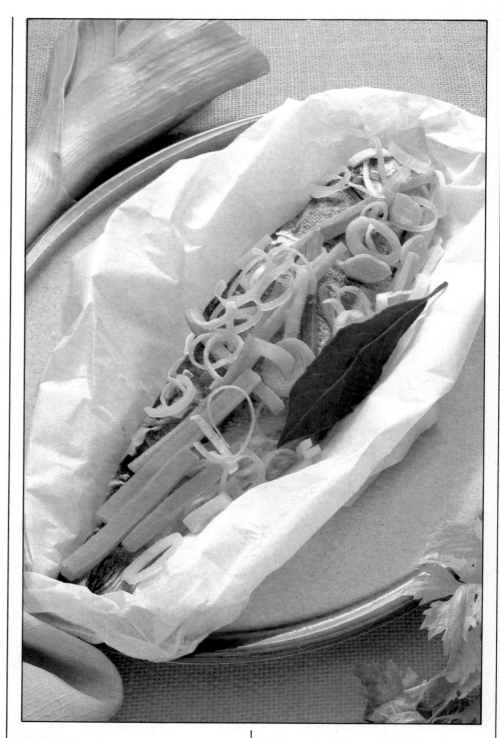

GARNISH
Lemon or lime wedges
Parsley sprigs

Cut the sardines, rinse well and pat dry. Place head to tail in a large, shallow dish. Heat the oil in a small bowl for 30 seconds on HIGH and

**This page: Trout en Papillote.
Facing page: Whole Poached Salmon.**

add the chopped shallot. Cook for 2 minutes on HIGH to soften the shallot. Stir in the mustard, white wine, chopped herbs and salt and

pepper. Loosely cover the sardines with plastic wrap or waxed paper, and cook on HIGH for 3 minutes. Turn the sardines over and spread with the mustard and herb mixture. Cook, uncovered, for 4 minutes on HIGH, or until the fish is cooked. Brown under a preheated broiler, if desired, before serving. May be served as an appetizer or as a main course with new potatoes and a green salad.

Whole Poached Salmon

PREPARATION TIME: 20 minutes

MICROWAVE COOKING TIME: 8-9 minutes per 1lb

SERVES: 6-8 people

3½ lb salmon, cleaned, with head and tail left on
Whole fresh herbs, such as dill or tarragon
Oil for brushing

GARNISH
Lemon slices or wedges
Sliced cucumber
Fresh herbs

Wash the salmon and pat dry. Place fresh herbs inside the cavity of the fish and brush the skin on both sides with oil. Use foil to cover the thin end of the tail and the head to prevent overcooking. Cover the foil with several thicknesses of plastic wrap. Make an incision along the skin on either side of the dorsal fin to allow steam to escape so that the skin does not burst. Lay the fish flat on the turntable, if it will fit, or curve it to fit the shape of the turntable. If curving the fish, tie loosely with string to hold the shape. Cook 8-9 minutes per 1lb on LOW or DEFROST. About halfway through the cooking time, uncover the head and tail and remove the string to allow the head and tail to cook through. To test the salmon to see if it is cooked, slip a sharp knife through one of the slits made on either side of the dorsal fin. If the blade passes through without resistance, the fish is cooked. Allow

the fish to cool slightly and then peel away the skin carefully. Start at the dorsal fin with a sharp knife and carry on peeling with a round-bladed table knife which should slip easily between the skin and the flesh. Carefully transfer the fish to a serving plate, removing the herbs inside the cavity. Garnish with cucumber, lemon slices or wedges and fresh herbs to serve. Serve hot with new potatoes and hollandaise sauce or cold with mayonnaise and a green salad.

Oysters à la Creme

PREPARATION TIME: 15 minutes

MICROWAVE COOKING TIME: 5 minutes

SERVES: 4 people

2 dozen oysters on the half shell or unopened
4 tbsps heavy cream
4 tbsps cream cheese
1 tbsp chopped parsley
Salt and pepper
Nutmeg

GARNISH
Coriander leaves

Scrub the oyster shells well, if unopened, and leave to soak in clean water for 2 hours. Arrange in a circle on the microwave turntable and cook on HIGH for 45 seconds-2 minutes. After 45 seconds insert a short-bladed knife near the hinge and prise open. If the oysters do not open easily, they need further cooking for up to 2 minutes. Remove any pieces of broken shell from the inside and place oysters in a circle on the turntable. Mix together the heavy cream, cream cheese, parsley and salt and pepper. Top each oyster with some of the cheese mixture. Sprinkle with nutmeg and heat through 2-3 minutes on MEDIUM. Garnish with coriander and serve immediately.

Right: Oysters à la Crème.

MEAT AND POULTRY

Poulet en Cocotte

PREPARATION TIME: 20 minutes

MICROWAVE COOKING TIME: 35-45 minutes

SERVES: 4-6 people

12-14 small onions
2 tbsps butter or margarine
1 clove garlic, crushed
2 tbsps flour
10oz canned beef consommé
½ cup dry white wine
12 small new potatoes, peeled
1 sprig fresh rosemary
1 sprig fresh marjoram or thyme
Salt and freshly ground black pepper
3lbs chicken
4oz mushrooms, left whole if small,
    quartered if large

Heat 2 cups water in a large bowl on HIGH until boiling. Drop in the onions and leave to stand for 2 minutes. Drain the onions, peel and trim the root ends. Melt the butter in a large casserole for 30 seconds on HIGH. Add the garlic and stir in the flour. Gradually pour on the consommé and white wine, stirring until well blended. Remove the leaves from the rosemary and the marjoram and add with salt and pepper. Truss the chicken legs, tuck the wing tips under and place the chicken in the casserole, spooning over the liquid. Place the new potatoes around the chicken and cover the dish tightly. Microwave on HIGH for 20-30 minutes, or until the meat in the thickest part of the thigh is no longer pink and the juices run clear. Baste the chicken frequently while cooking and stir the sauce to keep it smooth. Halfway through the cooking time add the peeled onions and re-cover the dish. In the last 5 minutes of cooking, add the mushrooms. Remove the chicken from the cooking liquid and cut into 8 pieces. Return the chicken pieces to the casserole and spoon over the sauce to serve. Alternatively, serve chicken whole, coated with sauce and surrounded by vegetables.

Kidneys Turbigo

PREPARATION TIME: 15 minutes

MICROWAVE COOKING TIME: 20 minutes

SERVES: 4 people

1 tbsp oil
8oz small pork sausages, skins pricked all
    over
12 lambs' kidneys, halved and cored
8oz button onions, peeled
4oz small mushrooms, left whole
1 cup beef stock
1 tbsp tomato paste
2 tbsps sherry
1 bay leaf
¼ tsp thyme
2 tbsps cornstarch dissolved in 4 tbsps
    cold water
1 tbsp chopped parsley
Salt and pepper

Heat a browning dish according to the manufacturer's directions, add the oil and heat for 30 seconds on HIGH. Add the sausages and cook on HIGH for about 5 minutes, turning over several times during cooking, until lightly browned. Remove the sausages from the browning dish to a casserole. Reheat the dish and brown the onions lightly. Add the onions to the sausages in the casserole along with the kidneys and mushrooms. Pour over stock and stir in the tomato paste. Add the sherry, bay leaf, thyme and salt and pepper and cover the dish. Cook on HIGH for 12 minutes, stirring frequently. Add the cornstarch and water mixture to the casserole and stir very well. Cook, uncovered, about 3 minutes or until the sauce thickens. Stir frequently after 1 minute. Remove the bay leaf before serving, and garnish with chopped parsley.

Roast Fillet of Beef with Herbs

PREPARATION TIME: 15 minutes plus marinating time

MICROWAVE COOKING TIME: 8-11 minutes plus standing time

SERVES: 6 people

½ cup red wine
2 tbsps red wine vinegar
3 tbsps oil
1 tsp each chopped tarragon, thyme,
    rosemary and parsley
2 tbsps Worcestershire sauce
1lb beef tenderloin

GARNISH
Fresh herbs

Combine all the ingredients for the marinade in a small, deep bowl and cook on HIGH for 2-3 minutes.

Facing page: Roast Fillet of Beef with Herbs (top) and Kidneys Turbigo (bottom).

Allow to cool completely. Place the beef in a plastic bag or a shallow dish. Pour over the marinade and turn the beef several times to coat thoroughly. If using a bag, tie securely and place on a plate or a dish. Chill for at least 4 hours, turning the meat several times. When ready to cook, place the beef on a microwave-proof roasting rack, tucking the thinner portion of the meat under slightly on the end. If desired, tie the meat at 1 inch intervals to help keep its shape. Cover 1-2 inches of each end of the beef with foil. Cook on HIGH for about 3 minutes and remove the foil from the beef. Lower the setting to MEDIUM and cook for 5-8 minutes longer, turning the beef over once. The internal temperature of the meat

This page: Poulet en Cocotte. Facing page: Duck with Peaches (top) and Lemon Pepper Chicken (bottom).

should register 130°F. Leave the meat to stand for 3 minutes before carving. Slice the meat thinly and surround with the fresh herbs to serve.

Lemon Pepper Chicken

PREPARATION TIME: 20 minutes

MICROWAVE COOKING TIME: 10 minutes

SERVES: 4 people

4 chicken breasts
Juice of 1 lemon
1 tbsp coarsely ground black pepper
Paprika
Salt

GARNISH
Lemon wedges
Watercress

Heat 4 metal skewers in a gas flame or on an electric burner. Skin the chicken breasts. When the skewers are red hot, make a criss-cross pattern on the chicken flesh with the hot skewers. It may be necessary to reheat the skewers after using once or twice. Place the chicken in a large casserole with the thinner end of the chicken breasts pointing towards the center. Sprinkle over the paprika, pepper, lemon juice and salt. Cover the dish tightly and cook 10 minutes on MEDIUM. It may be necessary to cook a further 5 minutes on MEDIUM if the chicken is not done. Baste occasionally with the juices during cooking. To serve, pour the pan juices back over the chicken and garnish with lemon slices and watercress.

Crispy Chicken

PREPARATION TIME: 15 minutes

MICROWAVE COOKING TIME: 9-12 minutes

SERVES: 4-6 people

3½ lbs chicken pieces

CRISPY COATING
1 cup crushed cornflakes
6 tbsps grated Parmesan cheese
½ tsp dry mustard
1 tsp paprika
½ tsp celery salt
½ tsp oregano
½ tsp parsley
Pepper

DIPPING MIXTURE
½ cup butter or margarine
2 eggs, beaten

Skin all the chicken pieces and remove any fat. Combine all the crispy coating ingredients and spread out evenly on a sheet of waxed paper. Melt the butter for 1 minute on HIGH and stir into the beaten eggs in a shallow dish. Dip the chicken into the egg and butter mixture or use a basting brush to coat each piece. Put the chicken pieces in the crumb mixture and lift the ends of the paper to help toss and coat the chicken. Place half the chicken in a glass dish, bone side down. Make sure the thickest pieces of the chicken are on the outside of the dish to start. Cover loosely with waxed paper. Cook on HIGH for 9-12 minutes. Rearrange and turn the chicken over halfway through the cooking time, and remove the paper. Keep the cooked chicken warm while cooking the remaining chicken. If necessary, cover the turntable with paper towels to reheat all of the chicken at once for 1-2 minutes.

Barbecued Spare Ribs

PREPARATION TIME: 15 minutes plus marinating time

MICROWAVE COOKING TIME: 20 minutes

SERVES: 4 people

MARINADE
3 tbsps Worcestershire sauce
1 tbsp soy sauce
3 tbsps tomato ketchup
1 tbsp honey
Gravy browning (optional)
3½ lbs pork spare ribs, cut into 1 rib pieces

Dissolve the marinade ingredients in a bowl and cook on HIGH for 1 minute. Leave to cool completely. Add the ribs to the marinade and stir to mix well. Cover and refrigerate for several hours, stirring the ribs occasionally. Transfer the ribs to a shallow dish or place in a microwave roasting dish. Cover with plastic wrap, pierced several times, and cook on HIGH for 10 minutes. Baste well with the marinade and turn the ribs over. Cook for a further 10 minutes on HIGH or until the ribs are tender. Serve with any remaining sauce.

Duck with Peaches

PREPARATION TIME: 20 minutes

MICROWAVE COOKING TIME: 18 minutes

SERVES: 4 people

4 breasts of duck, boned
4 tbsps butter or margarine
Salt and pepper
½ cup whole blanched almonds
1 tbsp cornstarch
1lb canned sliced peaches, drained and juice reserved
½ cup red wine
1 tbsp lemon or lime juice
1 bay leaf
Pinch cinnamon
Pinch nutmeg
2 tsps whole allspice berries

Heat a browning dish according to the manufacturer's directions. When hot, add the butter or margarine and allow to melt. Sprinkle both sides of each duck breast with salt and pepper. Place skin side down on the browning dish and press down well. Cook on the skin side for 6 minutes on HIGH. Turn the duck breasts over and cook a further 6 minutes on the other side. Remove the duck breasts to a covered casserole to stand while preparing the sauce. To brown the almonds for the sauce, reheat the browning dish briefly, add the almonds and heat for 1-2 minutes on HIGH, stirring occasionally until the almonds are a light golden brown. Mix the cornstarch with the peach juice, red wine, lemon juice, spices and bay leaf in a small, deep bowl or glass measure. Cook on HIGH for 6-7 minutes, stirring after 1 minute.

Facing page: Barbecued Spare Ribs (top) and Crispy Chicken (bottom).

Stir occasionally until thickened. Remove the bay leaf and add the browned almonds and the peaches to the sauce. Leave covered while finishing the duck. Cut each duck breast into thin slices and arrange on 4 serving plates. Spoon the peach sauce over the duck breasts to serve.

Tarragon Steak

PREPARATION TIME: 15 minutes

MICROWAVE COOKING TIME:
6 minutes for the sauce, as indicated in method for steak

SERVES: 4 people

4 fillet steaks, cut 1½ inches thick, brushed
   with oil on both sides
Salt
Freshly ground pepper
12 mushroom caps, fluted if desired

SAUCE
½ cup heavy cream
4 sprigs fresh tarragon
1 tsp Dijon mustard
Salt and pepper

First prepare the sauce. Pour the cream into a deep bowl or a glass measure. Remove the leaves from the sprigs of tarragon and leave whole or chop and combine with the cream. Cook the cream on HIGH for 6 minutes, until boiling and reduced and thickened. Stir in the mustard and the salt and pepper and leave covered while preparing the steaks. Heat a browning dish according to the manufacturer's directions. Sprinkle the steaks with salt and pepper and cook for 2 minutes on one side and 2½ minutes on the other for rare. For medium-rare, 2 minutes on one side and 3½ minutes on the other. For medium, 3 minutes on one side and 4½ minutes on the other. For well-done, 3 minutes on one side and 6 minutes on the other. Add the mushrooms at the same time as the steaks are cooking. For well-done steaks, remove the mushrooms halfway through cooking time. Remove the steaks and mushrooms to a serving plate and

keep warm. Pour the sauce into the browning dish and mix in the meat juices. Pour the sauce over the steaks to serve.

Marmalade Duckling

PREPARATION TIME: 15 minutes

MICROWAVE COOKING TIME:
40 minutes

SERVES: 3-4 people

4½-5lbs duckling
1 slice orange
1 slice onion
1 bay leaf
Salt

GLAZE
4 tbsps bitter orange marmalade, thin cut
4 tbsps soy sauce
½ cup chicken stock
2 tsps-1 tbsp cornstarch
Salt and pepper

GARNISH
Orange slices
Watercress

Place the slice of orange, slice of onion and bay leaf inside the duck cavity. Sprinkle the inside lightly with salt and pepper. Prick the duck skin all over with a fork and use some of the soy sauce from the glaze to brush on all sides of the duck. Sprinkle lightly with salt and place the duck breast side down on a microwave-proof roasting rack. Cook for 10 minutes on HIGH and drain well. Return the duck to the oven, reduce the power to MEDIUM and continue cooking for a further 15 minutes. Combine the remaining soy sauce with the orange marmalade. Turn the duck breast side up and brush with the glaze. Continue cooking for 15 minutes on MEDIUM, draining away the fat often and brushing with the glaze. Remove the duck from the roasting rack and leave to stand, loosely covered with foil, for 5 minutes before carving. Drain all the fat from the roasting dish but leave the pan juices. Combine the cornstarch,

chicken stock, salt and pepper and remaining glaze with the pan juices and pour into a small, deep bowl. Cook 2-3 minutes on HIGH until thickened. Remove the orange, onion and bay leaf from the cavity of the duck and put in a bouquet of watercress. Surround the duck with orange slices and spoon over some of the sauce. Serve the rest of the sauce separately.

Hamburgers

PREPARATION TIME: 15 minutes

MICROWAVE COOKING TIME:
As indicated in method

SERVES: 4 people

1lb ground beef
1 small onion, finely chopped
4 tbsps Worcestershire sauce or soy sauce
Salt and pepper
4 hamburger buns
Lettuce and tomato (optional)

Combine the meat, onions, salt and pepper and mix well. Hamburgers may be cooked on a plate or roasting rack or in a pre-heated browning dish. If using the browning dish method, add the Worcestershire or soy sauce to the hamburger mixture. Shape into 4 even-sized patties. Pre-heat the browning dish according to the manufacturer's directions. For medium-rare hamburgers cook for 2 minutes on HIGH on the first side and 1-2 minutes on HIGH on the second side. For well-done hamburgers, cook 2½ minutes on the first side and 2-3 minutes on the second. Standing time is not needed for hamburgers cooked in a browning dish. To cook hamburgers on a plate or roasting rack, shape into patties and brush with the Worcestershire or

Facing page: Hamburgers (top) and Tarragon Steak (bottom).

soy sauce on both sides. Arrange the hamburgers on a roasting rack or on a plate lined with paper towels. Cover the hamburgers with waxed paper to prevent spatters. Use the same cooking times and setting as for hamburgers cooked on the browning dish, but allow the hamburgers to stand for 1-2 minutes before serving.

This page: Marmalade Duckling.

REHEATING AND DEFROSTING

Beef and Vegetable Stew

PREPARATION TIME: 20 minutes

MICROWAVE COOKING TIME:
29 minutes

SERVES: 4 people

2 tbsps oil
1lb frying or rump steak
2 tbsps flour
1 clove garlic, crushed
½ cup red wine
1 cup beef stock
Bouquet garni (1 sprig thyme, 1 bay leaf,
  3 parsley stalks)
Salt and pepper
1 tsp tomato paste
2 large carrots, peeled and cut into
  matchsticks
3 sticks celery, cut into matchsticks
3 small onions, quartered
4oz mushrooms, quartered

Heat a browning dish according to
the manufacturer's directions.
Meanwhile, trim the meat and cut
into 1 inch pieces. Pour the oil into
the browning dish and quickly brown
the meat on all sides. Pour the meat
juices and oil into a casserole dish
and mix in the flour. Add the garlic
and gradually stir in the wine and
stock. Add the bouquet garni, cover
the dish and cook on HIGH for 6
minutes, stirring every 2 minutes
until thickened. Add the meat to the
dish and re-cover. Cook on HIGH
for a further 15 minutes or until the
meat is tender. Adjust the seasoning
and leave the casserole to stand,
covered. Meanwhile, place the carrot,
celery and onion in a small bowl with
4 tbsps water. Cover and cook on
HIGH for 4 minutes. Add the
mushrooms and re-cover the dish.
Cook a further 4 minutes on HIGH

or until the vegetables are tender.
Remove the bouquet garni from the
meat and drain the vegetables. If
freezing, allow both the meat and
vegetables to cool completely and
freeze them in separate containers. To
defrost, heat the meat for 6-8
minutes on DEFROST or LOW,
breaking up the chunks of meat as
they defrost. Allow to stand 10-20
minutes before reheating. Defrost the
vegetables on LOW or DEFROST
for 4 minutes then leave to stand
before reheating. To reheat, combine
the vegetables and the meat in a
serving dish and cover well. Cook on
HIGH for 12-15 minutes until heated
through. If refrigerating, combine the
meat and the vegetables in a
casserole or serving dish and cover.
To reheat, cook on HIGH for 12-15
minutes or until heated through.
Serve the stew with rice, pasta or
potatoes.

Salade de Legumes

PREPARATION TIME: 15 minutes

MICROWAVE COOKING TIME:
2-4 minutes

SERVES: 6 people

9-10oz frozen or canned artichoke hearts
1 red onion, chopped or 4 green onions,
  thinly sliced
1 clove garlic, minced
1 green pepper, seeded and chopped
1 tsp chopped fresh basil
1 tsp chopped fresh thyme
2 tsps chopped parsley
1lb canned navy beans, rinsed and
  drained or white kidney beans or butter
  beans
4 tomatoes, peeled, seeded and chopped

DRESSING
3 tbsps olive oil
2 tbsps white wine vinegar
½ tsp Dijon mustard
Pinch salt and pepper

GARNISH
1 head radicchio
Few leaves curly endive

If using frozen artichoke hearts, place
in a large casserole dish and cover.
Microwave on HIGH for 3-4
minutes, or until slightly warm. Stir
in the remaining ingredients, except
the dressing and garnish, and cook
for 2 minutes on HIGH to warm
through. Mix the dressing ingredients
and pour over the warm salad and
toss to coat. Serve warm. Cover and
chill for at least 2 hours before
serving. Arrange the radicchio and
endive leaves on serving plates and
pile on the salad. Spoon over any
excess dressing to serve.

Convenient Vegetable Casserole

PREPARATION TIME: 5 minutes

MICROWAVE COOKING TIME:
15 minutes

SERVES: 4 people

2 cans mushroom soup or 1 can
  condensed soup with an equal measure
  of water
2 tbsps cornstarch dissolved in 4 tbsps
  heavy cream
9-10oz frozen mixed vegetables
Pinch ground nutmeg
1 tbsp chopped parsley

TOPPING
1 package crisp fried onions

Mix the soup with the cornstarch and heavy cream. Cook, uncovered, on HIGH for 6-7 minutes, stirring occasionally after 1 minute until thickened. Break up the mixed vegetables to separate and add frozen to the sauce. Add the nutmeg and parsley and stir well. Pour into a casserole or serving dish and microwave on HIGH for 5-8 minutes or until heated through. Sprinkle on the crisp fried onions and heat 30 seconds on HIGH. Serve immediately.

Vegetable Stock

PREPARATION TIME: 15 minutes

MICROWAVE COOKING TIME:
15 minutes

MAKES: 4 cups

8oz carrots, roughly chopped
6 sticks celery, roughly chopped
1 turnip, roughly chopped (optional)
3 onions, chopped and the peel of one reserved for color
1 tomato, quartered and seeded
3 parsley stalks
1 whole clove
1 bay leaf
1 blade mace
2 sprigs thyme or other fresh herbs
6 black peppercorns
Pinch salt
4 cups water

FOR CHICKEN STOCK
Add 8oz chicken pieces (if including giblets, discard chicken livers)

FOR BEEF STOCK
Add 8oz shin of beef, cut into small cubes and browned for 8 minutes in a preheated browning dish

FOR FISH STOCK
Add skin, bones and trimmings from 8oz fish

Combine all the ingredients for the required stock in a large bowl. Half-cover the bowl with plastic wrap and cook on HIGH for 15 minutes. The stock will boil, so the bowl must be deep enough to contain it. Allow to stand for 15-20 minutes before straining. The stock will keep up to 3 days in the refrigerator. Alternatively, freeze the stock in ice cube trays for convenience. If the beef stock is not brown enough for your liking, a few drops of gravy browning can be added to the finished stock. Use the stock for soups and to prepare sauces and gravies.

Chicken Cacciatore

PREPARATION TIME: 20 minutes

MICROWAVE COOKING TIME:
35-45 minutes

SERVES: 4 people

3¼ lbs chicken, cut into 8 pieces and skinned
3 tbsps oil
1 medium onion, finely sliced
1 clove garlic, crushed
1 green pepper, seeded and thinly sliced
1 tbsp chopped fresh basil or 1½ tsps dried basil
1 bay leaf
Pinch ground nutmeg
4 tbsps red wine
6 tbsps chicken stock
8oz canned tomatoes, broken up
Salt and pepper
1 tbsp cornstarch mixed with 2 tbsps cold water
Grated Parmesan cheese (optional)

Place the oil and the onion in a large casserole dish and cook on HIGH for 3 minutes. Add the garlic, pepper, bay leaf, basil and nutmeg and a pinch of salt and pepper. Cover and cook on HIGH for 2 minutes. Pour in the wine, stock and tomatoes and stir well. Add the chicken and cook on MEDIUM for 30-40 minutes. About 6-7 minutes before the end of the cooking time, blend the cornstarch and the water and add to the

Right: Salade de Legumes (top) and Convenient Vegetable Casserole (bottom).

chicken, stirring in well. Cook until the sauce thickens. Allow to stand for 5 minutes before serving. To freeze, allow the chicken to cool completely and transfer to a serving dish or a freezer container. Cover well and store for up to 1 month. To thaw and reheat, microwave, uncovered, on HIGH for 15-20 minutes, stirring frequently. Sprinkle over grated Parmesan cheese, if desired, and serve with pasta or rice.

This page: Vegetable Stock. Facing page: Chicken Cacciatore (top) and Beef and Vegetable Stew (bottom).

EGG DISHES

Poached Eggs Hollandaise

PREPARATION TIME: 20 minutes

MICROWAVE COOKING TIME:
11-12 minutes

SERVES: 4 people

1lb fresh spinach, stems removed and
*   leaves well washed*
4 eggs

HOLLANDAISE SAUCE
1 stick butter
2 tbsps lemon juice
Pinch cayenne pepper
2 egg yolks
Salt and pepper
Paprika or nutmeg

Place the spinach in a roasting bag and secure loosely with string. Cook on HIGH for 5 minutes and drain very well, squeezing out excess moisture. Set aside while poaching the eggs. Pour 6 tbsps of hot water into each custard cup and add a drop of vinegar to each. Bring the water to the boil on HIGH for about 1½-2 minutes. Break an egg into each dish and pierce the yolk with a sharp knife or skewer. Arrange the dishes in a circle on the oven turntable and cook on HIGH for 2½-3 minutes or on MEDIUM for 3-3½ minutes. Give the dishes a half turn halfway through the cooking time. Loosen the eggs from the side of the dish with a knife and slip onto a draining spoon. Chop the spinach roughly and arrange in one large serving dish or four individual serving dishes and place an egg on top. Cover the dishes and keep warm while preparing the sauce. Place the butter for the sauce in a large glass measure or small, deep bowl and heat on HIGH for

1½ minutes. Mix the lemon juice with the cayenne pepper and egg yolks and whisk gradually into the hot butter. Cook on MEDIUM for 1 minute, whisking halfway through the cooking time. Make sure the sauce does not boil. If the sauce appears to be curdling, remove from the oven and dip the bowl or measure into cold water to stop the cooking. Whisk well and return to the oven for a further 1 minute or until thickened. Reheat the eggs and the spinach for 20 seconds on HIGH and pour over the sauce. Sprinkle either paprika or grated nutmeg on top of the sauce to serve.

Scrambled Eggs and Shrimp

PREPARATION TIME: 15 minutes

MICROWAVE COOKING TIME:
5-7½ minutes plus standing time

SERVES: 4 people

4 eggs
4 tsps butter or margarine
4 tbsps milk or light cream
1 tbsp chopped chives
2oz cooked, peeled shrimp
4 large ripe tomatoes
Salt and pepper

Place the butter in a glass measure or a small, deep bowl and cook on HIGH for about 30 seconds-1 minute. Beat the eggs with the milk and add a pinch of salt and pepper. Pour into the melted butter and cook on HIGH for 3-4½ minutes. Stir frequently while cooking to bring the set pieces of egg from the outside of the bowl to the center. When just

beginning to set, remove the eggs from the oven and stir in the chives and the shrimp. Allow to stand for 1-2 minutes to finish cooking. Meanwhile, cut the tomatoes into quarters or eighths but do not cut all the way through the base. Arrange the tomatoes in a circle on the turntable and heat through for 1-2 minutes on HIGH. To serve, press the tomatoes open slightly and fill each with some of the egg and shrimp mixture.

Asparagus and Tomato Omelet

PREPARATION TIME: 15 minutes

MICROWAVE COOKING TIME:
15 minutes

SERVES: 2 people

4oz chopped asparagus, fresh or frozen
2 tbsps water
6 tbsps milk
1 tsp flour
Salt and pepper
2 tomatoes, peeled, seeded and chopped
3 tbsps grated cheese
Paprika

Put the asparagus and water into a large casserole. Cover and cook for 5-6 minutes on HIGH. Leave to stand while preparing the omelet. Beat the egg yolks, milk, flour and salt and pepper together. Beat the egg whites until stiff but not dry and fold

Facing page: Poached Eggs Hollandaise (top) and Scrambled Eggs and Shrimp (bottom).

into the egg yolks. Melt the butter in a 9 inch glass pie dish for 30 seconds on HIGH. Pour the omelet mixture into the dish and cook on MEDIUM for 7 minutes or until softly set. Lift the edges of the omelet as it cooks to allow the uncooked mixture to spread evenly. Sprinkle with the cheese and spread on the drained asparagus and the chopped tomato. Fold over and cook for 1 minute on LOW to melt the cheese. Sprinkle with paprika and serve immediately.

Basic Custard Sauce

PREPARATION TIME: 5 minutes

MICROWAVE COOKING TIME: 3-4 minutes

MAKES: Approximately 1 cup

1 cup milk
1 vanilla pod
2 tbsps sugar
2 tsps cornstarch
2 egg yolks

Heat the milk and the vanilla pod for 2 minutes on HIGH and leave to stand for 10 minutes. Remove the vanilla pod from the milk. Mix together the sugar and the cornstarch in a small, deep bowl or a glass measure. Pour on the milk gradually, stirring constantly. Cook on HIGH for 3 minutes, stirring once or twice until the sauce thickens. Beat the egg yolks with 2 tbsps of the hot sauce, then pour into the bowl or measure and cook on LOW for 1 minute. Do not allow the sauce to boil or it will curdle. Cover with plastic wrap until ready to serve and then pour into a serving dish.

This page: Basic Custard Sauce. Facing page: Asparagus and Tomato Omelet.

VEGETABLES AND FRUIT

Stuffed Eggplants

PREPARATION TIME: 20 minutes

MICROWAVE COOKING TIME:
18-25 minutes

SERVES: 4 people

2 eggplants
1 tbsp butter or margarine
1 clove garlic, crushed
1 onion, finely chopped
1 small green pepper, seeded and chopped
2oz mushrooms, roughly chopped
2 cups canned tomatoes, chopped and
    juice reserved
1 tbsp tomato paste
2 tsps chopped basil
Pinch sugar
Salt and pepper

TOPPING
1 cup grated mozzarella cheese
1 tbsp dry breadcrumbs

Cut the eggplants in half lengthwise
and score the flesh lightly. Sprinkle
with salt and leave to stand for 20
minutes. Rinse well and pat dry.
Wrap each eggplant completely in
plastic wrap and cook on HIGH for
7-9 minutes. Leave to stand while
preparing the filling. Melt the butter
for 30 seconds on HIGH and add the
garlic and onion. Cook for 1-2
minutes on HIGH and add the green
pepper and mushrooms. Cook a
further 2-3 minutes on HIGH and
stir in the drained tomatoes and the
tomato paste. Add the basil, sugar,
salt and pepper and cover the bowl.
Cook 6-8 minutes and set aside.
Unwrap the eggplants and scoop out
the flesh, leaving a ¼ inch lining
inside the skin of each. Cut the flesh
roughly and add to the tomato
mixture. If the mixture looks dry, add
some of the reserved tomato juice.
Fill each eggplant shell and cook for
3 minutes on HIGH. Top with the
mozzarella cheese and sprinkle each
lightly with the breadcrumbs. Heat a
further 2-3 minutes on LOW to melt
the cheese before serving.

Dahl

PREPARATION TIME: 25 minutes

MICROWAVE COOKING TIME:
45 minutes plus 5-10 minutes
standing time

SERVES: 4 people

8oz lentils, brown or green
4 tbsps butter or margarine
1 large onion, finely chopped
1 clove garlic, crushed
1 red or green chili pepper, finely chopped
1 tsp cumin
1 tsp coriander
1 tsp turmeric
½ tsp cinnamon
½ tsp nutmeg
3 cups vegetable stock
Salt and pepper
1 bay leaf
Chopped coriander leaves

ACCOMPANIMENT
4-8 poppadoms

Cover the lentils with water and soak
overnight. Alternatively, microwave
10 minutes to boil the water and then
allow the lentils to boil for 2 minutes.
Leave to stand, covered, for 1 hour.
Melt the butter or margarine for
1 minute on HIGH in a large
casserole. Add the onion, garlic, chili
pepper and spices. Cook 4 minutes
on MEDIUM. Drain the lentils and
add to the casserole with the
vegetable stock. Cover and cook on
HIGH for 45 minutes, or until the
lentils are soft and tender. Allow to
stand, covered, 5-10 minutes before
serving. If desired, purée before
serving and add the chopped
coriander. To prepare the
poppadoms, brush each side lightly
with a little oil and cook one at a
time on HIGH for about 30 seconds,
or until crisp. To cook two together,
microwave for 1½-2 minutes.

Red Bean Pilaf

PREPARATION TIME: 20 minutes

MICROWAVE COOKING TIME:
1 hour 23 minutes plus standing time

SERVES: 4 people

1 cup red kidney beans
1½ cups long-grain rice
2 tbsps butter or margarine
1 green pepper, diced
4 green onions, chopped
2 tbsps chopped parsley
2 tbsps desiccated coconut
Cayenne pepper
Ground nutmeg
Salt and pepper

Cover the beans with water and
leave to soak overnight.
Alternatively, microwave 10 minutes
to boil the water, allow the beans to
boil for 2 minutes and leave to stand
1 hour, covered. Drain and cover

**Facing page: Red Bean Pilaff (top)
and Dahl (bottom).**

with fresh water and add a pinch of salt. Cook on MEDIUM for 55 minutes-1 hour. Allow to stand for 10 minutes before draining. The beans must be completely cooked. Save the cooking liquid to use as stock in other recipes if desired. Place rice in a large bowl or casserole dish and add 2 cups water and a pinch of salt. Cook for 10 minutes. Leave to stand for 5 minutes before draining. Heat the butter or margarine for 30 seconds on HIGH and add the pepper dice. Cook for 1 minute, stirring once or twice. Stir in the cayenne pepper, nutmeg, salt, pepper, rice and beans. Cook on HIGH for 1 minute. Add the green onions, parsley and desiccated coconut and cook a further 30 seconds on HIGH before serving.

Vegetable Stir-Fry

PREPARATION TIME: 20 minutes

MICROWAVE COOKING TIME:
7½ minutes

SERVES: 4 people

2 tbsps oil
4 spears broccoli
4oz pea pods, trimmed
4oz miniature corn
1 red pepper, seeded and sliced
½ cup water chestnuts, sliced
4oz mushrooms, sliced
1 clove garlic, minced
1 tbsp cornstarch
6 tbsps vegetable stock
4 tbsps soy sauce
2 tbsps sherry
4oz bean sprouts
2 green onions, sliced

Pre-heat a browning dish according to manufacturer's directions. Add the oil to the dish when hot. Cut off the broccoli flowerets and reserve them. Slice the stalks diagonally. Slice the miniature corn in half lengthwise. Put the sliced broccoli stalks and the corn together in the hot oil for 1 minute on HIGH. Add the red pepper, pea pods, water chestnuts, garlic, mushrooms and the broccoli flowerets and cook a further 1 minute on HIGH. Mix together the

cornstarch, vegetable stock, soy sauce and sherry in a glass measure or a small glass bowl and cook for 4 minutes on HIGH, stirring after 1 minute until thickened. Transfer the vegetables to a serving dish and pour over the sauce. Add the bean sprouts, green onions and cook a further 1 minute on HIGH. Serve immediately.

Cauliflower Mornay

PREPARATION TIME: 20 minutes

MICROWAVE COOKING TIME:
10-12 minutes plus standing time

SERVES: 4 people

1 head cauliflower

MORNAY SAUCE
2 tbsps butter or margarine
2 tbsps flour
1 cup milk
½ tsp Dijon mustard
½ cup grated Cheddar cheese
Salt and pepper

TOPPING
1 tbsp butter or margarine
3 tbsps dry brown breadcrumbs
Paprika

Remove all but the very pale green leaves of the cauliflower and wash well. Shake off the excess water and wrap the whole head of cauliflower in plastic wrap. Place upside down on a plate and cook on HIGH for 3 minutes. Turn over and cook an additional 3-4 minutes, or until the base is tender. Leave the cauliflower to stand, covered, for 3 minutes while preparing the sauce. Melt the butter for the sauce in a glass measure on HIGH for 1 minute. Stir in the flour and gradually add the milk. Stir continuously until the mixture is smooth. Add the mustard and salt and pepper and cook on HIGH for 1½-2 minutes, until smooth and thick. Stir in the cheese

Right: Vegetable Stir-Fry.

and leave to stand. Melt the butter for the topping for 30 seconds on HIGH and stir in the breadcrumbs and the paprika and set aside. Unwrap the cauliflower and place right-side-up in a casserole or other microwave-proof serving dish. Coat with the mornay sauce and sprinkle on the crumb topping. Heat through for 1-2 minutes on HIGH before serving.

Broccoli with Brown Butter

PREPARATION TIME: 10 minutes

MICROWAVE COOKING TIME: 13-16 minutes

SERVES: 4 people

1lb broccoli spears
6 tbsps butter

This page: Stuffed Eggplants. Facing page: Broccoli with Brown Butter (top) and Cauliflower Mornay (bottom).

1-2 tsps lemon juice
Chopped mixed herbs (optional)
Pinch pepper
Flaked toasted almonds

This page: Stuffed Tomatoes.
Facing page: Mashed Potatoes (top)
and Baked Potatoes (bottom).

Trim the broccoli spears to an even size and if the stalks are thick, trim them down slightly. Place in a shallow dish with the stalks to the outside and the flowerets in the center. Pour over 4 tbsps water and sprinkle lightly with salt. Cover with pierced plastic wrap and cook on HIGH for 8-10 minutes. Leave covered while preparing the butter. Place the butter in a deep glass bowl and microwave on HIGH for 5-6 minutes, or until a deep golden brown. Stir every 2-3 minutes. Skim the foam from the top as it develops. Add lemon juice to taste and the fresh herbs if desired. Add a pinch of black pepper and pour over drained broccoli to serve. Sprinkle on almonds.

Glazed Vegetables

PREPARATION TIME: 20 minutes

MICROWAVE COOKING TIME:
19-21 minutes plus standing time

SERVES: 4-6 people

2 tbsps butter or margarine
1 tbsp dark brown sugar
1-2 tbsps water or vegetable stock
2 carrots, peeled and cut into strips
2 salsify, peeled and cut into strips and/or
    2 turnips, peeled and cut into wedges
4oz large mushrooms, quartered
6oz button or pickling onions, peeled and
    left whole
Salt and pepper
2 tsps Dijon mustard
Fresh rosemary or thyme

Melt the butter in a large casserole for 30 seconds on HIGH. Stir in the brown sugar and stock and heat an additional 30 seconds on HIGH to help dissolve the sugar. Heat 2 cups water for 5-6 minutes on HIGH in a loosely covered bowl. When boiling, put in the onions and leave to stand for 2-3 minutes to loosen the peels. Drain well, peel and trim the root ends. Place the carrots, salsify and/or turnips and onions in the bowl with the butter and the sugar. Cook, uncovered, on HIGH for 2 minutes. Add the mushrooms, rosemary or thyme and a pinch of salt and pepper and mix well. Cover and cook on HIGH for 8 minutes or until the vegetables are tender. Stir in the mustard and cook an additional 1 minute on HIGH. Leave to stand for 1 minute and serve immediately.

Mashed Potatoes

PREPARATION TIME: 15 minutes

MICROWAVE COOKING TIME:
6-12 minutes plus standing time

SERVES: 4 people

1½ lbs potatoes, peeled
Salt and pepper
2 tbsps butter
4-6 tbsps milk
Pinch garlic powder

Cut the potatoes into even-sized pieces and put into a large bowl with a pinch of salt and 4 tbsps water. Cover and cook on HIGH for 5-10 minutes. Leave to stand for 5 minutes. Mash until smooth and then beat in the butter, pepper and garlic powder. Heat the milk in a small bowl until very hot, and beat into the potatoes a bit at a time (it may not be necessary to add all the milk). Serve immediately or reheat for 1-2 minutes, well covered. For a variation, cut the quantity of milk in half and add one beaten egg. Mix well and fill a pastry bag with a rosette tube. Pipe swirls of potato onto a plate covered with waxed paper. Chill thoroughly. Brush with additional beaten egg and sprinkle lightly with paprika. Cook on HIGH for 3-4 minutes until piping hot.

Baked Potatoes

PREPARATION TIME: 5 minutes

MICROWAVE COOKING TIME:
18 minutes

SERVES: 4 people

4 potatoes, 9oz each in weight
½ cup butter mixed with one of the
    following combinations:
1 tbsp chopped chives and 2 tsps Dijon
    mustard
1 tbsp chopped parsley and 2 tsps anchovy
    paste or essence
1 tsp chopped basil and 2 tsps tomato
    paste
1 clove garlic, crushed and 1 tbsp
    crumbled blue cheese

Scrub the potatoes well and pat them dry. Prick them 2 or 3 times with a fork and place in a circle towards the edge of the turntable. Cook for 18 minutes, turning over halfway through cooking. Wrap each potato in foil and allow to stand for 5 minutes before serving. Make a crosswise incision in the top of each potato and press at the base to open

Right: Glazed Vegetables.

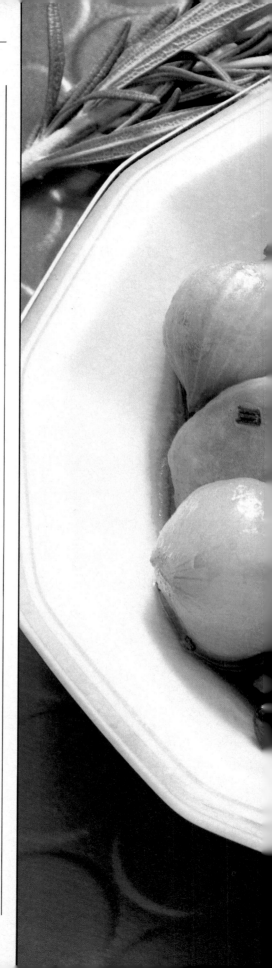

Above: Pears in White Wine and Cassis. Right: Plums in Port.

the cuts. Serve with one of the flavored butters. To prepare the butters, place the butter in a small bowl and soften for 20 seconds on HIGH. If the butter is not soft enough to mix, heat an additional 10 seconds on HIGH. Mix in the chosen flavoring ingredients and roll the butter into a cylinder shape in plastic wrap. Chill until firm and then cut into slices to serve.

Pears in White Wine and Cassis

PREPARATION TIME: 20 minutes

MICROWAVE COOKING TIME: 18-24 minutes

SERVES: 4 people

1 cup white wine
3 tbsps Creme de Cassis
½ stick cinnamon
Peel of ½ a lemon
1 cup granulated sugar
4 dessert pears, peeled

Combine the wine, cassis, cinnamon

stick and lemon peel in a deep bowl that will accommodate 4 pears snuggly. Cook on HIGH for 6-8 minutes, until piping hot. Stir in the sugar and microwave an additional 2 minutes on HIGH to dissolve. Leave the stems on the pears, but remove the eyes from the bottom of each. Place the pears stem side up. Cover the bowl with plastic wrap cutting a hole for each pear stem. This will keep the pears upright as they cook. Cook on HIGH for 10-14 minutes, or until the pears are tender. Remove the pears to a serving dish and take out the cinnamon stick and the lemon peel. If desired, the sauce may be thickened with 2 tbsps arrowroot or cornstarch before serving. Serve either hot or cold.

Honey and Brandy Peaches

PREPARATION TIME: 20 minutes

MICROWAVE COOKING TIME: 27-33 minutes

SERVES: 6 people

1 cup water
1 cup honey
1 tbsp lemon juice
4 tbsps brandy
6 ripe peaches

Place the water in a large bowl and cook for 2-2½ minutes or until hot. Stir in the honey and the lemon juice and blend well. Cook for a further 2-3 minutes, stirring every 1 minute. Remove from the microwave oven and leave to stand while preparing the peaches. Pour 4 cups water into a large bowl, cover and cook on HIGH for 8-11 minutes, or until boiling. Drop in 3 peaches at a time, and

leave to stand for 1-1½ minutes. Using a draining spoon, transfer the fruit to cold water. The skins should peel off easily. If not, repeat the procedure until the peaches peel easily. Repeat for the remaining 3 peaches and place all the peaches into the prepared syrup. Cover the bowl loosely and cook on MEDIUM for 7 minutes. Add the brandy and stir well. Leave the peaches to cool in the syrup. Serve warm or cold with whipped cream if desired.

Stuffed Tomatoes

PREPARATION TIME: 10 minutes

MICROWAVE COOKING TIME: 6 minutes

SERVES: 4 people

4 large ripe tomatoes
2 tbsps butter or margarine
1 shallot, finely chopped
8oz mushrooms, finely chopped
1 cup fresh white breadcrumbs
1 clove garlic, crushed
1 tbsp white wine
1 tsp Dijon mustard
1 tsp chopped parsley
1 tsp chopped oregano
¼ tsp thyme
Salt and pepper

Pour 2 cups water into a large bowl. Cover with plastic wrap and microwave on HIGH for 5-6 minutes, or until boiling. Place 2 tomatoes in the water and let stand for 1-1½ minutes. Remove the tomatoes to a bowl of cold water and peel off the skins. Repeat with the remaining 2 tomatoes. Remove the cores and cut the tops from the rounded ends. Scoop out the seeds, and strain the juice. Place the butter in a small bowl with the shallot and cook for 1 minute on HIGH. Add the

mushrooms, wine and garlic and cook for 2 minutes on HIGH. Stir in the breadcrumbs, mustard, herbs, seasoning and tomato juice. Mix well and fill the tomatoes with the mixture. Place the tomatoes in a circle in a shallow dish and place on the tops at a slight angle. Cook, uncovered, for 1-2 minutes on HIGH, depending upon the ripeness of the tomatoes. Serve hot and garnish with parsley if desired.

Plums in Port

PREPARATION TIME: 15 minutes

MICROWAVE COOKING TIME: 14 minutes

MAKES: Approximately 4 cups

1½ lbs plums, halved and stoned
3 cups granulated sugar
1½ cups ruby port or red wine
2 whole cloves or 1 cinnamon stick

Put the sugar and port or wine into a large, deep bowl. Put in the cloves or cinnamon stick and cook, uncovered, for 4-8 minutes on HIGH, stirring occasionally to help dissolve the sugar. Put in the plums and cover the bowl with plastic wrap and cook for 5 minutes on HIGH. Reduce the power to MEDIUM and cook a further 5 minutes. Remove the wrap and allow the plums to cool. Serve warm or cold with whipped cream or ice cream.

Facing page: Honey and Brandy Peaches.

Microwave

100 MICROWAVE SECRETS

PRESERVES AND PICKLES

Curried Fruit

PREPARATION TIME: 10 minutes

MICROWAVE COOKING TIME:
30-60 seconds plus 2-3 minutes
standing time

SERVES: 4 people

2 cups mixed dried fruit salad
2 tsps curry powder
2 tsps to 1 tbsp cornstarch
Juice of ½ a lemon
2 tbsps water

Place the dried fruit in a deep bowl.
Mix the curry powder, cornstarch,
lemon juice and water together.
Sprinkle over the fruit and cover
with plastic wrap. Cook on HIGH
for 30-60 seconds, or until the fruit is
plump and softened, stirring after
half the time. Leave to stand,
covered, 2-3 minutes. If the liquid
has not thickened enough, mix
additional cornstarch with enough
water to make a thick paste and fold
into the fruit. Cook a further
1 minute on HIGH to thicken. May
be served hot or cold with meat and
poultry.

Aromatic Oil

PREPARATION TIME: 10 minutes

MICROWAVE COOKING TIME:
1½-2 minutes

MAKES: 2 cups

2 cups vegetable oil or olive oil or a half-
and-half mixture
Peel of 1 lemon or 1 small orange
Fresh herbs such as rosemary, thyme or
tarragon

2 cloves garlic or 2 shallots
12 black peppercorns
6 whole cloves
6 allspice berries
4 juniper berries
2 bay leaves

Pour a little water into two 1 cup
bottles and sterilize for 2-3 minutes

**This page: Curried Fruit. Facing
page: Aromatic Oil (left) and
Rosemary Vinegar (right).**

on HIGH. Drain the bottles upside
down on paper towels. Choose from
the list of ingredients and divide
them equally between the two

bottles. Pour over the oil and heat the bottles for 1½-2 minutes on HIGH, uncovered. Cover and seal while still warm, and store in a cool, dark place for 1-2 weeks before using. Use in salad dressings and for sautéeing.

Pickled Orange Slices

PREPARATION TIME: 10 minutes

MICROWAVE COOKING TIME: 16 minutes

MAKES: Approximately 3 cups

3-4 oranges
1½ cups sugar
1 cup water
1 cup white wine vinegar
1 stick cinnamon
2 whole allspice berries
4 whole cloves

Slice the oranges into ¼ inch rounds, discard the ends and remove any seeds. Put the sugar, water, vinegar and whole spices into a bowl or into 2 cup sterilized jars. Cook, uncovered, for 6 minutes on HIGH. Put in the orange slices and cover with plastic wrap. Cook for 10 minutes on MEDIUM, or until the orange rind looks clearer. Remove the plastic wrap, seal and cover while still warm. Keep in the refrigerator.

Sweet Pickled Onions

PREPARATION TIME: 20 minutes

MICROWAVE COOKING TIME: 15 minutes

MAKES: Approximately 4 cups

4 cups button or pickling onions
1½ cups light brown sugar
2 cups cider, malt or white wine vinegar
½ cup water
1 tbsp mustard seed
½ cinnamon stick
Pinch salt

Put the onions in a large bowl and pour over enough water to cover.

Cook on HIGH for 1 minute. Drain and peel the onions. Put all the remaining ingredients together in a large bowl. Cook, uncovered, for 5 minutes on HIGH, stirring frequently. When the sugar has dissolved, remove the cinnamon. Put the onions in sterilized jars or into a large glass bowl. Spoon the pickling liquid over the onions and cook a further 5 minutes on HIGH. If cooked in a bowl, spoon into sterilized jars. Seal while still warm and cover. Keep in the refrigerator.

Rosemary Vinegar

PREPARATION TIME: 10 minutes

MICROWAVE COOKING TIME: 1½-2 minutes

MAKES: 2 cups

2 cups red or white wine vinegar or cider
  vinegar
2-4 sprigs fresh rosemary
12 black peppercorns

Pour a little water into two 1 cup bottles and sterilize on HIGH for 2-3 minutes. Drain the bottles upside down on paper towels. Place the sprigs of rosemary and the peppercorns in each bottle and pour on the vinegar. Heat, uncovered, for 1½-2 minutes on HIGH. Seal and cover the bottles while the vinegar is still warm. Leave in a cool, dark place for 1-2 weeks before using.

Three-Fruit Marmalade

PREPARATION TIME: 20 minutes

MICROWAVE COOKING TIME: 50-60 minutes

MAKES: 5-6lbs

4 limes
2 oranges
2 grapefruit
3 cups boiling water
7 cups granulated sugar

Squeeze the juice from the limes,

oranges and grapefruit and reserve. Cut away the peel and shred it thinly, coarsely or chop in a food processor as desired. Place the remaining pith and seeds into a piece of cheesecloth and tie into a bag. Place the juice, bag of pith and seeds and shredded peel into a large bowl. Add half the water and leave to stand for 30 minutes. Add the remaining water and cover the bowl with plastic wrap, piercing several times. Cook on HIGH for 25 minutes. Uncover the bowl and remove the cheesecloth bags and squeeze out the juice. Add the sugar and cook, uncovered, for 20-25 minutes or until the setting point is reached, stirring every 5 minutes. To test the setting point, put a plate into the freezer for 30 minutes. Drop a spoonful of the marmalade onto the plate and if it solidifies and wrinkles when the plate is tilted, setting point has been reached. Allow the marmalade to stand for 5 minutes. Sterilize the jars as for Aromatic Oil. Ladle the hot marmalade into the jars, seal and cover while still warm.

Rhubarb and Raspberry Jam

PREPARATION TIME: 10 minutes

MICROWAVE COOKING TIME: 13-15 minutes

MAKES: Approximately 4 cups

2 cups rhubarb, cut into small pieces
  (frozen or canned rhubarb, well drained
  may be substituted)
2 cups red raspberries
4 cups sugar
3 tbsps lemon juice
¼ cup pectin for every 2 cups cooked fruit
  (optional)

Put the rhubarb into a large bowl and cover with pierced plastic wrap. Cook for 2 minutes on HIGH and

Facing page: Pickled Orange Slices (top) and Sweet Pickled Onions (bottom).

add the raspberries. Re-cover the bowl and cook for 1 minute on HIGH. If using frozen or canned rhubarb, cook with the raspberries for 3 minutes on HIGH in a covered bowl. Add the sugar and lemon juice and stir well. Cook, uncovered, for 10 minutes on HIGH, stirring frequently. Measure the fruit and juice and add the necessary pectin, if using, stirring well to mix. Cook for a further 1 minute on HIGH. Test the jam by stirring with a wooden spoon. If it leaves a channel, the setting point has been reached. If not, cook a further 2-3 minutes on HIGH.

This page: Rhubarb and Raspberry Jam (top) and Three-Fruit Marmalade (bottom). Facing page: Cheesecake.

Sterilize jars as for Aromatic Oil and pour the hot jam into the jar. Seal and cover while the jam is still warm.

BAKING, DESSERTS AND BEVERAGES

Cheesecake

PREPARATION TIME: 20 minutes
plus chilling time

MICROWAVE COOKING TIME:
16-24 minutes

MAKES: 1 cake

FILLING
2 packages cream cheese
⅔ cup sugar
6 tbsps light cream or milk
Grated rind and juice of ½ a lemon
Pinch salt
4 eggs

CRUST
4oz graham crackers
3 tbsps butter or margarine
1 tbsp sugar

TOPPING
6 tbsps raspberry, strawberry or cherry
    preserve
1 tsp lemon juice

Microwave the cream cheese in a deep bowl for 1 minute on MEDIUM, or until softenend. Beat in the sugar, milk or cream and salt. Add the lemon juice and rind and the eggs gradually, beating continuously. Cook the mixture on HIGH for 4 minutes or until very hot and slightly thickened. Stir well every 2 minutes. Line a 9 inch microwave cake dish with a circle of waxed paper or 2 thicknesses of plastic wrap. Pour in the cheese mixture and leave to stand. To prepare the crust, grind the graham crackers in a food processor until fine. Cook the butter for 30 seconds- 1 minute on HIGH, pour onto the crackers and add the sugar. Process to mix and then sprinkle on top of the cheese mixture, pressing down lightly. Microwave on MEDIUM 7-15 minutes or until the cheese mixture is almost set. Rotate the dish a quarter turn every 3 minutes. A sharp knife inserted into the center should come out almost clean when the cake is done. The mixture will firm as it chills. When completely cool, refrigerate at least 8 hours or overnight. To serve, loosen the cheesecake from the edges of the dish and carefully turn out on to a plate.

Peel off the paper or plastic wrap and set aside while making the topping. Combine the preserves with the lemon juice and heat for 1 minute on HIGH. Drizzle over the cheesecake before serving.

Hot Chocolate

PREPARATION TIME: 5 minutes

MICROWAVE COOKING TIME: 4 minutes

MAKES: 4 cups

4 tbsps sugar
3 tbsps cocoa
3 cups milk
Pinch cinnamon
4 large or several small marshmallows

Place the sugar in a large glass pitcher with the cocoa. Add ½ cup milk and mix in gradually until smooth. Cook for 1 minute on HIGH and add the remaining milk, stirring well. Add the cinnamon and cook for 3 minutes further, until hot. Pour into 4 cups and top with the marshmallows.

Bombe aux Abricots

PREPARATION TIME: 2 hours

MICROWAVE COOKING TIME: 2 minutes

SERVES: 6-8 people

1 cup dried apricots
2 tbsps brandy
1½ pints vanilla ice cream
½ cup toasted, chopped hazelnuts

Place a 4 cup bombe mold or decorative mold into the freezer for 2 hours. Roughly chop the dried apricots and place them in a small bowl with the brandy. Cover well and microwave 30 seconds to 1 minute on HIGH and set aside to cool completely. Soften 1 pint vanilla ice cream for 1 minute on HIGH. Stir in the chopped toasted hazelnuts and if the ice cream is too soft, freeze again until of a spreading consistency.

Coat the base and sides of the mold with the hazelnut ice cream and freeze until firm. If the ice cream slides down the sides of the bowl during freezing, keep checking and pressing ice cream back into place. Heat the remaining ice cream on HIGH for 1 minute or until very soft. Stir in the brandied apricots. Freeze again until slushy. Pour into the center of the hazelnut ice cream and freeze until solid. About 30 minutes before serving, unmold the bombe by briefly dipping in warm water or wrapping a hot cloth around the outside of the mold. Alternatively, if the mold is microwave-proof, heat for 30 seconds on HIGH and unmold.

Irish Coffee

PREPARATION TIME: 5 minutes

MICROWAVE COOKING TIME: 6-8 minutes

MAKES: 4 cups

2½ cups hot water
1½ tbsps instant coffee
4 tbsps Irish whiskey
6 tbsps whipped cream

Place the water in a large glass pitcher and microwave on HIGH for 6-8 minutes or until boiling. Immediately stir in the instant coffee and stir until dissolved. Add the whiskey and sugar and reheat for 1 minute on HIGH. Pour into Irish coffee glasses and top with whipped cream. Serve at once.

Lemon Meringue Pie

PREPARATION TIME: 25 minutes

MICROWAVE COOKING TIME: 14-20 minutes

MAKES: 1 pie

Right: Bombe aux Abricots.

PIE CRUST
1⅓ cups graham cracker crumbs
6 tbsps butter or margarine
2 tbsps brown sugar

FILLING
1 cup sugar
4 tbsps cornstarch
1¾ cups water
3 eggs, separated

Grated rind and juice of 1 lemon
1 tbsp butter or margarine

MERINGUE
3 egg whites from the separated eggs
1 tsp cornstarch
¼ tsp cream of tartar
6 tbsps sugar

Place the graham crackers into a food

**This page: Lemon Meringue Pie.
Facing page: Hot Chocolate (left)
and Irish Coffee (right).**

processor and work until finely
ground. Melt the butter for 30
seconds on HIGH and add to the
crumbs with the machine running.
Add the sugar and press the mixture

into a 9 inch pie dish. Cook for 1½ minutes on HIGH, rotating the dish several times. Allow to cool while preparing the filling. Combine the sugar and cornstarch with 4 tbsps water in a small bowl. When well blended, stir in the remaining water gradually. Cook on HIGH for 6-8 minutes, or until thickened and clear. Stir every 2-3 minutes. Separate the eggs and beat the egg yolks lightly. Mix a little of the hot mixture into the egg yolks and then blend the yolks into the remaining mixture. Cook on HIGH for 1 minute, stirring well. Stir in the lemon peel and juice and the butter. Allow to cool slightly and then pour into the prepared pie crust. To prepare the meringue, place the egg whites in a deep mixing bowl with the cornstarch and cream of tartar. Beat until soft peaks form. Add the sugar a spoonful at a time, beating well between each addition. Continue beating until stiff peaks form. Spread the meringue over the top of the lemon mixture, covering the filling completely. Cook on MEDIUM for 3-6 minutes or until the meringue is set, turning the dish a half turn after 1½-3 minutes. The meringue may be browned under the broiler, if desired. Refrigerate the pie until chilled and serve cold.

Steamed Raspberry Jam Pudding

PREPARATION TIME: 20 minutes

MICROWAVE COOKING TIME: 5 minutes plus standing time

SERVES: 6 people

½ cup raspberry jam
½ cup butter or margarine
½ cup sugar
2 eggs
1 tsp vanilla extract
1 cup all-purpose flour
1 tsp baking powder
2 tbsps milk

Grease a 3 cup mixing bowl or decorative mold very well with butter or margarine. Put the jam into

the bottom of the mold and set aside. Cream the remaining butter or margarine and sugar until light and fluffy. Beat in the eggs 1 at a time and add vanilla extract. Sift in the flour and baking powder and fold in. If the mixture is too stiff, add up to 2 tbsps of milk to bring to a soft dropping consistency. Spoon the mixture carefully on top of the jam and smooth the top. Cover the top of the bowl or mold with 2 layers of plastic wrap, pierced several times to release the steam. Cook 5-8 minutes on HIGH. Leave to stand 5-10 minutes before turning out to serve. Serve with whipped cream or basic custard sauce.

Whole-wheat Bread

PREPARATION TIME: 1-2 hours

MICROWAVE COOKING TIME: 10-12 minutes

MAKES: 1 loaf

3 cups whole-wheat flour
1 cup all-purpose flour
1 tsp salt
1 cup milk
1 package active dry yeast
2 tbsps butter or margarine
1 tsp brown sugar

TOPPING
1 egg, beaten with a pinch of salt
Oatmeal or bran

Sift the flours and the salt into a large bowl. If topping with bran, reserve half the bran and return the rest to the bowl. Make a well in the center of the ingredients. Heat the milk for 15 seconds on HIGH. Stir in the butter to melt and the yeast to dissolve. Stir in the sugar and pour into the well in the center of the bowl and stir to incorporate gradually all the ingredients. Turn out onto a floured surface, and knead for 10 minutes. Put the dough into a lightly-greased bowl and turn over to coat all sides. Cover the yeast mixture with plastic wrap or a clean towel. Leave to rise for 1-1½ hours in

a warm place. Alternatively, place the bowl of dough in a dish of hot water and put into the microwave oven for 1 minute on HIGH or 4 minutes on LOW. Leave the dough to stand for 15 minutes and then repeat until the dough has doubled in bulk. This should cut the rising time in half. Shape the dough by punching it down and kneading again lightly for about 2 minutes. Roll the dough out to a rectangle and then roll up tightly. Seal the ends and tuck under slightly. Put into a lightly greased loaf dish, about 9 inches by 5 inches. Cover the loaf dish loosely and leave dough to rise in a warm place for about 30 minutes, or use the microwave rising method. Brush the top of the loaf with lightly beaten egg and sprinkle on the remaining bran or the oatmeal if using. Cook on MEDIUM for 6-8 minutes and give the dish a quarter turn every 1 minute. Increase the temperature to HIGH and cook for 1-2 minutes, rotating as before. The top should spring back when lightly touched if the bread is done. Leave in the dish for 5 minutes before removing to a wire rack to cool. If desired, when the bread is removed from the dish, oatmeal or bran may be pressed on the base and sides.

Mulled Wine

PREPARATION TIME: 5 minutes

MICROWAVE COOKING TIME: 4 minutes, plus standing time

MAKES: 4 cups

1 pint red wine
6 tbsps sugar
2 cinnamon sticks
Rind of half a lemon
6 cloves
4 tbsps brandy (optional)

Place the wine, sugar, cinnamon sticks, lemon peel and cloves in a large bowl. Cook for 4 minutes or

Facing page: Whole-wheat Bread (top) and Fruit Scones (bottom).

until boiling. Add the brandy, if using, and leave to stand, covered, for 5 minutes. Strain and serve warm. A cinnamon stick may be placed in each cup if desired.

Spiced Orange Tea

PREPARATION TIME: 5 minutes

MICROWAVE COOKING TIME: 6-10 minutes, plus standing time

MAKES: 4 cups

2½ cups hot water
Grated rind of half an orange
3 whole cloves
1 stick cinnamon
2 tea bags

Combine the water, orange peel and spices in a large bowl. Cover and microwave on HIGH for 6-10 minutes, or until boiling. Immediately add the tea bags and leave to stand 3-5 minutes. Remove the tea bags and take out the cinnamon with a slotted spoon. Serve with the orange rind, either hot or chilled.

Fruit Scones

PREPARATION TIME: 15 minutes

MICROWAVE COOKING TIME: 3-4 minutes

MAKES: 6-8 scones

2 cups all-purpose flour
1 tbsp baking powder
4 tbsps butter or margarine
2 tbsps sugar
¼ cup golden raisins
1 egg, beaten
4 tbsps milk

TOPPINGS
1 egg white, lightly beaten
2 tbsps sugar mixed with 1 tbsp ground cinnamon or crushed graham cracker crumbs or finely chopped walnuts or toasted almonds

Sift the flour, baking powder and a pinch of salt into a large bowl and cut in the butter or margarine until

the mixture resembles fine breadcrumbs. This may be done in a food processor. Add the sugar and the raisins and stir in by hand. Stir in the beaten egg and enough milk to form a soft dough. The dough should not be too sticky. Knead the dough lightly into a ball but do not over-work. Flatten by hand or with a rolling pin to about ½ inch thick. Cut into 2 inch rounds or squares. Place the scones in a circle on a microwave baking sheet and brush the tops with

This page: Steamed Raspberry Jam Pudding. Facing page: Mulled Wine (left) and Spiced Orange Tea (right).

lightly-beaten egg white. Sprinkle with your choice of toppings and microwave on HIGH for 3-4 minutes, changing the position of the scones from time to time as they cook. It may be necessary to microwave the scones in 2 batches. Serve warm.

Creme Caramel

PREPARATION TIME: 15 minutes

MICROWAVE COOKING TIME: 24-29 minutes

SERVES: 4-6 people

CARAMEL
½ cup water
½ cup granulated sugar

CUSTARD
3 eggs
4 tbsps sugar
1 tsp vanilla extract
Pinch salt
¾ cup light cream
¾ cup milk

To prepare the caramel, place the water and sugar in a deep bowl or a glass measure and stir well. Cook on HIGH for 10-12 minutes or until golden. Do not allow the syrup to become too dark as it will continue to cook when removed from the oven. Pour into a warm 7 inch soufflé dish or deep casserole dish, tilting the dish to swirl the caramel around the sides. Allow to cool and harden completely. Beat the eggs with the sugar, vanilla and a pinch of salt until light and fluffy. Combine the cream and the milk in a glass measure and heat on HIGH for 4 minutes. Gradually add to the egg mixture, stirring continuously. Strain the mixture over the caramel, cover the dish and place in a shallow dish with enough hot water to come 1-2 inches up the outside of the custard dish. Cook on LOW for 10-13 minutes, giving the dish a quarter turn every 2-3 minutes. When a knife is inserted into the center of the custard it should come out clean when the custard is done. Do not over-cook, however, as the custard will continue to cook while standing. When cool, chill in the refrigerator for several hours. To serve, loosen the custard carefully from the side of the dish and turn out onto a serving dish. Some of the caramel will remain in the bottom of the soufflé or casserole dish once the custard is turned out. If desired, 1oz semi-sweet chocolate or 1 tbsp coffee powder may be heated with the cream and milk and added to the custard for flavor variations.

Rhum Babas

PREPARATION TIME: 1 hour

MICROWAVE COOKING TIME: 5 minutes plus 1 minute standing time

MAKES: 12

⅔ cup milk
1 package active dry yeast
2 tsps sugar
⅔ cup butter or margarine
4 eggs
½ cup dried currants
Pinch salt

SYRUP
½ cup honey
6 tbsps water
3 tbsps brandy

Heat the milk for 30 seconds on HIGH. Mix in the sugar and yeast. Sift the flour and the salt into a large mixing bowl and warm for 15 seconds on HIGH. Make a well in the center of the flour and pour in the yeast mixture. Cover the yeast with a sprinkling of flour and leave until frothy, about 30 minutes. Stir together to form a batter. Soften the butter 30-40 seconds on HIGH and beat into the dough along with the eggs, by hand or machine. Work the dough for about 10 minutes until shiny and elastic. It will be very soft. Stir in the currants by hand. Butter 10-12 custard cups or individual molds thoroughly and spoon in the baba mixture. Cover with greased plastic wrap and leave in a warm place for 30-40 minutes. When the mixture has risen halfway up the sides of the cups, cook on HIGH for 5 minutes. The babas are done when the tops look dry. Leave to stand on a flat surface for 1 minute before turning out onto a rack. Place the honey and the water in a deep bowl and cook on HIGH for 7 minutes. Stir in the brandy and spoon the syrup over the babas to soak through. Serve with fresh fruit and cream.

Coconut Teacake

PREPARATION TIME: 20 minutes

MICROWAVE COOKING TIME: 9-11 minutes plus standing time

MAKES: 1 cake

4 tbsps butter or margarine
6 tbsps dark brown sugar
6 tbsps flaked coconut
4 tbsps chopped walnuts

CAKE
¾ cup butter or margarine
¾ cup sugar
3 eggs, beaten
1½ cups all-purpose flour
2 tsps baking powder
Milk

Line a 9 inch round cake dish with waxed paper. Place the butter in the bottom of the dish and cook on HIGH for 45 seconds-1 minute, or until the butter is melted and starting to bubble. Mix in the brown sugar, coconut and walnuts and spread evenly in the bottom of the dish. Set the dish aside while preparing the cake. Cream the butter with the sugar until light and fluffy. Beat in the eggs one at a time, beating well between each addition. Sift the flour with the baking powder and fold into the creamed mixture. Add enough milk to bring the mixture to a dropping consistency. Carefully pour over the coconut mixture in the cake dish. Cook on MEDIUM for 6 minutes, giving the dish a half turn halfway through the cooking time. Increase the setting to HIGH and continue to cook 2-4 minutes or until the cake springs back when lightly touched and begins to pull away from the sides of the dish. Let stand on a flat surface for 5 minutes before turning out onto a serving plate. Carefully remove the paper, scraping off any topping mixture and spreading it back onto the cake. Allow to cool and serve.

Coconut Teacake (top) and Rhum Babas (bottom).

Chocolate Ring Cake

PREPARATION TIME: 20 minutes

MICROWAVE COOKING TIME:
13-15 minutes plus standing time

SERVES: 6-8 people

1½ cups all-purpose flour
1½ tsps bicarbonate of soda
4 tbsps cocoa
1 cup sugar
⅔ cup butter or margarine
¾ cup evaporated milk
1 tbsp distilled white vinegar
2 eggs, beaten
Few drops vanilla extract

TOPPING
4oz white chocolate

Lightly grease a 6 cup cake ring. Sift the flour, soda and cocoa into a mixing bowl and add the sugar. Combine the evaporated milk and vinegar and set aside. Melt the butter or margarine on HIGH for 2-3 minutes or until liquid. Pour into the milk and vinegar and gradually add the beaten eggs. Pour into the dry ingredients and beat well. Pour into the cake ring and smooth down the top to level. Cook on HIGH for 10 minutes or until the top of the cake is only slightly sticky. Cool in the ring for 10 minutes then turn out onto a wire rack to cool completely. Melt the white chocolate in a small dish for 1-2 minutes on HIGH or until liquid. When the cake is cool, drizzle over the still warm white chocolate and allow to set completely before cutting the cake to serve.

Chocolate Mousse

PREPARATION TIME: 15 minutes plus chilling time

MICROWAVE COOKING TIME:
2½ minutes

SERVES: 4 people

7 tbsps unsalted butter
4 tbsps sugar
4 eggs, separated
8oz semi-sweet chocolate

4 tbsps coffee liqueur

DECORATION
Whipped cream
Coffee dragees or grated chocolate

Put the butter into a deep bowl and soften for 30 seconds on HIGH. Add the sugar and beat until light and fluffy. Gradually beat in the egg yolks. Chop the chocolate roughly and place in a small bowl with the coffee liqueur. Microwave on MEDIUM for 2 minutes or until the chocolate is completely melted. Combine the chocolate with the butter mixture and beat for 5 minutes or until the mixture is light and fluffy. Whisk the egg whites and fold into the mixture. Spoon into small dessert dishes and chill until firm. Decorate with a rosette of whipped cream and one coffee dragee or sprinkle with grated chocolate. Serve cold.

Liqueur à l'Orange

PREPARATION TIME: 15 minutes

MICROWAVE COOKING TIME:
3-4 minutes

MAKES: 3 cups

3 oranges
8oz sugar
1 pint brandy

Peel 1 of the oranges and scrape off any white pith. Set the peel aside and cut all the oranges in half and squeeze the juice. Combine orange peel and juice and sugar in a large bowl. Cook on HIGH for 3-4 minutes or until boiling. Stir frequently to help dissolve the sugar. Allow to boil for 30 seconds. Cool completely and strain the juice. Combine with the brandy and pour into a bottle. Seal well and leave to stand in a cool, dark place for 1 month before serving. Shake the bottle occasionally while storing, to mix.

Right: Chocolate Ring Cake.

This page: Eau de Framboise (left), liqueur à l'Orange (center) and Crème de Menthe (right). Facing page: Chocolate Mousse (top) and Creme Caramel (bottom).

Creme de Menthe

PREPARATION TIME: 10 minutes

MICROWAVE COOKING TIME: 9-10 minutes

MAKES: 2 cups

1½ cups sugar
1 cup water
6 sprigs mint or 1 tsp mint extract
Few drops green food coloring
1½ cups vodka

Combine the sugar, water and mint in a very large bowl. Microwave on HIGH 4-5 minutes or until boiling. Stir frequently to help dissolve the sugar. Allow to boil for 5 minutes. Watch closely, and do not allow the mixture to caramelize. Allow to cool and then remove the mint. Add mint extract, if using, and cool. Stir in the food coloring and vodka. Pour into a bottle and seal. Leave to stand in a cool, dark place for 1 month before serving. Shake the bottle occasionally while storing.

Eau de Framboise

PREPARATION TIME: 10 minutes

MICROWAVE COOKING TIME: 7-10 minutes

MAKES: 2 cups

1lb frozen or canned raspberries in syrup
1½ cups sugar
1½ cups vodka

Cook the raspberries on MEDIUM in a large bowl for 4-5 minutes. If frozen, break up as the berries defrost. Drain the juice into a large bowl and set the raspberries aside. Stir the sugar into the juice and

microwave on HIGH for 3-5 minutes, stirring until the sugar dissolves. Allow the mixture to boil rapidly. Cool completely and then add the reserved raspberries and vodka. Pour into a bottle and leave to stand in a cool, dark place, well sealed, for 1 month. Shake the bottle occasionally to mix. Strain before serving.

Molasses Cookies

PREPARATION TIME: 20 minutes

MICROWAVE COOKING TIME: 12-18 minutes

MAKES: 24 Cookies

½ cup butter or margarine
½ cup dark brown sugar
1 egg
2 tbsps molasses
2 tsps baking powder
2 cups whole-wheat flour
Pinch salt
1 tsp allspice
½ tsp ginger

FROSTING
4 cups powdered sugar
4 tbsps hot water
Yellow food coloring (optional)
Juice of 1 lemon
Zest of 1 lemon, cut in thin strips

Beat the sugar and the butter together until light and fluffy. Gradually beat in the egg and then stir in the molasses and sift in the baking powder, flour, salt and spices. Stir together well and drop in 1 inch balls on wax paper on a plate or microwave baking sheet. Arrange in a circle of 8 balls. Cook on MEDIUM for 2-3 minutes per batch, until the tops look set. Remove with the paper and cool on a flat surface. Repeat with the rest of the mixture and when cool, remove them from the paper and place on a wire rack. To prepare the frosting, mix the powdered sugar and hot water together. Add the food coloring, if using, lemon juice and lemon zest. Once the cookies are cool, coat with the frosting and leave to set completely before serving.

Microwave Meringues

PREPARATION TIME: 15 minutes

MICROWAVE COOKING TIME: 6 minutes

SERVES: 8-10 people

MERINGUES
1 egg white
4 cups powdered sugar (all the sugar may not be needed)
Food colorings such as red, green or yellow
Chopped toasted nuts or sifted cocoa powder
Flavoring extracts
Powdered sugar
Whipped cream

Beat the egg white lightly and sift in the powdered sugar until the mixture forms a pliable paste that can be rolled out like pastry. Add chosen coloring and flavoring with the powdered sugar. The mixture may be divided and several different colorings and flavoring may be used. Roll the dough to a thin sausage shape about ½ inch thick. Cut into small pieces and place well apart on wax paper on a plate or microwave baking sheet. Flatten the pieces slightly. Cook for 1 minute on HIGH or until dry. The meringues will triple in size. Leave to cool on a wire rack. The meringue mixture may be rolled to a ½ inch thickness and a very small pastry cutter used to cut out different shapes. These meringues will be slightly larger than those made by the first method. When the meringues are cool, sandwich them together with whipped cream and sprinkle lightly with powdered sugar. Serve with a fresh fruit salad, fruit sauce or chocolate sauce, if desired.

Right: Microwave Meringues (top) and Molasses Cookies (bottom).

Microwave

100 MICROWAVE SECRETS

LOW CALORIE DESSERTS

Apple Snow

PREPARATION TIME: 15 minutes	
MICROWAVE COOKING TIME: 5½-7 minutes	
SERVES: 4 people	
TOTAL CALORIES: 385	

1lb dessert apples, peeled, cored and sliced
1 tsp finely grated lemon zest
2 egg whites
2 tbsp sugar
2 drops almond extract
½ oz slivered almonds

Put the apple and lemon zest in a medium bowl, cover tightly and cook for 4-5 minutes on HIGH until pulpy. Purée in the blender. Beat the egg whites until stiff and fold half the mixture into the apple purée. Beat the sugar and almond extract into the remaining beaten whites. Half-fill four sundae dishes with the purée and pile the mallow on top. Arrange the dishes in a circle in the microwave and cook uncovered for 1½-2 minutes on HIGH until the mallow puffs up. Sprinkle with slivered almonds and quickly brown at a 6 inch distance from a hot broiler.

Rhubarb, Orange and Strawberry Comfort

PREPARATION TIME: 5 minutes	
MICROWAVE COOKING TIME: 10-12 minutes	
SERVES: 4-6 people	
TOTAL CALORIES: 202	

1lb canned rhubarb, cut into 1 inch lengths
¼ tsp ground ginger
1 10½ oz can mandarin orange segments in natural juice
Liquid sweetener
2 tbsp low fat natural yogurt
6oz strawberries, halved and rinsed
2 tbsp crunchy muesli

Put the rhubarb in a large bowl, add

This page: Rhubarb, Orange and Strawberry Comfort (top) and Apple Snow (bottom). Facing page: Hot Fruit Salad Cups.

the ground ginger and strain in the juice from the mandarin oranges. Cover and cook for 10-12 minutes on HIGH, stirring twice during cooking until the rhubarb is mushy. Mix in

sweetener to taste. Stir in the yogurt and fold in the orange segments, cover and leave to cool. Reserve four strawberries for decoration and thinly slice the remainder. Mix the sliced strawberries into the rhubarb, then spoon the mixture into individual goblets. Just before serving, sprinkle with the muesli and top with a half or whole strawberry.

Tipsy Berries

PREPARATION TIME: 5 minutes

MICROWAVE COOKING TIME:
7 minutes plus chilling

SERVES: 4-6 people

TOTAL CALORIES: 408

2 tbsps sugar
1 cup sweet red wine
2 tbsps tequila
Low calorie sweetener
1lb raspberries
4oz blackcurrants } *or use all*
4oz redcurrants } *blackcurrants*

Mix the sugar and the wine in a medium bowl and cook uncovered for 2 minutes on HIGH. Stir until the sugar is dissolved. Cook uncovered for 5 minutes, then stir in the tequila and add liquid sweetener to taste. Trim and rinse the fruit and place in a serving bowl, then pour the syrup over. Chill thoroughly in the refrigerator, stirring occasionally.

Hot Fruit Salad Cups

PREPARATION TIME: 10 minutes

MICROWAVE COOKING TIME:
6½ minutes

SERVES: 4 people

TOTAL CALORIES: 457

2 large oranges
2 tbsps sugar
1 tsp rum
1 small dessert apple
1 slice fresh or canned pineapple
1 banana
¼ oz shelled pistachios, skinned and
   chopped

Halve the oranges and put in a shallow dish, cut side down. Cook uncovered for 2 minutes on HIGH until the juice can be easily squeezed. Gently squeeze the juice and scrape out most of the flesh. Set the shells aside. Stir the sugar into the juice and cook uncovered for 1-1½ minutes on HIGH until boiling. Stir, then cook uncovered for 2 minutes on HIGH. Add the rum. Core and cube the apple, cut the pineapple into wedges and peel and slice the banana, and mix all the fruit into the juice. Cook uncovered for 30 seconds on HIGH, then stir and cook for a further 30 seconds on HIGH. Spoon the fruit into the orange shells and pour the syrup over. Decorate with pistachio nuts.

Blackberry and Raspberry Molds

PREPARATION TIME: 5 minutes

MICROWAVE COOKING TIME:
7 minutes plus setting time

SERVES: 4 people

TOTAL CALORIES: 290

8oz fresh or frozen blackberries
8oz fresh or frozen raspberries
Approximately 1 cup fresh orange juice
2 tbsps cold water
2 tsp gelatin
Liquid sweetener
4 rosettes whipping cream

Put the blackberries in one bowl and the raspberries in another and cook each separately, uncovered, for 3 minutes on HIGH or until the juice runs freely. Strain the juices into a wide-necked jug and make up to 1¼ cups with the orange juice. Put the water into a small dish or glass and cook for 30 seconds on HIGH until hot but not boiling. Sprinkle the gelatin over the surface and stir thoroughly. Cook for 20 seconds on HIGH, then stir until the gelatin is completely dissolved. Leave to cool for a few moments before pouring into the fruit juices. Stir in liquid sweetener to taste. Chill until just beginning to set. Divide the blackberries between four tall glasses and cover with the juice. Refrigerate until set, then top up with the raspberries. Decorate each with a rosette of cream.

Home Made Yogurt

PREPARATION TIME: 5 minutes

MICROWAVE COOKING TIME:
12-13 minutes plus setting time

MAKES:
approximately 2½ cups

TOTAL CALORIES: 262

2 cups skimmed milk
4 tbsps skimmed milk powder
4 tbsps low fat yogurt

Put the milk in a large bowl and cook uncovered for 2 minutes on HIGH. Stir and cook for a further 2-3 minutes on HIGH until the milk boils. Reduce the setting and cook uncovered for 8 minutes on DEFROST (35%), stirring occasionally until the milk is slightly reduced. Whip in the milk powder and leave to cool until comfortable to the touch. Whip in the yogurt, then pour into a wide-necked flask or divide between the glasses in a yogurt maker. Cover and leave for 8 hours until the yogurt is just set, then refrigerate covered for a further 3-4 hours.

Chocolate Creams

PREPARATION TIME: 5 minutes

MICROWAVE COOKING TIME:
5 minutes plus chilling time

SERVES: 4 people

TOTAL CALORIES: 568

¼ cup cocoa powder, sifted
⅓ cup custard powder
2½ cups skimmed milk

Facing page: Home Made Yogurt (top) and Tipsy Berries (bottom).

Low calorie sweetener
1 milk coated chocolate Graham cracker,
*   grated*

Mix the cocoa and custard with a little of the cold milk in a medium bowl. Whip in the remaining milk and cook uncovered for 5 minutes on HIGH, whipping frequently until thickened. Add sweetener to taste. Divide the cream between four individual molds and leave to cool for 30 minutes, then cover with plastic wrap and refrigerate until cold. Remove the plastic wrap and decorate the tops of the creams with grated cracker.

Coffee Soufflés

PREPARATION TIME: 20 minutes

MICROWAVE COOKING TIME:
40 seconds

SERVES: 4 people

TOTAL CALORIES: 795

½ cup double strength hot black coffee
1 tbsp powdered gelatin
2 eggs, separated
2 tbsp sugar
¾ cup canned evaporated milk, well
*   chilled*
½ tsp vanilla extract
1 small bar dairy flake chocolate, finely
*   crushed*
4 rosettes whipping cream

Cut four strips wax paper and attach to four individual custard cups with an elastic band, making sure that the collars protrude 1 inch above the rims. Put half the coffee in a medium jug and heat uncovered for 30 seconds on HIGH. Sprinkle on the gelatin and stir to dissolve. If necessary return to the microwave for a further 10 seconds. Beat the egg yolks and sugar until thick and mousse-like. Beat in the remaining coffee, then mix in the dissolved gelatin. In another bowl whip the milk and vanilla extract until very thick, then fold into the coffee mixture. Leave in a cool place until on the point of setting, then beat the egg whites until stiff and fold into the mixture. Pour evenly into the prepared dishes and chill until set. With the aid of a round-bladed knife dipped into hot water, remove the paper collars. Decorate the soufflés with crushed, flaked chocolate and a cream rosette.

This page: Blackberry and Raspberry Molds. Facing page: Chocolate Creams (top) and Apple and Cherry Sponge Cakes (bottom).

and vanilla extract together until thick. Fold in the flour and the chopped apple. Divide the mixture between approximately fifteen double thickness paper cases and sprinkle the cherries over each. Arrange five at a time in a circle in the microwave and cook for 45 seconds to 1 minute on HIGH until the cakes are just dry on top. Do not overcook.

Baked Bananas Sauce au Poire

PREPARATION TIME: 15 minutes

MICROWAVE COOKING TIME: 6 minutes

SERVES: 4 people

TOTAL CALORIES: 375

1 large orange
2 ripe pears
Low calorie sweetener
4 small bananas

Pare thin strips of orange and shred finely. Put into a jug, cover with cold water and cook on FULL POWER for 2 minutes or until tender. Drain and set aside. Halve the orange and squeeze the juice of one half into a blender. Remove and chop the segments from the remaining half of orange and set aside. Peel, core and cut up the pears, and blend with the orange juice to a smooth purée, adding sweetener to taste. Peel the bananas and put into a small dish. Cook uncovered for 2 minutes on HIGH, then reposition the fruit, placing the two outside bananas into the middle. Pour the pear purée over the bananas and cook uncovered for 2 minutes on HIGH. Top with the chopped orange and decorate with the reserved shreds. Serve immediately.

Apple and Cherry Sponge Cakes

PREPARATION TIME: 15 minutes

MICROWAVE COOKING TIME: 2-3 minutes

MAKES: approximately 15

TOTAL CALORIES: 590

2 large eggs
Pinch cream of tartar
2 tbsps sugar
½ tsp vanilla extract
½ cup all-purpose flour, sifted
1 dessert apple, peeled, cored and finely chopped
⅛ cup candied cherries, finely chopped

Beat the eggs, cream of tartar, sugar

This page: Coffee Soufflés. Facing page: Baked Bananas Sauce au Poire.

Microwave
FREEZER TO MICROWAVE

Microwave
FREEZER TO MICROWAVE

Food budgets go much further with a freezer and microwave in the house. Buy food in its season when it's cheapest, and freeze for later use, cooked or uncooked. Either way, defrosting in the microwave is quick and easy. Once you master the principles of freezing and microwave cooking and defrosting you will see what good friends these two appliances can be.

With the defrosting and reheating abilities of a microwave oven menu planning can become crisis-free. Most ovens incorporate an automatic defrosting control in their setting programs. If your oven does not have this facility, use the lowest temperature setting and employ an on/off technique. In other words, turn on for 30 seconds-1 minute and then let the food stand for a minute or two before repeating the process. This procedure allows the food to defrost evenly without starting to cook at the edges.

Always cover the food when defrosting or reheating. Plastic containers, plastic bags and freezer-to-table ware can be used to defrost food in. Meals can be placed on paper or plastic trays and frozen. Cover with plastic wrap or wax paper. It is usually advisable to defrost food first and then cook or reheat it, but there are exceptions to this rule, so be sure to check instructions on pre-packaged foods before proceeding. Foods frozen in blocks, such as spinach or casseroles, should be broken up as they defrost.

Bread rolls and coffee cakes can be placed on paper plates or covered in paper towels to reheat or defrost. These materials will help protect the food and will absorb the moisture which comes to the surface and could otherwise make the foods soggy. If you want a crisp crust on reheated bread, slip a sheet of foil under the paper towel, and don't cover completely.

When reheating foods in a sauce, stir occasionally to distribute heat evenly. Spread food out in an even layer for uniform heating. Sauces and gravies can be poured over sliced meat and poultry to keep it moist while reheating. To tell if reheating is completed, touch the bottom of the plate or container; if it feels hot, then the food is ready. Foods can be arranged on plates in advance and reheated without over-cooking or drying out, an advantage when entertaining. With a microwave oven you can spend more time with your guests than by yourself in the kitchen!

All the recipes in this book were prepared in an oven with a 700 watt maximum output. For 500 watt ovens add 40 seconds for each minute stated in the recipe. For 600 watt ovens add 20 seconds for each minute stated in the recipe. If using a 650 watt oven only a slight increase in overall time is necessary.

SOUPS

Potato Soup

PREPARATION TIME: 10 minutes	
MICROWAVE COOKING TIME: 21 minutes	
SERVES: 4 people	

4 cups diced potatoes
3 tbsps butter or margarine
1 onion, thinly sliced
1 cup water
3 cups milk
2 tbsps chopped fresh dill or 1 tbsp dried
    dill
1 bay leaf
Salt and pepper
Nutmeg

GARNISH
Fresh dill

Put the potatoes, butter and onions into a large bowl. Cover with plastic wrap and pierce several times. Cook for 10 minutes on HIGH. Add the milk, water, dill, bay leaf, seasoning and nutmeg and cook for 7 minutes on HIGH. Leave to stand, covered, for 1 minute. Uncover the soup and allow to cool slightly. Remove the bay leaf and pour half the soup into a food processor or blender and purée until smooth. Repeat with remaining soup. Adjust the seasoning and the consistency and if too thick, add more milk or water. Allow the soup to cool and pour into a freezer container, leaving 1 inch headspace; seal. Store up to 3 months. To defrost and reheat, cook on LOW/DEFROST for 12 minutes in the freezer container without lid. Transfer the soup to a large bowl and leave to stand 10 minutes. Cook on MEDIUM HIGH to HIGH for 10 minutes. Break up the soup with

This page: Carrot and Orange Soup. Facing page: Cream of Mushroom Soup (top) and Potato Soup (bottom).

a fork and stir every 5 minutes until the soup is hot. Serve garnished with the fresh dill.

Carrot and Orange Soup

PREPARATION TIME: 15 minutes	
MICROWAVE COOKING TIME: 24 minutes	
SERVES: 4 people	

1 cup chopped carrots
1 onion, peeled and finely chopped

Red Pepper Soup

PREPARATION TIME: 15 minutes

MICROWAVE COOKING TIME: 15 minutes

SERVES: 4 people

3 red peppers, seeded and chopped
3 tomatoes, seeded and roughly chopped
1 medium onion, peeled and finely chopped
4 cups chicken or vegetable stock
2 tbsps cornstarch
Salt and pepper

GARNISH *(after defrosting)*
½ red pepper, finely chopped
Chopped parsley

Place the peppers, tomatoes and onions in a large bowl with the stock, salt and pepper. Stir in the cornstarch. Loosely cover and cook on HIGH for 15 minutes, stirring often. Allow the soup to stand for 1-2 minutes and then purée in a food processor or blender. Allow the soup to cool completely and pour into a freezer container. Seal well and freeze up to 3 months. To defrost and reheat, follow the directions for Tomato and Basil Soup. When the soup has defrosted completely, reheat for 2-3 minutes on HIGH with the diced red pepper garnish. Sprinkle with chopped parsley just before serving.

2 cups diced potatoes
3 cups vegetable or chicken stock
3 tbsps butter or margarine
1 cup milk
1 orange
1 tsp ground ginger
Pinch sugar
Salt and pepper

Combine the carrots, potatoes and onion in a large, deep bowl. Cover loosely and cook for 10 minutes on HIGH. Add the stock, milk, ginger and the juice of the orange, reserving the peel. Add a pinch of sugar, salt and pepper and re-cover the bowl. Cook for further 10 minutes on HIGH. Leave to stand, covered, for 1 minute. Meanwhile, scrape the white pith from the orange peel and cut the peel into short, thin strips. Put into a small bowl and just cover with water. Cook on HIGH for 2 minutes to soften the peel. Drain and rinse in cold water and set aside. Uncover the soup and allow to cool slightly. Pour half the soup into a food processor or blender and purée until smooth. Repeat with remaining soup. Mix in reserved orange peel strips and pour the soup into a freezer container. Allow to cool, seal and store for up to 3 months. To defrost and reheat, follow the instructions for Potato Soup. The soup may also be served chilled. If desired, serve garnished with a swirl of cream.

Winter Vegetable Soup

PREPARATION TIME: 25 minutes

MICROWAVE COOKING TIME: 15 minutes

SERVES: 4-6 people

3½ cups vegetable stock
1 potato, peeled and diced
½ small rutabaga, peeled and diced
1-2 turnips, depending upon size, peeled and diced
1 carrot, peeled and diced

This page: Red Pepper Soup. Facing page: Winter Vegetable Soup (top) and Hot and Sour Soup (bottom).

½ small head white cabbage, shredded
1 leek, thinly sliced and well washed
1 bouquet garni (1 bay leaf, 1 sprig thyme,
    3 parsley stalks)
2 tsps tomato paste (optional)
Salt and pepper
2 tbsps chopped parsley

Combine the stock, bouquet garni, potato, rutabaga, turnips and carrots in a large, deep bowl. Loosely cover and cook for 10 minutes on HIGH. Add the cabbage and leeks and cook a further 5 minutes on HIGH. Add the tomato paste, if using, salt and pepper. Allow the soup to cool completely and remove the bouquet garni. Pour the soup into a freezer container, leaving 1 inch headspace on top. Seal and freeze for up to 3 months. To defrost and reheat, cook for 10 minutes on DEFROST and stand 10 minutes, stirring occasionally to help break-up the soup. Do not over-stir; the vegetables should remain whole. When the stock and the vegetables have defrosted, pour the soup into a bowl or serving dish and reheat on HIGH for 4-5 minutes before serving. Add the chopped parsley just before serving and adjust the seasoning.

Parsnip and Carrot Soup

PREPARATION TIME: 10 minutes

MICROWAVE COOKING TIME:
10 minutes

SERVES: 4 people

8oz parsnips, peeled and finely chopped or
    grated
8oz carrots, peeled and finely chopped or
    grated
1 cup stock or water
2 cups milk
Pinch ground nutmeg
Salt and pepper
1 small bunch chives, snipped
2-5oz light cream

Place the parsnips, carrots, water, salt and pepper and nutmeg into a large, deep bowl. Cover and cook on HIGH for 10 minutes, stirring

occasionally. Add the milk and leave the soup to stand for 1 minute. Uncover and allow to cool slightly. Pour the soup into a blender or food processor and purée until smooth. Add the chives and allow the soup to cool completely. Pour into a freezer container, seal and store for up to 3 months. To defrost and reheat, follow the instructions for Potato Soup. Just before serving, stir in the cream.

Cream of Mushroom Soup

PREPARATION TIME: 10 minutes

MICROWAVE COOKING TIME:
17 minutes

SERVES: 4 people

12oz mushrooms, cleaned and finely
    chopped
1 shallot, finely chopped
2 tbsps butter or margarine
3 tbsps all-purpose flour
1 sprig rosemary
2 cups chicken or vegetable stock
1½ cups milk
Salt and pepper
Pinch nutmeg
2 tbsps dry sherry
⅓ cup heavy cream

Put the mushrooms, shallot and butter into a large glass bowl. Cover loosely and cook on HIGH for 4 minutes, or until the mushrooms are soft. Stir occasionally. Add the flour and stir in well. Add the sprig of rosemary and gradually add the stock and milk. Add salt, pepper and nutmeg and re-cover the bowl. Cook a further 6 minutes on HIGH, or until boiling. Stir several times during cooking. Allow the soup to stand for 1-2 minutes, covered. Purée the soup in a food processor or blender, if desired, in 2 batches. Allow the soup to cool completely and then pour into a freezer container. Freeze for up to 3 months. To defrost and reheat, follow the instructions for Potato Soup. Just before reheating, stir in the sherry and the heavy cream. Adjust the seasoning and serve.

Split Pea Soup with Bacon

PREPARATION TIME: 15 minutes

MICROWAVE COOKING TIME:
40 minutes-1¼ hours

SERVES: 4 people

4 slices bacon, bones and rind removed
2 shallots, finely chopped
6 cups hot water
1 cup dried green split peas
2 small carrots, thinly sliced
1 tsp chopped thyme
1 tbsp chopped parsley
1 bay leaf
1½-3 cups vegetable stock
Salt and pepper
Dash Worcestershire sauce

Combine the bacon and the shallots in a large, deep bowl. Cover with paper towels and cook on HIGH for 2-3 minutes, or until the bacon is brown. Add the remaining ingredients and cover the bowl loosely. Cook on HIGH for 40 minutes-1¼ hours, or until the peas are soft, stirring every 10 minutes. Remove the bay leaf and allow the soup to cool completely. Purée in a food processor and add stock to bring soup to the consistency of unwhipped cream. Pour the soup into a freezer container, leaving 1 inch headspace. Seal well and freeze for up to 3 months. To defrost and reheat, follow instructions for Potato Soup. Garnish with fresh chopped parsley before serving, if desired.

Hot and Sour Soup

PREPARATION TIME: 15 minutes

MICROWAVE COOKING TIME:
18-20 minutes

SERVES: 4 people

1 chicken breast
4 cups hot water
2 carrots, thinly sliced on the diagonal
2 sticks celery, cut in thin diagonal slices

Facing page: Parsnip and Carrot Soup (top) and Split Pea Soup with Bacon (bottom).

4oz sliced mushrooms
2 tbsps cornstarch
2 tbsps white wine or rice vinegar
1 tbsp soy sauce
Dash sesame oil and tabasco
1 egg, slightly beaten

Combine the chicken, water, carrot and celery in a large, deep bowl. Cover loosely and cook on HIGH 8-10 minutes, or until the chicken is no longer pink. Turn the meat over and stir the ingredients from time to time. Remove the chicken and vegetables and reserve the stock. Allow the chicken to cool and remove the skin and bones. Cut the chicken into thin shreds. Add the chicken and mushrooms to the stock and cook a further 4-6 minutes on HIGH. Mix the cornstarch, vinegar, soy sauce, sesame oil and tabasco, and stir into the stock. Cook on HIGH 1-2 minutes, or until slightly thickened. Allow the soup to cool completely and combine with the reserved carrot and celery. Pour into a freezer container and cover well. Be sure to leave 1 inch headspace in the container before sealing. Store for up to 3 months. To defrost and reheat, follow the instructions for Winter Vegetable Soup. When soup is piping hot, pour in the beaten egg in a thin stream, stirring constantly.

Tomato and Basil Soup

PREPARATION TIME: 10 minutes

MICROWAVE COOKING TIME: 20-25 minutes

SERVES: 4 people

2 8oz cans tomatoes
2 onions, finely chopped
2 cups beef or chicken stock
1 tbsp tomato paste
2 tbsps chopped basil
Pinch ground allspice
1 bay leaf
Pinch sugar
Salt and pepper
4 tbsps red wine
2 tbsps cornstarch

GARNISH (*after defrosting*)
Fresh basil leaves

Put the tomatoes and their juice, onions, stock, tomato paste, basil, allspice and salt and pepper into a large bowl. Cook, uncovered, for 12-15 minutes on HIGH, stirring occasionally. Add a pinch of sugar if necessary, to bring out the tomato flavor. Sieve the tomatoes, extracting as much pulp as possible. Add basil and blend the wine and cornstarch and stir into the soup. Cook, uncovered, for 8-10 minutes on HIGH, stirring often until thickened. Allow the soup to cool completely and pour into a freezer container, leaving 1 inch headspace. Seal well and store for up to 3 months. To defrost and reheat, warm for 10 minutes on DEFROST. Stand for 10 minutes, breaking-up the soup with a fork as it defrosts. When completely melted, pour the soup into a serving dish and reheat 4-5 minutes on HIGH, or until hot. Garnish with fresh basil leaves before serving.

Italian Onion Soup

PREPARATION TIME: 10 minutes

MICROWAVE COOKING TIME: 22-33 minutes

SERVES: 4-6 people

1½ lbs onions, thinly sliced

16oz can plum tomatoes
2 tbsps butter or margarine
2 tbsps all-purpose flour
½ cup red wine
2 cups beef stock
¼ tsp basil
¼ tsp oregano
Tomato paste
1 bay leaf
Salt and pepper

GARNISH (after defrosting)
4 slices French bread, toasted and
    buttered
2 tbsps Mozzarella cheese, grated
2 tbsps Parmesan cheese, grated

Place the onions and butter in a large bowl and loosely cover. Cook on HIGH for 12-16 minutes, stirring occasionally. Stir in the flour and add the tomatoes and their juice, wine, stock, basil, oregano and bay leaf. Add a pinch of salt and pepper and re-cover the bowl. Cook on HIGH for 8 minutes, stirring occasionally. Reduce the setting to LOW and cook a further 4 minutes. Leave to stand, covered, for 1-2 minutes. Adjust the seasoning and add enough tomato paste to give a good tomato color and flavor. Allow the soup to

cool completely and remove the bay leaf. Pour the soup into a freezer container, leaving 1 inch headspace. Seal well and freeze for up to 3 months. Defrost and reheat as for French Onion Soup. Combine the cheeses and sprinkle onto the slices of toasted French bread. Place on a plate and cook on LOW until the cheese starts to melt. Broil conventionally until lightly browned, and place on top of the hot soup to serve.

French Onion Soup

PREPARATION TIME: 10 minutes	
MICROWAVE COOKING TIME: 30-34 minutes	
SERVES: 4-6 people	

1½ lbs onions, thinly sliced
2 tbsps butter or margarine
2 tbsps all-purpose flour
½ cup dry cider or white wine
4 cups beef stock
¼ tsp thyme
1 bay leaf
Salt and pepper
2 tbsps brandy

Facing page: Italian Onion Soup (top) and French Onion Soup (bottom). Above left: Tomato and Basil Soup. Above right: Creamy Spinach Soup.

GARNISH (after defrosting)
4 slices French bread, toasted and
    buttered
½ cup Gruyere or Swiss cheese

Place the onions and the butter in a large bowl and loosely cover. Cook on HIGH for 12-16 minutes, stirring occasionally. Stir in the flour and add the wine or cider, stock, thyme, bay leaf, salt and pepper. Re-cover the bowl and cook on HIGH for 10 minutes. Stir occasionally. Reduce the setting to LOW and cook a further 8 minutes. Leave the bowl to stand, covered, for 1-2 minutes. Remove the bay leaf and allow the soup to cool completely. Pour into a freezer container, leaving 1 inch headspace. Seal well and freeze for up to 3 months. To defrost and reheat, warm for 10 minutes on LOW or DEFROST and stand 10 minutes, breaking the soup up occasionally with a fork, but taking care not to break-up the onions. Once the soup has completely defrosted, add brandy, pour into a serving dish and reheat for 4-5 minutes on HIGH. Top the bread with the grated cheese and place on a plate. Cook on LOW until the cheese begins to melt and then broil conventionally until lightly browned. Top the soup with the cheese toast and serve immediately.

Creamy Spinach Soup

PREPARATION TIME: 15 minutes

MICROWAVE COOKING TIME: 21 minutes

SERVES: 4-6 people

2lbs fresh spinach, washed and stems removed
2 tbsps butter or margarine
1 shallot, finely chopped
2 tbsps all-purpose flour
1½ cups chicken or vegetable stock
¼ tsp marjoram
Squeeze lemon juice
Grated nutmeg
Salt and pepper
1½ cups milk
½ cup cream
1 bay leaf

GARNISH (after defrosting)
Thinly sliced lemon or 1 hard-boiled egg, chopped

Put the washed spinach into a roasting bag and tie loosely. Stand the bag upright in the oven and cook for 5 minutes on HIGH, or until the spinach is just wilted. Turn bag once. Put the butter and shallot into a large bowl, cover and cook for 5 minutes on HIGH. Stir in the flour and cook a further 2 minutes on HIGH. Add the stock, marjoram, bay leaf and grated nutmeg. Cook for 2 minutes on HIGH, stirring occasionally, until thickened. Add the spinach, salt, pepper and lemon juice and cook for 3 minutes on HIGH. Stir the milk into the soup and pour the soup into a food processor or blender and purée in 2 batches until smooth. Allow the soup to cool completely

and pour into a freezer container. Seal and freeze for up to 3 months. To defrost and reheat, follow the instructions for Potato Soup. Before serving, add the cream and adjust the seasoning. Serve garnished with thin slices of lemon or chopped hard-boiled egg.

Salad Soup

PREPARATION TIME: 10 minutes

MICROWAVE COOKING TIME: 20 minutes

SERVES: 4-6 people

2-3 potatoes, peeled and diced
6 green onions, finely chopped
½ head lettuce, shredded
4oz fresh spinach leaves, washed and stems removed
1 small bunch watercress, well washed and thick stems removed
½ cucumber, peeled and grated
2 tbsps chopped parsley
1½-2 cups chicken or vegetable stock
2 cups milk
Pinch nutmeg
Pinch cayenne pepper
Salt and pepper
½ cup light cream

GARNISH (after defrosting)
Natural yogurt
Chopped parsley

Put the potatoes into a large bowl and cover loosely. Cook for 7 minutes on HIGH, stirring occasionally. Add the vegetables, herbs and stock to the potatoes and re-cover the bowl. Cook for further 5 minutes on HIGH. Stir in the milk and add the nutmeg, cayenne pepper, salt, pepper and cream. Leave the soup to stand, covered, for 1-2 minutes and then pour into a blender or food processor. Purée the soup until smooth, and allow to cool completely. Pour into a freezer container, leaving at least 1 inch headspace. Seal well and freeze for up to 3 months. To defrost and reheat, follow the instructions for Potato Soup. Serve garnished with spoonfuls of natural yogurt sprinkled with chopped parsley.

Lima Bean and Ham Soup with Mint

PREPARATION TIME: 15 minutes

MICROWAVE COOKING TIME: 10 minutes

SERVES: 4-6 people

2oz butter or margarine
2 onions, finely chopped
1 tbsp all-purpose flour
4 cups chicken or vegetable stock
1lb frozen lima beans
1 bouquet garni (1 bay leaf, 1 sprig thyme, 3 parsley stalks)
8oz cooked ham, cut into small cubes
1 tbsp chopped mint
1 tbsp chopped parsley
2 egg yolks
½ cup heavy cream
Salt and pepper

GARNISH (after defrosting)
Fresh mint leaves

Place the butter and the onions in a large, deep bowl and cook for 2 minutes on HIGH, loosely covered, to soften the onions. Stir in the flour and gradually add the stock. Add the beans, bouquet garni, chopped mint, chopped parsley and salt and pepper. Re-cover the bowl and cook a further 10 minutes on HIGH, or until the beans are very tender. Remove the bouquet garni and allow the soup to cool slightly. Purée in a food processor or blender in 2 batches until smooth and sieve if desired. Add the ham to the soup and allow the soup to cool completely. Pour into a freezer container, leaving 1 inch headspace. Seal and freeze for up to 3 months. Defrost and reheat as for Potato Soup. Serve garnished with whole fresh mint leaves.

Facing page: Salad Soup (top) and Lima Bean and Ham Soup with Mint (bottom).

APPETIZERS

Chicken Liver Pâté

PREPARATION TIME: 8 minutes

MICROWAVE COOKING TIME:
9 minutes

SERVES: 4 people

1lb chicken livers
1 shallot, finely chopped
1 clove garlic, crushed
1 large sprig rosemary
3 tbsps butter
1 tbsp parsley
1 tbsp Madeira or sherry
1 tbsp cream
Nutmeg
Salt and pepper

GARNISH *(after defrosting)*
Juniper berries
Small sprigs rosemary

Pick over the livers, removing any discolored parts. Put the livers, shallot, garlic, rosemary and half the butter into a bowl. Cover with pierced plastic wrap and cook for 6 minutes on HIGH, stirring once. Remove the rosemary and put the mixture into a food processor with the Madeira and parsley. Purée until smooth and stir in the cream. Allow the mixture to cool and then add the remaining butter. Purée again to mix well. Divide the pâté between 4 small dishes and allow to cool completely. Cover well and freeze for up to 2 months. To defrost and serve, warm the pâté on DEFROST for about 2 minutes. Turn and rearrange the dishes often, taking care that the edges of the pâté do not heat up. Allow the pâté to stand for at least 20 minutes before serving to complete the defrosting process. Garnish with fresh rosemary and juniper berries.

Kipper Pâté

PREPARATION TIME: 10 minutes

MICROWAVE COOKING TIME:
2½-3½ minutes

SERVES: 4 people

8oz kipper fillets
4 tbsps butter or margarine
3 tbsps heavy cream

This page: Mushrooms à la Grecque. Facing page: Kipper Pâté (top) and Chicken Liver Pâté (bottom).

1 tbsp lemon juice
1 tsp grated horseradish or horseradish sauce
Pinch salt
Coarsely ground black pepper

GARNISH (*after defrosting*)
Lemon slices

Place the kippers in a small, shallow dish and cover loosely. Cook on HIGH for 2-3 minutes or until the fish breaks easily. Remove the skin and any bones and set the fish aside. Melt the butter for 30 seconds on HIGH in a deep bowl. Combine the butter and kippers in a food processor and purée until smooth. Add the lemon juice, cream and horseradish sauce and work until blended. Taste and add salt, if desired, and stir in the coarsely-ground black pepper by hand. Divide the mixture among 4 serving dishes and smooth the top. Alternatively, freeze in 1 container. Allow to cool completely before freezing and cover well. May be kept for up to 1 month. To defrost before serving, heat for 2 minutes on LOW or DEFROST, making sure the mixture does not begin to heat up. Leave to stand for 10 minutes to complete the defrosting. Serve garnished with lemon slices and hot or melba toast.

Pinwheels

PREPARATION TIME: 20 minutes

MICROWAVE COOKING TIME: 3½-6½ minutes

SERVES: 6-8 people

6oz ham, finely chopped
2 tbsps garlic and herb soft cheese
2 tbsps prepared mayonnaise
6 black olives, pitted and chopped
2 tbsps chopped pecans or walnuts
6 slices whole-wheat bread
4 tbsps butter or margarine
1 egg
4 tbsps sesame seeds

Mix the ham, cheese, mayonnaise, olives and nuts and set aside. Trim the crusts from the bread and roll each slice of bread until very thin. Spread each slice with the ham mixture and roll up as for a jelly roll. Melt the butter in a shallow dish for 30-45 seconds on HIGH. Beat the egg lightly and slowly beat into the butter. Coat the rolls in the butter and egg mixture and then roll in the sesame seeds to coat thoroughly. Chill to firm and then wrap each roll individually and freeze for up to 2 weeks. To serve, unwrap the rolls and slice each into 6 pieces with a sharp knife. Place the slices in circles on two plates. Microwave each plate on HIGH for 3-6 minutes or until the pinwheel slices are hot. Turn the plate once or twice during cooking.

Mushrooms à la Grecque

PREPARATION TIME: 15 minutes

MICROWAVE COOKING TIME: 10 minutes

SERVES: 4 people

1lb mushrooms, quartered if large
2 tbsps butter or margarine
4oz canned plum tomatoes, drained and broken up
½ tsp coriander seeds, slightly crushed
½ tsp cumin seeds, slightly crushed
½ tsp fennel seeds, slightly crushed
2 tbsps tomato paste
Juice of half lemon
1 tbsp chopped parsley
2 tsps chopped fresh coriander leaves
1 clove garlic, crushed
2 shallots, finely chopped
Salt and pepper
2 tbsps cornstarch
3 tbsps dry white wine
Salt and pepper

Place the mushrooms and butter in a large, deep bowl. Cook on HIGH for 5 minutes. Stir in the remaining ingredients except for the wine and cornstarch. Cook a further 2 minutes on HIGH, loosely covered. Take some of the hot sauce and pour into the cornstarch and white wine mixture and return it to the bowl. Stir well and cook a further 3 minutes on HIGH until the cornstarch thickens. Allow to cool completely and divide among individual serving dishes or a large freezer container. Cover well and freeze for up to 3 weeks. To defrost, cook gently on DEFROST or LOW for 10 minutes, breaking up occasionally with a fork, but being careful not to break up the mushrooms. Leave to stand 10 minutes. May be served hot or cold with toast or pitta bread.

Gnocchi Verde

PREPARATION TIME: 20 minutes

MICROWAVE COOKING TIME: 10-13 minutes

SERVES: 6-8 people

1½ lbs fresh spinach, well washed and
   stalks removed, or 10oz frozen, chopped
   spinach
¾ cup Fontina or Gruyere cheese, finely
   grated
2 tbsps Parmesan cheese, grated
1 clove garlic, crushed
½ cup fresh white breadcrumbs
¼ tsp oregano
Salt and pepper
Pinch nutmeg
1 egg, beaten

Cook the spinach in a roasting bag or loosely covered bowl for 4-5 minutes on HIGH, or until wilted. Alternatively, cook the frozen spinach 4-5 minutes on HIGH, or until defrosted. Drain the spinach well, pressing out any excess liquid. Add all the remaining ingredients, adding the egg gradually to bind the mixture together. Shape the mixture into 1 inch balls. Place on a plate

Facing page: Pinwheels (top) and Gnocchi Verde (bottom). This page: Pork and Peppercorn Pâté.

lined with wax paper and cover loosely. Freeze until firm and then pack in a container. Keep in the freezer for up to 2 weeks. To serve, place the balls well apart on a plate or microwave-proof baking sheet. Cook from frozen for 2 minutes on HIGH. Reduce the power to MEDIUM and cook for further 4-6 minutes, re-arranging once or twice. Serve hot.

Pork and Peppercorn Pâté

PREPARATION TIME: 10 minutes

MICROWAVE COOKING TIME: 15 minutes

SERVES: 6-8 people

8oz ground pork
8oz ground veal
4oz ham, minced
4oz pork liver
3oz ground pork fat
1 clove garlic, crushed
4 tbsps brandy
Ground allspice
¼ tsp thyme
2 tsps green peppercorns
2 tsps pink peppercorns

Pinch sugar
Salt and pepper
4 tbsps dry white wine
2 tbsps cornstarch
4 tbsps Gruyere cheese, grated
Dry breadcrumbs

Barely trim the ends of the fennel and cut the bulbs in half, lengthwise. Remove the core and place the bulbs in a shallow dish with 4 tbsps water. Cover loosely and cook 6-10 minutes on HIGH or until just tender. Remove from from the cooking liquid and allow to cool. Combine all the sauce ingredients in a glass measure or a small, deep bowl. Cook on HIGH for 5 minutes, stirring once or twice until thickened. Place 2 fennel halves in each of 4 serving dishes. Spoon over the sauce, leaving some of the fennel showing. Sprinkle with cheese and then lightly sprinkle with breadcrumbs. Allow to cool completely and cover each dish well. Alternatively, arrange in 1 serving dish. Freeze for up to 1 month. To defrost, heat on LOW or DEFROST for 5 minutes. Leave to stand for 5-10 minutes to complete the defrosting. To reheat, cook for 5 minutes on HIGH, and brown under a broiler before serving if desired.

8oz sliced bacon
Salt and pepper

Remove skin and ducts from the liver and chop in a food processor once or twice. Add the ground meats, ham, pork fat, garlic, brandy, allspice and thyme. Process to blend but do not over-work. Stir in the peppercorns by hand. Line a loaf dish with the strips of bacon and press in the pâté mixture on top. Fold any overlapping strips of bacon over the top of the pâté and cover it well. Cook on MEDIUM for 6 minutes and then leave to stand for 5 minutes. Cook a further 10 minutes on MEDIUM. Cover with foil, press down and weight. Leave to stand for 2 hours to firm up and then store in the freezer for up to 1 month. Defrost as for Pâté aux Herbes. Serve sliced with salad and French bread.

This page: Fennel Provençale.
Facing page: Coquilles au Poisson Fumé (top) and Sweet and Sour Cocktail Meatballs (bottom).

Fennel Provençale

PREPARATION TIME: 20 minutes

MICROWAVE COOKING TIME: 16-20 minutes

SERVES: 4 people

4 small bulbs fennel

SAUCE
8oz canned plum tomatoes
1 clove garlic, crushed
2 shallots, finely chopped
1 tbsp capers
1 tbsp chopped black olives
2 tsps chopped basil
1 tbsp chopped parsley

Coquilles au Poisson Fumé

PREPARATION TIME: 15 minutes

MICROWAVE COOKING TIME: 12 minutes

SERVES: 4 people

1½ lbs smoked haddock or cod
1¼ cups milk
1 bay leaf
6 black peppercorns
1 tbsp butter or margarine
1 shallot, finely chopped
4oz small mushrooms, quartered or sliced
2 tbsps cornstarch
4 tbsps dry white wine
1 pimento cap, chopped

TOPPING
4 tbsps dry breadcrumbs
4 tbsps Parmesan cheese
2 tbsps butter
Paprika

Place the fish and half the milk in a shallow dish. Add the bay leaf and peppercorns and cover loosely. Cook on HIGH for 2 minutes and set aside to cool in the liquid. Skin the fish and remove any bones. Flake the fish and set it aside. Reserve the cooking liquid from the fish. Melt the butter or margarine in a small, deep bowl and add the shallot and mushrooms. Cook for 5 minutes on HIGH. Strain on the cooking liquid from the fish and add the remaining milk. Mix the cornstarch with the wine and stir into the sauce. Cook a further 5 minutes on HIGH, stirring occasionally until thickened. Stir in the chopped pimento and the reserved flaked fish. Divide the mixture between 4 small dishes and smooth the top. Melt the remaining butter and mix together the breadcrumbs and the Parmesan cheese. Sprinkle on top of each dish and drizzle over the melted butter. Sprinkle lightly with paprika and allow to cool completely. Cover well and freeze for up to 1 month. To defrost, cook for 7 minutes on DEFROST or LOW and allow 5 minutes standing time. Reheat on HIGH for 3 minutes and brown under a broiler if desired before serving.

Stuffed Zucchini

PREPARATION TIME: 10 minutes

MICROWAVE COOKING TIME: 18 minutes

SERVES: 4 people

4 even-sized zucchini
1 tbsp butter or margarine
1 shallot, finely chopped
1 cup milk
2 tbsps cornstarch
16 pimento-stuffed olives, roughly chopped
1 tbsp chopped parsley
½ tsp chopped basil

TOPPING
4 tbsps dry breadcrumbs
4 tbsps Parmesan cheese, grated
2 tbsps butter
Salt and pepper

GARNISH (after defrosting)
Stuffed olives
Fresh basil leaves

Trim the ends of the zucchini and cut them in half, lengthwise. Place in a large, shallow dish with 4 tbsps water. Cover loosely with plastic wrap and cook for 4-5 minutes on HIGH. Rinse in cold water until completely cooled and drain. Carefully scoop out the flesh with a teaspoon, leaving a thin lining of flesh inside the skin. Meanwhile, melt the butter in a small, deep bowl and cook the shallot to soften. Reserve 4 tbsps of milk and add the rest to the shallot. Combine the milk with the cornstarch and add to the bowl. Cook until thickened, about 2-3 minutes on HIGH, stirring once or twice. Add the chopped herbs and the olives. Add the chopped flesh from the zucchini to the sauce mixture and stir well. Add salt and pepper to taste and fill the zucchini shells with the mixture. Sprinkle over the mixture of dry breadcrumbs and Parmesan cheese and melt the remaining butter for 30 seconds on HIGH. Drizzle over the zucchini and place them in a serving dish. Cover well and freeze for up to 1 month. To defrost, heat on LOW or DEFROST for about 4 minutes. Leave to stand approximately 5 minutes and then reheat on HIGH for 3-5 minutes or until piping hot. Broil if desired before serving. Garnish with olives and basil.

Sweet and Sour Cocktail Meatballs

PREPARATION TIME: 25 minutes

MICROWAVE COOKING TIME: 7-11 minutes

SERVES: 4-6 people

8oz ground pork or beef
1 clove garlic, minced
2oz unblanched almonds, finely chopped
Salt and pepper
SAUCE
8oz canned pineapple pieces, drained and ⅓ cup juice reserved
1 tbsp brown sugar
2 tsps cornstarch
¼ tsp ground ginger
1 tbsp white wine vinegar
1 tbsp soy sauce
1 tbsp tomato ketchup

Combine the meatball mixture and shape into 1 inch balls. Place in a circle on a plate or shallow baking dish and cook for 4 minutes, or until the meatballs are firm and no longer pink. Rearrange the meatballs once during cooking. Set the pineapple pieces aside while mixing together the sauce ingredients. Cook the sauce in a glass measure or a deep bowl for 3-7 minutes on HIGH, or until thickened. Combine the sauce with the pineapple and the meatballs and stir carefully. Allow to cool completely and arrange in a serving dish. Cover tightly and freeze for up to 1 month. To defrost, cook on LOW or DEFROST for about 4 minutes, stirring the mixture as it defrosts. Leave to stand for 5 minutes and repeat until completely defrosted. Cook a further 6 minutes on HIGH, stirring once or twice.

Chicken and Tongue Rolls

PREPARATION TIME: 15 minutes

MICROWAVE COOKING TIME: 10 minutes

SERVES: 4 people

4 chicken legs
4 slices smoked tongue
2 tbsps grated Parmesan cheese
1 tbsp grated Gruyere or Cheddar cheese
1 tbsp chopped parsley
1 tbsp white wine
Salt and pepper

Remove the bones from the chicken legs and flatten them out. Divide the tongue equally between each chicken leg. Mix together with the grated

Facing page: Stuffed Zucchini.

cheeses, parsley and salt and pepper. Place a spoonful of the mixture on top of each piece of tongue. Roll-up the chicken and tie the rolls with string two or three times. Place the rolls in a shallow dish with the white wine and partially cover. Cook the rolls on HIGH for 5 minutes. Turn over once during cooking and cook a further 5 minutes on HIGH. Allow the rolls to cool, covered, in the cooking liquid. When cool, remove the string and cover tightly. Freeze for up to 1 month. To defrost, use either LOW or DEFROST and heat for 5 minutes. Leave to stand for 5 minutes and repeat the process until completely defrosted. Reheat 4-5 minutes on HIGH if desired. Slice each roll into rounds and serve hot or cold, garnished with parsley and tomatoes if desired.

Stuffed Mushrooms

PREPARATION TIME: 8 minutes
MICROWAVE COOKING TIME: 6-8 minutes
SERVES: 6 people

6 large or 12 small mushrooms
4oz ham, finely chopped
½ cup fresh white breadcrumbs
6 tbsps finely chopped walnuts
1 egg, beaten
1 bunch chives, snipped
1 tbsp chopped parsley
1 tbsp Dijon mustard
Dry breadcrumbs
3 tbsps butter
Salt and pepper

Clean the mushrooms, trimming the stalks and chopping them finely. Mix the mushroom stalks with the ham, white breadcrumbs, walnuts, herbs, mustard and seasoning. Gradually beat in the egg to bind together. Pile the mixture on top of the mushrooms and set them aside. Melt the butter for 30 seconds on HIGH and set aside to cool slightly. Sprinkle the dry breadcrumbs on top of the mushrooms and drizzle over the melted butter. Place on a plate and freeze in one layer. Cover well and

keep in the freezer for up to 1 month. To defrost, cook on LOW or DEFROST for about 4 minutes, rotating the mushrooms occasionally. To reheat, increase the setting to HIGH and cook for about 5 minutes. The mushrooms may be browned under a broiler just before serving.

Pâté aux Herbes

PREPARATION TIME: 20 minutes
MICROWAVE COOKING TIME: 20 minutes
SERVES: 4 people

10oz chopped frozen spinach
1lb ground pork
1 onion, peeled and chopped
2 cloves garlic, crushed
4 tbsps chopped fresh mixed herbs
⅔ cup heavy cream
1 small can ham cut in ½ inch thick strips
8oz bacon
Salt and pepper
1 egg, beaten

Cook the spinach in a large bowl or casserole for 5 minutes on HIGH,

This page: Pâté aux Herbes. Facing page: Stuffed Mushrooms (top) and Chicken and Tongue Rolls (bottom).

breaking it up as it cooks. Drain well to remove any excess water. Combine with the pork, onion, garlic, herbs, cream and salt and pepper. Add the egg and stir thoroughly together. Line a 1lb glass loaf dish with the strips of bacon. Press ½ of the pork and spinach mixture into the dish on top of the bacon. Lay the ham strips on top. Repeat with remaining spinach and pork mixture. Cover the dish well and cook for 20 minutes on MEDIUM. Leave to stand until cool. Place a weight on top of the dish and leave in the refrigerator for 2 hours, or until firm. Cover tightly and freeze for up to 2 months. To defrost, heat gently on LOW or DEFROST for 10 minutes, rearranging the dish occasionally and not allowing the mixture to get too hot. Leave to stand for 10 minutes and then repeat the process until defrosted. Allow to cool and serve with salad and French bread.

MAIN MEALS

Stuffed Peppers

PREPARATION TIME: 20 minutes

MICROWAVE COOKING TIME:
28-31 minutes

SERVES: 4-6 people

3 large peppers, red, yellow and green
   variety
¾ lb ground beef
1 onion, finely chopped
½ cup rice, cooked
½ cup raisins
2 tbsps chopped walnuts
1 tbsp Worcestershire sauce
2 tsps brown sugar
2 tsps wine vinegar
Salt and pepper

SAUCE
1lb canned tomatoes
1 bay leaf
2 tsps chili powder
1 clove garlic, crushed
1 tbsp tomato paste
1 tbsp cornstarch mixed with 2 tbsps
   water
Salt and pepper

Cut the peppers in half and remove the cores and seeds. Place them in 1 layer in a shallow dish with 4 tbsps water. Cover loosely and cook for 4 minutes on HIGH. Leave to stand, covered, while preparing the filling. Cook the beef for 5-6 minutes on MEDIUM in a casserole dish. Add the onion and increase the setting to HIGH. Cook 4-6 minutes further, breaking the meat up with a fork frequently while cooking. Stir in the remaining ingredients. Drain the peppers and fill with the meat. Combine all the sauce ingredients except the cornstarch in water, in a glass measure. Cook for 12 minutes on HIGH, or until boiling. Combine the cornstarch and water and stir into the sauce. Cook a further 3 minutes, stirring frequently after 1 minute. Allow to cool slightly, remove the bay leaf and purée the sauce. Strain if desired. Pour over the peppers in a serving dish and allow to cool. Cover well and freeze for up

This page: Chicken Paprika. Facing page: Stuffed Peppers.

to 3 months. Defrost 10-15 minutes on LOW or DEFROST and allow to stand for 10 minutes. Cook 10 minutes on HIGH to reheat and serve.

Beef Ragôut

PREPARATION TIME: 20 minutes

MICROWAVE COOKING TIME:
29 minutes

SERVES: 4 people

2 tbsps oil
1lb frying steak
1 tbsp flour
1 clove garlic, crushed
½ cup red wine
1 cup beef stock
Bouquet garni (1 sprig thyme, 1 bay leaf,
    3 parsley stalks)
Salt and pepper
1 tsp tomato paste (optional)
2 large carrots, peeled and cut into
    matchsticks
2 roots of salsify, peeled and cut into
    matchsticks
2 small leeks, thinly sliced and well
    washed
4oz mushrooms, quartered

Heat a browning dish according to the manufacturer's directions. Meanwhile trim the meat and cut it into 1 inch pieces. Pour the oil into the browning dish and quickly brown the meat on all sides. Pour the meat juices and oil into a casserole dish and mix in the flour. Add the garlic and gradually stir in the wine and the stock. Add the bouquet garni, cover the dish and cook on HIGH for 6 minutes, stirring every 2 minutes until thickened. Add the meat and the bouquet garni to the dish and re-cover. Cook on HIGH for a further 15 minutes, or until the meat is tender. Adjust the seasoning and leave the casserole to stand, covered. Meanwhile, place the carrot and the salsify in a small bowl with 4 tbsps water. Cover and cook on HIGH for 4 minutes. Add the leeks and the mushrooms and re-cover the dish. Cook a further 4 minutes on HIGH, or until the vegetables are tender. Drain. Remove the bouquet garni from the meat and allow the meat to cool completely. Allow the vegetables to cool completely and freeze the meat and the vegetables in separate containers for up to 3 months. To defrost, heat the meat for 6-8 minutes on LOW or DEFROST, breaking up the chunks

of meat as they defrost. Allow to stand 10-20 minutes before reheating. Defrost the vegetables on LOW or DEFROST for 4 minutes and leave to stand before reheating. To reheat, combine the vegetables and the meat in a serving dish and cover well. Cook on HIGH for 12-15 minutes until heated through. Serve with rice, pasta or potatoes.

Spiced Pork Casserole

PREPARATION TIME: 15 minutes

MICROWAVE COOKING TIME:
16-21 minutes

SERVES: 4 people

2 tbsps oil
1lb pork fillet, cut in 1 inch cubes
1 onion, finely sliced
¼ tsp ground turmeric
½ tsp ground coriander
¼ tsp ground allspice
2 tbsps flour
1 cup chicken or vegetable stock
Juice and grated rind of 1 orange
Salt and pepper
8 dried apricots
2 tbsps golden raisins
2 tbsps currants

Heat a browning dish according to the manufacturer's directions. When hot, add half the oil and quickly brown the pork on all sides. Place the onion in a large bowl or casserole with the remaining oil, cover loosely and cook on HIGH for 3 minutes. Stir in the spices and the flour and then add the stock, orange juice and rind and cover the bowl. Cook on HIGH for a further 3 minutes. Stir well and add the contents of the browning dish, salt and pepper and the dried fruit. Cook, uncovered, on HIGH for 10-15 minutes, stirring several times during cooking. Adjust the seasoning and allow to cool completely. Fill a serving dish or a freezer container with the casserole and seal well. Freeze for up to 2 months. To defrost, keep the casserole covered and heat on LOW or DEFROST for 4-6 minutes, breaking-up large pieces of the casserole as it defrosts. Allow to

stand, covered, for 10-20 minutes before reheating. Reheat on HIGH for 12-14 minutes and serve with rice.

Chicken Paprika

PREPARATION TIME: 20 minutes

MICROWAVE COOKING TIME:
36-47 minutes plus standing time

SERVES: 4 people

3¼ lbs chicken, cut into 8 pieces and
    skinned
3 tbsps oil
1 medium onion, finely sliced
1 clove garlic, crushed
1 red pepper, seeded and thinly sliced
1 tbsp mild paprika
Pinch cayenne pepper (optional)
½ cup chicken stock
8oz canned tomatoes, broken-up
Salt and pepper
1 tbsp cornstarch mixed with 2 tbsps cold
    water

GARNISH
Natural yogurt or sour cream if desired

Place the oil and onion in a large casserole dish and cook on HIGH for 3 minutes. Add the garlic, peppers, paprika, cayenne pepper if using and salt and pepper. Cover and cook on HIGH for 2 minutes. Pour in the stock and tomatoes and stir well. Add the chicken and cook on MEDIUM for 30-40 minutes. Blend the cornstarch and the water and add to the chicken, stirring well. Cook for 6-7 minutes on MEDIUM or until the sauce thickens. Allow to stand for 5 minutes. Allow to cool completely and transfer to a serving dish or freezer container. Cover well and store for up to 2 months. To thaw and reheat, cook, uncovered, on LOW or DEFROST for 15 minutes, stirring frequently. Leave to stand 10 minutes and reheat on HIGH for 10-12 minutes. When

**Facing page: Beef Ragôut (top) and
Spiced Pork Casserole (bottom).**

cubes of lamb, stirring to brown. Add the garlic and the spices and cook for 5 minutes on HIGH, stirring frequently. Pour the contents of the browning dish into a casserole, add the onions and sprinkle on the flour. Stir to mix thoroughly and pour on the stock. Add tomato paste. Cover and cook on HIGH for 10 minutes. Stir in the peppers and the onions and cook for a further 10 minutes on HIGH. Allow to cool completely and put into a freezer container or a serving dish. Freeze for up to 3 months. Microwave on LOW or DEFROST for 5 minutes breaking-up the ingredients as they defrost. Allow the curry to stand for 5 minutes and then repeat the defrosting for another 5 minutes. Leave to stand 10 minutes. Repeat if necessary. When completely defrosted, stir in the coconut and heat for 8 minutes on HIGH. Add the yogurt and the tomatoes and cook for a further 2 minutes on HIGH, or until heated through. Serve with rice.

Chicken Korma

PREPARATION TIME: 15 minutes
MICROWAVE COOKING TIME: 20 minutes
SERVES: 4 people

2 tbsps butter or margarine
1 onion, chopped
2 apples, peeled, cored and chopped
1 tbsp curry paste
1 tbsp flour
1 cup chicken or vegetable stock
1 tsp lime juice
1 tsp tomato paste (optional)
1lb chicken, skinned, boned and diced
Salt and pepper
½ cup roasted cashews
½ cup natural yogurt

Melt the butter for 30 seconds on HIGH in a bowl. Add the onion and

thoroughly hot, spoon yogurt or sour cream over the top, if using, and serve with pasta.

Lamb Masala

PREPARATION TIME: 15 minutes
MICROWAVE COOKING TIME: 30 minutes
SERVES: 4 people

1 tbsp oil
1lb lamb fillet, cut into 1 inch pieces
2 cloves garlic, crushed
2 tbsps garam masala
1 tsp ground cumin
1 tsp ground coriander
½ tsp ground ginger
Pinch ground cloves
Pinch ground cinnamon
1 small red pepper, seeded and sliced
1 small green pepper, seeded and sliced
1 onion, sliced
1½ tbsps flour
½ cup stock
2 tsps tomato paste
2 tsps desiccated coconut
2 tbsps natural yogurt
3 tomatoes, quartered and cored
Salt and pepper

Heat a browning dish according to the manufacturer's directions. When hot, pour in the oil and add the

This page: Spicy Lamb Chops. Facing page: Lamb Masala (top) and Chicken Korma (bottom).

apples and cook, uncovered, on HIGH for 4 minutes, stirring occasionally. Add the curry paste, flour, stock, lime juice and tomato paste if using. Stir together well and cook on HIGH for 2 minutes. Stir in the diced chicken and cover the bowl. Cook on HIGH for 3 minutes and then stir well. Cook a further 3-5 minutes on HIGH until the apple has disintegrated and the chicken is cooked. Stir in the cashews and allow the curry to cool completely. Put into a freezer container or a serving dish, cover well and freeze for up to 2 months. Heat for 5 minutes on LOW or DEFROST, breaking-up the ingredients as they defrost. Leave the curry to stand for 5 minutes and then heat again on LOW or DEFROST for 5 minutes, or until completely defrosted. Leave to stand 10 minutes to complete defrosting. Reheat for 8 minutes on HIGH and stir in the yogurt. Cook a further 2 minutes on HIGH and serve with rice or poppadums. To prepare poppadums in the microwave oven, brush each side lightly with oil and cook one at a time on HIGH for about 30 seconds, or until crisp.

Piquant Liver

PREPARATION TIME: 20 minutes

MICROWAVE COOKING TIME: 14-15 minutes

SERVES: 4 people

2 tbsps butter or margarine
2 onions, thinly sliced
2 tbsps flour mixed with a good pinch of salt and pepper
1lb lambs' or calves' liver, thinly sliced
½ cup beef stock
2 tbsps white wine vinegar
½ tsp marjoram
1 tbsp chopped parsley

Put the butter or margarine and the onions into a bowl and cook on HIGH for 2-3 minutes, stirring occasionally. Skin the liver and remove any large ducts or tubes. Toss in the seasoned flour and shake off the excess. Mix any remaining flour

with the stock and vinegar. Layer the liver and onions in a shallow baking dish. Add the marjoram and parsley to the stock mixture and pour over the liver. Cover the dish with pierced plastic wrap and cook on HIGH for 10-12 minutes, stirring occasionally. Allow to cool completely before wrapping and freezing. Store up to 6 weeks. To defrost, microwave on LOW or DEFROST for 8-10 minutes and allow to stand for about 10 minutes. Reheat on HIGH for 10-12 minutes, stirring occasionally. Serve with saffron rice.

Kidneys Turbigo

PREPARATION TIME: 15 minutes

MICROWAVE COOKING TIME: 20 minutes

SERVES: 4 people

1 tbsp oil
8oz small pork sausages, skins pricked all over
12 lambs' kidneys, halved and cored
8oz button onions, peeled
4oz small mushrooms, left whole
1 cup beef stock
1 tbsp tomato paste
2 tbsps sherry
1 bay leaf
¼ tsp thyme
2 tbsps cornstarch dissolved in 4 tbsps cold water
1 tbsp chopped parsley
Salt and pepper

Heat a browning dish according to the manufacturer's directions. Add the oil and cook for 30 seconds on HIGH. Add the sausages and cook on HIGH for about 5 minutes, turning over several times during cooking, until lightly browned. Remove the sausages from the browning dish to a casserole. Reheat the dish and brown the onions lightly. Add the onions to the sausages in the casserole along with the kidneys and the mushrooms. Pour over the stock and stir in the tomato paste. Add the sherry, bay leaf, thyme and salt and pepper and cover the dish. Cook on HIGH for

about 12 minutes, stirring frequently. Add the cornstarch and water mixture to the casserole and stir very well. Cook, uncovered, about 3 minutes or until the sauce thickens. Stir frequently after 1 minute. Remove the bay leaf and allow the casserole to cool completely. Freeze in the casserole dish or another serving dish. Cover well and keep in the freezer for up to 6 weeks. To defrost, warm on LOW or DEFROST for 10-12 minutes, with a 3 minute interval after each 5 minutes of defrosting. Reheat for 7-10 minutes on HIGH and garnish with chopped parsley.

Spicy Lamb Chops

PREPARATION TIME: 20 minutes

MICROWAVE COOKING TIME: 17½-19½ minutes

SERVES: 4 people

2 tbsps oil
1 tsp ground cumin
1 tsp ground coriander
1 tsp chili powder
1 tbsp red wine vinegar
4 tbsps orange juice
1 tbsp soft brown sugar
1 tsp tomato paste
1 tsp Worcestershire sauce
1 cup beef or chicken stock
4 lamb chump chops
1 onion, sliced
1 small red and 1 small green pepper, seeded and sliced
2oz salted peanuts
Pepper
2 tbsps cornstarch mixed with 4 tbsps water

Heat the oil in a shallow dish for 30 seconds on HIGH. Stir in the spices and all the remaining marinade ingredients. Heat for 2 minutes on HIGH and set aside to cool. When cold, place in the lamb chops and turn them once or twice to coat evenly. Leave to marinate for about

Facing page: Kidneys Turbigo (top) and Piquant Liver (bottom).

Veal with Fennel and Tomato

PREPARATION TIME: 15 minutes

MICROWAVE COOKING TIME:
16-21 minutes

SERVES: 4 people

2 tbsps oil
1lb lean veal, cut into 1 inch cubes
1 medium onion, finely sliced
¼ tsp fennel seed, crushed
1 tsp chopped basil
1 bay leaf
1 clove garlic, crushed
12oz canned plum tomatoes
2 tsps tomato paste
½ cup red wine
2 tbsps cornstarch
1 bulb fennel, trimmed and thinly sliced

Heat a browning dish according to the manufacturer's instructions. When hot, add the oil to the dish and quickly brown the veal on all sides. Remove the veal, add the onions to the dish and stir to brown lightly. Transfer the veal and onions to a casserole dish and add the fennel seed, basil, bay leaf and garlic. Stir in the canned tomatoes and the tomato paste. Cover the dish and cook on HIGH for 10-15 minutes, stirring halfway through cooking. Add salt and pepper and leave to stand while preparing the fennel. Put the fennel slices into a small bowl or casserole with 4 tbsps water. Cover and cook for 6 minutes on HIGH. Leave both the veal and the fennel to cool and pack them separately into freezer containers. Freeze for up to 2 months. To defrost, follow the instructions for Beef Ragôut. When defrosted, combine the fennel and the veal in a serving dish, cover, and cook on HIGH for 12-15 minutes, or until heated through. Serve with rice or pasta.

1 hour in the refrigerator. Heat a browning dish according to the manufacturer's instructions. When hot, lift the chops from the marinade and drain them. Place them on the hot browning dish and press down firmly. Cook, uncovered, for 5 minutes on HIGH. Turn the chops over and lower the temperature to MEDIUM or ROAST and cook for 3-4 minutes. Set aside to cool. Meanwhile, combine the remaining marinade with the onions and the peppers. Cook, uncovered, for 5 minutes on HIGH and add the cornstarch and water mixture. Stir well and cook 2-3 minutes or until thickened. Add the peanuts and allow the sauce to cool. Arrange the

This page: Shrimp and Chicken Pilaf. Facing page: Veal with Fennel and Tomato (top) and Chicken Dijon (bottom).

lamb chops in a serving dish that will go into the freezer. Pour over the cooled sauce and cover well. Freeze for up to 2 months. To defrost, microwave on LOW or DEFROST for 5 minutes. Allow the dish to stand for 5 minutes and then repeat the defrosting for a further 5 minutes or until completely defrosted. To reheat, microwave on HIGH for 10-15 minutes or until all the ingredients are hot.

Chicken Dijon

PREPARATION TIME: 15 minutes
plus overnight soaking for lentils

MICROWAVE COOKING TIME:
21-26 minutes

SERVES: 4 people

2 tbsps oil
1½ lbs chicken pieces, skinned
12 button onions
1 tbsp flour
1½ cups chicken stock
2 tbsps Dijon mustard
1 tsp coarsely ground black pepper
4oz red lentils
Salt
Bouquet garni
1 tbsp chopped parsley

Heat a browning dish according to the manufacturer's directions. Pour the oil into the browning dish when it is hot and add the chicken pieces, a few at a time. Turn them to brown quickly on all sides and remove them to a bowl. Reheat the browning dish and brown the button onions quickly and place them with the chicken. Add the flour to the browning dish and cook 1 minute on HIGH to brown slightly. Pour over some of the chicken stock to deglaze the browning dish and add to the chicken. Pour over the remaining stock and stir in the Dijon mustard and coarsely ground black pepper. Add the lentils, salt and bouquet garni. Cover loosely and cook on HIGH for 15-20 minutes, stirring occasionally. Allow to cool and remove the bouquet garni. Arrange in a serving dish and cover well. Freeze for up to 2 months. Defrost for 10-12 minutes on a LOW or DEFROST setting. Allow the chicken to stand for 3-5 minutes at 5 minute intervals during defrosting if the outside edges of the casserole begin cooking before the middle has defrosted. Reheat on HIGH for 10-12 minutes and sprinkle with the chopped parsley before serving. Serve with potatoes or pasta.

Fisherman's Pie

PREPARATION TIME: 15 minutes

MICROWAVE COOKING TIME:
26-28 minutes

SERVES: 4 people

1lb fish and shellfish (mixture of whitefish, smoked fish, shrimp and mussels)
1½ lbs potatoes, peeled
2 tbsps butter or margarine
4 tbsps hot milk
Salt and pepper

SAUCE
2 tbsps butter or margarine
2 tbsps flour
Milk
3 tbsps chopped parsley
Dash tabasco
Salt and pepper

GLAZE
1 egg, beaten with a pinch of salt

Skin the fish and remove any bones. Cut into chunks, place in a large bowl and cover with pierced plastic wrap. Cook on HIGH for 4 minutes. Add the mussels to the bowl and cook for a further 2 minutes on HIGH. Leave to stand, covered, while preparing the potatoes. Place the potatoes in a bowl with 4 tbsps water, cover and cook on HIGH for 10-12 minutes or until tender. Drain well and mash with butter and hot milk until smooth. Season with salt and pepper. Melt the butter for the sauce in a glass measure for 30 seconds on HIGH. Stir in the flour and measure the juices from the fish. Make up to 1 cup with cold milk. Stir the milk and fish juices into the flour and butter and whisk well. Cook on HIGH for 6 minutes, whisking several times during cooking to prevent lumps from forming. Stir in the parsley and add salt and pepper and a dash of tabasco. Arrange the fish and mussels in a casserole dish and add the shrimp. Pour the sauce over the fish and smooth down. Spoon or pipe the mashed potato on top in a lattice pattern. Allow the pie to cool completely and then freeze until the potato is firm. Cover the pie well and freeze up to 2 months. Heat the pie for 10 minutes on LOW or DEFROST, leaving a 3 minute interval between each 5 minute defrosting period. Glaze the potato with the beaten egg and cook on HIGH for 12-15 minutes, or until heated through. Brown under a preheated broiler before serving.

Cauliflower and Ham Mornay

PREPARATION TIME: 15 minutes

MICROWAVE COOKING TIME:
18-25 minutes

SERVES: 4 people

1 medium sized cauliflower, broken into large flowerets
4oz ham, cut into cubes or strips

MORNAY SAUCE
2 tbsps butter or margarine
2 tbsps flour
1 cup milk
Salt and pepper
Dash Worcestershire sauce
Dash tabasco
1 cup Cheddar cheese, grated

Place the cauliflower flowerets in a bowl or casserole with 3 tbsps water. Cover and cook on HIGH for 10-15 minutes, stirring gently occasionally. Drain the cauliflower and mix with the ham. Arrange in a shallow serving dish. Melt the butter or margarine for the sauce in a glass measure for 1-2 minutes on HIGH. Stir in the flour and gradually beat in the milk. Cook on HIGH for 7-8 minutes, whisking occasionally to prevent lumps from forming. Season with salt and pepper, Worcestershire sauce and tabasco. Stir in half the cheese. Pour the sauce over the cauliflower and ham and sprinkle on the remaining cheese. To freeze, allow to cool completely and cover well. Freeze for up to 1 month. To defrost, heat on LOW or DEFROST for 15-20 minutes, taking the dish out of the oven and leaving it to stand for 2-3 minutes at 5 minute intervals if outside edges begin to cook before the middle is defrosted. To reheat, cook on HIGH for 5-7 minutes and brown under a hot broiler if desired.

Facing page: Fisherman's Pie (top) and Cauliflower and Ham Mornay (bottom).

Chicken Veracruz

PREPARATION TIME: 25 minutes	
MICROWAVE COOKING TIME: 38 minutes	
SERVES: 4 people	

1lb chicken, skinned and boned
2 tbsps oil
2 medium onions, diced
2 tsps chili powder
1 clove garlic, crushed
2 tsps dried oregano
2 tsps cumin seed, slightly crushed
1 tsp cayenne pepper
Salt
1 tbsp cornstarch mixed with 2 tbsps
    water
1 cup chicken stock
8oz canned tomatoes
15oz canned chickpeas, drained and
    rinsed
1 small red pepper, seeded and diced
1 small green pepper, seeded and diced
1 small yellow pepper, seeded and diced

Cut the chicken into small cubes. Place the oil and the onions in a bowl with the chili powder and cook on HIGH for 3 minutes or until the onion softens. Add the remaining ingredients except the chickpeas and peppers and stir well. Cover and cook on HIGH for 10 minutes. Turn down to LOW or DEFROST and cook for 20 minutes or until the chicken is tender. Add the chickpeas and peppers and cook for a further 5 minutes on HIGH. Allow to cool completely before transferring to a serving dish or a freezer container. Cover well and store for up to 2 months. To thaw and reheat, cook on LOW or DEFROST for 10-12 minutes, stirring from time to time. Leave to stand 10 minutes. Reheat on HIGH 7-10 minutes. Serve with rice.

Pork Normande

PREPARATION TIME: 20 minutes	
MICROWAVE COOKING TIME: 48 minutes	
SERVES: 4 people	

2 tbsps butter or margarine
2-3 pork fillets, thinly sliced
2 shallots, finely chopped
1 cooking apple, peeled, cored and
    chopped
½ cup dry cider
½ cup chicken or vegetable stock
1 tsp lemon juice
1 tsp crumbled sage
Salt and pepper
½ cup golden raisins
1 tbsp cornstarch mixed with 2 tbsps
    water
4 tbsps heavy cream

GARNISH (after defrosting)
2 apples, cored and thinly sliced
2 tbsps brown sugar
2 tbsps chopped parsley

Pre-heat a browning dish according to the manufacturer's directions. When hot, melt the butter and add the pork and shallots and stir to brown. Return the browning dish to the oven and cook on HIGH for 5 minutes, stirring frequently. Pour the contents of the browning dish into a casserole and add the apple, cider, stock, lemon juice, sage and salt and pepper. Cover the dish and cook on MEDIUM for about 40 minutes. Stir the cornstarch and water mixture into the sauce and cook for 2-3 minutes on HIGH, or until thickened. Add the cream and the raisins and stir well. Allow to cool completely and then put into a serving dish or freezer container. Reserve the garnish for later use. Freeze for up to 2 months. To defrost, warm on LOW or DEFROST for 5 minutes, breaking-up the ingredients as they thaw. Allow the pork to stand for 5 minutes and then repeat the process until completely defrosted. To reheat, cook on HIGH for 10-15 minutes. To garnish, heat a browning dish according to the manufacturer's directions and when hot place on the sliced apples. Sprinkle over the brown sugar and turn the apples frequently to glaze. Cook for approximately 2-3 minutes on HIGH. Arrange the apples on top of the pork and sprinkle with chopped parsley to serve.

or until all the ingredients are hot. Do not over-cook the shrimp. Sprinkle with Parmesan cheese to serve.

Tarragon Chicken

PREPARATION TIME: 10 minutes

MICROWAVE COOKING TIME: 19 minutes

SERVES: 4 people

4 tbsps butter or margarine
1 clove garlic, crushed
2 shallots, finely chopped
2oz small mushrooms, left whole
4 chicken breasts, skinned and boned
2 tbsps chopped fresh tarragon
Salt and pepper
1 cup chicken stock
2 tbsps cornstarch
½ cup heavy cream
Squeeze lemon juice

GARNISH *(after defrosting)*
Fresh tarragon sprigs

Heat the butter or margarine in a large casserole dish for 1-2 minutes on HIGH. Add the garlic, shallot and mushrooms. Cover and cook on HIGH for 2 minutes. Arrange the chicken on top of the mushrooms and sprinkle over the tarragon. Reserve 4 tbsps chicken stock to mix with the cornstarch and add the rest of the stock to the chicken. Cover and cook on MEDIUM or ROAST for 12 minutes. Stir occasionally during cooking. Add the cornstarch and stock mixture to the chicken and stir well. Cook for 2-3 minutes on HIGH, uncovered, or until thickened. Stir in the double cream and adjust the seasoning. Add the lemon juice and allow the chicken to cool completely. Put into a freezer container or arrange in a serving dish, cover well and freeze for up to 2 months. To thaw, heat on LOW or DEFROST for 5 minutes and then leave to stand for 5 minutes. Repeat the process until completely defrosted. To reheat, cook on HIGH for 10-15 minutes, stirring occasionally. Garnish with fresh tarragon leaves before serving.

Shrimp and Chicken Pilaf

PREPARATION TIME: 15 minutes

MICROWAVE COOKING TIME: 30-40 minutes

SERVES: 4-6 people

4 tbsps butter or margarine
12oz chicken, skinned, boned and cut into thin shreds
1 onion, sliced
1 red pepper, seeded and sliced
1 green pepper, seeded and sliced
3oz mushrooms sliced
2oz unblanched almonds, roughly chopped
2 sticks celery, sliced
1 clove garlic, crushed
1 tsp turmeric
1 tsp basil, chopped
2 tbsps parsley, chopped
Salt and pepper
1½ cups cooked rice
8oz frozen peeled shrimp
½ cup grated Parmesan cheese

Facing page: Chicken Veracruz. This page: Tarragon Chicken (top) and Pork Normande (bottom).

Melt the butter for 30 seconds on HIGH in a large casserole. Add the chicken and cover the dish. Cook on HIGH for 6-8 minutes, stirring occasionally. Add all the remaining ingredients except the shrimp, cheese and rice. Cook together well and cook for a further 5 minutes on HIGH, stirring occasionally. Stir in the rice and allow the mixture to cool completely. Pack into a freezer container, separately from the shrimp and reserve the cheese to finish. Freeze for up to 2 months. To defrost, warm on LOW or DEFROST for 5 minutes, breaking the ingredients up as they defrost. Leave to stand, covered, for 5 minutes and heat again on LOW or DEFROST for a further 5 minutes or until completely defrosted. Reheat for 5 minutes on HIGH and stir in the frozen shrimp. Reheat a further 5 minutes on HIGH

VEGETABLES AND SNACKS

Ratatouille

PREPARATION TIME: 30 minutes

MICROWAVE COOKING TIME: 10-15 minutes

SERVES: 4-6 people

1 large eggplant, sliced, scored and salted
1lb zucchini, thinly sliced
1 large onion, thinly sliced
1 green pepper, cored and thinly sliced
1lb tomatoes, skinned and chopped
2 tbsps olive oil
1 clove garlic, crushed
1 tsp chopped thyme
2 tsps chopped basil
Salt and pepper

Rinse eggplant and pat dry. Mix all the ingredients together in a large bowl. Cover with plastic wrap and microwave on HIGH for 10-15 minutes. Adjust the seasoning and allow to cool completely. Freeze in a serving dish or deep container. To thaw, warm on LOW or DEFROST for 10-12 minutes, breaking-up the ingredients as they thaw. May be served hot or cold. Reheat 5-7 minutes on HIGH.

Stuffed Baked Potatoes

PREPARATION TIME: 30 minutes

MICROWAVE COOKING TIME: 19 minutes plus standing time

SERVES: 4-8 people

4 large potatoes, scrubbed but not peeled
2 tbsps butter or margarine
2 shallots, finely chopped
4 strips bacon, diced
4 mushrooms, finely chopped
2 tbsps frozen peas

½ cup grated Cheddar cheese
Paprika

Prick the potato skins well and then arrange the potatoes on paper towels on the oven turntable. Cook on HIGH for 15 minutes, turning the potatoes over and re-arranging after half the cooking time. Wrap each potato in foil and leave to stand 5 minutes until soft. Melt the butter in a small bowl and add the onion

This page: Stuffed Baked Potatoes. Facing page: Eggplant Parmesan (top) and Ratatouille (bottom).

and bacon and cook on HIGH for 2 minutes, until the onion has softened and the bacon is brown. Add the mushrooms and peas and cook a further 2 minutes on HIGH. Cut a large slice from the top of each potato and scoop out all the potato

flesh, leaving a thin lining inside each shell. Mash the potato until smooth and add 3-4 tbsps milk. Add salt and pepper and mix in the butter and vegetable mixture. Fill each potato skin and allow to cool completely. Sprinkle with cheese and wrap each potato separately. Freeze for up to 1 month. To thaw, unwrap the potatoes and place them on paper towels on the oven turntable. Cover them loosely with plastic wrap and cook on HIGH for 9 minutes. Re-arrange once or twice during cooking. Remove the covering and sprinkle with paprika. Cook a further 1 minute on HIGH. Leave to stand 2-3 minutes before serving.

Sloppy Joes

PREPARATION TIME: 20 minutes

MICROWAVE COOKING TIME: 6-7 minutes

SERVES: 6-8 people

1lb ground beef and pork mixed
1 onion, finely chopped
10oz can tomato soup
2 tsps Worcestershire sauce
1 green pepper, finely chopped
2 tsps Dijon mustard
1 tsp tomato ketchup
2 tsps cider vinegar
2 tsps brown sugar
Salt and pepper
4 baps or hamburger buns, frozen

Combine the ground meats and the onion in a casserole dish and cook, uncovered, on HIGH for 6-7 minutes. Break-up the meat with a fork as it cooks. Strain off any fat or liquid. Stir in the soup, Worcestershire sauce, chopped pepper, mustard, ketchup, vinegar, sugar and salt and pepper. Allow to cool completely and seal in freezer container. Cover well and freeze for up to 2 months. Freeze the rolls separately. To thaw, uncover the container and cook on HIGH for 7-8 minutes stirring occasionally to break-up the ingredients. During the last minute or two of cooking, add the rolls, wrapped in paper towels. When the rolls have defrosted and are warm, split them and fill with the Sloppy Joe mixture.

Muffin Pizzas

PREPARATION TIME: 25 minutes

MICROWAVE COOKING TIME: 10-11 minutes

SERVES: 4-8 people

8oz canned tomatoes, drained
1 clove garlic, crushed
¼ tsp oregano
¼ tsp basil
1 tbsp tomato paste
Salt and pepper
4 muffins, split
4 slices salami, chopped
2oz mushrooms, sliced
1½ cups grated Mozzarella cheese
2 tbsps Parmesan cheese

Place the tomatoes, garlic, herbs, tomato paste and seasoning in a bowl. Cover loosely and cook on HIGH for 4-5 minutes until thick, stirring once or twice. Leave to cool. Spread some of the tomato mixture on each muffin half and sprinkle over the chopped salami and mushrooms. Top with Mozzarella cheese and Parmesan cheese. Wrap each muffin pizza separately and freeze for up to 1 month. To thaw, unwrap the pizza and place on a plate lined with paper towels. Cook on HIGH for 6 minutes, re-arranging the pizzas once or twice during cooking. Leave to stand for 2-3 minutes before serving.

Eggplant Parmesan

PREPARATION TIME: 30 minutes

MICROWAVE COOKING TIME: 15-20 minutes

SERVES: 4 people

2 medium eggplant, halved, scored and sprinkled with salt
2 tbsps oil
1 onion, finely chopped
1 clove garlic, crushed
1 green pepper, seeded and diced
15oz canned tomatoes
1 tsp chopped basil
¼ tsp oregano
2 tbsps cornstarch mixed with 4 tbsps red or white wine
Dash cayenne pepper
Salt and pepper
1 cup grated Parmesan cheese
Paprika

Leave the eggplant to stand for 30 minutes and then rinse and drain well. Scoop out the flesh, leaving a thin shell of eggplant inside the skin. Chop the flesh and heat the oil in a casserole for 1 minute on HIGH. Add the onion and the eggplant flesh and cook for 1 minute on HIGH. Pour in the tomatoes and add the garlic, green pepper and herbs. Cover and cook on HIGH for 10 minutes. Add salt and pepper and the cornstarch and white wine mixture. Cook a further 3-5 minutes on HIGH, or until thickened. Spoon into the eggplant shells and allow to cool completely. Sprinkle on the cheese and place the eggplant into a serving dish. Cover well and freeze for up to 1 month. Defrost on LOW or DEFROST for 5 minutes. Sprinkle on paprika and cook on HIGH for 7 minutes, or until hot and the cheese has melted. May be browned under pre-heated broiler if desired.

Tricolor Vegetable Purées

PREPARATION TIME: 25 minutes

MICROWAVE COOKING TIME: 21-27 minutes

SERVES: 6-8 people

LEEK PURÉE
2lbs leeks, trimmed and well washed
2 tbsps butter
2 tbsps heavy cream
Salt and pepper
Pinch nutmeg

CARROT PURÉE
1lb carrots, peeled and thinly sliced

Facing page: Sloppy Joes (top) and Muffin Pizzas (bottom).

ground coriander. Allow all the purées to cool completely and freeze each separately in freezer containers. Cover well and keep for up to 1 month. Defrost each purée separately on LOW or DEFROST for 2 minutes and leave to stand for 5 minutes. Repeat the process until the purées are defrosted. Spoon the purées into a serving dish and cook on HIGH for 6-8 minutes until hot.

Pommes Dauphinoise

PREPARATION TIME: 25 minutes

MICROWAVE COOKING TIME: 15-16 minutes

SERVES: 4-6 people

1 tbsp butter
1lb potatoes, peeled and thinly sliced
Salt and pepper
2 cloves garlic, crushed
1 cup heavy cream
1 tbsp cornstarch mixed with 2 tbsps cold milk
Paprika

Grease a round, shallow baking dish with the butter. Layer the potatoes into the dish with salt, pepper and garlic in between each layer. Mix the cream with the cornstarch and milk mixture. Cook on HIGH for 3-4 minutes, stirring after 1 minute. Cook until thickened and pour over the potatoes. Sprinkle the top with paprika and cook on HIGH for 12 minutes. Allow to stand for 5 minutes and then cool completely. Cover the dish well and freeze for up to 3 weeks. Thaw on LOW or DEFROST for 10 minutes. Reheat on HIGH for 8 minutes without stirring.

1 sprig fresh thyme
2 tbsps butter
2 tbsps heavy cream
Pinch sugar
Salt and pepper

TURNIP PURÉE
1lb turnips, peeled and roughly chopped
2 tbsps butter
2 tbsps heavy cream
Salt and pepper
Pinch ground coriander

To prepare the leek purée, slice the leeks thinly and place in a bowl with 3 tbsps water. Cook on HIGH for 7-10 minutes, or until very tender. Drain and purée in a food processor until smooth. Add the butter, cream,

salt, pepper and grated nutmeg and allow to cool completely. For the carrot purée, place the carrots in a bowl with the sprig of thyme and 3 tbsps water. Cover loosely and cook on HIGH for 6-8 minutes until tender. Drain and remove the sprig of thyme. Purée in a food processor until almost smooth. Beat in the butter, cream, sugar and salt and pepper to taste. The mixture will not be completely smooth. For the turnip purée, place the turnips in a bowl with 3 tbsps water. Cover and cook on HIGH for 8-9 minutes, or until very tender. Drain well and then mash by hand or purée in a food processor until smooth. Beat in the butter, cream, salt, pepper and

Honey and Lemon Parsnips

PREPARATION TIME: 10 minutes

MICROWAVE COOKING TIME: 10 minutes

SERVES: 4 people

*1lb young parsnips, peeled, trimmed and
    sliced
Rind and juice of 1 small lemon
3 tbsps honey
Pinch salt and pepper*

Remove the cores from the parsnips
if they are tough. Combine the
parsnips with the remaining
ingredients in a large casserole and
cover with plastic wrap pierced to
release steam. Cook on HIGH for
10 minutes and then allow to stand
for 2 minutes, covered. Allow to cool
completely and freeze in a micro-
proof serving dish. Cover well and
keep for up to 1 month. Thaw on
LOW or DEFROST for 5 minutes

**Facing page: Tricolor Vegetable
Purées (top) and Honey and Lemon
Parsnips (bottom). This page:
Pommes Dauphinoise (top) and
Pommes Duchesse (bottom).**

and then leave to stand until
completely thawed at room
temperature. Reheat on HIGH for
5-8 minutes until very hot and glazed.

Pommes Duchesse

PREPARATION TIME: 30 minutes
MICROWAVE COOKING TIME: 12-14 minutes
SERVES: 6-8 people

*1lb potatoes, scrubbed but not peeled
2 tbsps water
3-4 tbsps milk
1 large egg, beaten
Salt and pepper*

Prick the skins of the potatoes with a
fork and place them with the water in
a casserole dish. Cover and cook on
HIGH for 10-12 minutes until tender.
Drain the potatoes, cut in half and
scoop out the flesh. Mash the
potatoes well with a potato masher
or with an electric whisk. Heat the
milk for 1 minute and add to the
potatoes with butter and seasoning.
Beat together well and leave to cool
completely. Mix in half the beaten
egg and fill a pastry bag with the
potato mixture. Using a large rosette
tube, pipe out swirls of potato on a
micro-proof baking sheet. Make sure
that the swirls of potato do not have
a hole in the center. Cook on HIGH
for 1 minute. Brush with beaten egg
and cook a further 1 minute on
HIGH, or until glaze has set. Cool
completely and freeze 2-3 hours,
unwrapped. When solid, wrap well
and freeze for up to one month.
Reheat on HIGH for 3 minutes or
until piping hot. Brown quickly
under a pre-heated broiler if desired.

Curried Vegetables

PREPARATION TIME: 30 minutes
MICROWAVE COOKING TIME: 13-16 minutes
SERVES: 6-8 people

*1 tbsp oil
1 onion, finely chopped
1 green chili pepper, seeded and finely
    chopped
1 small piece fresh ginger, peeled and
    grated
2 cloves garlic, crushed
½ tsp ground coriander
½ tsp ground cumin
1 tsp ground turmeric
2 potatoes, peeled and diced
1 eggplant, cut into small cubes
1 small cauliflower, cut into flowerets
14oz canned tomatoes, drained
½ cup vegetable or chicken stock*

8oz okra, trimmed and washed
1 cup roasted, unsalted cashews
4 tbsps desiccated coconut
4 tbsps natural yogurt

Heat the oil in a large bowl or casserole dish for 1 minute on HIGH. Add the onion, chili pepper, ginger and garlic. Cook on HIGH for 1 minute further. Add the spices and cook an additional 1 minute on HIGH. Add the potatoes, eggplant and tomatoes. Cover loosely and cook on HIGH for 8-10 minutes or until the potatoes and eggplant are almost tender. Add the cauliflower, okra and stock. Cover loosely and cook on HIGH for 3-4 minutes, or until the vegetables are almost tender. Add the cashews and the desiccated coconut. Add salt and pepper to taste and allow the vegetables to cool completely. Freeze in a container or a serving dish, well covered. Thaw on LOW or DEFROST for 10 minutes, stirring occasionally. Leave to stand 10 minutes, then reheat on HIGH for 6-10 minutes. Serve hot, topped with natural yogurt.

This page: Curried Vegetables.
Facing page: Almond Savarin.

BAKING AND DESSERTS

Almond Savarin

PREPARATION TIME:
45 minutes-1 hour

MICROWAVE COOKING TIME:
18-21 minutes

SERVES: 6-8 people

½ cup sliced almonds
8oz bread flour
1 tsp salt
½ cup milk
2 tsps fresh yeast, crumbled
2 tsps sugar
3 eggs, slightly beaten
⅓ cup butter

SYRUP
½ cup water
6 tbsps amaretto
4 tbsps water
⅔ cup sugar

GARNISH
Fresh fruit
Whipped cream

Place the almonds in a baking dish or a glass bowl and cook on HIGH for 6-8 minutes, shaking the bowl or dish occasionally. Once the almonds begin to brown, watch them carefully. Sift the flour and salt into a large, glass bowl and cook on HIGH for 20-30 seconds to warm the flour. Pour the milk into a glass measure and heat for 30 seconds on HIGH, or until lukewarm. Stir in the yeast and sugar until well mixed. Gradually beat in the eggs. Make a well in the center of the flour and pour the yeast and egg mixture into the middle. Stir with a wooden spoon to gradually bring in the flour from the sides of the bowl and mix to a smooth batter. The batter will be slightly gluey and elastic. Cover the bowl with plastic wrap and warm for 10-15 seconds on HIGH to start the yeast working. Leave the bowl in a warm place until the batter doubles in bulk, about 45 minutes. Melt the butter on HIGH for 1 minute and allow to cool slightly. Beat into the risen batter with a wooden spoon until it is completely mixed in. Stir in the almonds. Once the mixture is smooth and elastic, pour into a well buttered microwave-proof ring mold, cover with plastic wrap and warm again for 10-15 seconds on HIGH. Leave to double in bulk, as before. Cook, uncovered, on HIGH for about 5-6 minutes until just firm to the touch. The top will still look moist. Allow to cool briefly in the dish and then turn out onto a wire rack to finish cooking completely.

GARNISH
*Orange zest or blackberries or small
bunches of red or blackcurrants*

Put the sugar, lime and orange juice
and water into a deep bowl.
Microwave on HIGH for 2 minutes,
stir to help dissolve the sugar and
microwave a further 2 minutes on
HIGH. Cool and add the burgundy.
Pour into a shallow freezer container
and freeze until slushy. Spoon into a
food processor or whisk with an
electric mixer to break up ice crystals
and then return to the freezer
container, cover and freeze until
solid. To serve, soften quickly in the
microwave for 15-20 seconds on
HIGH, keeping the container
covered. Stir the mixture until
crumbly and spoon into serving
dishes. Decorate with orange zest or
blackberries or the small bunches of
red or blackcurrants.

St. Clement's Sorbet

PREPARATION TIME: 20 minutes
plus freezing

MICROWAVE COOKING TIME:
6 minutes

SERVES: 4-6 people

1¼ cups sugar
1 cup water
4-5 lemons, depending upon size
4-6 oranges, depending upon size
4 tbsps orange liqueur

GARNISHES (to serve)
*Citrus peel or mint leaves or desiccated
coconut*

Combine the sugar and water in a
large bowl. Cook, uncovered, on
HIGH for about 5 minutes, or until
boiling. Stir well and heat a further
1 minute on HIGH, or until the sugar
dissolves. Allow to cool. Grate the
rind of 1 lemon and 1 orange and add
to the syrup. Squeeze the juice from
the remaining lemons and oranges
and strain into the syrup. Reserve
strips of peel if desired for garnishing.
Stir the liqueur into the syrup and
chill. Freeze in ice cube trays until
solid. To serve, place cubes in a food
processor, 6-8 at a time, and process

Meanwhile combine the water and
the amaretto with the sugar and stir
well. Bring the mixture to the boil on
HIGH. This takes about 5 minutes.
Continue cooking for a further
2 minutes on HIGH. Allow the syrup
to cool. Return the savarin to the
cleaned ring mold and pierce all over
with a skewer. Pour the syrup over
the savarin and leave it to soak in.
Turn the savarin out onto a plate or a
very large freezer container and cool
completely. Cover well and freeze for
up to 2 months. To defrost, heat on
HIGH for 1 minute and then leave to
finish defrosting at room temperature.
Fill the center of the savarin with
fresh fruit and cream to serve.

*This page: **Parfait au Cassis (top)
and Frozen Wine Cream (bottom).**
Facing page: **Burgundy Granita
(right) and St. Clement's Sorbet
(left).***

Burgundy Granita

PREPARATION TIME: 15 minutes

MICROWAVE COOKING TIME:
4 minutes

SERVES: 4-6 people

⅓ cup sugar, plus 2 tbsps
Juice of ½ a lime and ½ an orange
1 tbsp water
½ bottle burgundy

quickly until smooth. Serve immediately. Prepare citrus peel garnish, scrape all the pith off the strips and then cut them into very fine shreds. Place them in a bowl with 2 tbsps water and cook on HIGH for 2 minutes to soften. Drain and dry. Sprinkle on top of the sorbet to serve. Alternatively, garnish with mint leaves or desiccated coconut. Keeps in the freezer, well sealed, for up to 3 months.

Crêpes Suzette

PREPARATION TIME: 25 minutes

MICROWAVE COOKING TIME: 24 minutes

SERVES: 4-6 people

PANCAKES
1 cup all-purpose flour
Pinch salt
1 egg
½ pint milk
1 tbsp oil

SAUCE
⅓ cup butter
4 tbsps sugar
Grated rind and juice of 1 orange
Grated rind and juice of ½ lemon
4 tbsps brandy or orange liqueur

GARNISH
Thin orange slices

Sift the flour and salt into a bowl. Make a well in the center and add the egg and half of the milk. Beat well, drawing in the flour from the sides of the bowl gradually. Gradually beat in the remaining milk and the oil. Allow the batter to stand for 30 minutes before using. Fry the pancakes in a small crêpe pan lightly greased with oil. Makes about 12-15 pancakes. Fold the pancakes into triangle shapes and arrange in a shallow dish. To make the sauce, put the butter into a glass measure and cook on DEFROST for 5 minutes, or until melted. Stir in the sugar to dissolve. Add the orange juice and rind, lemon juice and rind and the brandy or orange liqueur. Microwave on HIGH for 2 minutes and stir well. Pour over the pancakes and allow to cool completely. Cover

well with plastic wrap and freeze for up to 2 weeks. To thaw, cook on HIGH for 5 minutes. Leave to stand for 5 minutes and if necessary reheat a further 2-3 minutes on HIGH before serving. Garnish with thin orange slices. NOTE: pancakes may also be frozen separately, packed between pieces of wax paper or plastic wrap. Wrap well and freeze for up to 2 months. Thaw in the microwave oven for 2 minutes on LOW or DEFROST and then leave to stand at room temperature to finish defrosting.

Parfait au Cassis

PREPARATION TIME: 25 minutes

MICROWAVE COOKING TIME: 12 minutes

SERVES: 6 people

1½ cups blackcurrants, fresh or canned
2 tbsps Creme de Cassis
3 egg yolks
1 cup soft brown sugar
1 cup light cream
1 cup heavy cream

GARNISH
Whole blackcurrants
Mint leaves

Purée the blackcurrants and sieve to remove the seeds. Add the cassis and freeze until slushy. Whisk the yolks and sugar until thick and mousse-like. Heat the light cream on HIGH for 2 minutes in an uncovered bowl. Add the cream gradually to the eggs and sugar, stirring constantly. Place the bowl in a dish of hot water. Water should be at the same level as the mixture. Loosely cover the bowl and heat on LOW for 10 minutes, stirring frequently. Cool quickly over ice, stirring occasionally. Whip the heavy cream and fold in. Freeze in a shallow container 2-3 hours, until almost solid. Quickly process or beat the cream mixture and pour it into a bowl. Process the blackcurrants and fold into the cream mixture for a marbled effect. Do not over-fold. Freeze in glass micro-proof serving dishes. Soften in the refrigerator for

30 minutes before serving, or warm on HIGH for 20 seconds. Garnish with blackcurrants and/or mint leaves. Serve with cookies.

Frozen Wine Cream

PREPARATION TIME: 20 minutes plus freezing

MICROWAVE COOKING TIME: 15 minutes

SERVES: 4-6 people

1½ lbs white seedless grapes
1½ cups sweet white wine
¾ cup sugar
1½ cups heavy cream, lightly whipped

Remove the grapes from the stems and place in a deep bowl with the wine. Cover loosely and cook on MEDIUM for 7 minutes, or until the grapes are soft. Remove from the oven and allow to cool completely. Purée in a food processor or blender and then sieve to remove the skins. Add food coloring if desired. Allow to cool completely and then mix with the cream. Place in a bowl or decorative mold and cover well. Freeze for up to 2 months. To defrost, allow to thaw at room temperature if the bowl or mold is metal. If the container is microwave-proof, warm on LOW or DEFROST for 2-3 minutes. Turn out and garnish with a small bunch of green grapes and mint leaves.

Crêpes au Chocolat

PREPARATION TIME: 25 minutes

MICROWAVE COOKING TIME: 5 minutes

SERVES: 4-6 people

PANCAKES
Follow recipe for Crêpes Suzette

Facing page: Crêpes au Chocolat (top) and Crêpes Suzette (bottom).

HIGH for 10 minutes. Stir the plums and set them aside to cool completely. Put the butter or margarine into a large mixing bowl. Cook on MEDIUM to MEDIUM HIGH for about 2 minutes, or until melted. Stir in the crushed snaps and the almonds. Cook on HIGH for 2 minutes. Stir well after 1 minute. Carefully spoon the biscuit crumble over the plums. Allow the topping and plums to cool completely and then cover well. To thaw, microwave on DEFROST or LOW for 10 minutes, stand for 5 minutes and then microwave on HIGH for 5 minutes. Brown quickly under a broiler if desired.

Pineapple Upside-Down Cake

PREPARATION TIME: 20 minutes

MICROWAVE COOKING TIME: 8 minutes plus 5 minutes standing time

SERVES: 6 people

2 tbsps butter
¾ cup soft, light brown sugar
¾ cup walnut halves
6-8 cocktail cherries or candied cherries
8oz canned sliced pineapple, well drained or fresh pineapple, peeled and sliced
½ cup butter or margarine
2 eggs, beaten
1 cup all-purpose flour with 1 tsp baking powder
½ cup finely crushed graham crackers

Place the 2 tbsps butter in a small glass bowl and melt for 30 seconds on HIGH. Stir in the sugar and heat a further 40-50 seconds on HIGH, or until the sugar has partially dissolved. Spread over the base of a 8 inch round cake dish. Place 4-5 whole walnut halves in a circle in the middle of the dish. Cut cherries in half and place rounded side down in

FILLING
8oz semi-sweet chocolate, finely grated

GARNISH
Powdered sugar
Fresh or frozen raspberries

Prepare the pancakes as for the Crêpes Suzette recipe. Allow the pancakes to cool completely and fill each with the grated chocolate. Fold into triangles or roll-up into cigar shapes. Cover well and freeze for up to 1 month. To reheat, place on a serving dish and cover loosely. Cook on HIGH for 4-5 minutes until the pancakes are hot and the chocolate is melted. Allow to cool slightly, garnish with raspberries and sprinkle over sifted powdered sugar.

Plum and Ginger Crisp

PREPARATION TIME: 15 minutes

MICROWAVE COOKING TIME: 12 minutes

SERVES: 4-6 people

1lb plums
3-4oz raw sugar

TOPPING
5 tbsps butter or margarine
8oz plain ginger snaps, crushed
½ cup sliced almonds

Wash, halve and stone the plums. Put into a micro-proof baking dish and toss with the sugar. If the plums are very sweet, do not add all the sugar. Cover the dish loosely and cook on

This page: Rum-Raisin Bread Pudding (top) and Plum and Ginger Crisp (bottom). Facing page: Pineapple Upside-Down Cake.

a circle around the walnuts. Cut pineapple rings in half and place half circles around the walnuts and cherries in a pinwheel design. Beat butter or margarine and remaining sugar until light and fluffy. Beat in the eggs gradually. Chop any remaining cherries, walnuts and pineapple and stir into the cake mixture. Sift in flour with the baking powder and stir in cracker crumbs. Spoon carefully over the topping and smooth the top. Cook on HIGH for 6-7 minutes. When the cake is done it will pull away from the sides of the dish and a wooden pick inserted into the center will come out clean.
Cool completely, wrap and freeze in the baking dish for up to 3 months. To thaw, unwrap and re-heat in the baking dish on HIGH for 5 minutes. Leave to stand for 3 minutes before turning out onto a serving dish. Serve warm with cream, ice cream or lightly sweetened natural yogurt.

Rum-Raisin Bread Pudding

PREPARATION TIME: 15 minutes plus soaking time

MICROWAVE COOKING TIME: 14 minutes

SERVES: 4 people

2 cups milk
8oz whole-wheat bread
4 tbsps dark rum
1 cup raisins
½ cup raw sugar
1 tbsp golden syrup or honey
2 eggs, slightly beaten
2oz butter or margarine
2 tsps mixed spice

Pour the milk into a small bowl and heat for 1 minute on HIGH. Tear the bread into small pieces, put into the bowl with the milk and leave to stand for 2-3 hours to soak. Combine the rum and the raisins in a small bowl and heat for 1 minute on HIGH. Leave to stand while the bread soaks. Reserve half the sugar and combine the remaining half with the honey or

golden syrup, eggs and 1 tsp mixed spice. Add to the bread mixture and stir well. Add the raisins and rum. Melt the butter or margarine on HIGH for 10-20 seconds and pour over the bread. Mix the butter or margarine in and pour into a lightly greased micro-proof baking dish. Cook on HIGH for 12-14 minutes, or until firm. Remove from the oven and sprinkle with the remaining sugar and mixed spice. To freeze, allow to cool completely and wrap well. Keep for up to 3 months. To thaw, heat on DEFROST or LOW for 3 minutes. Reheat on HIGH for 2 minutes.

Fruit and Almond Cake

PREPARATION TIME: 20 minutes

MICROWAVE COOKING TIME: 13-16 minutes

MAKES: 1 cake

⅔ cup margarine
¾ cup dark brown sugar
3 eggs, beaten
1½ cups all-purpose flour
2 tsps baking powder
2-3 drops almond extract
2 tbsps ground almonds
½ cup seedless raisins
½ cup dried apricots, roughly chopped
½ cup glacé cherries, rinsed and roughly chopped

Cream the margarine and sugar until light and fluffy. Add the beaten eggs, one at a time, beating well between each addition. Beat in the almond extract and ground almonds and fold in the flour. Add the raisins, apricots and cherries. If the mixture is very thick, add enough milk to bring to dropping consistency. Lightly grease a large ring mold and sprinkle with sugar. Spoon the cake mixture into the prepared mold and smooth the top. Cook on MEDIUM HIGH for 12-14 minutes, increase the setting to HIGH and cook a further 1-2 minutes, or until just set. Allow to stand for 15 minutes and turn out onto a wire rack. Allow to cool completely and wrap well. Freeze for up to 3 months. To defrost, unwrap

and cover with a paper towel. Warm on LOW or DEFROST for 5 minutes and then leave to stand to defrost at room temperature. When completely defrosted, sprinkle the top with a little sifted powdered sugar.

Banana-Date Walnut Loaf

PREPARATION TIME: 15 minutes

MICROWAVE COOKING TIME: 6 minutes

MAKES: 1 loaf

2 eggs
4 tbsps milk
1 tbsp molasses
½ cup margarine
1½ cups all-purpose flour
2 tsps baking powder
⅓ cup soft brown sugar
⅓ cup chopped dates
1 small banana, sliced
½ cup chopped walnuts

Put the eggs, milk, molasses, margarine, flour and brown sugar into a large mixing bowl. Beat until well mixed. Add baking powder and fold in the dates, banana and walnuts. Spoon into a lightly greased 6 cup microwave bread dish. Cook on HIGH for about 6 minutes, giving the dish a half turn halfway through cooking time. Allow the bread to stand in the dish for 10 minutes before turning out. Allow to cool completely and wrap well. Freeze for up to 3 months. To defrost, unwrap and cover the loaf with paper towels. Thaw on LOW or DEFROST for 5 minutes and then leave to stand to continue defrosting at room temperature.

Facing page: Fruit and Almond Cake (top) and Banana-Date Walnut Loaf (bottom).

Rhubarb Apricot Compôte

PREPARATION TIME: 10 minutes

MICROWAVE COOKING TIME:
6 minutes

SERVES: 4 people

*1lb fresh young rhubarb, cut into 1 inch
  pieces
Finely grated rind and juice of 1 orange
1 tbsp apricot jam
1 small can apricot halves*

Place the rhubarb, orange rind and
juice and the jam into a 3 cup mixing
bowl. Cover loosely and cook on
HIGH for 6 minutes. Stir well and
set aside to cool. Drain the apricots
and chop them roughly, reserving a
few whole for garnish, if desired. Add
to the rhubarb and chill. Put into a
serving dish or freezer container and
cover well. Freeze for up to 3 weeks.
To thaw, warm on LOW or
DEFROST for 12 minutes, breaking-
up the fruit gently as it defrosts.
Leave to stand for 10 minutes and
then reheat for 1 minute on HIGH if
desired. Compôte may also be served
cold with yogurt, ice cream or
whipped cream.

Apricot Pudding

PREPARATION TIME: 10 minutes

MICROWAVE COOKING TIME:
6-10 minutes

SERVES: 4-6 people

BATTER
*14½ oz canned apricot halves
4 tbsps butter or margarine
4 tbsps sugar
1 egg, slightly beaten
1 cup all-purpose flour with 1 tsp baking
  powder
3-4 tbsps milk
Few drops almond extract*

SAUCE
*Reserved apricots and juice
Juice of ½ lemon
1 tbsp cornstarch*

Drain half the apricot halves well and
reserve the juice and the remaining

apricots. Chop the drained apricots
and set them aside. Beat the
margarine or butter to soften and
gradually beat in the sugar until light
and fluffy. Gradually add the egg,
beating well between each addition.
Sift in the flour with the baking
powder, if using, and fold together.
Stir in the chopped apricots and as
much milk as necessary to bring the
batter to dropping consistency. Add
the almond extract. Grease a 2 cup
pudding basin or micro-proof mixing
bowl with margarine and spoon in
the pudding batter, smoothing the
top. Cook, uncovered, for 3-5
minutes or until the top is almost set
but still moist. Leave the pudding to
stand for 5 minutes. Allow to cool

**This page: Chocolate Cherry
Pudding (top) and Apricot Pudding
(bottom). Facing page: Poires Belle
Helene (top) and Rhubarb Apricot
Compôte (bottom).**

completely and wrap well. Purée the
apricots and juice in a food processor
or blender. Add the lemon juice and
cornstarch and mix well. Pour into a
glass measure and cook on HIGH for
3-5 minutes, or until thickened.
Cover the top of the sauce with a
circle of wax paper and leave to cool
completely. Pour the sauce into a
serving dish, jug or freezer container
and cover well. Freeze the pudding
and sauce separately for up to
3 months. To thaw the pudding, heat

on LOW or DEFROST 1½-2 minutes and leave to stand for 10 minutes. Reheat on HIGH for 2 minutes. Heat the sauce on LOW or DEFROST for 2 minutes and leave to stand for 2 minutes. Reheat on HIGH for 1 minute. Turn out the pudding into a serving dish and pour over the sauce. Serve with whipped cream if desired.

Jamaican Mousse Cake

PREPARATION TIME: 25 minutes
MICROWAVE COOKING TIME: 4 minutes
SERVES: 6-8 people

6oz semi-sweet chocolate
3 tbsps dark rum
½ cup heavy cream
1 tbsp strong black coffee
1 tbsp raw sugar
2 large bananas, peeled and mashed until smooth
3 eggs, separated

TO DECORATE
½ cup cream, whipped
Chocolate curls

Break-up the chocolate, place in a bowl and cook on HIGH for 3 minutes, or until melted. Stir in the rum and cream and beat until smooth. Dissolve the sugar in the coffee for 1 minute on HIGH. Add to the chocolate mixture and beat in the bananas. Add the egg yolks, one at a time, beating well between each addition. Whisk the egg whites until stiff and then gently fold into the chocolate and banana mixture. Spoon into a loose-based or springform mold. Chill for 2 hours, cover and freeze for up to 1 month. Thaw at room temperature until mixture loosens from the sides. Unmold the mousse but leave on the base. If the base is metal, carefully slide the mousse off onto a serving plate. Use cream to decorate the top and add chocolate curls just before serving. Serve partially frozen.

Chocolate Cherry Pudding

PREPARATION TIME: 10 minutes
MICROWAVE COOKING TIME: 8½ minutes
SERVES: 4-6 people

⅓ cup softened butter or margarine
⅓ cup soft brown sugar
¾ cup all-purpose flour with 1 tsp baking powder
2 tbsps cocoa
2 eggs
2 tbsps milk

SAUCE
15oz morello cherries, drained and pitted
2 tbsps cornstarch
2 tbsps kirsch (optional)
Few drops almond extract

Beat the butter until softened and gradually beat in the sugar until light and fluffy. Lightly beat the eggs and add them gradually to the butter and sugar mixture. Sift the flour with the baking powder, and the cocoa powder and fold in carefully. Add enough milk to bring the mixture to dropping consistency. Spoon into a lightly greased 3 cup micro-proof pudding basin. Cook on HIGH for 3½-4 minutes, until well risen and springy to the touch. Set aside to cool completely. Combine the cornstarch with the drained syrup from the cherries in a glass measure. Cook on HIGH for 3 minutes, stirring after 1 minute. When thickened, add the kirsch, if using, and almond extract. Allow the sauce to cool completely and stir in cherries. Freeze the pudding and the sauce separately for up to 1 month. To thaw the pudding, heat on LOW or DEFROST for 1½-2 minutes and leave to stand for 10 minutes. Reheat on HIGH for 2 minutes. Heat the sauce on LOW or DEFROST for 2 minutes and leave to stand for 2 minutes. Reheat on HIGH for 1 minute. Turn the pudding out into a serving dish and pour over the sauce. Serve with whipped cream if desired.

Poires Belle Helene

PREPARATION TIME: 20 minutes
MICROWAVE COOKING TIME: 7 minutes
SERVES: 4 people

1 cup water
Juice of 1 small lemon
2 tbsps sugar
4 ripe dessert pears, approximately the same size
4oz semi-sweet chocolate
3 tbsps heavy cream

GARNISH
Angelica or mint leaves
Whipped cream

Mix together the water, lemon juice and sugar in a bowl that will accommodate the 4 pears snugly. Peel the pears, leaving on the stems but removing the eyes in the bottom. Place pears stem side up in the bowl and cover with plastic wrap pierced with holes for the stems. Cook on HIGH for 3 minutes. Baste the pears with the cooking liquid, re-cover and cook a further 2 minutes on HIGH. Allow to cool completely. Remove the pears from the bowl. Place chocolate in a deep bowl and microwave on HIGH for 1½ minutes. Add 4 tbsps of the pear cooking liquid and stir well. Microwave on HIGH for 30 seconds. Stir to blend and fold in the cream. Cool completely and freeze the pears and the sauce separately. The pears may be frozen in a serving dish if desired. Cover both well. To thaw the pears, warm on LOW or DEFROST for 5 minutes and leave to stand for 10 minutes. Reheat for 1 minute on HIGH if desired, or serve cold. Defrost the sauce 2 minutes on LOW or DEFROST and leave to stand for 2 minutes. If desired, reheat the sauce for 1 minute on HIGH. Pour the sauce over the pears and garnish each pear with angelica cut into leaf shapes or with fresh mint

Facing page: Jamaican Mousse Cake.

leaves. Serve with whipped cream. Pears and sauce may be frozen for up to 3 weeks.

Lemon-Lime Cheesecake

PREPARATION TIME: 25 minutes

MICROWAVE COOKING TIME: 2½ minutes plus standing time

SERVES: 6-8 people

6 tbsps butter or margarine
6oz graham crackers, finely crushed
1lb cream cheese
1 cup sugar
Grated rind and juice of 1 small lemon
*   and 1 lime*
3 eggs
1 tbsp powdered gelatine
A few drops of green and yellow food
*   coloring (optional)*

GARNISH
½ cup whipped cream
Thin lemon and lime slices

Place the butter in a small bowl and cook for 2 minutes on MEDIUM, or until melted. Stir in the crushed crackers and press firmly into a lightly-greased loose-based dish and chill. Beat the cheese and sugar together until light and fluffy. Remove 2 tbsps of the juice to a small custard cup and add the remaining juice and rind to the cheese and mix thoroughly. Sprinkle the gelatine on top of the reserved juice and leave to soak. Separate the eggs and beat the yolks gradually into the cheese mixture. Heat the gelatine for 30 seconds on HIGH and leave to stand for 2 minutes until clear. Pour the cleared gelatine into the cheese mixture and stir well. Whip the egg whites in a large bowl until they form stiff peaks, and fold into the cheese mixture. Pour the cheesecake mixture on top of the cracker crust and chill until set. To freeze, remove the cheesecake from the dish but leave on the base. Freeze, uncovered, until firm and then wrap well. Freeze for up to 2 weeks. Best thawed overnight in the refrigerator or in a cool place for 2 hours. When defrosted, unwrap the cheesecake and remove the base

if metal. Place the cheesecake on a serving plate. Cook on HIGH for 2 minutes and then on LOW or DEFROST for 8 minutes. Leave to stand until completely defrosted. Decorate with rosettes of cream and thin slices of lemon and lime.

Raspberry Yogurt Cake

PREPARATION TIME: 25 minutes plus chilling

MICROWAVE COOKING TIME: 4-6 minutes

SERVES: 6-8 people

This page: Lemon-Lime Cheesecake. Facing page: Raspberry Yogurt Cake.

BASE
4 tbsps butter or margarine
4oz graham crackers, crushed

FILLING
1 tbsp powdered gelatine
3 tbsps water
1½ lbs raspberries
4 tbsps sugar
1 cup natural yogurt
1 tbsp raspberry liqueur or grenadine syrup

Chocolate-Raspberry Meringue Cake

PREPARATION TIME: 20 minutes

MICROWAVE COOKING TIME: 13-16 minutes

SERVES: 6-8 people

1½ cups all-purpose flour
1½ tsps bicarbonate of soda
4 tbsps cocoa
1 cup sugar
⅔ cup butter or margarine
¾ cup evaporated milk
1 tbsp distilled white vinegar
2 eggs, beaten
Few drops vanilla extract
8oz frozen raspberries

TO FINISH
3 egg whites
1 tsp cornstarch
¼ tsp cream of tartar
6 tbsps sugar
Toasted flaked coconut

Lightly grease a 6 cup cake ring. Sift the flour, soda and cocoa into a mixing bowl and add the sugar. Combine the evaporated milk and vinegar and set aside. Melt the butter or margarine on HIGH for 2-3 minutes or until liquid. Pour into the milk and vinegar and gradually add the beaten eggs. Pour into the dry ingredients and beat well. Pour into the cake ring and smooth down the top to level. Cook on HIGH for 10 minutes or until the top of the cake is only slightly sticky. Cool in the ring for 10 minutes then turn out onto a wire rack to cool completely. When cool cut in half around the middle and scoop out some of the crumbs on the top and bottom half to form a channel. Fill with the frozen raspberries, sandwich the cake together and cover it well. Freeze up to 2 months. Thaw the cake for 2 minutes on DEFROST and set aside. To prepare the meringue, place the egg whites, cornstarch and cream of tartar in a mixing bowl. Beat until soft peaks form. Add the sugar, a spoonful at a time, continuing to beat until stiff peaks form. Spread the meringue over the cake and cover

Heat the butter on HIGH for 2-3 minutes until melted. Stir in the crushed crackers. Press onto the base of a loose-bottom dish and leave in the refrigerator to set. Sprinkle the gelatine over the water in a small bowl and leave to soak. Combine the raspberries and sugar in a large bowl and cook for 1-2 minutes on HIGH, stirring occasionally. Mash with a fork and then sieve out the seeds if desired. Warm the gelatine on HIGH for 1 minute until dissolved. Combine the yogurt with the raspberry purée and pour in the gelatine, stirring constantly. Add the liqueur or grenadine syrup and pour

This page: Chocolate-Raspberry Meringue Cake. Facing page: White and Dark Chocolate Bombe.

on top of the cracker base and leave to set in the refrigerator. Freeze, remove from the dish but leave on the base. Freeze, unwrapped, until firm. Wrap well and return to the freezer for up to 1 month. Best thawed overnight in the refrigerator or in a cool place for about 2 hours. Alternatively, defrost as for Lemon-Lime Cheesecake. Garnish with rosettes of whipped cream and whole raspberries if desired.

completely. Sprinkle on the toasted coconut and microwave on MEDIUM 3-6 minutes or until the meringue is set.

White and Dark Chocolate Bombe

PREPARATION TIME: 30 minutes plus freezing

MICROWAVE COOKING TIME: 4½ minutes

SERVES: 6-8 people

½ pint dark chocolate ice cream
2 tsps coffee powder
1 tbsp hot water
1 pint vanilla ice cream
4oz white chocolate, broken up
2oz amaretti biscuits, coarsely crushed

Place a 4 cup bombe mold or bowl into the freezer for 2 hours. Soften the dark chocolate ice cream on HIGH for 1 minute. Mix together the coffee powder and hot water in a small bowl and heat for 1 minute on HIGH. Stir into the chocolate ice cream. If the ice cream is too soft, freeze again until of spreading consistency. Coat the base and sides of the mold or bowl with the dark chocolate ice cream and freeze until firm. If the ice cream slides down the sides of the bowl during freezing, keep checking and pressing the ice cream back into place. Heat the vanilla ice cream on HIGH for 2 minutes or until very soft and almost liquid. Set aside and melt the white chocolate in a small bowl for 1 minute on HIGH or until soft. Fold the white chocolate into the vanilla ice cream and re-heat 2-3 minutes. Stir in the crushed biscuits. Freeze the ice cream until slushy and then pour into the center of the dark chocolate ice cream, cover and freeze until solid. Half an hour before serving, unmold the bombe by briefly dipping in warm water or wrapping a hot cloth around the outside. Alternatively, if the mold is microwave-proof, heat for 30 seconds on HIGH and unmold. Decorate the top with grated semi-sweet or white chocolate.

Microwave
FISH DISHES

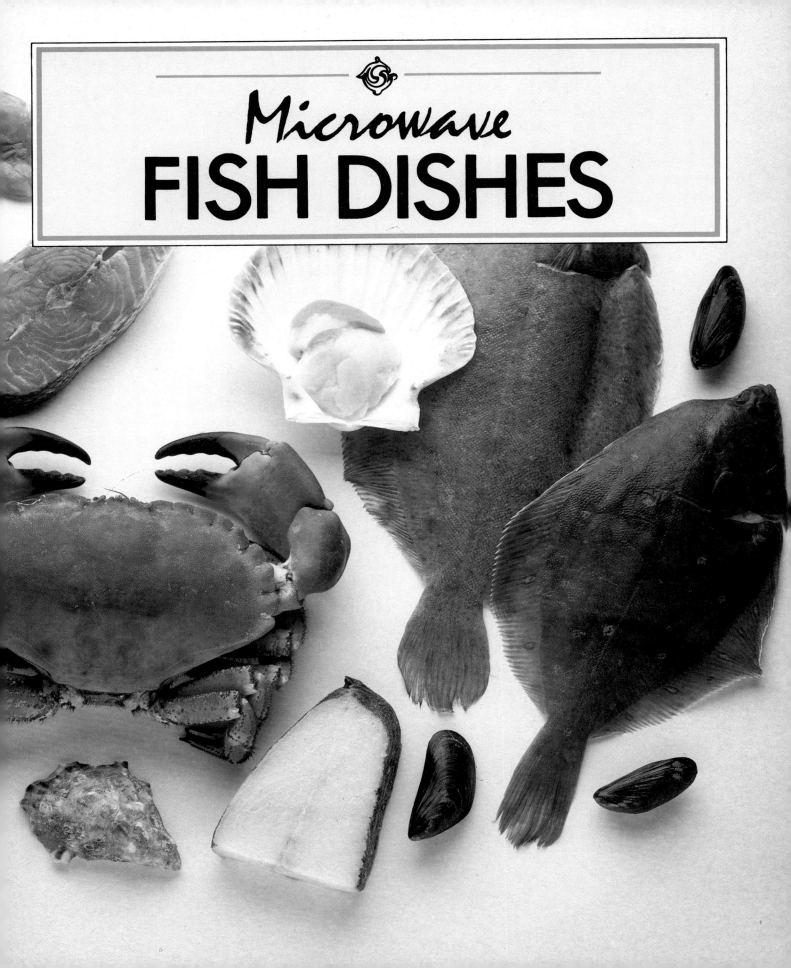

Microwave
FISH DISHES

A microwave oven is a fish kettle par excellence. In fact, many people prefer microwaved fish and shellfish to that cooked by conventional methods. Microwave cooking retains the natural moisture of food, something that is important in well-prepared fish. Fish and shellfish both require quick cooking, so the microwave oven really comes into its own.

Poaching is the fish cooking method that the microwave oven performs best. Use a shallow dish or a cooking bag and add white wine or water and lemon juice with peppercorns, onion slices and aromatic herbs, spices and vegetables. In a microwave oven all the flavor cooks into the fish, and low evaporation means plenty of liquid to make a good sauce.

A whole fish, such as a salmon or sea bass, can easily be poached providing the fish is not too large to allow it to turn freely. It is best to choose a fish no heavier than 2lbs in weight. Use a large cooking bag, securely tied, or a large, shallow dish covered with plastic wrap. Wrap the head and tail with foil to keep them from over-cooking and falling off. Cook 7-10 minutes on HIGH, or slightly longer on MEDIUM. The fish will continue to cook as it stands, so keep it covered while preparing sauces to accompany the fish. If you are not sure whether the fish is cooked, check close to the bone in an inconspicuous place. The flesh should be firm and opaque.

Even frying is possible, after a fashion, in a microwave oven. Dredge fish fillets or small whole fish with seasoned flour, and preheat a browning dish. Briefly fry in butter on both sides to get a light brown, slightly crisp coating; a surprising result from a microwave oven.

Shellfish need careful cooking in a microwave oven or they toughen. Cook them no longer than 3 minutes on the highest setting, or add them to a hot sauce at the last minute.

In the classification of fish there are four main categories: Flat fish, such as sole and flounder; Round fish, such as trout; Shellfish and Smoked fish. Flat fish and round fish may be subdivided into oily fish, such as trout and salmon, and whitefish, such as sole or cod. Whatever fish you choose, your microwave oven will help you cook it to perfection.

Microwave
FISH DISHES

SOUPS

Waterzoi

PREPARATION TIME: 20 minutes

MICROWAVE COOKING TIME:
12-14 minutes plus 2 minutes
standing time

SERVES: 4-6 people

*1lb whitefish such as turbot, monkfish, cod
    or freshwater fish such as pike or perch,
    skin and bones reserved*
*Bouquet garni (1 bay leaf, sprig thyme,
    parsley stalks)*
6 black peppercorns
1 tbsp lemon juice
2 shallots, finely chopped
½ cup dry white wine
*4oz carrots, peeled and cut into thin
    rounds*
2 sticks celery, thinly sliced
*2 leeks, cut into thin rounds and well
    washed*
Salt and pepper
Scant 1 cup heavy cream
3 tbsps chopped parsley

Combine the fish bones and
trimming with 1½ cups water and
bouquet garni in a large, deep bowl.
Cook for 10 minutes on HIGH and
then strain. Discard the bouquet
garni and the fish bones and
trimmings. Combine the fish stock,
shallots, wine, carrots, celery and
leeks in a large, deep bowl. Loosely
cover and cook about 6 minutes on
HIGH, or until the vegetables are
nearly tender. Cut the fish into 2
inch pieces and add to the bowl.
Season with salt and pepper, re-cover
the bowl and cook a further 6-8
minutes on HIGH or until done. Stir
in the heavy cream and leave the
soup to stand for 2 minutes before
serving. Top each bowl with a
sprinkling of chopped parsley before
serving. The soup will be thin.
Waterzoi is often served with an
accompaniment of boiled potatoes.

**This page: Seafood Minestrone.
Facing page: Cream of Flounder
Soup with Paprika (top) and
Waterzoi (bottom).**

Seafood Minestrone

PREPARATION TIME: 20 minutes

MICROWAVE COOKING TIME:
15 minutes plus 2 minutes
standing time

SERVES: 4 people

1 small leek, trimmed, cut into 2 inch
    strips and well washed
½ carrot, peeled and cut into 2 inch strips
1 celery stalk, trimmed and cut into 2 inch
    strips
1 zucchini, ends trimmed and cut into
    2 inch strips
1 clove garlic, crushed
2 cups dry white wine
3 cups fish or vegetable stock
2 tsps chopped fresh oregano or 1 tsp dried
    oregano
1 bay leaf
4oz uncooked langoustines
4oz clams or cockles, shelled
4oz mussels, shelled
4oz cooked, peeled shrimp
¾ cup small pasta shells
1 tbsp tomato paste

Cut all the vegetables and place in a
large, deep bowl. Add the garlic,
wine, stock, herbs and tomato paste.
Season with salt and pepper and
loosely cover the bowl. Cook on
HIGH for about 8 minutes, or until
the vegetables are just barely tender.
Add the langoustines and the pasta
shells and re-cover the bowl. Cook
for 5 minutes on HIGH. Add the
clams or cockles and the mussels and
cook a further 2 minutes on HIGH,
or until all the seafood and the pasta
shells are cooked. Add the shrimp
and leave the soup to stand for
2 minutes.

Crabmeat Bisque

PREPARATION TIME: 15 minutes

MICROWAVE COOKING TIME:
17 minutes

SERVES: 4 people

1lb crabmeat, fresh or frozen
3 tbsps butter or margarine
1 shallot, finely chopped

3 tbsps flour
2 cups fish or vegetable stock
2 tsps tomato paste
1 bay leaf
Salt and pepper
1 cup milk
½ cup heavy cream
Dash tabasco
2 tbsps dry sherry

GARNISH

4 tbsps sour cream
4 tsps chopped parsley

Pick over the crabmeat carefully to
remove any pieces of shell or
cartilage. Place the butter in a large,
deep bowl and cook for 30 seconds
on HIGH to melt. Add shallot and
cook for 2 minutes on HIGH, stirring
once or twice. Stir in the flour and
then add the stock, bay leaf, tomato
paste, salt and pepper. Cover and
cook on HIGH for 5 minutes, stirring
frequently. Add the milk and
crabmeat and cook a further 3-4
minutes on HIGH. Allow to cool
slightly then pour into a food
processor or blender and purée.
Return the soup to the rinsed out
bowl and add the cream and sherry.
Heat through for 1 minute on HIGH
and serve. Garnish each serving with
a spoonful of sour cream and
chopped parsley.

New England Clam Chowder

PREPARATION TIME: 15 minutes

MICROWAVE COOKING TIME:
16 minutes

SERVES: 4 people

2lbs unshelled clams or 2 10oz cans clams
1 cup water, mixed with 1 tsp lemon juice
1 bay leaf
2 tbsps butter
1 onion, finely chopped
4 strips bacon, rind and bones removed
2 tbsps flour
2 cups diced potatoes
3½ cups milk
¼ tsp thyme
2 tbsps chopped parsley

Salt and pepper
Light cream as necessary

Scrub the clam shells well and
discard any that are broken or open.
Put the clams into a large bowl with
the water, lemon juice and bay leaf.
Cover loosely and cook for 2
minutes on HIGH, or until the
clam shells open. Stir the clams
occasionally. Strain the liquid
through a fine sieve and reserve it.
Remove the clams from their shells
and set aside. If using canned clams,
reserve the liquid. Add the butter
into a large, deep bowl and heat for
30 seconds on HIGH. Dice the
bacon and add it to the bowl along
with the onion. Cover loosely and
cook on HIGH for 3 minutes. Stir in
the flour, potatoes, milk, reserved
clam liquid, thyme, parsley and salt
and pepper. Cook for 10 minutes on
HIGH, stirring occasionally. Add the
clams and, if the soup is very thick,
some of the cream to thin it down.
Cook for 1 minute on HIGH. Serve
immediately.

Cream of Flounder Soup with Paprika

PREPARATION TIME: 20 minutes

MICROWAVE COOKING TIME:
18-21 minutes plus 2 minutes
standing time

SERVES: 4 people

⅓ cup butter or margarine
2 shallots, finely chopped
2 cloves garlic, crushed
1 tbsp paprika
1 stick celery, diced
½ bulb fennel
1 leek, white part only, well washed and
    finely sliced
1 small potato, peeled and diced
1 carrot, peeled and diced
3 tbsps flour

**Facing page: Crabmeat Bisque (top)
and New England Clam Chowder
(bottom).**

Curried Shrimp Soup

PREPARATION TIME: 15 minutes

MICROWAVE COOKING TIME:
8-9 minutes plus standing time

SERVES: 4 people

3 tbsps butter or margarine
3 tbsps flour
1 tbsp curry powder
1 shallot, finely chopped
1 apple, peeled, quartered, cored and cut
into dice
2 cups fish or vegetable stock
2 cups milk
12oz-1lb cooked, peeled shrimp

GARNISH
½ cup natural yogurt

Melt the butter and add the curry
powder and cook for 1 minute on
HIGH. Stir in shallot and apple and
cook for a further 2 minutes on
HIGH. Stir in the flour and when
well blended pour on the stock. Stir
well and cook for a further 4 minutes
on HIGH, or until thickened. Leave
to cool. Pour into a food processor or
blender and purée until smooth. Add
the milk and cook 1-2 minutes on
HIGH. Add the shrimp and stand for
2-3 minutes before serving. Garnish
with natural yogurt.

2 cups dry white wine
2 cups fish or vegetable stock
1 bouquet garni (bay leaf, sprig thyme,
parsley stalks)
1lb flounder fillets, skinned
1 cup heavy cream

GARNISH
1 reg pepper, seeded and cut into small
dice

Melt the butter in a large, deep bowl
for 30 seconds on HIGH. Add the
shallots, garlic, paprika, celery, fennel,
leek, potato and carrot. Loosely
cover the bowl and cook 10 minutes,
or until the vegetables are soft. Stir in
the flour. Add the wine, fish stock,
bouquet garni and fish. Cover the
bowl loosely and cook a further

**This page: Curried Shrimp Soup.
Facing page: Bouillabaisse.**

6-8 minutes or until the fish is done.
Allow to cool slightly and remove
the bouquet garni. Pour the soup
into a blender or food processor and
purée until smooth. Strain if desired.
Return the soup to the rinsed-out
bowl, add the cream and season with
salt and pepper. Add the red pepper
garnish and re-heat the soup
2-3 minutes on HIGH to partially
cook the garnish. Allow the soup to
stand, covered, 2 minutes before
serving.

Bouillabaisse

PREPARATION TIME: 15 minutes

MICROWAVE COOKING TIME:
10 minutes

SERVES: 4 people

12oz assorted fish (e.g. monkfish, red
snapper, cod, whitefish)
8oz assorted cooked shellfish (shrimp,
lobster, scallops, crab)
2 leeks, cleaned and thinly sliced
1 small bulb fennel, sliced
2 tbsps olive oil
2 tomatoes, skinned, seeded and roughly
chopped
1 tbsp tomato paste
3 cups water

½ cup white wine
1 clove garlic, crushed
1 strip orange rind
Few shreds saffron
1 bay leaf
1 tsp lemon juice
1 tbsp chopped parsley
Salt and pepper

GARNISH
4 slices French bread, toasted
¼ cup prepared mayonnaise mixed with
    1 clove garlic, crushed, and a pinch of
    cayenne pepper

Cut fish into 1 inch pieces. Remove shells from shellfish and cut crab and lobster into small pieces. Put the leeks, fennel, garlic and olive oil into a large casserole. Cover and cook for 3 minutes on HIGH. Add the rind, saffron, bay leaf, lemon juice, water and wine. Stir in the tomato paste and seasoning and mix well. Add fish and tomatoes and cook for 5 minutes, covered, on HIGH. Add shellfish and parsley, and cook for 2 minutes on HIGH. Leave to stand, covered, for 2 minutes before serving. Mix the mayonnaise, garlic and cayenne pepper and spread on the pieces of toasted French bread. Place bread in the bottom of the serving dish and spoon over the soup.

Zuppa di Pesce

PREPARATION TIME: 15 minutes

MICROWAVE COOKING TIME:
18-20 minutes

SERVES: 4 people

2lbs whitefish such as monkfish, halibut,
    turbot or cod, skinned and boned and
    cut into bite-size pieces
Reserved fish trimmings and bones
2 onions, peeled and chopped
3 cloves garlic, crushed
2 tomatoes, skinned and chopped
Sprig of fresh oregano
1 bay leaf
Grated rind of 1 orange
½ cup dry white wine
Salt and pepper
Gravy browning

GARNISH
Chopped parsley

Combine the reserved fish trimmings and bones with ⅓ of the onion and 5 cups water in a large, deep bowl. Cook on HIGH for 10 minutes and then strain. Discard the onion and fish bones and trimmings. Cook the remaining onion and the garlic in a large, deep bowl for about 1 minute on HIGH. Add the fish pieces, tomatoes, oregano, bay leaf, orange rind, wine and salt and pepper. Pour over the strained stock and cover the bowl loosely. Cook for 6-8 minutes on HIGH, or until the fish is done. Add a few drops gravy browning for color, if desired. Remove the bay leaf and oregano before serving. Garnish with chopped parsley.

Sweet Potato and Scallop Soup

PREPARATION TIME: 20 minutes

MICROWAVE COOKING TIME:
15-18 minutes

SERVES: 4 people

1 medium onion, finely chopped
1½ lbs sweet potatoes, peeled and sliced
2 medium potatoes, peeled and sliced
3½ cups fish or vegetable stock
1 bay leaf
Salt and pepper
6-8 scallops with roes attached
1 cup heavy cream
2oz butter

Place the onions, sweet potatoes and potatoes in a large, deep bowl. Loosely cover and cook for 4-6 minutes on HIGH, or until the vegetables are nearly soft. Add the stock, bay leaf, salt and pepper and cover the bowl. Cook an additional 4 minutes on HIGH or until the vegetables are very soft. Remove the roes from the scallops and set them aside. Cut the white part of the scallops into 4 pieces and add to the soup. Cook another 3 minutes on HIGH or until the scallops are just tender. Allow the soup to stand for 2 minutes and remove the bay leaf. Pour the soup into a food processor or blender and purée until smooth. Place the scallop roes in a small bowl with 1 tbsp water. Cover loosely and cook 2 minutes on HIGH, or until the roes are done. Allow to cool, mash with the butter and place in the refrigerator to chill. Return the soup to the rinsed out bowl and add the cream. Cook, uncovered, for a further 4-6 minutes on HIGH to heat through. Before serving, top with a spoonful of the scallop roe butter and swirl through the soup.

Oyster Stew (right) and Sweet Potato and Scallop Soup (far right).

Oyster Stew

PREPARATION TIME: 15 minutes
MICROWAVE COOKING TIME:
20 minutes
SERVES: 4 people

1½ lbs canned or frozen oysters
2 tbsps butter
1 onion, finely sliced

2 carrots, peeled and cut into dice
4 potatoes, peeled and diced
2 tbsps flour
2 cups fish or vegetable stock
1 bay leaf
¼ tsp thyme
2 tbsps chopped parsley
Salt and pepper
2 cups milk

Melt the butter for 30 seconds on HIGH in a large, deep bowl. Add the onion, carrot and potatoes and cook for 8 minutes on HIGH, stirring frequently. Sprinkle on the flour and stir in the stock. If using canned oysters, strain the liquid and substitute it for part of the fish stock. Add the bay leaf, thyme, parsley, salt and pepper and loosely cover the

bowl. Cook on HIGH for 4-6 minutes, or until the potatoes are almost tender. Add the oysters and milk and cook for a further 2 minutes on HIGH. Allow to stand for 2 minutes before serving.
Note: frozen oysters are available from Chinese markets.

Solianka (Russian Salmon Stew)

PREPARATION TIME: 20 minutes

MICROWAVE COOKING TIME: 12-14 minutes plus 2 minutes standing time

SERVES: 4-6 people

This page: **Cream of Smoked Haddock Soup. Facing page: Zuppa di Pesce (top) and Solianka (Russian Salmon Stew) (bottom).**

1 tbsp butter or margarine
1 onion, finely chopped
1 tbsp flour
3 cups fish or vegetable stock
1 cup canned tomatoes, broken-up
1lb salmon, skinned and cut into chunks
1 bouquet garni (bay leaf, sprig thyme and parsley stalks)
2 tbsps chopped parsley
Salt and pepper
4 dill pickles, chopped
2 tbsps capers
6 black olives, pitted and chopped

Melt the butter or margarine 30 seconds on HIGH in a large, deep bowl. Add the onion and cook 4 minutes to soften. Stir in the flour and add the stock and tomatoes. Cook a further 4 minutes on HIGH, stirring occasionally. Add the salmon, bouquet garni, parsley and salt and pepper. Cover and cook 4-6 minutes or until the salmon is done. Add the pickles, capers and olives and leave to stand, covered, 2 minutes. Remove the bouquet garni before serving.

Matelote

PREPARATION TIME: 20 minutes

MICROWAVE COOKING TIME: 14-16 minutes plus 2 minutes standing time

SERVES: 4-6 people

2 tbsps butter or margarine
2 shallots, finely chopped
1 medium potato, peeled and cubed
8oz monkfish, turbot or cod, skinned and cut into chunks
1 wing of skate, skinned and cut into 4 pieces through the bone
1 cup dry cider or white wine
2 cups fish or vegetable stock
1 bouquet garni (bay leaf, sprig of thyme and parsley stalks)
1 cup shelled mussels
1 cup peeled, cooked shrimp
Salt and pepper
5-6 tbsps heavy cream

GARNISH
Chopped parsley

Melt the butter or margarine in a large, deep bowl for 30 seconds on HIGH. Add shallots and potato and cook for 4 minutes on HIGH. Add monkfish and skate and cook 4 minutes on HIGH. Pour over the cider and stock, and add the bouquet garni, salt and pepper. Cover and cook 6-8 minutes on HIGH or until potato and fish are tender. Add the mussels during the last 2 minutes of cooking. If desired, remove skate and flake fish away from the bones.

Return fish to the soup and discard bones. Stir in the shrimp and cream and leave to stand for 2 minutes. Remove the bouquet garni before serving and garnish with chopped parsley. Accompany with French bread if desired.

Bourride

PREPARATION TIME: 15 minutes

MICROWAVE COOKING TIME: 20-23 minutes plus standing time

SERVES: 4 people

1lb monkfish, turbot or John Dory, skinned
2 small leeks, well washed and chopped
2 cloves garlic
2 large potatoes, peeled and sliced
1 bouquet garni
Zest of 1 orange
Salt and pepper
½ cup heavy cream
2 tomatoes, seeded and chopped

GARLIC CROUTONS
3 tbsps olive oil
1 clove garlic, crushed
4 slices bread, crusts removed
Salt and pepper
Pinch paprika

Cut the fish into even-sized pieces. It is not necessary to remove the bones unless desired. Put the fish and the leeks, garlic, orange peel, bouquet garni and potatoes into a large, deep bowl. Cover with 2 cups water. Loosely cover the bowl and cook the fish on HIGH for 15 minutes. Set aside for 2 minutes. Pour the cream into a glass measure and cook for 3-4 minutes on HIGH, or until boiling. Meanwhile, prepare the croutons. Cut the bread into even-sized cubes and toss with the oil and the crushed garlic. Sprinkle with salt and pepper and spread the bread out onto a flat plate. Sprinkle lightly with paprika and cook on HIGH for 1½-2 minutes, or until the croutons are firm but not crisp. Stir and turn the croutons several times during cooking. Allow

them to stand for 5 minutes before serving. Add the cream to the soup and season with salt and pepper. Add the tomatoes and re-heat the soup 1-2 minutes on HIGH. Serve topped with the garlic croutons.

Cream of Smoked Haddock Soup

PREPARATION TIME: 15 minutes

MICROWAVE COOKING TIME: 19-20 minutes

SERVES: 4 people

1lb smoked haddock fillets, skinned
2 cups hot fish or vegetable stock
8oz potatoes, peeled and diced
1 large onion, peeled and chopped
2 sticks celery, peeled and diced
2 cups milk
Salt and pepper
1 tbsp lemon juice

GARNISH
2 hard-boiled eggs, chopped
2 tbsps chopped parsley

Place the fish in a shallow dish and pour over a few spoonfuls of stock. Loosely cover the dish and cook for 4-5 minutes or until the fish is done. Flake the fish finely, discarding any bones. Set aside. Place the potatoes, onion, celery and remaining stock in a bowl. Cover loosely and cook for about 10 minutes, stirring occasionally during cooking. Add the milk. Add the fish to the potato mixture, season with salt and pepper and stir in the lemon juice. Loosely cover and cook for a further 5 minutes on HIGH. Allow the soup to stand for about 2 minutes before serving. Garnish with the chopped hard-boiled egg and parsley.

Facing page: Matelote (top) and Bourride (bottom).

Microwave
FISH DISHES

APPETIZERS

Salmon and Green Peppercorn Terrine

PREPARATION TIME: 25 minutes

MICROWAVE COOKING TIME: 16-18 minutes

SERVES: 6-8 people

12 large spinach leaves
12oz plaice or sole fillets, skinned
1lb salmon
1 cup fresh white breadcrumbs
5 tbsps light cream
1 egg white, lightly beaten
1 shallot, finely chopped
1 cup heavy cream, lightly whipped
1 tbsp green peppercorns
Salt

Wash the spinach leaves and remove the stalks. Place the leaves in a bowl and cover loosely with plastic wrap and cook on HIGH, in the water that clings to the leaves, for 30 seconds to 1 minute. Rinse with cold water and pat dry with paper towels. Use the leaves to line the base and sides of a terrine or loaf dish, leaving the ends of the leaves overlapping the dish. Place shallot in a small bowl and loosely cover. Cook 1 minute on HIGH to soften. Cut the plaice or sole fillets into long, thin strips. Skin the salmon and remove any bones. Cut into small pieces. Place in a food processor or blender with the breadcrumbs, light cream, egg white, shallot and salt. Process to a smooth purée. Fold in the heavy cream and green peppercorns by hand. Spread ⅓ of the salmon mixture into the bottom of the terrine dish on top of the spinach leaves. Arrange half of the plaice or sole strips on top and then cover with another ⅓ of the salmon mixture. Repeat with the remaining fish strips and salmon mixture. Fold the spinach leaves over the top of the mixture and cover the dish loosely with plastic wrap. Place the terrine in a shallow dish half filled with hot water. Cook on MEDIUM for 14-16 minutes. Remove the terrine and leave to cool slightly. Serve hot with a Hollandaise sauce from the recipe for Lobster Asparagus Hollandaise, or cold with mayonnaise mixed with the grated rind and juice of ½ a lemon.

This page: **Salmon and Green Peppercorn Terrine. Facing page: Moules Dijonnaise.**

clean bowl and cook for 1 minute on HIGH. Stir in the shrimps and spoon into 6 small custard cups, pressing the mixture down firmly. Spoon over any remaining butter, cover and chill until firm. To serve, turn out the shrimps onto small dishes and garnish with lemon wedges and parsley sprigs. Serve with the toast. May be prepared a day in advance and kept in the refrigerator.

Seafood in Garlic Sauce

PREPARATION TIME: 20 minutes

MICROWAVE COOKING TIME: 10-13 minutes

SERVES: 4 people

1¼ lbs of the following shellfish: jumbo shrimp, shelled oysters, shelled mussels, scallops, squid cleaned and cut in rings, lobster tails cooked and sliced, crab claws shelled
2 tbsps white wine or dry sherry

SAUCE
1½ tbsps salted black beans
1 tbsp water
3 tbsps lemon juice
½ cup fish or vegetable stock
2 tbsps soy sauce
Dash sesame oil
1½ tbsps cornstarch
1 clove garlic, finely minced
Pinch red pepper flakes

GARNISH
4 leaves of a Chinese cabbage
2 green onions, shredded

Place any uncooked seafood in a small bowl with the 2 tbsps white wine or sherry. Loosely cover and cook 3-5 minutes on MEDIUM, stirring occasionally. Cook until the seafood is just tender and set aside. Crush the black beans and combine with the water for the sauce. Set aside until ready to use. Combine the remaining sauce ingredients in a small bowl. Cover loosely and cook on HIGH for about 5 minutes, stirring occasionally after 1 minute. When the sauce has thickened, add the black beans and water, and the cooking liquid from the seafood. Stir

Spicy Potted Shrimps

PREPARATION TIME: 5 minutes plus chilling

MICROWAVE COOKING TIME: 3 minutes

SERVES: 4 people

12oz cooked fresh or frozen shrimp
¾ cup unsalted butter
1 tsp grated nutmeg
½ tsp ground ginger
½ tsp freshly ground pepper
½ tsp hot paprika

GARNISH
Lemon wedges
Small parsley sprigs

This page: Seafood in Garlic Sauce. Facing page: Masala Shrimp (top) and Spicy Potted Shrimp (bottom).

ACCOMPANIMENT
Melba toast or hot whole-wheat toast triangles

If using frozen shrimp, dry well on paper towels. To clarify the butter, heat on MEDIUM for 2 minutes. Leave the butter to stand for about 15 minutes. Skim the salt from the top of the butter and carefully pour or spoon off the clear butter oil, leaving the milky sediment in the bottom of the dish. Combine the clarified butter and the spices in a

well and add all the seafood to the sauce. Cover loosely and heat through on MEDIUM 2-3 minutes. To serve, place 1 of the Chinese cabbage leaves on each plate and fill with the seafood mixture. Sprinkle the seafood with green onions and serve immediately.

Shrimp Gratinée

PREPARATION TIME: 10 minutes

MICROWAVE COOKING TIME: 4 minutes

SERVES: 4 people

1lb peeled, cooked shrimp
1 cup heavy cream
½ tsp ground mustard
Salt and pepper
2 tbsps butter or margarine
4 tbsps dry breadcrumbs
4 tbsps grated Cheddar and Parmesan
    cheese mixed
Pinch paprika (optional)

Place the shrimp in individual microproof serving dishes. Mix the cream and the mustard together and add a pinch of salt and pepper. Pour the cream mixture over the shrimp and set aside. Melt the butter for 30 seconds to 1 minute on HIGH. Stir in the breadcrumbs and the cheese. Sprinkle an equal amount of the crumb and cheese mixture over each dish of shrimp. Cook on HIGH for 3 minutes and then brown quickly under a hot broiler. If not broiling, sprinkle with paprika before cooking for 3 minutes. Serve immediately.

Kipper and Mushroom Pâté

PREPARATION TIME: 15 minutes

MICROWAVE COOKING TIME: 5 minutes 40 seconds

SERVES: 4-6 people

2 double kipper fillets
½ cup butter or margarine
2oz small mushrooms sliced
Grated rind and juice of ½ lemon

Scant 1 cup heavy cream
Pepper
Pinch nutmeg
Pinch cayenne pepper

Place the kippers in a shallow dish and dot with 2 tbsps of the butter. Loosely cover the dish and cook for 5 minutes on HIGH, or until the fish flakes. Drain any juices and reserve. Remove the skin and any bones from the kippers. Slice the mushrooms and combine them in a small dish with 1oz butter. Loosely cover and cook for 30 seconds on HIGH. Set the mushrooms aside. Soften the remaining butter for 10 seconds on HIGH. Combine with the kippers, cooking juices, lemon juice and rind in a food processor or blender. Season with pepper, nutmeg and cayenne pepper and process to a smooth purée. Whip the cream lightly and fold into the kipper mixture by hand. Reserve about 12 mushroom slices and fold the rest into the kipper mixture. Divide between 6 small custard cups, or pack into 1 large dish. Garnish with the mushroom slices and chill for at least 1 hour. Serve the pâté with hot toast and lemon wedges.

Moules Dijonnaise

PREPARATION TIME: 5 minutes

MICROWAVE COOKING TIME: 9 minutes

SERVES: 4 people

2lbs fresh mussels in the shell
1 tbsp butter or margarine
1 shallot, finely chopped
1 clove garlic, crushed
½ cup white wine
2 tsps flour
2 tbsps Dijon mustard
½ cup heavy cream
2 tsps parsley, chopped
2 tsps tarragon, chopped
Salt and pepper

Wash the mussels in cold water and scrub them well. Discard any that do not shut when tapped or have broken shells. Put the butter into a large bowl and cook for 30 seconds

on HIGH. Add the shallot, garlic, wine, seasoning and mussels. Cover with plastic wrap and cook for 5 minutes on HIGH, or until the shells open. Stir several times during cooking. Discard any mussels that do not open. Remove the mussels from the bowl, put into a serving dish and keep warm. Strain the liquid and set it aside. Put the flour into a clean bowl and gradually pour on the mussel cooking liquid, stirring well to mix. Cook, uncovered, for 2 minutes on HIGH, or until thick. Stir in the mustard, cream, chopped herbs, salt and pepper. Heat through for 1 minute on HIGH. Pour over the mussels and serve with French bread.

Masala Shrimp

PREPARATION TIME: 15 minutes

MICROWAVE COOKING TIME: 11-12 minutes plus 2 minutes standing time

SERVES: 4 people

1½ lbs jumbo shrimp
2 tbsps oil
1 small onion, finely chopped
2 cloves garlic, crushed
1 tsp ground coriander
1 tsp ground cumin
1 tsp ground mustard
1 tsp ground ginger

**Kipper and Mushroom
Pâté (right) and Shrimp
Gratinée (below).**

Crabmeat Mushrooms

PREPARATION TIME: 8 minutes

MICROWAVE COOKING TIME:
6-8 minutes

SERVES: 4 people

4 very large flat mushrooms, washed with
*   stalks removed*
4oz crabmeat
½ cup fresh white breadcrumbs
⅓ cup finely chopped walnuts
1 egg, beaten
1 bunch chives, snipped
1 tbsp chopped parsley
1 tbsp Dijon mustard
Dry breadcrumbs
3 tbsps butter

Chop the stalks finely and mix with
the crabmeat, fresh breadcrumbs,
walnuts, herbs, mustard and salt and
pepper. Beat in the egg gradually to
bind the mixture together. It should
not be too wet. Pile some of the
mixture on top of each mushroom
and place them on a plate in a circle.
Cook for 3-5 minutes on HIGH. Set
aside and melt the butter for 30
seconds on HIGH. Sprinkle the dry
breadcrumbs over the mushrooms
and spoon some of the melted butter
on top. Cook for a further 1 minute
on HIGH. Brown under a broiler
before serving.

Shrimp, Bacon and Cucumber-filled Avocados

PREPARATION TIME: 15 minutes

MICROWAVE COOKING TIME:
4½ minutes

SERVES: 4 people

4 strips bacon, rindless and boneless
3oz cooked, peeled shrimp
½ cucumber, peeled, seeded and diced
½ cup garlic and herb soft cheese
2 large ripe avocados
Juice of 1 lemon
Dash of tabasco
Salt and pepper

TOPPING
2 tbsps butter or margarine
4 tbsps dry breadcrumbs

1 tsp ground turmeric
¼ tsp ground cinnamon
Pinch cayenne pepper
4 tomatoes, peeled, seeded and diced
2 tsps tomato paste
Juice of ½ lime
Salt and pepper
6 tbsps natural yogurt
2 tsps garam masala

GARNISH
Lime wedges
Coriander leaves

Remove the shells from the shrimp
but leave on the very tail ends. Wash,
de-vein and pat dry. Put the oil,
onion, garlic and spices into a bowl.
Cover loosely with plastic wrap and
cook on HIGH for 2 minutes. Mix in

**This page: Japanese Shrimp
Custard. Facing page: Shrimp,
Bacon and Cucumber-filled
Avocados (top) and Crabmeat
Mushrooms (bottom).**

the tomatoes, tomato paste, lime
juice and salt. Cook on HIGH for
3-4 minutes, until the tomatoes have
pulped. Add the shrimp and cook on
HIGH for 3-4 minutes, or until the
shrimp are tender and pink. Stir in
the yogurt and leave to stand for
about 2 minutes before serving.
Divide the shrimp between 4 serving
dishes and sprinkle each serving with
some of the garam masala. Garnish
with lime wedges and coriander
leaves.

4 tbsps grated Parmesan cheese
Paprika

Heat a browning dish according to the manufacturer's directions and when hot brown the bacon for 1 minute per side. Crumble it into a small bowl. Add the shrimp, cucumber, garlic and herb cheese, salt and pepper and a dash tabasco. Cut the avocados in half and remove the stones. Scoop out the flesh, leaving a ¼ inch lining on the inside of the shell. Sprinkle the scooped out flesh and the shell with lemon juice. Add the avocado flesh to the other ingredients in the bowl and pour in the remaining lemon juice. Mix the ingredients thoroughly, but do not over mix. Spoon the filling into the avocado shells, sprinkle on the cheese and breadcrumbs. Melt the butter for 30 seconds on HIGH and spoon some over each avocado. Cook for 3 minutes on HIGH and then brown under a pre-heated broiler. If not broiling, sprinkle lightly with paprika before cooking for 3 minutes. Serve immediately.

Japanese Shrimp Custard

PREPARATION TIME: 15 minutes
MICROWAVE COOKING TIME: 7-9 minutes
SERVES: 4 people

4 jumbo shrimp shelled, but with tail ends left on
4 pea pods, trimmed
¼ small red pepper, seeded and cut into strips
½ cup bean sprouts
4 mushrooms, sliced

CUSTARD
4 eggs
1 cup chicken, fish or vegetable stock
½ tsp light soy sauce
1 small piece ginger, grated
Salt and pepper

GARNISH
4 green onions, thinly sliced or shredded

Prepare the shrimp, sprinkle lightly with salt and pepper and place one in each of 4 microproof custard cups so that the tails stick out of the dish. Place the pea pods, pepper and mushrooms in a glass dish, cover loosely and cook for 1 minute on HIGH. Divide the vegetables evenly among the 4 dishes. Mix together the custard ingredients and pour over. Cover each dish with plastic wrap and place in a circle in a larger shallow dish. Pour hot water around the custard cups to come ¼ of the way up the sides. Cook on MEDIUM for about 6-8 minutes, turning the dishes and rearranging them occasionally. Cook until softly set. Leave to stand, covered, 10 minutes before serving. Serve warm or chilled, garnished with the green onions.

Oysters Mornay

PREPARATION TIME: 20 minutes
MICROWAVE COOKING TIME: 5 minutes
SERVES: 4 people

2 dozen oysters on the half shell

SAUCE
2 tbsps butter
2 tbsps flour
¼ tsp ground mustard
Pinch nutmeg
Pinch cayenne pepper
1 cup milk
½ cup finely grated Cheddar cheese
Salt and pepper

GARNISH
Black lumpfish caviar

Place the butter for the sauce in a glass meaure and cook on HIGH for 1 minute. Stir in the flour and add

Facing page: Oysters Mornay.

the mustard, nutmeg, cayenne pepper and a pinch of salt and pepper. Gradually pour on the milk, stirring continuously. Cook for a further 2 minutes on HIGH, stirring once until smooth and thick. Stir in the cheese to melt. Place the oysters on a plate or directly on the turntable of the oven. Spoon some of the sauce into each oyster and heat for 2 minutes on MEDIUM. Top each oyster with a spoonful of caviar to serve.

Coquilles St. Jacques Parisienne

PREPARATION TIME: 15 minutes

MICROWAVE COOKING TIME: 17-22 minutes

SERVES: 4 people

3 tbsps butter or margarine
4oz mushrooms, quartered
2 shallots, finely chopped
3 tbsps flour
Salt and pepper
¼ tsp chopped fresh thyme
1 tbsp chopped parsley
4 tbsps dry white wine
½ cup fish stock
8-12 scallops, depending upon the size
½ cup heavy cream
2 tomatoes, peeled, seeded and cut into thin strips

TOPPING
2 tbsps butter or margarine
½ cup dry breadcrumbs
2 tbsps grated Parmesan cheese

Place the butter or margarine, mushrooms and shallots in a small dish and cook on HIGH for 2-3 minutes, stirring once or twice. Add the flour, salt, pepper, thyme, and parsley, mixing well. Gradually add the wine and the fish stock, stirring constantly. Cook 1 minute on HIGH to slightly thicken. If the scallops are large, cut into quarters, but leave the roe whole. Add the scallops to the sauce, partially cover the bowl and cook on HIGH for 5-6 minutes, stirring halfway through the cooking time. Add the cream and lower the setting to MEDIUM to cook for 3-4 minutes, stirring occasionally. Add the tomatoes to the scallops and leave to stand for 2 minutes. To prepare the topping, place the butter in a small bowl and cook on HIGH for 30 seconds. Stir in the breadcrumbs and the Parmesan cheese. Divide the scallop mixture between 4 shells or small dishes and sprinkle with the crumb mixture. Loosely cover with plastic wrap and cook for 7-8 minutes on MEDIUM or MEDIUM HIGH until hot, rearranging the shells or dishes halfway through the cooking time. Serve hot.

Quick Salmon Mousse

PREPARATION TIME: 15 minutes

MICROWAVE COOKING TIME: 4-6 minutes

SERVES: 4 people

1lb salmon
1 bay leaf
4 tbsps water
½ cup low fat soft cheese
½ tsp tomato paste
2 tsps chopped dill
1 tbsp lemon juice
Salt
Dash tabasco
4 tbsps mayonnaise
4oz sliced smoked salmon

GARNISH
Cucumber slices
Lemon slices
Fresh dill

Place the fish in a small casserole with the bay leaf and the water. Cover and cook 4-6 minutes on HIGH or until the fish flakes. Remove the skin and bones and put the fish into a food processor or blender. Reserve the liquid. Process the fish with the cheese, tomato paste, lemon juice, dill, salt and tabasco until smooth. Add reserved liquid as necessary if the mixture is too thick. Spoon into mounds on 4 small serving dishes and chill until firm. Before serving, spread 1 tbsp of mayonnaise carefully over each mound of salmon mousse. Cut the slices of smoked salmon to size and press onto the mayonnaise carefully to completely cover the mousse. Leave at room temperature for about 30 minutes before serving. Garnish with the cucumber slices, lemon slices and fresh dill. Serve with melba toast or hot buttered whole-wheat toast.

Moules Bourguignonne

PREPARATION TIME: 20 minutes

MICROWAVE COOKING TIME: 7-8 minutes

SERVES: 4 people

1lb fresh mussels in their shells
3 tbsps butter or margarine
1-2 cloves garlic, crushed
⅓ cup dry breadcrumbs
1 tbsp chopped parsley
2 tsps lemon juice
Salt and pepper
Paprika

Wash the mussels in cold water and scrub the shells well. Discard any mussels that do not shut when tapped, or that have broken shells. Put the cleaned mussels into a large bowl with 4 tbsps water. Cover with plastic wrap and cook on HIGH for 5 minutes. Stir the mussels once or twice while cooking. Discard any mussels that have not opened. Put the butter or margarine in a small bowl and soften on HIGH for 30 seconds. Add the garlic, and cook a further 30 seconds on HIGH. Stir in the breadcrumbs, parsley, lemon juice, salt and pepper. Remove the top shells from the mussels and arrange them in their half shells in individual serving dishes. Top each mussel with a small spoonful of the garlic-breadcrumb mixture and sprinkle with paprika. Return the dishes to the oven and re-heat 1-2 minutes on MEDIUM before serving.

Pickled Herring

PREPARATION TIME: 20 minutes

MICROWAVE COOKING TIME: 6-8 minutes

SERVES: 4 people

4 herrings, gutted and boned
½ cup white wine vinegar
½ cup water
1 onion, peeled and sliced

Coquilles St. Jacques Parisienne
(above) and Moules
Bourguignonne (right).

This page: Quick Salmon Mousse. Facing page: Marinated Salmon (top) and Pickled Herring (bottom).

4 peppercorns
4 allspice berries
2 tsps mustard seed
1 bay leaf
1 large sprig fresh dill
Salt

Separate all the fish into two whole fillets and remove the heads, tails and fins. Place the fillets in a shallow dish, scatter over the onions and set aside. Mix the vinegar, water peppercorns, allspice berries, mustard seed, bay leaf, dill and salt in a glass measure and cook for 6-8 minutes on HIGH. Allow to cool slightly and then pour over the fish. Leave the fish to cool in the liquid, cover and leave in the refrigerator overnight. Serve the fish with some of the onions on a bed of lettuce, and garnish with sprigs of fresh dill if desired.

Marinated Salmon

PREPARATION TIME: 20 minutes

MICROWAVE COOKING TIME: 6-8 minutes

SERVES: 6 people

½ cup dry white wine
2 tsp white wine vinegar or lemon juice
1 cinnamon stick
1 tsp coarsely ground white peppercorns
1 onion, finely chopped
1 tbsp crushed coriander seeds
2 whole cloves
2 tsps sugar
4 tbsps oil
1lb salmon, filleted and skinned

GARNISH
Curly endive or watercress

Combine the white wine, vinegar, spices, sugar and onion in a glass measure. Cook for 6-8 minutes on HIGH. Stir in the oil and allow to cool slightly. Cut the salmon across the grain into thin slices and arrange in a large, shallow dish. Pour over the white wine and spice mixture and leave to cool at room temperature. Cover and put into the refrigerator for at least 4 hours. Serve arranged on a bed of curly endive and spoon over a bit of the marinade.

MAIN DISHES

Sea Bass with Fennel and Orange Sauce

PREPARATION TIME: 25 minutes

MICROWAVE COOKING TIME: 18-22 minutes

SERVES: 2-3 people

1 sea bass weighing 1lb 12oz, cleaned and
  trimmed
2 tbsps butter
Salt and pepper
1 tbsp lemon juice

FENNEL AND ORANGE SAUCE
1 medium bulb fennel, cored and sliced
Juice and grated rind of 1 orange
1 tbsp butter
1½ tbsps flour
Salt and pepper
¼ cup milk
3 tbsps heavy cream
Salt and pepper
1 tbsp aquavit (optional)
Fennel tops
1 orange, sliced

Cut three slits in each side of the sea
bass and cover the head and tail with
foil. Melt 2 tbsps butter in a large,
shallow dish. Place the sea bass in the
butter and turn several times to coat
evenly. Sprinkle over some salt and
pepper and lemon juice. Loosely
cover and cook for 8-10 minutes on
HIGH. Turn the fish over halfway
through the cooking time.
Alternatively, curve the fish to fit the
turntable, brush with melted butter
and secure head to the tail with
loosely-tied string. Cover well with
plastic wrap. Leave to stand, covered,
while preparing the sauce. Reserve
the green tops of the fennel for
garnish and place the sliced fennel

and orange juice in a small, deep
bowl. Reserve the orange rind for
later use. Cover the bowl and cook
on HIGH for 6-7 minutes. Remove
the fennel from the bowl with a
draining spoon and chop finely by
hand or in a food processor. Reserve
the cooking liquid. Melt the butter

**This page: Fish Peperonata. Facing
page: Trout with Almonds (top)
and Sea Bass with Fennel and
Orange Sauce (bottom).**

on HIGH for 30 seconds in a glass
measure or small, deep bowl. Add
the flour and salt and pepper.
Gradually stir in the milk and when

This page: Salmon Steaks with Sauce Choron. Facing page: Shrimp Newburg (top) and Scampi Provençale (bottom).

smooth add the fennel cooking liquid. Cook 3 minutes on HIGH, stirring after 1 minute and frequently thereafter until the sauce is smooth and thick. Stir in the fennel and the cream and heat a further 1-2 minutes on HIGH. Add the orange rind and stir in the aquavit, if using. Place the sea bass on a large serving plate and spoon over some of the sauce. Serve the rest of the sauce separately and garnish the fish with the orange slices and whole or chopped fennel tops.

Langoustine Provençale

PREPARATION TIME: 15 minutes

MICROWAVE COOKING TIME: 10 minutes

SERVES: 4 people

2 tbsps olive oil
1 onion, finely chopped
1 clove garlic, crushed
1 14oz can plum tomatoes
5 tbsps dry white wine
1 bay leaf
¼ tsp thyme
1 tsp basil
1 tbsp chopped parsley
Salt and pepper
2 tbsp cornstarch

1½ lbs langoustine, shelled
Salt and pepper

Combine the olive oil, onion and garlic in a deep bowl and cook for 5 minutes on HIGH, stirring frequently. Add the tomatoes, wine, herbs and bay leaf, salt and pepper and stir well. Heat for 2 minutes on HIGH. Mix the reserved tomato juice with the cornstarch and add to the sauce. Cook 1 minute on HIGH and stir well. Add the langoustine to the sauce and cook for 2 minutes on HIGH or until they are tender and pink and the sauce has thickened. Serve with rice.

Shrimp Newberg

PREPARATION TIME: 10 minutes

MICROWAVE COOKING TIME: 12 minutes

SERVES: 4 people

1 cup heavy cream
1 tbsp tomato paste
½ tsp paprika
Pinch cayenne pepper
8oz crabmeat, fresh or frozen
4oz cooked, peeled shrimp
2 tbsps sherry
Salt and pepper
2 egg yolks

GARNISH
Chopped parsley

Pour the cream into a glass measure and heat for 6 minutes on HIGH, or until just boiling. Whisk in the tomato paste, paprika and a pinch of cayenne pepper, cover and set aside. Combine the crabmeat, shrimp and sherry in a small bowl. Cook for 4 minutes on MEDIUM. Cover and set aside. Beat the egg yolks in a small bowl and add 2 or 3 spoonfuls of the hot cream to the eggs and whisk well. Return the eggs to the rest of the cream and cook the sauce on MEDIUM for 3-4 minutes, whisking every 15 seconds until thickened. Combine the hot cream mixture with the crabmeat and shrimp and stir well. Serve on toast or rice, garnished with chopped parsley.

Poisson Suprême

PREPARATION TIME: 20 minutes

MICROWAVE COOKING TIME:
12-13 minutes

SERVES: 4 people

4 large flounder fillets, skinned
4 tbsps dry white wine
1 bay leaf
2 parsley stalks
4 black peppercorns
2 tbsps butter or margarine
1 shallot, finely chopped
3oz mushrooms, sliced
2 carrots, peeled and cut into thin 2 inch
   strips
3 sticks celery, cut into thin 2 inch strips
2 tbsps flour
1 cup milk
2 tsps chopped fresh thyme or tarragon
2 tbsps heavy cream
Salt and white pepper

Fold the fish fillets in half and place
in a shallow dish, thin ends toward
the middle of the dish. Pour over the
white wine and add the bay leaf,
parsley stalks and peppercorns.
Cover loosely and cook for 5-6
minutes, or until the fish is tender.
Pour off and reserve the cooking
juices. Leave the fish covered while
preparing the sauce. Place the butter
in a deep bowl and melt for 30
seconds on HIGH. Stir in the shallot
and cook for 2 minutes on HIGH,
stirring occasionally until softened.
Add the carrots and celery and
loosely cover the bowl. Cook for 6
minutes on HIGH, stirring frequently
until the carrots and celery are
almost tender. Add the mushrooms
and stir in the flour carefully.
Gradually add the milk, stirring
constantly. Re-cover the dish and
cook a further 2 minutes on HIGH,
stirring occasionally to keep the
sauce smooth. Add the thyme, cream
and salt and pepper. Place the fish in
a serving dish, cover with the sauce
and re-heat for 1 minute on HIGH.
Serve with rice or new potatoes.

Paupiettes aux Fines Herbes

PREPARATION TIME: 20 minutes

MICROWAVE COOKING TIME:
10-12 minutes

SERVES: 4 people

3 tbsps butter or margarine
2 shallots, finely chopped
1 tbsp chopped parsley
1 tbsp chopped chervil, fresh thyme, fresh
   tarragon and chives, mixed
1 cup fresh breadcrumbs
¼ tsp ground mace
1 tbsp lemon juice
Salt and pepper
4 double sole fillets, skinned and cut in
   half
4 tbsps dry white wine
½ cup heavy cream

Melt the butter in a small bowl for
30 seconds on HIGH. Use some of
the butter to lightly grease 8 small
custard cups. Add the chopped
shallot to remaining butter in the
bowl and cook for 2 minutes on
HIGH, stirring once or twice. Add
the parsley and the mixed herbs,
breadcrumbs, mace, salt and pepper

and stir well. Divide the filling into 8
portions and spread on the skinned
side of each sole fillet. Roll the fillets
up and place 1 fillet in each greased
cup. Pour some of the white wine
into each cup and cover loosely with
plastic wrap. Arrange the cups in a

Paupiettes aux Fines Herbes (left)
and Poisson Suprême (bottom left).

circle on the oven turntable and cook for 4-6 minutes on HIGH, rearranging the cups halfway through the cooking time. Leave the cups to stand, covered, while preparing the sauce. Pour the heavy cream into a glass measure and cook, uncovered, for 5 minutes on HIGH or until boiling rapidly. Allow to boil 1-2 minutes and remove from the oven. Carefully pour away any cooking liquid from the cups of fish through a fine strainer into the cream. Invert the cups onto serving plates and lift off carefully. Add salt and pepper to the sauce and pour around the paupiettes to serve.

Sweet and Sour Fish

PREPARATION TIME: 20 minutes

COOKING TIME: 4-5 minutes

SERVES: 4 people

1lb sole or plaice fillets
4oz canned, sliced water chestnuts
8oz canned pineapple chunks, ¼ cup juice reserved
1 green pepper, seeded and sliced
Juice of 1 lemon
1-2 tbsps brown sugar
1 tbsp light soy sauce
1 tbsp tomato ketchup
1 tbsp cornstarch
3 green onions, shredded
3 tomatoes, peeled and quartered
Salt and pepper

Skin the fish fillets and fold them in half. Place in a large casserole, thinner ends of the fillets toward the middle of the dish. Pour over enough water to come ¼ inch up the sides of the fillets. Cover the dish loosely and cook for 2 minutes on HIGH. Set aside and keep warm. Drain the water chestnuts and place them in a small bowl with the pineapple chunks and the green pepper. Mix the reserved juice from the pineapple with the lemon juice, brown sugar, soy sauce, ketchup, and cornstarch. Pour over the pineapple, water chestnuts and green pepper in a small bowl and cook for 2-3 minutes on HIGH, stirring often until thickened.

Drain off the cooking liquid from the fish and add the tomatoes, green onions, salt and pepper. Cook for a further 1 minute on HIGH. Arrange the fish on a serving plate and pour over the sauce. Serve with rice or crisp noodles.

Trout with Almonds

PREPARATION TIME: 10 minutes

MICROWAVE COOKING TIME: 10 minutes

SERVES: 4 people

½ cup butter
½ cup sliced almonds
4 even-sized trout, cleaned

GARNISH
Watercress
Lime slices or wedges

Pre-heat a browning dish according to the manufacturer's instructions. Add half the butter and heat until beginning to brown. Add the almonds and stir to brown slightly. Remove the almonds and the browned butter to a dish and set aside. Pat the trout dry. Re-heat the browning dish. Melt remaining butter and, when very hot, add trout and cook on HIGH for 2 minutes. Turn the trout over and cook a further 2 minutes. Re-position the trout occasionally during cooking. Repeat with remaining 2 trout. Serve the trout topped with the almonds and any remaining butter. Garnish with watercress and lime.

Fish Peperonata

PREPARATION TIME: 20 minutes

COOKING TIME: 10-12 minutes

SERVES: 4 people

1½ lbs monkfish tails, skinned, boned and cut into 1 inch pieces
¼ cup water
2 tbsps lemon juice
1 bay leaf
4 peppercorns
1 tbsp tomato paste

2 cloves garlic, crushed
1 onion, thinly sliced
1 red pepper, seeded and sliced
1 green pepper, seeded and sliced
1 yellow pepper, seeded and sliced
1 tbsp cornstarch mixed with 2 tbsps cold water
1 tbsp chopped fresh basil or 2 tsps dried basil
1 tbsp chopped parsley
Salt and pepper
8 tomatoes, skinned, seeded and sliced

Place the fish, water, lemon juice, bay leaf and peppercorns in a shallow dish. Cover loosely and cook for about 4-6 minutes, or until fish is tender. Strain the liquid and reserve. Set the fish aside and keep warm. Mix the fish cooking liquid and tomato paste in a small bowl. Add the garlic and onion and cook 2 minutes on HIGH. Stir well and add the peppers and cook a further 1 minute on HIGH. Mix some of the hot liquid with the cornstarch and water and then return it to the dish with the herbs. Cook 2 minutes, stirring often after 1 minute. Add the tomatoes and fish and cook 1 minute more to heat through. Serve with rice or pasta.

Salmon Steaks with Sauce Choron

PREPARATION TIME: 15 minutes

MICROWAVE COOKING TIME: 11-15 minutes

SERVES: 4 people

4 salmon steaks, about 1½ lbs in total weight
½ cup butter
3 egg yolks
Juice and rind of 1 orange
1 tbsp lemon juice
Salt and pepper
2 tbsps heavy cream

GARNISH
1 small orange, sliced

Facing page: Sweet and Sour Fish.

Tuck in the ends of the salmon steaks and secure with wooden picks. Arrange in a round dish with the secured ends toward the middle of the dish. Cover loosely and cook on MEDIUM 8-12 minutes, or until just cooked. Turn the fish over halfway through the cooking time. Leave covered while preparing the sauce. In a glass measure melt the butter for 1 minute on HIGH. Beat the egg yolks with the orange juice and rind, lemon juice and salt and pepper. Gradually stir the mixture into the butter. Cook on LOW for 15 seconds and whisk. Repeat every 15 seconds until the sauce thickens, about 3 minutes. Place the glass measure in iced water if the sauce starts to curdle. Stir in the cream. Arrange salmon on a serving dish and pour over some of the sauce. Garnish with the orange slices and serve the rest of the sauce separately.

Jambalaya

PREPARATION TIME: 20 minutes

MICROWAVE COOKING TIME: 14-17 minutes

SERVES: 4 people

8oz spicy sausage, such as Pepperoni or Merguez, skinned and diced
8oz cooked ham, cubed
1 green pepper, seeded and cut into 1 inch pieces
1 medium onion, peeled and roughly chopped
1 clove garlic, peeled and finely chopped
1 red or green chili, seeded and finely chopped
2 tbsps olive oil
10oz canned tomatoes
1 tbsp tomato paste
2 tbsps white wine or lemon juice
1 tsp chopped marjoram
1 bay leaf
¼ tsp grated fresh nutmeg
Salt and pepper
4oz peeled, cooked shrimp
2 tomatoes, peeled, seeded and cut into large pieces
1½ cups cooked long grain rice

Place the sausage, ham, green pepper, onion, garlic, chili and olive oil in a large casserole or deep bowl. Stir to

coat all the ingredients in oil and cover the bowl loosely. Cook for 6-7 minutes or until the onion and pepper are almost tender. Mix the canned tomatoes, tomato paste and white wine or lemon juice and add to the bowl. Add the marjoram, bay leaf, grated nutmeg, salt and pepper and loosely cover the bowl. Cook for 2-3 minutes on HIGH, and add the shrimp, tomatoes, rice and salt and pepper. Re-cover the bowl and cook a further 4 minutes, or until all the ingredients are hot. Remove the bay leaf before serving. Serve with lightly cooked okra.

This page: Jambalaya. Facing page: Chinese Fish.

Chinese Fish

PREPARATION TIME: 20 minutes

MICROWAVE COOKING TIME: 8-9 minutes

SERVES: 4 people

2 bream, gray mullet or red snapper, cleaned, 2lbs in total weight
4 tbsps dry white wine
3 tbsps light soy sauce
3 tbsps water
1 3 inch piece fresh ginger, peeled

Herring Lyonnaise

PREPARATION TIME: 15 minutes

MICROWAVE COOKING TIME: 17-18 minutes

SERVES: 4 people

4 tbsps butter or margarine
2 large onions, sliced
4 herrings, cleaned
2 tbsps dry white wine
3 tbsps chopped parsley

Heat a browning dish according to the manufacturer's directions. Put in half the butter and allow to brown slightly. Add the sliced onions and cook for 5 minutes on HIGH, stirring frequently until lightly browned. Remove the onions from the browning dish and set them aside. Melt the rest of the butter and add the fish. Cook the herrings for 5 minutes per side. Remove the herrings to a serving dish and top with the onions and keep warm. Add the white wine to the juices in the browning dish and cook for 1 minute on HIGH. Stir in the parsley and pour the mixture over the fish. Heat through 1-2 minutes on HIGH before serving.

Stuffed Trout

PREPARATION TIME: 20 minutes

MICROWAVE COOKING TIME: 14 minutes

SERVES: 4 people

4 tbsps butter
1½ cups fresh white breadcrumbs
2 tsps chopped fresh basil
2 tsps chopped parsley
1 clove garlic, crushed
4oz cooked peeled shrimp, roughly chopped
Salt and pepper
1 egg, beaten
4 trout, cleaned and boned
Juice of 1 lemon

This page: Codfish Valencia. Facing page: Herring Lyonnaise (top) and Stuffed Trout (bottom).

2 sticks celery, cut in 3 inch lengths and finely shredded
2 carrots, cut as for celery
4 green onions, cut as for celery
½ cup sliced bamboo shoots, cut in very thin strips
1 tbsp cornstarch mixed with 2 tbsps cold water
2 tsps oyster sauce
Dash sesame oil

Make three slashes in each side of the fish and place them in a shallow dish. Pour over the wine, soy sauce and water. Cut a thin slice lengthwise from the ginger and add it to the fish with salt and pepper. Reserve the remaining ginger. Cover the fish loosely and cook on HIGH for 4 minutes. Turn over. Shred the remaining ginger finely. Add to the fish with the rest of the vegetables and bamboo shoots. Re-cover the dish and cook a further 4 minutes, or until the fish is done. Remove the fish and vegetables to a serving dish, cover and keep warm. Strain cooking liquid into a glass measure and stir in the cornstarch and oyster sauce. Cook on HIGH for 2 minutes, or until thickened, stirring halfway through. Stir in the sesame oil and pour over the fish and vegetables to serve.

GARNISH
Lemon slices
Whole fresh basil leaves

Place the butter in a small bowl and heat for 30 seconds on HIGH to melt. Stir in the breadcrumbs, herbs, shrimp, salt and pepper and enough egg to bind the mixture together. Sprinkle the insides of the trout lightly with salt and pepper and fill each with some of the stuffing. Place the trout in a large, shallow dish and sprinkle with lemon juice. Cover loosely with plastic wrap and cook for 6 minutes on HIGH. Carefully reposition the trout, re-cover the dish and cook for another 7 minutes on HIGH. Allow to stand for 3 minutes before serving. Garnish with lemon slices and basil leaves.

Sweet and Sour Fish Balls

PREPARATION TIME: 20 minutes

MICROWAVE COOKING TIME: 13 minutes

SERVES: 4 people

Breadcrumbs made from 2-4 slices white
* bread with crusts removed*
2 medium onions, grated
1lb whitefish
1 egg, beaten with 1 tbsp cream
Salt and pepper

SAUCE
1½ tbsps cornstarch
½ cup light brown sugar
4 tbsps water
8oz canned pineapple pieces, juice
* reserved*
6 tbsps cider or wine vinegar
4 tbsps soy sauce
2 tbsps tomato ketchup
1 green pepper, seeded and sliced
1 clove garlic, crushed
1 small piece ginger, grated
2 tomatoes, peeled and quartered
4 green onions, sliced into 1 inch diagonal
* pieces*
Salt and pepper

Place half the breadcrumbs and the onions in a food processor and grate. Add the fish and process until broken down. Add the egg and

cream, salt and pepper and work to mix thoroughly. If the mixture is too thick add a bit more cream. If too thin, add some of the reserved breadcrumbs until thick enough to shape. Divide into 16 pieces and roll into balls. Arrange in a shallow dish, cover loosely and cook on HIGH for 3 minutes. Rearrange the fish balls and cook a further 3 minutes on HIGH. Keep covered and set aside. Combine cornstarch, sugar, reserved pineapple juice and water. Add the vinegar, soy sauce and ketchup and stir thoroughly. Cook 5 minutes on highest setting or until thick. Stir after the first minute's cooking and occasionally thereafter. Add the green pepper, ginger, garlic, salt and pepper and cook for 1 minute on HIGH. Add the pineapple pieces, tomatoes and onions and cook a further 1 minute on HIGH. Pour over the fish balls and serve with rice.

Codfish Valencia

PREPARATION TIME: 20 minutes

MICROWAVE COOKING TIME: 13-14 minutes

SERVES: 4 people

2 tbsps butter
1 large onion, sliced
1 clove garlic, crushed
2 14oz cans plum tomatoes
2 tbsps tomato paste
Grated rind and juice of ½ orange
1 bay leaf
2 tsps oregano
1 tbsp lemon juice
2lbs cod fillets or steaks
1 tbsp cornflour mixed with 2 tbsps dry
* white wine*
Salt and pepper
2oz large green olives, pitted

GARNISH
½ cup unblanched almonds, roughly
* chopped*
1 tbsp finely chopped parsley

Place the butter in a bowl and cook on HIGH for 30 seconds to melt. Add the onion and the garlic and cook on HIGH for 2 minutes to soften slightly. Add the tomatoes,

tomato paste, orange rind and juice, bay leaf, oregano and cook for 3-4 minutes, stirring occasionally. Add the olives and stir in the cornstarch and white wine mixture. Cook a further 1-2 minutes on HIGH, stirring halfway through. Cook until the cornstarch thickens. Set the sauce aside while cooking the fish. Place fish in a shallow dish with the lemon juice. Cover loosely and cook 4-5 minutes, turning the fish over half way through the cooking time. Pour the sauce into a microproof serving dish and place the fish on top. Sprinkle with nuts and parsley and heat through for 1 minute on HIGH. Serve with rice.

Shrimp Creole

PREPARATION TIME: 20 minutes

MICROWAVE COOKING TIME: 10-13 minutes plus 2 minutes standing time

SERVES: 4 people

1lb uncooked shrimp, peeled
1 onion, thinly sliced
3 sticks celery, thinly sliced
1 clove garlic, crushed
1 tbsp olive oil
2 tbsps cornstarch
8oz canned tomatoes with the juice
½ cup dry white wine or water
4 tbsps tomato ketchup
1 bay leaf
1 tbsp chopped parsley
½ tsp oregano, fresh or dried
½ tsp thyme, fresh or dried
Pinch cayenne pepper
Salt and pepper
Pinch sugar
1 green pepper, seeded and chopped

De-vein the shrimp and set them aside. In a deep, medium size bowl or casserole, combine the onion, celery, garlic and olive oil. Cook, uncovered, on HIGH for 3 minutes to slightly soften the vegetables. Stir halfway

Facing page: Sweet and Sour Fish Balls (top) and Shrimp Creole (bottom).

through the cooking time. Mix the cornstarch with the canned tomatoes, breaking the tomatoes up with a fork. Add the wine or water, ketchup, bay leaf, parsley, oregano, thyme, cayenne pepper, salt and pepper. Cover and cook on HIGH for 3 minutes. Stir after 1 minute's cooking time and frequently thereafter. If the sauce has not thickened, cook an additional 1-2 minutes on HIGH. Taste the sauce and add a pinch of sugar if necessary, to bring out the tomato flavor. Add the green pepper and the shrimp and cook for 4-7 minutes on medium, or until they are tender and pink. Stir halfway through the cooking time. Cover and leave to stand for 2

minutes before serving. Accompany with rice.

Seafood and Bacon Kebabs with Pineapple and Avocado

PREPARATION TIME: 20 minutes

MICROWAVE COOKING TIME:
8 minutes

SERVES: 4 people

12 small scallops
12 jumbo shrimp
6 strips bacon, rind and bones removed
1 small avocado, peeled and cut into 1

inch pieces
1 small can pineapple pieces

BASTE
2 tbsps reserved pineapple juice
2 tsps lemon juice or lime juice
2 tsps soy sauce or Worcestershire sauce
Salt and pepper

If the scallops are very large cut them in half. Shell the shrimp, leaving the shell on the very tail end. De-vein if necessary. Stretch the bacon strips by scraping them with the back of a knife several times. Cut each strip in half. Wrap the scallops in the bacon. Thread the scallops and shrimp onto wooden skewers, alternating with the avocado and the pineapple pieces. Mix together the baste and brush over the surface of the kebabs, making sure the avocados are well covered. Place the kebabs on a rack or on a plate lined with paper towels. Cook on MEDIUM for about 5 minutes, turning once. Brush the kebabs frequently with the basting mixture while cooking. Increase the setting to HIGH and cook a further 3 minutes to crisp the bacon. Serve the kebabs on rice and pour over any remaining basting mixture.

Monkfish Kebabs

PREPARATION TIME: 1 hour

MICROWAVE COOKING TIME:
9 minutes

SERVES: 4 people

1lb monkfish, cut into 1 inch pieces
1 small green pepper, cut into 1 inch pieces
1 small red pepper, cut into 1 inch pieces
8 even-sized mushrooms
4 bay leaves

MARINADE
2 tbsps oil
1 tbsp white wine or lemon juice
1 tbsp chopped thyme and parsley, mixed
Dash Worcestershire sauce
Salt and pepper

This page: Lobster Thermidor. Facing page: Seafood and Bacon Kebabs with Pineapple and Avocado (top) and Monkfish Kebabs (bottom).

Thread the fish, peppers, mushrooms and bay leaves onto wooden skewers, alternating the ingredients, and place in a large, shallow dish. Mix the marinade together and pour over the fish kebabs. Cover and leave in the refrigerator for 1 hour. Cook on the roasting rack on HIGH for 4 minutes. Brush with marinade and rearrange. Cook a further 5 minutes or until the fish is tender. Serve on a bed of rice.

Lobster Thermidor

PREPARATION TIME: 20 minutes

MICROWAVE COOKING TIME: 15-19 minutes

SERVES: 4 people

2 medium lobsters, cooked
1 tbsp butter or margarine
4oz mushrooms, quartered
2 shallots, finely chopped
¼ tsp paprika
2 tsps flour
½ cup heavy cream
2 tsps chopped parsley
2 tsps marjoram
2 tbsps sherry or brandy
Salt and pepper

TOPPING
1 tbsp butter or margarine
4 tbsps fine dry breadcrumbs
2 tbsps grated Cheddar or Parmesan
   cheese

Cut the lobsters in half and remove the tail meat. Remove the black intestinal line, if present, and chop the meat roughly. Use the green tomalley and the coral if desired. Leave the legs and the claws attached and rinse out the shells. Leave to drain upside down on paper towels. Melt 1 tbsp butter in a medium-size bowl for 30 seconds on HIGH. Add the mushrooms and shallot and cook on HIGH for 2 minutes. Stir in the flour and add the paprika. Cook a further 30 seconds on HIGH, stirring once. Add the flour and cream and cook on medium for 3-4 minutes, stirring often until thickened. Add the herbs, sherry or brandy, salt and pepper to the sauce. Add the lobster meat and stir well. Divide the

mixture evenly between the lobster shells and place them on the oven turntable. Cover loosely with plastic wrap and cook on HIGH for 5 minutes. Rearrange the lobsters once during cooking. Melt the butter for the topping for 30 seconds on HIGH and stir in the breadcrumbs. Sprinkle over the lobsters when cooked and top with the cheese. Cook a further 30 seconds on HIGH to melt the cheese, or brown under a pre-heated broiler.

Tuna au Poivre

PREPARATION TIME: 5 minutes

MICROWAVE COOKING TIME: 10-11 minutes plus heating browning dish

SERVES: 4 people

4 6oz tuna steaks
1 tbsp oil
2 tbsps green peppercorns
1 tbsp brandy
6 tbsps crème fraiche or sour cream
Pinch salt

Brush the tuna steaks on both sides with the oil. Crush the peppercorns using a mortar and pestle or with a rolling pin and press onto one side of the tuna steaks. Pre-heat a browning dish to the maximum time the manufacturer allows and then immediately add the tuna steaks, peppercorn side up. Cook, uncovered, for 7 minutes on HIGH. Cook an additional 1 minute if the fish does not flake easily when tested. When the fish steaks are done, remove them to a serving dish and

Tuna au Poivre (above) and Raie au Beurre Noir (right).

Curried Shrimp with Bananas, Pineapple and Cashews

PREPARATION TIME: 20 minutes

MICROWAVE COOKING TIME: 12-16 minutes

SERVES: 4 people

2 tbsps oil
1 onion finely chopped
1 clove garlic, crushed
2 tsps turmeric
2 tsps ground coriander
½ tsp ground cumin
¼ tsp each ground cinnamon, nutmeg and ginger
2 tbsps flour
1½ cups fish or vegetable stock
1 tsp lime juice
2 tsps mango chutney
4oz canned pineapple pieces
1 large or 2 small bananas, peeled and cut into chunks
½ cup roasted, unsalted cashew nuts
12oz peeled, cooked shrimp

GARNISH
Desiccated coconut

Put the oil into a deep bowl and add the onion and garlic. Cover loosely and cook on HIGH for 3-4 minutes, or until the onion softens. Stir in the spices and the flour and cook for a further 2 minutes on HIGH, stirring frequently. Gradually pour in the stock and add the lime juice and mango chutney. Cook for 6-8 minutes or until boiling, stirring frequently. Add the drained pineapple, bananas and cashews and stir well. Add the shrimp and cook on HIGH for 1-2 minutes, or until the shrimp and the fruit are heated through. Serve with rice and sprinkle with desiccated coconut.

keep them warm. Add the brandy to the browning dish and heat for 30 seconds on HIGH. Stir the cream into the juices remaining in the dish and add a pinch of salt to taste. Spoon the sauce over the tuna steaks and serve immediately.

Raie au Beurre Noir

PREPARATION TIME: 10 minutes

MICROWAVE COOKING TIME: 12-14 minutes

SERVES: 4 people

4 skinned wings of skate, about 1½ lbs in total weight
⅓ cup butter
2 tbsps capers

Juice of 1 lemon
2 tsps chopped parsley
Salt and pepper

Arrange skate wings thin edge toward the middle of a casserole dish. Cover and cook on HIGH 8-10 minutes. Leave covered while preparing butter sauce. Heat a browning dish according to manufacturer's instructions. Add the butter and cook until golden. Add capers and stir in the butter for 1 minute. Re-heat until the butter is a nut-brown color, add lemon juice, parsley, salt and pepper and pour over the fish to serve. Garnish with whole sprigs of parsley if desired.

This page: Curried Shrimp with Bananas, Pineapple and Cashews. Facing page: Salmon with Parsley Caper Sauce (top) and Cod Steaks with Mushrooms and Pink Peppercorns (bottom).

Cod Steaks with Mushrooms and Pink Peppercorns

PREPARATION TIME: 15 minutes

MICROWAVE COOKING TIME: 9-11 minutes

SERVES: 4 people

4-8 cod steaks, depending upon size
½ cup white wine
1 bay leaf
2 shallots, finely chopped
2 tbsps butter or margarine
1½ cups sliced mushrooms
2 tbsps flour
½ cup milk
2 tsps pink peppercorns
2 tsps chopped parsley
Grated nutmeg
Salt and pepper

Put the cod and wine into a casserole with the thin ends of the steaks pointing towards the middle of the dish. Add the bay leaf and shallot. Cover loosely and cook for 6 minutes on HIGH. Leave covered and set aside. Melt the butter in a small bowl for 30 seconds on HIGH. Add the mushrooms, cover loosely and cook for 1 minute on HIGH to soften slightly. Stir in the flour and milk and strain on the cooking liquid from the fish. Add the peppercorns, parsley, a pinch of grated nutmeg and salt and pepper. Cook, uncovered, for 2-3 minutes on HIGH, stirring often until thickened. Remove the skin and bone from the cod steaks if desired and spoon over some of the sauce to serve. Serve the remaining sauce separately.

Halibut Chasseur

PREPARATION TIME: 10 minutes

MICROWAVE COOKING TIME: 19-21 minutes

SERVES: 4 people

2 tsps butter or margarine
3 shallots, peeled and finely chopped
1 clove garlic, crushed
2 tsps cornstarch
½ cup dry white wine

2 tbsps tomato paste
½ tsp mixed chopped parsley, thyme and marjoram
Salt and pepper
8oz mushrooms, sliced
8oz halibut steaks
4 tbsps water
Pinch sugar

Combine the butter or margarine, shallots and garlic in a small bowl, cover and cook 3 minutes on HIGH, or until the shallots are soft. Stir in the cornstarch and add the wine, tomato paste, herbs, salt and pepper. Cook, uncovered, for 2 minutes on HIGH. Whisk well. Add the mushrooms and cook, uncovered, 5-6 minutes on HIGH, stirring occasionally until the mushrooms are done and the sauce has thickened. Cover the sauce and set it aside. Arrange the halibut steaks in a shallow dish and pour over the water. Cover loosely and cook for 6-8 minutes on HIGH or until the fish is done. Transfer the fish to a serving plate and pour the cooking juices into the mushroom sauce. Adjust the seasoning and add a pinch of sugar, if desired, to bring out the tomato flavor. Spoon some of the sauce over the fish and re-heat, uncovered, for 2 minutes on HIGH. Serve the remaining sauce separately.

Sole Veronique

PREPARATION TIME: 20-25 minutes

MICROWAVE COOKING TIME: 12-15 minutes

SERVES: 4 people

2 sole, filleted (flounder may be substituted)
1 slice onion
1 bay leaf
1 sprig thyme
2 parsley stalks
Black peppercorns
½ cup dry white wine
½ cup water
2 tbsps butter or margarine
2 tbsps flour
4 tbsps heavy cream
1 cup white grapes (preferably seedless variety)

2 tsps lemon juice
2 tsps chopped parsley
Salt

Trim and skin the fillets and turn the ends under so that all the fillets are the same length. Place them in a large, shallow dish and add the onion slice, bay leaf, sprig of thyme, parsley stalks and peppercorns. Pour over the wine and the water and loosely cover the dish. Cook for 5-7 minutes on HIGH, or until the fish is tender. Remove the fish to a serving plate, cover and keep warm. Reserve the fish cooking liquid. Melt the butter in a deep bowl or glass measure for 30 seconds on HIGH. Stir in the flour and then gradually add the fish cooking liquid. Cook the sauce for 3-4 minutes on HIGH, stirring after 1 minute and frequently thereafter. Stir in the cream and the parsley and add salt and pepper to taste. Place the grapes in hot water for a few minutes and then peel them. If not seedless variety, cut the grapes in half and remove the seeds. Add the grapes to the sauce along with the lemon juice. Pour over the fish and reheat for 3 minutes on MEDIUM before serving.

Salmon with Parsley Caper Sauce

PREPARATION TIME: 15 minutes

MICROWAVE COOKING TIME: 8 minutes

SERVES: 4 people

4 salmon steaks, about 1 inch thick
1 cup water
1 bay leaf
3 parsley stalks
1 sprig thyme
4 black peppercorns
Juice of 1 lemon
2 tbsps butter or margarine
2 tbsps flour
1 tbsp chopped parsley
1 tbsp small capers

Facing page: Halibut Chasseur (top) and Sole Veronique (bottom).

4 tbsps double cream
Salt and pepper

Place the salmon steaks in a casserole with the thin ends of the steak towards the middle of the dish. Pour over the water and add the bay leaf, parsley stalks, thyme, lemon juice and peppercorns. Cover the dish loosely and cook for 5-6 minutes on HIGH. Set aside while preparing the sauce. Melt the butter or margarine in a small, deep bowl for 30 seconds on HIGH. Stir in the flour and strain on the cooking liquid from the fish. Cook 2 minutes on HIGH, stirring often until thickened. Add the parsley and capers and stir in the cream. Add salt and pepper and heat the sauce a further 1 minute on HIGH. Skin and bone the salmon steaks if desired and pour over some of the sauce to serve. Serve the remaining sauce separately.

Smoked Haddock with Peas and Pasta

PREPARATION TIME: 15 minutes

MICROWAVE COOKING TIME: 10-12 minutes

SERVES: 4 people

8oz pasta shells, cooked
8oz smoked haddock fillets (cod may be substituted)
1 cup milk
2 tbsps butter or margarine
2 tbsps flour
3 tbsps frozen peas
1 tbsp chopped chives
1 tbsp chopped parsley
1 hard-boiled egg, chopped
Salt and pepper

Place the smoked fish in a large, shallow dish and pour over 6 tbsps of the milk, reserving the rest. Cook 4-5 minutes on HIGH and leave it standing, covered, while preparing the sauce. Melt the butter or margarine for 30 seconds on HIGH in a deep bowl or glass measure. Stir in the flour and pour on the reserved milk. Strain the fish cooking liquid into the bowl and stir well. Cook on

This page: Smoked Haddock with Peas and Pasta. Facing page: Halibut Dieppoise.

HIGH for 3 minutes, stirring once or twice. Add the frozen peas to the sauce along with the chives and parsley. Cook a further 2-3 minutes on HIGH, or until the sauce is thick and the peas are cooked. Skin and flake the fish, removing any bones. Add to the sauce with the chopped hard-boiled egg and salt and pepper. Stir carefully. Toss with drained pasta shells. Heat through 1 minute on HIGH before serving.

Halibut Dieppoise

PREPARATION TIME: 15 minutes

MICROWAVE COOKING TIME: 10-11 minutes

SERVES: 4 people

4 halibut steaks
3 tbsps dry white wine
½ cup water
1 bay leaf
1 sprig thyme
2 parsley stalks
Black peppercorns
2 tbsps butter or margarine
2 shallots, finely chopped
3oz small mushrooms, quartered

2 tbsps flour
2 tsps chopped fresh thyme
2 tsps chopped parsley
Salt and pepper
1 cup canned or frozen mussels
1 cup cooked, peeled shrimp
2 tomatoes, skinned, seeded and cut into
   small dice
Salt and pepper
4 tbsps cream

Place the halibut steaks in a shallow dish and pour over the wine, water and add the bay leaf, sprig thyme, parsley stalks and peppercorns. Loosely cover the dish and cook the fish 5-7 minutes on HIGH, or until tender. Transfer the fish to a serving dish, cover and keep it warm. Melt the butter or margarine in a glass measure or deep bowl for 30 seconds on HIGH. Add the shallots and cook for 2 minutes on HIGH, stirring once or twice, until the shallots soften. Add the mushrooms and cook a further 1 minute on HIGH. Stir in the flour and strain on the liquid from the fish. Stir well and cook, uncovered, 3-5 minutes on HIGH or until thickened. Add the chopped herbs, mussels and shrimp. Stir in the cream and cook a further 1 minute on HIGH. Add the tomatoes and leave the sauce to stand for 1 minute to heat them through. Pour over the fish and cook a further 1 minute on HIGH, uncovered, before serving.

Microwave FISH DISHES

SNACKS AND CANAPÉS

Smoked Fish in a Potato

PREPARATION TIME: 20 minutes

MICROWAVE COOKING TIME:
26-32 minutes

SERVES: 4 people

4 large baking potatoes
½ cup milk
4 small smoked haddock fillets
4 tbsps water
1 tbsp butter or margarine
1 tsp mild curry powder
1 tbsp chopped chives
Salt and pepper

SAUCE
2 tbsps butter or margarine
2 tbsps flour
Pinch dry mustard
Pinch cayenne pepper
1 cup milk
½ cup grated cheese
Salt and pepper

GARNISH
Paprika

Wash the potatoes and prick the skins several times with a fork. Bake the potatoes 10-12 minutes on HIGH. Wrap them in foil and leave to stand 5 minutes. Place the smoked haddock fillets in a shallow dish with the 4 tbsps water. Loosely cover and cook 5 minutes on HIGH, or until the fish is tender. Set the fish aside while heating the milk on HIGH for 5 minutes. Melt 1 tbsp butter or margarine in a deep bowl for 30 seconds on HIGH. Stir in the curry powder and cook a further 1 minute on HIGH. Cut a slice off the top of each potato and scoop out the pulp, leaving a border inside the skin. Skin and flake the smoked haddock,

removing any bones. Put an equal portion of fish inside each potato shell. Add the scooped out potato to the curry powder and butter in the bowl and mash well with a fork. Gradually pour in the hot milk and continue mashing until smooth. It may not be necessary to add all the milk, but the potato must be soft, while still holding its shape. Set aside while preparing the sauce. Melt the remaining butter or margarine in a

This page: Smoked Salmon and Trout Canapés (outer) and Kipper and Cheese Potato Canapés (inner). Facing page: Smoked Fish in a Potato (top) and Smoky Cheese and Shrimp Spread (bottom).

small, deep bowl. Stir in the flour, mustard and cayenne pepper. Gradually beat in the milk and cook

3-5 minutes on HIGH, stirring frequently, until thickened. Add the grated cheese, salt and pepper to taste and stir well. Spoon an equal amount of the sauce mixture over the smoked haddock in each potato shell. Pipe or spoon the potato mixture on top and sprinkle with paprika. Cook for 3-4 minutes on HIGH to heat through completely before serving.

Crabmeat Pea Pods

PREPARATION TIME: 20 minutes

MICROWAVE COOKING TIME: 2 minutes

SERVES: 4 people

4-6oz pea pods, even-sized if possible

FILLING
½ cup fresh or frozen crabmeat
4oz cream cheese
1 tbsp finely chopped parsley
2 tsps black poppy seeds
2 tsps paprika
Dash tabasco
1 tbsp milk (optional)

Blanch the pea pods for 1 minute on HIGH with 4 tbsps water in a loosely-covered bowl. Rinse under cold water and dry well. Carefully open one side of each pea pod to form a pocket. Mix all the filling ingredients together and spoon into a pastry bag fitted with a ½ inch plain tube and pipe the filling into each pea pod. Arrange on a serving dish and heat for 30 seconds on HIGH. Garnish the dish with watercress if desired.

Kipper and Cheese Potato Canapés

PREPARATION TIME: 25 minutes

MICROWAVE COOKING TIME: 12-17 minutes

MAKES: 8

6oz new potatoes, scrubbed but unpeeled
1 double kipper fillet

2 tbsps butter or margarine
1 tbsp snipped chives
4 tbsps sour cream or natural yogurt
Salt and pepper
½ cup finely grated Cheddar cheese
Paprika

Lightly prick the potato skins with a fork and place on paper towels, spaced well apart. Cook for 4-6 minutes, turn over and rearrange and then cook a further 4-6 minutes or until soft. Split in half and scoop out the flesh, leaving a thin border of potato inside the skins. Place the kipper fillet in a shallow dish and loosely cover. Cook 2-3 minutes on HIGH, skin and remove any bones. Flake the fish and add to the potato. Add the sour cream or yogurt, chives, salt and pepper and mix well, mashing the potato. Fill each potato shell with some of the kipper mixture, mounding it well. Sprinkle with cheese and paprika and cook 2 minutes on HIGH until hot. Serve immediately.

Stuffed Garlic Shrimp

PREPARATION TIME: 15 minutes

MICROWAVE COOKING TIME: 4-5 minutes

SERVES: 4 people

8 uncooked jumbo shrimp with the shell on the very ends of the tails left on
2 tbsps dry white wine
1 package garlic and herb cheese
½ tsp coarsely ground pepper
Chopped parsley

Split the shrimp down the back and remove the intestinal tract. You need to cut about ⅔ of the way through the shrimp and press the shrimp open to flatten slightly. Place the shrimp cut-side up in a shallow dish in one layer. Press plastic wrap or wax paper directly over the shrimp to keep them open. Cook on MEDIUM for 2 minutes or until almost tender. Mix the garlic and herb cheese with the ground pepper and pipe or spoon into each shrimp. Heat, uncovered, a further 2-3 minutes on MEDIUM or until the shrimp are completely cooked. Sprinkle well with chopped parsley before serving.

Smoky Cheese and Shrimp Spread

PREPARATION TIME: 15 minutes

MICROWAVE COOKING TIME: 5 minutes

SERVES: 4 people

1 tbsp butter or margarine
1 shallot, finely chopped
1½ cups shredded smoky cheese
3 tbsps cream
4 fl oz cooked, peeled shrimp, roughly chopped
4oz cream cheese
Salt and pepper
Paprika

Melt the butter in a small, deep bowl for 30 seconds on HIGH. Add the shallot and cook for 1 minute on HIGH to soften. Add the smoky cheese to the bowl and stir in the cream. Cook for 4 minutes on MEDIUM, or until the cheese has melted. Add the shrimp, cream cheese and salt and pepper. Stir well

Crabmeat Pea Pods (above right) and Stuffed Garlic Shrimp (far right).

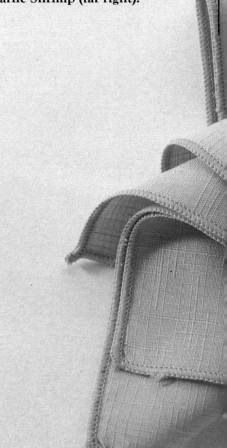

to soften the cheese and completely blend the mixture. Allow to cool and then chill. Leave at room temperature for at least 15 minutes before serving and sprinkle lightly with paprika. Serve with crudites or crackers.

Shrimp and Caviar Tartlets

PREPARATION TIME: 20 minutes

MICROWAVE COOKING TIME: 5-6 minutes

MAKES: 12

12 slices whole-wheat bread, crusts removed
1 tbsp butter or margarine
4oz peeled, cooked shrimp, roughly chopped
4oz fromage blanc or low fat soft cheese
2 tsps snipped chives
Dash tabasco
Salt and pepper

GARNISH
Black or red lumpfish caviar

Roll out the slices of bread to flatten slightly. Cut into 3 inch rounds with a pastry cutter. Melt the butter for 30 seconds on HIGH and brush over both sides of the bread rounds. Mold into small custard cups and cook for 3 minutes on HIGH until crisp. Remove from the custard cups and place on a serving plate. Fill each shell with chopped shrimp. Mix the fromage blanc or soft cheese with the chives, salt and pepper. Put a spoonful on top of the shrimp in each tartlet shell and heat for 2-3 minutes on MEDIUM. Top each tartlet with caviar before serving.

Smoked Salmon and Trout Canapés

PREPARATION TIME: 15 minutes

MICROWAVE COOKING TIME: 1-2 minutes

MAKES: 12-16

8 slices brown bread, toasted and cut into 2 inch squares or triangles

⅓ cup unsalted butter
2 tbsps cream cheese
1 smoked trout, skinned and boned
4oz smoked salmon
1 tbsp lemon juice
1 tbsp creamed horseradish
1 tsp chopped fresh dill
Salt and pepper

GARNISH
Small sprigs of fresh dill

Soften the butter 10-20 seconds on HIGH in a small bowl. Spread on the toast squares or triangles and set them aside. Flake the smoked trout fillets and add to the cream cheese. Cut half of the smoked salmon very finely and add to the cream cheese. Reserve the remaining salmon. Add the lemon juice, horseradish, chopped dill, and salt and pepper to the fish and cream cheese and mix thoroughly. Divide the mixture among all the pieces of toast, mounding it well. Cut the remaining salmon into thin strips and place a cross of two strips over the top of each canapé. Place on a serving dish and heat through for 1-2 minutes on MEDIUM. Serve garnished with small sprigs of dill. If desired, cucumbers sliced into ¼ inch rounds may be used as a base for the canapés. In this case, omit the butter from the recipe.

Crab au Gratin

PREPARATION TIME: 15 minutes

MICROWAVE COOKING TIME: 6-8 minutes

SERVES: 4 people

2 tbsps dry white wine
1 stick celery, finely chopped
1 shallot, finely chopped
1 7oz jar Cheddar cheese spread
4 tbsps light cream or milk
6oz fresh or frozen crabmeat
4 slices brown bread toast, crusts removed
Paprika
Salt and pepper

Place the white wine in a deep bowl and add the celery and onion.

Loosely cover the bowl and cook 2-3 minutes on HIGH, stirring once or twice, until the vegetables are softened. Stir in the Cheddar cheese spread and heat on MEDIUM for 1-2 minutes, or until softened. Stir in the cream and the crabmeat and heat a further 2 minutes on MEDIUM until piping hot. Arrange the toast in a microproof baking dish and spoon over the cheese-crabmeat mixture. Sprinkle with paprika and heat through 1-2 minutes on HIGH. May be browned under a pre-heated broiler before serving.

Scrambling Shrimp

PREPARATION TIME: 15 minutes

MICROWAVE COOKING TIME: 4-5 minutes plus standing time

SERVES: 4 people

1 tbsp butter or margarine
2 green onions, finely chopped
¼ green pepper, seeded and cut into small dice
¼ red pepper, seeded and cut into small dice
4 eggs, beaten with pepper and salt
3oz peeled, cooked shrimp

Melt the butter in a medium-sized bowl on HIGH for 30 seconds. Add the onion and peppers and partially cover the bowl. Cook for 2-3 minutes on HIGH or until slightly softened. Add the eggs to the bowl and cook on HIGH for about 1 minute. Stir well and add the shrimp. Cook a further 1 minute on HIGH or until softly scrambled. Leave to stand for 1 minute before serving. Serve on buttered toast or muffins if desired.

Facing page: Scrambling Shrimp (top) and Crab au Gratin (bottom).

Tacos Veracruz

PREPARATION TIME: 15 minutes

MICROWAVE COOKING TIME:
6 minutes

SERVES: 4 people

TOPPING
1 ripe avocado, peeled and mashed
2 tomatoes, seeded and chopped
1 small clove garlic, crushed
1 tbsp lime or lemon juice
Salt and pepper

FILLING
1 tbsp oil
1 shallot, finely chopped
½ green pepper, chopped
1 tsp ground cumin
½ red or green chili pepper, finely chopped
4 tbsps tomato paste
6 tbsps water
Salt and pepper
4oz cooked, peeled shrimp, roughly
    chopped
Salt and pepper
4 taco shells

First mix the topping ingredients
together, cover and set aside. Heat
the oil in a small, deep bowl for 30
seconds on HIGH. Add the shallot,
green pepper, cumin and chili pepper
and cook 2-3 minutes to soften
slightly. Stir once or twice during
cooking. Add the tomato paste and
water. If the sauce is too thick add an
additional spoonful of water. Add the
salt and pepper and stir in the
shrimp. Cook 2-3 minutes on
MEDIUM to heat the shrimp
through. Spoon into the taco shells
and top with the avocado mixture.

Pizzas Marinara

PREPARATION TIME: 10 minutes

MICROWAVE COOKING TIME:
2 minutes

SERVES: 4 people

4 tbsps tomato paste
1 tbsp dry white wine
1 tbsp water
2 green onions, chopped

½ tsp oregano
1 clove garlic, crushed
4oz shrimp, canned or frozen mussels,
    canned or fresh clams or cockles, or a
    combination of all three
8 anchovy fillets
4 black olives, pitted and sliced
2 tsps capers
¼ cup grated Mozzarella cheese
2 tbsps grated Parmesan cheese
Salt and pepper
4 English muffins, split

Mix the tomato paste with the wine,
water, onion, oregano, garlic, salt and
pepper. Spread on the muffin halves.
Arrange the shellfish on top with a
cross of anchovies. Add the olives
and capers and sprinkle on the
Mozzarella cheese. Sprinkle the

**This page: Shrimp and Caviar
Tartlets. Facing page: Tacos
Veracruz (top) and Pizzas Marinara
(bottom).**

Parmesan cheese on last and arrange
the pizzas on a paper towel on a plate
on the oven turntable. Cook 2-4
minutes on HIGH, changing the
postition of the pizzas once or twice
during cooking. Leave to stand 1
minute before serving. Pizzas may be
quickly browned under a pre-heated
broiler if desired. Serve hot.

Microwave
WHOLEFOOD

What are wholefoods? Simply the best ingredients with no additives, no artificial colorings, flavorings or preservatives, and with none of the essential nutrients taken away. Who eats them? Anyone who wants to combine a healthy style of eating and who enjoys eating delicious food which ranges over the cuisines of many countries. Wholefood dishes vary from familiar favorites in a new guise, to unusual and exotic dishes which will delight the adventurous cook and bring enthusiastic praise from those who eat the results

A wholefood diet is not necessarily vegetarian, but it does make use of many interesting and perhaps slightly unusual ingredients.

The dishes tend to be high in fiber, but low in fats, salt and sugar. Wholefood meals are often lower in calories and more satisfying than their conventional counterparts. In addition, wholefoods are inexpensive to buy and, because many are dried, they are easy to store. In combination with your microwave oven, they form some of the tastiest and healthiest "convenience foods" around.

Many of the ingredients are available in your supermarket, but for more variety, browse through your local health food or wholefood shop. The variety of grains, beans, nuts, dried fruits and different flours is astonishing. One of the great pleasures of wholefood cooking and eating is discovering the enormous range of new and unusual ingredients available. Don't be afraid to try out unfamiliar foods because you don't know how to prepare them. The basic preparation methods generally fall into only a few categories.

Most dried grains, such as rice, barley, wheatgrains and groats are first rinsed several times in cold water to remove the grain dust.

Rice and pasta need nearly as much cooking by microwave methods as by conventional ones. However, both pasta and rice cook without sticking together and without the chance of overcooking. This is because most of the actual cooking is accomplished during the standing time. All kinds of rice and all types of pasta benefit from being put into hot water with a pinch of salt and 1 tsp oil in a deep bowl. There is no need to cover the bowl during cooking but, during standing time, a covering of some sort will help retain heat. Ease long spaghetti into the bowl gradually as it softens. Drain rice and pasta and rinse under hot water to remove starch. Both pasta and rice can be reheated in a microwave oven without loss of texture.

Many of the pre-cooked grain products such as bulgur wheat and couscous, or finely ground grains such as polenta, are even quicker to prepare. These types are combined with water without rinsing, and cooked, covered in the case of bulgur wheat and couscous, or uncovered in the case of polenta, for approximately 5 minutes on HIGH. Most of the cooking water will be absorbed. Allow them to stand for a few minutes, fluff with a fork, or give a good stir, and they are ready to form the basis of a delicious meal.

Beans require a bit more forethought, but are also easily prepared. The microwave oven offers great time savings when used to re-hydrate pulses – dried peas, beans and lentils. Cover the pulses with water in a large bowl and heat on a HIGH setting to bring to the boil, which takes about 10 minutes. Allow the pulses to boil for about 2 minutes and then leave to stand for one hour. This cuts out overnight soaking. The pulses will cook in about 45 minutes-1 hour depending on what variety is used. This is about half the conventional cooking time. Make sure pulses are cooked completely; it can be dangerous to eat them uncooked.

If you are already cooking with wholefoods, you will be pleasantly surprised to find out how the microwave can be used to speed up and improve your cooking. If you have never tried wholefoods before, you are in for a treat – delicious and healthy meals made quickly and easily, thanks to your microwave!

PASTA

Lasagne Rolls

PREPARATION TIME: 35 minutes

MICROWAVE COOKING TIME: 15 minutes

SERVES: 4 people

8oz lasagne
1 tsp oil
2½ cups cottage cheese
½ cup Parmesan cheese, grated
2 cups spinach, finely chopped
¼ cup pine nuts
1 egg, beaten
½ tsp salt
1 cup tomato paste
¾ cup water
2 tsps mixed herbs

Cook the lasagne, two or three sheets at a time, in boiling water to which you have added 1 tsp oil. Place a few sheets in the water, microwave for 1-2 minutes on HIGH, or until they are just soft, but not fully cooked. Set aside the cooked sheets separately to prevent them from sticking together. Cook the spinach for 5 minutes on HIGH with no additional water, if frozen, or 3 minutes on HIGH with a small amount of water, if fresh. Drain and mix into the cottage cheese. Add the beaten egg, pine nuts, Parmesan cheese and salt, and set aside. Prepare a sauce by combining the tomato paste with the water and herbs. Place a large spoonful of the cottage cheese mixture on each sheet of lasagne and roll them up. Arrange the rolls in a dish, and pour over the sauce. Bake for 10 minutes on HIGH, or until the lasagne is fully cooked and most of the liquid is absorbed. Check halfway through the cooking time and add extra water if the dish seems dry. Once you've tasted this casserole, I'm

sure you will agree that the extra preparation time was worthwhile.

Pasta Paprika

PREPARATION TIME: 20 minutes

MICROWAVE COOKING TIME: 13 minutes

SERVES: 4 people

12oz green or whole-wheat fettucini, fresh or dried

1 tsp oil
1 large onion, chopped
1 clove garlic, crushed
3 peppers, one green, one red and one yellow, sliced
1 tbsp olive oil
16oz can tomatoes, sieved
2 tsps paprika
¼ cup Parmesan cheese, grated

This page: Lasagne Rolls. Facing page: Pasta Paprika (top) and Creamy Spiced Noodles (bottom).

Place the pasta in a large bowl, pour over boiling water to cover and add 1 tsp oil. Cook for 5 minutes on HIGH, or until the pasta is just tender. If using fresh pasta, cook for only 2 minutes on HIGH. Allow the pasta to stand in the water while you prepare the sauce. Combine the onion, garlic and sliced peppers with the olive oil and cook for 4 minutes on HIGH. Add the tomatoes and paprika. Stir this sauce into the drained pasta, sprinkle with the Parmesan cheese and cook for 4 minutes on HIGH. The red and yellow peppers add a bright note to this delicious quick supper dish, but if they are unavailable, green peppers may be substituted.

Sweet and Sour Noodles

PREPARATION TIME: 15 minutes

MICROWAVE COOKING TIME: 10-15 minutes

SERVES: 4 people

12oz whole-wheat noodles
1 tsp oil
2 tbsps butter or margarine
1 onion, finely chopped
1 green pepper, finely chopped
2 tbsps sugar
1 tsp vinegar
1 tsp prepared mustard
½ tsp paprika
14oz can tomatoes, chopped
4 eggs

Place the noodles in a large bowl, pour over boiling water to cover and add 1 tsp oil. Cook for 5-10 minutes on HIGH, or until the noodles are just tender. If using fresh pasta, cook for only two minutes on HIGH. Drain and set aside. Combine the onion, pepper and butter and cook for 3 minutes on HIGH to soften. Add the sugar, vinegar, spices and tomatoes and cook for a further 2 minutes on HIGH. Mix this sauce into the cooked noodles and bake for 2 minutes on HIGH. Make four indentations in the noodles with the back of a spoon and break an egg into each. Cover the dish, and

microwave on MEDIUM for 1 minute, or until the eggs are set. Alternatively, prepare in individual casserole dishes.

Creamy Spiced Noodles

PREPARATION TIME: 15 minutes

MICROWAVE COOKING TIME: 11-16 minutes

SERVES: 4 people

12oz whole-wheat noodles, fresh or dried
1 tsp oil
1 tbsp arrowroot
1 cup yogurt or fromage frais
¼ cup raisins
½ tsp curry powder
8oz smoked fish
3 onions, finely chopped
2 tbsps butter

Place the noodles in a large bowl, pour over boiling water to cover and

This page: Spaghetti with Pine Nuts. Facing page: Macaroni and Blue Cheese (top) and Sweet and Sour Noodles (bottom).

add 1 tsp oil. Cook for 5-10 minutes on HIGH, or until they are just tender. If using fresh noodles, cook for only 2 minutes on HIGH. Dissolve the arrowroot in a little water and stir into the yogurt or fromage frais. Mix in the curry powder and raisins. Remove the skin and any bones from the fish and flake it. Cook the flaked fish, onions and butter for 4 minutes on HIGH. Mix in the yogurt sauce and combine with the cooked and drained noodles. Bake for 2 minutes on HIGH. Use any smoked fish you like for this quick and tasty casserole, and vary the strength of the curry powder to suit your taste!

then stir in the blue cheese, reserving ½ cup for the topping. Cook for a further 1 minute on HIGH to melt the cheese. Combine the apple, onion, garlic and oil and cook for 3 minutes on HIGH to soften. Mix into the sauce then stir in the cooked macaroni. Sprinkle the reserved cheese on top and microwave on HIGH for 4 minutes. This dish can be made with Danish Blue for more economical meals, but try using one of the luxurious Italian blue cheeses, such as Gorgonzola, for special occasions.

Spaghetti with Pine Nuts

PREPARATION TIME: 10 minutes

MICROWAVE COOKING TIME: 8-9 minutes

SERVES: 4 people

12oz fresh or dried spaghetti
1 tbsp oil
1 large onion, sliced
1 clove garlic, crushed
1 cup pine nuts
6 tbsps olive oil
¼ cup fresh parsley, chopped or 2 tbsps dried parsley
14oz can artichoke hearts, drained and cut into bite-sized pieces
¼ cup Parmesan cheese, grated

Place the pasta in a large bowl, pour over boiling water to cover, and add 1 tbsp oil. Cook for 5 minutes on HIGH, or until the pasta is just tender. If using fresh pasta, cook for only two minutes on HIGH. Allow to stand in the water while you prepare the sauce. Combine the onion and garlic with the olive oil and cook for 2 minutes on HIGH. Add the parsley, pine nuts and artichoke hearts and cook for a further 1 minute on HIGH. Drain the pasta, and toss in this sauce until well coated. Mix in the Parmesan cheese and serve immediately. The pine nuts and artichoke hearts make this simple pasta dish something special. Serve it with a crisp green salad for a complete meal ready in minutes.

Macaroni and Blue Cheese

PREPARATION TIME: 15 minutes

MICROWAVE COOKING TIME: 16 minutes

SERVES: 4 people

12oz whole-wheat macaroni
1 tsp oil
2 tbsps butter or margarine
2 tbsps whole-wheat flour
2 tbsps arrowroot
1 tsp dried tarragon
½ tsp salt
2 cups milk
2 cups blue cheese, crumbled
2 apples, chopped
2 onions, sliced
1 clove garlic, crushed
1 tbsp oil

Place the pasta in a large bowl, pour over boiling water to cover and add 1 tsp oil. Cook for 5-10 minutes on HIGH, or until the pasta is just tender. If using fresh pasta, cook for only 2 minutes on HIGH. Drain the pasta to prevent it from becoming soggy. To prepare the sauce, combine the milk, butter, flour, arrowroot, tarragon and salt in a small bowl and mix well. Microwave for 2 minutes on HIGH and stir very well. Cook for a further 2 minutes on HIGH,

Vegetable Lasagne

PREPARATION TIME: 20 minutes

MICROWAVE COOKING TIME:
15 minutes

SERVES: 4 people

8oz lasagne, fresh or dried
1½ lbs sliced vegetables, for example, a
*   mixture of tomatoes, zucchini and*
*   beans*
3 cups cottage cheese
1 cup Parmesan cheese, grated
8oz sliced mozzarella cheese
2 cups strained fresh tomatoes
½ cup water
2 tsps dried mixed herbs

Combine the strained tomatoes,
water and herbs to make a sauce. Mix
together the cottage cheese and
Parmesan cheese, reserving ¼ cup
Parmesan for the topping. Pour a
little of the tomato sauce into the
bottom of a deep casserole dish,
place 2-3 sheets of uncooked lasagne
on top, followed by a thin layer of
sliced vegetables, some cottage
cheese and sliced mozzarella.
Continue layering until the
vegetables and cheese have been used
up. End with a few sheets of lasagne,
and pour over the remaining sauce.
Sprinkle over the reserved Parmesan
cheese and cook for 15 minutes on
HIGH, or until the lasagne is cooked
and most of the liquid has been
absorbed. Check halfway through the
cooking time, and add extra water if
the dish seems dry. Brown under a
preheated broiler if desired. This is a
simple and quick way of preparing a
baked lasagne. It produces such a
light and tasty result that it is sure to
become a favorite. It also makes an
impressive party dish.

Spaghetti with Mussel Sauce

PREPARATION TIME: 15 minutes

MICROWAVE COOKING TIME:
7-12 minutes

SERVES: 4 people

12oz whole-wheat spaghetti, fresh or dried
1 tsp oil

SAUCE
8oz can mussels, drained
4 tbsps butter
2 cloves garlic, crushed
1 onion, finely chopped
1 cup white wine
¼ cup fresh parsley, chopped or 2 tbsps
*   dried parsley*
4 tomatoes, peeled, seeded and cut in
*   strips*

Place the spaghetti in a large bowl,
pour over boiling water to cover, and
add 1 tsp oil. Cook for 5-10 minutes
on HIGH, or until the pasta is just
tender. If using fresh pasta, cook for
only 2 minutes on HIGH. Drain and
set aside. To prepare the sauce,
combine the butter, garlic and onion
and microwave for 2 minutes on
HIGH. Add the wine, mussels and
parsley and cook for a further 2
minutes on HIGH. Toss the tomatoes
and cooked spaghetti in this sauce,
and serve immediately. Cockles or
shrimp can be substituted for the
mussels, if preferred. Be sure to use
only seafood which has been packed
in brine, as vinegar will spoil the
sauce.

**This page: Spaghetti with Mussel
Sauce. Facing page: Vegetable
Lasagne.**

NUTS

Indonesian Chicken

PREPARATION TIME: 20 minutes

MICROWAVE COOKING TIME:
8-13 minutes

SERVES: 4 people

4 chicken portions, skinned or 4 boneless
 chicken breasts, skinned

SAUCE
2 onions, finely chopped
2 cloves garlic, crushed
2 tbsps butter
1 cup crunchy peanut butter
1 cup water or chicken stock
1 tbsp vinegar
1-2 tsps chili powder, to taste
½ tsp salt

To make the sauce, combine the
onion, garlic and butter and
microwave on HIGH for 2 minutes.
Mix in the remaining sauce
ingredients and cook for a further
2 minutes on HIGH. Set aside while
you prepare the chicken. If using
chicken portions, microwave on
HIGH for 8 minutes or until the
chicken is fully cooked. Chicken
breasts will need only 3-4 minutes on
HIGH. Arrange the cooked chicken
in a casserole and pour over the
sauce. Microwave for 2 minutes on
HIGH, or until the sauce is fully
heated. This unusual sauce makes
chicken into something special. Serve
the chicken and sauce over rice, with
green vegetables to accompany. The
peanut sauce is very versatile. Serve
it with other meats, or simply over a
dish of mixed grains or brown rice
and vegetables for a real vegetarian
treat!

Sweet and Sour Peanuts

PREPARATION TIME: 15 minutes

MICROWAVE COOKING TIME:
4 minutes

SERVES: 4 people

⅓ cup brown sugar
5 tbsps wine vinegar
3 tbsps soy sauce
1 tbsp arrowroot

**This page: Indonesian Chicken.
Facing page: Sweet and Sour
Peanuts (top) and Curried
Cashews (bottom).**

1 red pepper, chopped
1½ cups bean sprouts
1 cup unsalted roasted peanuts
8oz can bamboo shoots

Combine the sugar, vinegar, soy sauce and arrowroot and cook for one minute on HIGH. Add the remaining ingredients and microwave for 3 minutes on HIGH, or until the pepper is softened. Serve over brown rice, or Mixed Grains and Seeds for an exotic, but quickly made meal.

Stuffed Mushrooms with Sunflower Seeds

PREPARATION TIME: 10 minutes

MICROWAVE COOKING TIME: 1 minute

SERVES: 4 people

4 large flat mushrooms
¼ lb smooth pâté
2 tbsps sunflower seeds
Few snipped chives
2 tbsps water

Wipe the mushrooms and remove the stems. Place upside down in a dish and fill the caps with the pâté. Sprinkle the sunflower seeds and chives on top. Add the water and microwave on HIGH for 2 minutes. These stuffed mushrooms make a delightful and interesting appetizer to any meal. If you like, double the quantities and serve them with hot buttered whole-wheat toast for a meal on their own.

Curried Cashews

PREPARATION TIME: 15 minutes

MICROWAVE COOKING TIME: 9 minutes

SERVES: 4 people

1 medium onion, finely chopped
1 green pepper, chopped
1 tbsp oil
1 tbsp mustard seeds
1 tsp ground cumin
1 tsp coriander
1 tsp garam masala
2 cups bean sprouts
1 cup chopped or broken cashews

¼ cup raisins
2 cups tomato juice

GARNISH
Cucumber slices
Coriander leaves

Combine the onion, pepper and oil in a casserole for 2 minutes on HIGH. Add the spices and cook, covered, for 1 minute on HIGH. Add the nuts, raisins, bean sprouts and tomato juice and cook for a further 5 minutes on HIGH, or until the juice has thickened. Serve this nutritious and spicy dish over plain brown rice or Mixed Grains and Seeds.

Creamy Beans

PREPARATION TIME: 10 minutes

MICROWAVE COOKING TIME: 5-10 minutes

SERVES: 4 people

1lb fresh or frozen green beans
½ tsp nutmeg
Pinch salt
¼ cup shredded, toasted almonds
½ cup fromage frais or sour cream

Cook the beans in a covered casserole for 3 minutes on HIGH in 2 tbsps water if fresh, or for 5-10 minutes on HIGH, with no additional water if frozen. Sprinkle

1 cup grated Cheddar cheese
¾ cup finely chopped walnuts

Wash the cauliflower and break into flowerets. Wash and shred the cabbage. Place vegetables in a covered casserole with 6 tbsps of water and cook for 5-10 minutes on HIGH, or until the vegetables are cooked, but still slightly crunchy. Combine the butter, flour and milk in a small bowl and mix well. Cook for 4-5 minutes on HIGH, stirring well halfway through the cooking time. Add the walnuts and cheese. Combine the sauce and the vegetables and cook, uncovered, for 3 minutes on HIGH. Allow to stand a few minutes before serving. This makes a delicious light lunch or supper served on its own. For a more substantial meal, try serving it on top of hot buttered whole-wheat toast.

Savory Bread Pudding

PREPARATION TIME: 15 minutes
MICROWAVE COOKING TIME: 3 minutes
SERVES: 4 people

2 cups whole-wheat or granary bread, cut into cubes
1 large onion, chopped
1 clove garlic, crushed
½ cup sunflower seeds
½ cup walnuts or hazelnuts, chopped
1 tbsp dried herbs
½ tsp salt
1½ cups chicken or vegetable stock

Mix together all of the dry ingredients, making sure that they are well distributed. Pour on the stock and stir to moisten. Cook, covered, for 3 minutes on HIGH. Allow to stand for a few minutes before serving. Savory Bread Pudding is a perfect accompaniment to roast chicken. If you don't eat meat, serve it with a selection of winter vegetables such as Brussels sprouts or cabbage.

on the nutmeg, salt, and shredded almonds, then mix in the fromage frais or sour cream. Serve immediately. This recipe makes a nice vegetable accompaniment to a grain casserole. Try it with Spinach Rice, or Lamb with Bulgur. Serve it over buttered noodles for a simple, but elegant meal.

Facing page: Creamy Beans (top) and Cauliflower and Cabbage in Walnut and Cheese Sauce (bottom). This page: Savory Bread Pudding (top) and Stuffed Mushrooms with Sunflower Seeds (bottom).

Cauliflower and Cabbage in Walnut and Cheese Sauce

PREPARATION TIME: 15 minutes
MICROWAVE COOKING TIME: 12-18 minutes
SERVES: 4 people

1 cauliflower
1 small green cabbage

SAUCE
¼ cup butter
4 tbsps whole-wheat flour
2 cups milk

GRAINS

Bran and Oat Meatloaf

PREPARATION TIME: 20 minutes

MICROWAVE COOKING TIME: 31-32 minutes

SERVES: 4 people

1lb lean ground beef
1 egg
2 tbsps bran
¼ cup rolled oats
1 small onion, chopped
1 cup milk
1 tsp mixed dried herbs
1 tsp salt

TOMATO SAUCE
1lb canned tomatoes
3 tbsps tomato paste
1 clove garlic, crushed
1 onion, roughly chopped
1 green pepper, diced
1 tbsp cornstarch
2 tbsps cold water
Salt and pepper
Sugar (optional)

Mix together all the ingredients for the meatloaf and place the mixture in a loaf-shaped dish. (Remember, if the meat is frozen you can thaw it quickly in the microwave.) Smooth the top and cook for 15 minutes on HIGH. Leave to stand for 10 minutes before turning out. To prepare the sauce, combine tomatoes and their juice, paste and garlic. Cook, uncovered, on HIGH for 8 minutes or until boiling. Add the onion and green pepper and cook 5 minutes on HIGH. Combine cornstarch with the water and stir into the sauce. Cook 3-4 minutes on HIGH, or until thickened. Season with salt and pepper and add a pinch of sugar if desired. The addition of oats and bran adds extra fiber and extra flavor to this meatloaf. You can serve it with either tomato sauce or chutney. It goes particularly well with mashed potatoes, and if there is any left over, it makes delicious sandwiches.

This page: Bran and Oat Meatloaf. Facing page: Polenta Provençal (top) and Lamb with Bulgur (bottom).

Mixed Grains and Seeds

PREPARATION TIME: 5 minutes

MICROWAVE COOKING TIME: 20 minutes

SERVES: 4 people

½ cup brown rice
¼ cup wheat grains
⅓ cup rye grains
⅓ cup barley or oat groats
⅓ cup sunflower seeds
⅓ cup sesame seeds
2 cups water
1 cup grated cheese (optional)
2 tbsps butter (optional)

Measure the grains and seeds into a casserole and rinse well in several changes of cold water. Cook in the water, for approximately 20 minutes, until the rice and barley are soft. Drain off any excess water and let stand, covered, for 5 minutes before serving. This dish can be easily varied by making use of other grains and seeds. It makes an excellent base on which to serve curries and tomato dishes, and makes a nice change from plain brown rice. With the addition of 1 cup grated cheese and 2 tbsps butter it becomes a simple supper dish on its own.

Wheat Grain Cauliflower Cheese

PREPARATION TIME: 10 minutes

MICROWAVE COOKING TIME: 10 minutes

SERVES: 4 people

1 large cauliflower
¼ cup wheat grains
1 cup water
1 cup milk
2 tbsps whole-wheat flour
1 tbsp arrowroot
2 tbsps butter
½ cup grated Cheddar cheese
2 tbsps grated Parmesan cheese

Wash the cauliflower, break it into flowerets and cook it in a covered dish on HIGH for 5 minutes, using only the water that clings to the flowerets. Cook the wheatgrains in the water for 20-25 minutes on HIGH, or until they are chewy. Drain and reserve half the grains for topping. To make the sauce, combine the milk, whole-wheat flour, arrowroot and butter in a large bowl and stir well. Cook for 5 minutes on MEDIUM, stirring or whisking well halfway through the cooking time. Add the cheeses and the remaining wheat grains, stir well and cook for a further 2 minutes on MEDIUM, or until the cheese is melted. Pour the sauce over the cauliflower, sprinkle on reserved grains and brown under a broiler if desired. For a more substantial meal, try serving this over hot buttered whole-wheat toast.

Polenta Provençal

PREPARATION TIME: 15 minutes

MICROWAVE COOKING TIME: 11 minutes

SERVES: 4 people

1¼ cups polenta
4 cups water
1 tsp salt
1 cup grated Cheddar cheese or 3 tbsps grated Parmesan cheese
1lb sliced zucchini
1lb tomatoes, roughly chopped or 14oz can tomatoes
1 clove garlic, crushed or finely chopped
2 tsps dried basil
1 tsp dried oregano
½ tsp dried rosemary

Combine the polenta and water in a large container and cook, uncovered, on HIGH for 5 minutes. Stir very well and add the salt. Mix in the Cheddar or Parmesan cheese, and cook for a further 1 minute on HIGH. Set aside. Combine the vegetables and herbs in a separate casserole dish and cook for 5 minutes on HIGH. Serve the vegetables on top of the polenta, with additional Parmesan cheese sprinkled on top if desired. Try substituting sliced green beans or carrots for a delicious variation when zucchini are out of season.

Lamb with Bulgur

PREPARATION TIME: 15 minutes

MICROWAVE COOKING TIME: 16 minutes

SERVES: 4 people

1lb lamb fillet, cut into chunks
1 large onion, chopped
1 cup bulgur wheat
1 red pepper, seeded and cut into chunks
1 tbsp oil
1½ cups chicken or lamb stock
½ tsp salt
Chopped mint
Chopped parsley

Place the onion and oil in a casserole dish and cook for 2 minutes on HIGH. Add the lamb and cook for a further 4 minutes on HIGH. Stir in the bulgur, red pepper and the stock. Cover and cook for 10 minutes on HIGH. All of the liquid should be absorbed. Let stand, covered, for 5 minutes and fluff the bulgur with a fork before serving. This is a very nice winter dish and goes well with green beans. Try it with Creamy Beans and Almonds (see recipe).

Facing page: Mixed Grains and Seeds (top) and Wheat Grain Cauliflower Cheese (bottom).

Cheese Sandwich Souffle

PREPARATION TIME: 20 minutes	
MICROWAVE COOKING TIME: 21 minutes	
SERVES: 4 people	

8 slices whole-wheat or granary bread
1 tbsp prepared mustard
1½ cups Cheddar cheese, grated
1 large tomato, sliced
2 large eggs, beaten
2 cups milk
1 tsp mixed herbs
Pinch salt

Spread the mustard over 4 of the slices of bread and divide the sliced tomato and grated cheese over these slices. Use the remaining bread to cover. Place the sandwiches in a dish which they nearly fill and pour over a mixture of the beaten eggs, milk, herbs and salt. Let this mixture soak in well. Cover the dish and bake for 1 minute on HIGH, followed by 20 minutes on MEDIUM, or until the egg and milk mixture has set. Brown under the broiler, if desired, before serving. Unlike a true souffle, there is no need to rush this dish to the table! It is delicious hot or cold.

Chickpeas and Bulgur Wheat

PREPARATION TIME: 10 minutes	
MICROWAVE COOKING TIME: 10 minutes	
SERVES: 4 people	

1½ cups chickpeas, cooked
1 tbsp vegetable oil
2 small onions
1 medium-sized red pepper, chopped
¼ cup bulgur wheat
8 tbsps tomato paste
2 cups stock or water

To cook the chickpeas in the microwave, pour boiling water over them and leave to soak for at least 2 hours. Drain, then cook them in 4 cups of water for 25 minutes on HIGH. Cook the onion and red

pepper in the oil for 2 minutes on HIGH. Add the cooked chickpeas, bulgur wheat and the tomato paste dissolved in the stock. Cover and cook for 8 minutes on HIGH. Let stand, covered, for 5 minutes before serving. As an alternative you can use canned chickpeas, or chickpeas previously cooked by any other method. When pre-cooked chickpeas are used this becomes a quick and colorful main dish.

This page: **Chickpeas and Bulgur Wheat.** Facing page: **Cheese Sandwich Souffle (top) and Mexican Rice (bottom).**

Mexican Rice

PREPARATION TIME: 15 minutes	
MICROWAVE COOKING TIME: 35 minutes	
SERVES: 4 people	

1¼ cups brown rice
2 cups water
3 cups Edam or other mild cheese, grated

1 tsp ground cumin
1 tsp turmeric
1 tsp chili powder
1lb couscous
3 cups water
1 tsp salt

Combine the lamb, onion and garlic in a casserole and cook for 5 minutes on HIGH. Add the rest of the vegetables, the dried apricots, spices and the cooked chickpeas and microwave for a further 15 minutes on HIGH. To cook the chickpeas in the microwave, pour boiling water over them and leave to soak for at least 2 hours. Drain, then cook them in 4 cups water for 25 minutes on HIGH. Set the stew aside while you prepare the couscous. Place the couscous in a bowl with the salt and pour on the water. Leave to stand for at least 5 minutes, until the couscous has swollen and absorbed most of the liquid. Cover the bowl and microwave on HIGH for 5 minutes. Remove the cover and fluff up the couscous with a fork. Serve the stew on top of the couscous. For those who eat meat, this is a tempting variation on the couscous theme.

4oz can mild or hot chili peppers, to taste or 1 sweet red pepper, chopped
2 cups cottage cheese
3 cloves garlic, crushed
1 large onion, chopped
½ tsp salt

Cook the rice in the water for 20 minutes on HIGH. Drain and mix with the onion, chilis or red pepper, garlic and salt. In a separate bowl mix together the cheeses, reserving ¼ cup of the Edam for a topping. Layer the rice and cheese mixtures in a casserole, beginning and ending with a rice layer. Sprinkle on the reserved cheese and cook for 15 minutes on HIGH. Allow to stand for 5 minutes before serving. You can make this dish hot and spicy or mild but tasty depending on whether you choose to use chilis or a sweet red pepper.

**This page: Vegetable Couscous.
Facing page: Lamb Couscous.**

Lamb Couscous

PREPARATION TIME: 25 minutes

MICROWAVE COOKING TIME:
30 minutes

SERVES: 6 people

1lb lamb fillet, cut into chunks
2 onions, cut into chunks
1 green pepper, sliced
1 large potato, diced
4 carrots, sliced
2 small turnips, diced
1 cup chickpeas, cooked (see below)
14oz can tomatoes, roughly chopped
1 cup dried apricots, chopped
1 tsp ground coriander

Vegetable Couscous

PREPARATION TIME: 25 minutes

MICROWAVE COOKING TIME:
30 minutes

SERVES: 6 people

8oz zucchini, sliced
1 green pepper, sliced
2 onions, cut into chunks
1 large potato, diced
4 carrots, sliced
2 small turnips, diced
1 cup chickpeas, cooked (see below)
½ cup raisins
½ cup dried apricots, chopped
2 cups water or vegetable stock
3 cloves garlic, finely chopped or crushed
1 tsp ground coriander
1 tsp ground cumin
1 tsp turmeric

1 tsp chili powder
1lb couscous
3 cups water
1 tsp salt

Combine the onions, garlic, potato, carrots, turnips and green pepper in a casserole with the vegetable stock (or the water) and cook for 5 minutes on HIGH. Add the zucchini, cooked chickpeas, raisins, apricots and spices and cook for a further 15 minutes on HIGH. To cook the chickpeas in the microwave, pour boiling water over them and leave to soak for at least 2 hours. Drain, then cook them in 4 cups water for 25 minutes on HIGH. Set the vegetable stew aside while you prepare the couscous. Place the couscous in a bowl with the salt and pour on the water. Leave to stand for at least 5 minutes, until the couscous has swollen and absorbed most of the liquid. Cover the bowl and microwave on HIGH for 5 minutes. Remove the cover and fluff up the couscous with a fork. Serve the vegetable stew on top of the couscous. Couscous is a popular dish in North Africa, where it is normally cooked by steaming over an accompanying stew. The microwave makes it quick and easy to prepare.

Herb and Cheese Cobbler

PREPARATION TIME: 20 minutes
MICROWAVE COOKING TIME: 16 minutes
SERVES: 4 people

2½ cups frozen mixed vegetables
2 tbsps butter
2 tbsps whole-wheat flour
1¼ cups milk
1 tsp arrowroot
1 tsp mixed herbs
Pinch salt

TOPPING
4 tbsps butter
1 cup grated Cheddar cheese
1 cup bran

½ cup whole-wheat flour
1 tsp baking powder
½ cup milk
¼ tsp salt

Cook the frozen vegetables in a casserole, uncovered, for 4 minutes on HIGH. Set aside while you prepare the sauce. Place the butter, flour, mixed herbs, arrowroot, milk and a pinch of salt in a small bowl and stir well. Cook for 2 minutes on HIGH, then stir again. Cook for a further 2 minutes, then mix very well and combine with the vegetables. To prepare the topping, combine all the 4dry ingredients in a bowl and rub in the butter until the mixture has the texture of breadcrumbs. Stir in the milk to make a soft dough. Roll out ½ inch thick on a floured surface and cut into 8 rounds. Place the rounds on top of the filling and bake, uncovered, for 10 minutes on HIGH. Let stand for a few minutes before serving. You can also use an equivalent amount of fresh vegetables if preferred for this warming winter dish.

Vegetarian Tomale Pie

PREPARATION TIME: 30 minutes
MICROWAVE COOKING TIME: 20 minutes
SERVES: 4 people

1 cup lentils, cooked or soaked overnight
2 cups stock
1 cup lentils, cooked
1 large onion, chopped
1 clove garlic, finely chopped or crushed
1 tbsp oil
1lb fresh tomatoes, roughly chopped, or 14oz can of tomatoes
1 cup frozen corn
3 tbsps tomato paste dissolved in 1 cup water or stock from the lentils
1 medium green pepper, chopped
1 tbsp chili powder
1 tsp salt

TOPPING
1½ cups cornmeal

2 cups milk
1 tbsp butter or margarine
2 eggs, beaten
1 tsp salt
2 cups grated Cheddar cheese

If uncooked lentils are used, add the soaked and drained lentils to the stock and cook for 15 minutes on HIGH, until soft. Place the oil in a casserole with the onions and garlic, and cook for 2 minutes on HIGH. Add the cooked lentils, tomatoes, tomato paste dissolved in the liquid, corn, green pepper, chili powder, salt and water, cover and cook for 3 minutes on HIGH. Next combine the cornmeal, milk, butter and salt in a bowl and cook on MEDIUM for 5 minutes. Stir in the eggs and half of the cheese. Spread this batter over the lentil mixture, cover and bake for 10 minutes on HIGH. Sprinkle on the remaining grated cheese and cook, uncovered, for a further 2 minutes on high to melt the cheese, or brown under the broiler. If you eat meat, try replacing the lentils with 1lb ground beef. Add the meat to the onions and garlic and cook for 5 minutes on HIGH, then proceed as normal.

Spinach Rice

PREPARATION TIME: 20 minutes
MICROWAVE COOKING TIME: 32 minutes
SERVES: 4 people

1lb fresh spinach, chopped or 1lb frozen chopped spinach
1 small onion, finely chopped
1½ cups brown rice
2 cups water

Facing page: Vegetarian Tomale Pie (top) and Herb and Cheese Cobbler (bottom).

3 tbsps chopped fresh parsley, or 1½ tbsps
　　dried parsley
2 large eggs
1 cup milk
2 tbsps Worcestershire sauce
4 tbsps Parmesan cheese
1 tsp salt

If using fresh spinach, wash well and chop. Cook, covered, in a large casserole for 2 minutes on HIGH, in only the water that clings to the leaves. Set aside. Frozen spinach may be placed directly in a covered casserole dish and microwaved for 5 minutes on HIGH. Wash the rice several times in cold water and cook, uncovered, in the water for approximately 20 minutes on HIGH, or until the rice is tender, but slightly chewy. Drain any excess water. Combine the eggs, milk, Worcestershire sauce, cheese and salt in a small bowl and whisk very well. Cook for 4 minutes on HIGH, stirring well after half the cooking time. Add the cooked rice and the sauce to the spinach in the large casserole dish and mix well. Cook, uncovered, for 5 minutes on HIGH. Let stand for a few minutes before serving. This dish can be served hot, but it is also delicious served cold as a colorful grain salad.

Mixed Grain Kedgeree

PREPARATION TIME: 15 minutes

MICROWAVE COOKING TIME:
24 minutes

SERVES: 4 people

¼ cup brown rice
¾ cup oats
⅓ cup barley
⅓ cup wheat grains
2 cups water
½ lb smoked fish
2 medium onions, finely chopped
¼ cup raisins
2 tbsps butter
Salt and pepper to taste
1 hard-boiled egg, sliced
Coriander

Remove the skin and de-bone the

fish, if necessary. Flake the meat and cook with the onions, raisins and butter for 4 minutes on HIGH. Set aside. Combine the grains and cook in the water for 20 minutes, or until tender. Drain any excess liquid. Mix-in the cooked fish, onions and raisins and add salt and pepper to taste. Garnish with slices of hard-boiled egg and coriander. Any combination of grains could be used as a basis for this dish. Try it using Mixed Grains and Seeds.

Spanish Barley

PREPARATION TIME: 15 minutes

MICROWAVE COOKING TIME:
26 minutes

SERVES: 4 people

1½ cups barley
2 cups water
1 tbsp oil
1 large onion, chopped

This page: Mixed Grain Kedgeree.
Facing page: Spinach Rice (top) and
Spanish Barley (bottom).

1 clove garlic, finely chopped or crushed
1 green pepper, chopped
14oz can tomatoes, roughly chopped
1 tsp paprika
1 tsp salt

Cook the barley in the water for 20 minutes on HIGH. Drain any excess liquid, and set the barley aside. Mix the chopped onion, garlic, and green pepper with the oil in a casserole and cook on HIGH for 2 minutes. Add the seasonings, tomatoes and the cooked barley. Cook for 4 minutes on HIGH. Let the dish stand for 5 minutes or more before serving to allow the flavor to develop. The paprika gives this dish its distinctive taste. Spanish Barley makes a colorful and tasty main dish. It can also be served cold.

PULSES

Pease Pudding

PREPARATION TIME: 1 hour

MICROWAVE COOKING TIME:
14 minutes

SERVES: 4 people

1 cup dried peas or green split peas,
    cooked and puréed using a small
    amount of the cooking liquid
1 large onion, finely chopped
1 large carrot, finely chopped
2 tbsps butter
1 tbsp arrowroot
½ cup milk
1 egg, beaten
½ tsp marjoram
½ tsp savory
1 tsp salt
Pepper to taste

GARNISH
Tomato slices

To cook the peas in the microwave,
pour on boiling water to cover and
allow to soak for at least 2 hours, or
follow the instructions in the
introduction for re-hydrating pulses.
Microwave on HIGH for 10 minutes
and 1 hour on MEDIUM or until the
peas are soft. Drain, and reserve a
small amount of the cooking liquid.
To make the purée, either liquidize
the peas in a blender or food
processor, or rub them through a
sieve, using the reserved cooking
liquid as necessary. Mix the chopped
carrot, onion, beaten egg and herbs
into the purée and set aside.
Combine the milk, butter and
arrowroot in a bowl and mix well.
Microwave on HIGH for 2 minutes
and stir well. Combine with the
purée and turn into a lightly-greased
basin or ring mold. Cover and
microwave on MEDIUM for 12
minutes. Allow to cool for a few
minutes before turning out. Pease
Pudding is traditionally served with
bacon or ham, but if you don't eat
meat, try it with a cheese omelet.

This page: Pease Pudding. Facing
page: Brown Beans with Sweet
Apples (top) and Succotash
(bottom).

Succotash

PREPARATION TIME: 1 hour

MICROWAVE COOKING TIME:
16 minutes

SERVES: 4 people

2¼ cups butter beans, cooked
3 cups frozen corn
1 medium onion, chopped
1 green pepper, chopped
2 tbsps butter
½ cup yogurt
1 tsp arrowroot

To cook the butter beans in the microwave, pour over boiling water to cover and allow to soak for at least 2 hours, or follow the instructions in the introduction for re-hydrating pulses. Drain and cover with fresh water. Microwave on HIGH for 10 minutes and on MEDIUM for 1 hour or until soft. The butter beans may also be cooked by any other method. If canned beans are used, remember that cooked beans are approximately double the volume and weight of uncooked beans. Combine the onions and pepper with the butter, and microwave for 2 minutes on HIGH. Add the cooked beans and the frozen corn and microwave for 4 minutes on HIGH. Mix the arrowroot into 1 tbsp of the yogurt, then add the rest of the yogurt. Stir this stabilized yogurt into the beans and corn before serving. Succotash is often served with bacon, but if you don't eat meat try it with a tomato dish.

Stir-Fried Beans and Sprouts

PREPARATION TIME: 1 hour

MICROWAVE COOKING TIME:
6 minutes

SERVES: 4 people

1 cup adzuki beans, cooked
3 cups bean sprouts
1 onion, sliced
1 green pepper, sliced
1 tbsp oil
¼ cup soy sauce

To cook the beans in the microwave, pour over boiling water and leave to soak for at least 2 hours, or follow the instructions in the introduction for re-hydrating pulses. Drain, cover with fresh water and microwave on HIGH for 10 minutes, or until the beans are soft. Alternatively, use beans cooked by any other method. Remember that cooked beans are approximately twice the weight and volume of uncooked beans. Combine the oil, sliced pepper, onion and bean sprouts and cook for 2 minutes on HIGH. Add the cooked beans and soy sauce, mix well and microwave for 4 minutes on HIGH. This is a stir-fry with a difference! Try serving it over brown rice for a complete meal.

Pinto Beans with Sweet Apples

PREPARATION TIME: 1 hour

MICROWAVE COOKING TIME:
10 minutes

SERVES: 4 people

2¼ cups pinto beans
½ lb sweet apples
½ lb piece smoked bacon, cut into chunks
1 cup cider or water
1 tbsp arrowroot
Salt and pepper to taste
Gravy browning

To cook the beans in the microwave, pour over boiling water to cover and allow them to soak for at least two hours, or follow the instructions in the introduction for re-hydrating pulses. Drain and cover with fresh water. Microwave for 10 minutes on HIGH and 1 hour on MEDIUM, or until the beans are soft. The beans can also be cooked by any other method. If canned beans are used, remember that cooked beans are approximately double the weight and volume of uncooked beans. Core and slice the apples, but don't peel them, and combine with the cooked beans, bacon and cider. Microwave for 10 minutes on HIGH. Make a thin paste by mixing the arrowroot with a little water and stir this into the stew. Add gravy browning for color if desired. Cook for a further 1 minute on HIGH. Let stand for at least 10 minutes before serving to allow the flavors to develop. This stew is even tastier if made the day before and reheated for 5 minutes on HIGH. This hearty Dutch dish is traditionally served with boiled potatoes.

Garbure

PREPARATION TIME: 1 hour

MICROWAVE COOKING TIME:
23 minutes

SERVES: 4 people

2¼ cups haricot beans, cooked
4 carrots, sliced
2 leeks, chopped
1 large potato, diced
4 cups chicken or vegetable stock, or
    water
1 tsp marjoram
1 tsp thyme
½ tsp paprika
Salt and pepper, to taste
1 small cabbage, shredded

To cook the haricots in the microwave, pour on boiling water and allow to soak for at least 2 hours, or follow the instructions in the introduction for re-hydrating pulses. Drain and cover with fresh water. Microwave on HIGH for 10 minutes and 1 hour on MEDIUM, or until the beans are soft. Alternatively, the beans may be cooked by any other

Facing page: Stir-Fried Beans and Sprouts.

method. Remember that cooked beans are approximately twice the volume and weight of uncooked beans. Combine the potato, carrots, leeks, haricots and stock. Cook, covered, for 20 minutes on HIGH. Spread the shredded cabbage on top, cover and cook for a further 3-4 minutes on HIGH, or until the cabbage is soft. Ladle this tasty French country stew over thick slices of whole-wheat bread for a hearty meal.

This page: Bean Hotchpotch. Facing page: Garbure (top) and Chicken and Chickpeas (bottom).

Chicken and Chickpeas

PREPARATION TIME: 1 hour

MICROWAVE COOKING TIME: 27 minutes

SERVES: 4 people

4 chicken portions, skins removed
1½ cups chickpeas, cooked
1 large onion, finely chopped
5 cloves of garlic, finely chopped
1 tbsp oil
1lb tomatoes, roughly chopped or 14oz can tomatoes, chopped
1 tbsp parsley
½ cup water
Salt and pepper to taste
3oz okra, trimmed and sliced

To cook the chickpeas in the microwave, pour on boiling water and allow to soak for at least 2 hours, or follow the instructions in the introduction for re-hydrating pulses. Drain and cover with fresh water. Microwave on HIGH for 10 minutes and on MEDIUM for 1 hour, or until the beans are soft. Alternatively, the beans may be cooked by any other method. Remember that cooked beans are approximately twice the volume and weight of uncooked beans. Place the onions and garlic in a casserole with the oil, and microwave on HIGH for 2 minutes. Add the remaining ingredients and cook, covered, on HIGH for 25 minutes, or until the chicken is very well cooked. Add okra during the last 2 minutes of cooking time. Serve this delicious north African stew with plenty of brown bread to mop up the juices.

Bean Hotchpotch

PREPARATION TIME: 1 hour

MICROWAVE COOKING TIME: 20 minutes

SERVES: 6 people

2¼ cups haricot or other white beans, cooked
1lb bacon, diced
1lb carrots, thinly sliced
½ lb parsnips, thinly sliced
½ lb onions, roughly chopped
Salt and pepper to taste
2 tsps arrowroot (optional)
Parsley, chopped

To cook the beans in the microwave, pour over boiling water and leave to soak for at least 2 hours, or follow the instructions in the introduction for re-hydrating pulses. Drain and cover with fresh water. Microwave on HIGH for 10 minutes and on MEDIUM for 1 hour, or until the beans are soft. Alternatively, the beans may be cooked by any other method. Remember that cooked beans are approximately twice the weight and volume of uncooked beans. Combine all the ingredients in a large casserole and cook, covered,

for 20 minutes on HIGH, or until the vegetables are soft. If desired, the liquid can be thickened by dissolving the arrowroot in a little water. Stir this paste into the stew with the parsley and microwave, uncovered, for a further 2 minutes on HIGH. This hearty Dutch dish is really a meal in itself. Serve it with fresh whole-wheat rolls to soak up the juices.

Boston Baked Beans

PREPARATION TIME: 1 hour

MICROWAVE COOKING TIME:
35 minutes

SERVES: 4 people

2¼ cups haricot beans, cooked
2 tbsps molasses
1 tbsp brown sugar
1 tbsp dry mustard
2 large onions, roughly chopped
½ lb bacon, roughly chopped or 1 large bacon bone
2 cups water
½ tsp salt
Pepper to taste
2 tsps arrowroot (optional)

Combine the beans, bacon or bone and onions in a casserole. To cook the beans in the microwave, pour over boiling water and leave to soak for at least 2 hours, or follow the instructions for re-hydrating pulses in the introduction. Drain and cover with fresh water. Microwave on HIGH for 10 minutes and on MEDIUM for 1 hour, or until the beans are soft. Alternatively, the beans may be cooked by any other method. Remember that cooked beans are approximately twice the volume and weight of uncooked beans. Mix together the molasses, brown sugar, mustard powder, salt, pepper and water and pour over the beans. Add extra water if the beans are not covered. Cook, uncovered, for 35 minutes on HIGH. If desired, the sauce can be thickened by dissolving the arrowroot in a little water. Stir this paste into the beans and microwave on HIGH for a

further 2 minutes. Leave to stand for at least 10 minutes before serving, to allow the flavors to develop. This dish tastes even better when reheated. Thirty-five minutes may seem like a long time in a microwave, but it is considerably shorter than the 8-10 hours required to cook this American classic by conventional means. Try it served with Boston Brown Bread.

South American Beans and Rice

PREPARATION TIME: 1 hours

MICROWAVE COOKING TIME:
30 minutes

SERVES: 4 people

1¾ cups pinto beans, cooked
1½ cups brown rice
1 onion, finely chopped
1 green pepper, sliced
1 clove garlic, crushed
1 tbsp oil
4 cups chicken stock

To cook the beans in the microwave, pour on boiling water and allow to soak for at least 2 hours, or follow the instructions for re-hydrating pulses in the introduction. Drain and cover with fresh water. Microwave on HIGH for 10 minutes and on MEDIUM for 1 hour, or until the beans are soft. Alternatively, the beans may be cooked by any other method. Remember that cooked beans are approximately twice the volume and weight of uncooked beans. Place the onion, pepper and garlic in a casserole with the oil and cook on HIGH for 2 minutes. Add the remaining ingredients and microwave, covered, for 30 minutes on HIGH or until the rice is cooked and most of the liquid has been absorbed. For an authentic touch, serve this dish with slices of cooked banana or plantain.

Facing page: Boston Baked Beans (top) and South American Beans and Rice (bottom).

that cooked beans are approximately twice the volume and weight of uncooked beans. Mix together the cooked kidney beans, frozen corn and sauce. Place this mixture in a casserole and cover with the topping. Bake, covered, for 10 minutes on HIGH. Sprinkle on the reserved cheese and cook for a further 2 minutes on HIGH. This dish may also be browned under the broiler, if desired. Chili Corn Pie is a substantial meal on its own. A green salad makes a refreshing and colorful contrast.

Cassoulet

PREPARATION TIME: 1 hour

MICROWAVE COOKING TIME: 31 minutes

SERVES: 4 people

2¼ cups haricot beans, cooked
1lb lamb fillet, cut into pieces
2 onions, sliced
2 cloves of garlic, finely chopped
2 carrots, sliced
1 tbsp oil
1lb tomatoes, roughly chopped or 14oz can
    tomatoes, chopped
½ cup red wine
1 bay leaf
1 tsp thyme
1 tsp rosemary
2 cups whole-wheat breadcrumbs
2 tbsps bran

To cook the beans in the microwave, pour on boiling water and allow to soak for at least 2 hours, or follow the instructions in the introduction for re-hydrating pulses. Drain and cover with fresh water. Microwave on HIGH for 10 minutes and on MEDIUM for 1 hour, or until the beans are soft. Alternatively, the beans may be cooked by any other

Chili Corn Pie

PREPARATION TIME: 2 hours

MICROWAVE COOKING TIME: 15 minutes

SERVES: 4 people

1 cup red kidney beans, cooked
1½ cups frozen corn

CHILI SAUCE
1lb tomatoes, chopped or 14oz can
    tomatoes, chopped
1 onion, chopped
¼ cup wine vinegar
¼ cup brown sugar
½ tsp salt
½ tsp cinnamon
½ tsp ginger
½ tsp mustard seeds
½ tsp chili powder

TOPPING
1¼ cups polenta
2 cups milk or water
1 tbsp butter or margarine
2 large eggs, beaten
2 cups Cheddar cheese, grated

First prepare the topping. Combine the polenta, milk or water, butter and salt in a bowl. Add the beaten eggs and half of the grated cheese. Cook for 5 minutes on MEDIUM. Stir very well after cooking. Set aside. Next prepare the sauce by combining all the sauce ingredients. To cook the kidney beans in the microwave, cover with boiling water and soak for at least 2 hours, or follow the instructions in the introduction for re-hyrdrating pulses. Drain and cover with fresh water. Microwave on HIGH for 10 minutes and MEDIUM for 2 hours, or until the beans are soft. Alternatively, the beans may be cooked by any other method. If canned beans are used, remember

This page: Cassoulet. Facing page: Dhal (top) and Chili Corn Pie (bottom).

method. Remember that cooked beans are approximately twice the volume and weight of uncooked beans. Place the oil, onions, garlic, carrots and lamb in a casserole dish and microwave on HIGH for 3 minutes. Add the beans, tomatoes, herbs and wine. Cover and cook on HIGH for 25 minutes, or until the carrots are soft. Mix together the breadcrumbs and the bran and spread over the top of the stew. Press this topping down lightly so that it absorbs some of the juice. Microwave, uncovered, for a further 3 minutes on HIGH. This is an example of wonderful French country cooking and can be made quickly and easily in the microwave.

Barbecued Beans

PREPARATION TIME: 1 hour

MICROWAVE COOKING TIME: 16 minutes

SERVES: 4 people

2½ cups haricot or kidney beans, cooked
½ lb Frankfurters or saveloys cut into thick slices
¼ cup brown sugar
1lb tomatoes, roughly chopped or 14oz can tomatoes
2 tbsps Worcestershire sauce
½-1 tsp chili powder, to taste
1 tsp mustard powder
1 tsp salt
½ tsp pepper
1 tsp arrowroot

To cook the beans in the microwave, pour over boiling water and allow to soak for at least 2 hours, or follow the instructions in the introduction for re-hydrating pulses. Drain and cover with fresh water. Microwave on HIGH for 10 minutes and on MEDIUM for 1 hour, or until the beans are soft. Alternatively, use beans cooked by any other method. Remember that cooked beans are approximately twice the volume and

weight of uncooked beans. Combine all the ingredients, except for the arrowroot, in a casserole and bake for 15 minutes on HIGH. Make a paste by dissolving the arrowroot in a little water and stir this into the beans. Microwave for a further minute on HIGH. Allow to stand for at least 10 minutes before serving, to allow the flavors to develop. Barbecued Beans is a good dish to make in advance, it freezes well and the flavor is even better when defrosted and reheated in the microwave.

Tuna Butter Bean Bake

PREPARATION TIME: 1 hour

MICROWAVE COOKING TIME: 9 minutes

SERVES: 4 people

2¼ cups butter beans, cooked
6oz can tuna, drained
1½ cups frozen peas
1¼ cups milk
2 tbsps whole-wheat flour
2 tsps arrowroot
2 tbsps butter or margarine
1 cup Cheddar cheese, grated

To cook the butter beans in the microwave, pour over boiling water to cover and leave to soak for at least 2 hours, or follow instructions in the introduction for re-hydrating pulses. Drain and cover with fresh water. Microwave on HIGH for 20 minutes and on MEDIUM for 1 hour, or until the beans are soft. Alternatively, beans cooked by any other method may be used. Remember that cooked beans are approximately twice the volume and weight of uncooked beans. Combine the cooked butter beans, drained tuna and frozen peas in a casserole. Prepare a sauce by combining the milk, arrowroot, butter and half of the grated cheese in a bowl. Microwave on HIGH for 2 minutes, stir very well and cook for a further 2 minutes on HIGH. Mix this sauce into the beans, sprinkle the

reserved cheese on top and bake for 5 minutes on HIGH. You can substitute other frozen vegetables for the peas if you wish. Try this dish with corn for a tasty variation.

Dhal

PREPARATION TIME: 50 minutes

MICROWAVE COOKING TIME: 4 minutes

SERVES: 4 people

1 cup red lentils, cooked
1 small onion, chopped
1 clove garlic, crushed
¼ cup oil
1 tsp coriander
1 tsp turmeric
1 tsp fenugreek
½ tsp cumin
½ tsp chili powder
1 tbsp wine vinegar

To cook the lentils in the microwave, pour over boiling water to cover and soak for at least 15 minutes. Drain and cover with 3 cups fresh water. Microwave on HIGH for 15 minutes and on MEDIUM for 50 minutes, or until the lentils are soft. Drain any excess liquid. Combine the onion, garlic and oil and cook for 2 minutes on HIGH. Mix in spices and vinegar to form a thick paste. Add the cooked lentils and stir well. Microwave for 4 minutes on HIGH. Allow to stand for 5 minutes before serving, to allow the flavors to develop. This is a delicious spicy version of an Indian classic. Serve it with warm pitta bread or, for a more substantial meal, try it over brown rice with a spoonful of natural yogurt and chopped green onions on top.

Facing page: Barbecued Beans (top) and Tuna Butter Bean Bake (bottom).

Fresh and Dried Beans Provençal

PREPARATION TIME: 1 hour

MICROWAVE COOKING TIME: 7 minutes

SERVES: 4 people

1 cup green flageolet beans, cooked
3 cups fresh or frozen green beans
1lb tomatoes, chopped or 14oz can
   tomatoes, chopped
1 clove garlic, crushed
2 tsps dried basil
1 tsp dried oregano
½ tsp dried rosemary
Parmesan cheese, to taste

To cook the flageolets in the microwave, pour on boiling water to cover and soak for at least two hours, or follow the instructions in the introduction for re-hydrating pulses. Drain and cover with fresh water. Microwave on HIGH for 10 minutes and MEDIUM for 1 hour, or until the flageolet beans are soft. Alternatively, beans may be cooked by any other method. If canned beans are used, remember that cooked beans are approximately double the volume and weight of uncooked beans. Mix all the ingredients in a casserole and cook, uncovered, for 7 minutes on HIGH, stirring once halfway through cooking time. The green beans and red tomatoes make this a colorful dish. Serve it over brown rice or cooked polenta, and pass the Parmesan cheese separately.

Microwave
WHOLEFOOD
BAKING

Ginger Nuts

PREPARATION TIME: 20 minutes

MICROWAVE COOKING TIME:
1 minute per batch

MAKES: approximately 3 dozen

½ cup brown sugar
¾ cup butter
½ cup molasses
3 eggs
2 tbsps milk
2 tsps vinegar
4½ cups whole-wheat flour
1½ tsps soda
2 tsps ginger
½ tsp cinnamon
Pinch ground cloves
½ cup hazelnuts, chopped

Cream together the margarine, sugar, molasses, vinegar, milk and eggs. Mix in the baking soda, salt and spices, then add the flour. Finally, stir in the chopped hazelnuts. The dough should be very stiff, add extra flour if necessary. Drop by rounded teaspoonful around the edge of a plate which has been covered with wax paper. Microwave, 6-8 at a time, for 1 minute on HIGH. Remove to a rack to cool. If you find your molasses as "slow as molasses in January," place the jar in the oven and microwave for 30 seconds on HIGH. You will find it much easier to handle.

Facing page: Fresh and Dried Beans Provençal. This page: Peanut Butter Bran Cookies (left) and Ginger Nuts (right).

Muesli Cookies

PREPARATION TIME: 20 minutes

MICROWAVE COOKING TIME:
2 minutes per batch

MAKES: approximately 3 dozen

½ cup brown sugar
½ cup margarine
1 egg
2 cups whole-wheat flour
1 cup sugarless muesli
1 tsp vanilla extract
½ tsp baking soda
½ tsp baking powder
Pinch salt
4 tbsps dried currants

Cream together the margarine, sugar and egg. Mix in the baking powder, soda, salt and vanilla, then add the muesli, currants and flour. The dough should be very stiff; add extra flour if necessary. Drop by rounded teaspoonfuls around the edge of a plate which has been covered with wax paper. Microwave for 2 minutes on HIGH. Remove to a rack to cool. As with Sunflower Carob Cookies, these can be baked from frozen. Baked cookies also freeze successfully, ready for any unexpected guests.

Date Walnut Cake

PREPARATION TIME: 15 minutes

MICROWAVE COOKING TIME:
8 minutes

MAKES: 1 loaf

1 cup sugarless dates, chopped
6 tbsps margarine
½ cup water
1 cup whole-wheat flour
2 tsps baking powder
½ tsp baking soda
½ cup walnuts, chopped
1 tsp cinnamon
4 tbsps demerara sugar

Place the water, margarine, cut into pieces, and the dates in a bowl and

microwave on HIGH for 3 minutes. Mash the dates with a fork, then stir in the remaining ingredients. Cook in the loaf dish, which has been lined with wax paper, for 5 minutes on MEDIUM. Allow to cool for 5 minutes, then turn out onto a rack to finish cooling. Sprinkle with demerara sugar before leaving to cool. Serve in slices with coffee or tea.

**This page: Date Walnut Cake.
Facing page: Muesli Cookies (top)
and Flapjacks (bottom).**

Banana Bran Bread

PREPARATION TIME: 20 minutes

MICROWAVE COOKING TIME:
12 minutes

MAKES: 1 loaf

½ cup butter or margarine
½ cup brown sugar
2 medium eggs
2 large, very ripe bananas, mashed
¼ cup yogurt
1 cup bran
1½ cups whole-wheat flour
1 tsp baking powder
½ tsp baking soda
½ tsp salt
½ cup toasted bran

Cream together the butter or margarine and sugar. Add the eggs, mashed bananas and yogurt. Mix in the baking powder, baking soda and salt, and stir in the bran and flour. Mix thoroughly. Turn the batter into a lightly greased loaf dish. Cover the top loosely with plastic wrap and cover the sides of the dish with aluminum foil, shiny side out. Cook in the microwave for 10 minutes on HIGH. Remove the foil, sprinkle on toasted bran, and cook for a further 2 minutes on HIGH. Remove the plastic wrap and leave the loaf to cool in the dish for 10 minutes before turning out. This tea bread is particularly delicious served cold, sliced and spread with fresh butter.

Flapjacks

PREPARATION TIME: 10 minutes

MICROWAVE COOKING TIME:
4 minutes

MAKES: 16 wedges

½ cup margarine
2 tbsps honey
¼ cup whole-wheat flour
1¼ cups rolled oats
¼ cup sesame seeds
1 tsp cinnamon

Place the margarine in a mixing bowl and cook for 2 minutes on HIGH to melt. Mix in the honey and the dry ingredients. Pat the mixture onto a dinner plate which has been covered with wax paper. It should be at least ½ inch thick. Bake for 2½ minutes on HIGH. Cut into 16 wedges while still warm. Leave the flapjacks to cool before serving, otherwise they will crumble. If they do, all is not lost because flapjack crumbs make a very nice crumble topping for fruit.

Boston Brown Bread

PREPARATION TIME: 15 minutes

MICROWAVE COOKING TIME:
8-10 minutes

MAKES: 1 large loaf

1 cup yogurt
Scant ½ cup molasses
1 tbsp butter
¼ cup raisins
½ cup plus 1 tbsp all-purpose flour
½ cup plus 1 tbsp whole-wheat flour
¾ cup polenta
1 tsp baking soda
1 tsp salt

Melt the butter for 1 minute on HIGH. In a large bowl or food processor, mix together the melted butter, yogurt and molasses. Combine the dry ingredients, add to the mixture and stir well. Bake, covered with plastic wrap, in one or more well-greased loaf containers, for 10 minutes on HIGH. The bread rises quite a lot during cooking, so fill the containers no more than half full. Allow to cool slightly before removing from the containers. Serve warm, either plain or with butter. This bread freezes well, and can be easily reheated by wrapping it in plastic wrap and placing it in the microwave for 5 minutes on HIGH, if frozen, or 2 minutes on HIGH if at room temperature. In Boston this bread is the traditional accompaniment to Boston Baked Beans, but it is also good with cheese dishes or served hot with butter as a tea bread.

Apple Spice Ring

PREPARATION TIME: 20 minutes

MICROWAVE COOKING TIME:
7 minutes

MAKES: 1 8 inch ring

1lb eating apples, grated
⅔ cup ground hazelnuts
1 cup whole-wheat flour
½ cup bran
¼ cup brown sugar (optional)
1 egg, beaten
1½ tsps baking powder
1 tsp cinnamon
Pinch nutmeg
Pinch cardamom
¼ cup milk

Combine the grated apples with the dry ingredients, beat in the egg and stir in the milk until well mixed. The batter will be stiff. Turn into an 8 inch ring mold. Smooth the top and allow to stand for a few minutes before baking for 3 minutes on HIGH followed by 4 minutes on MEDIUM, or until the cake is set, but still moist. Allow to cool slightly before turning out onto a rack to finish cooling. This cake can be made with or without sugar, and ground almonds may be substituted for the hazelnuts. Either way, it's simply delicious!

Facing page: Banana Bran Bread (top) and Boston Brown Bread (bottom).

Sunflower Carob Cookies

PREPARATION TIME: 20 minutes

MICROWAVE COOKING TIME: 16 minutes

MAKES: 3-4 dozen cookies

1 cup margarine or butter
1 cup brown sugar
2 large eggs
1 cup bran
2 cups rolled oats
2 cups whole-wheat flour
1 cup sunflower seeds
2 cups carob drops (semi-sweet or dark chocolate drops may be substituted)
2 tsps vanilla extract
1 tsp soda
1 tsp salt

Cream together the margarine, eggs, sugar, vanilla, soda and salt. Mix in the bran, oats and flour. The dough should be very stiff; if not, add more flour. Finally, stir in the sunflower seeds and carob drops, making sure they are well distributed in the dough. Drop the dough by rounded teaspoonfuls around the edge of a dinner plate which has been covered with wax paper or baking parchment. Most dinner plates will accommodate 6 cookies at a time. Bake on HIGH for two minutes. Allow to cool for a few minutes before removing to a rack to finish cooling. You can also form the dough into a 2 inch diameter log, cover with foil and freeze. Whenever you want a few cookies, simply cut off the desired number of ¼ inch thick slices and bake as described above for 2 minutes and 15 seconds. This is one way to make sure these popular cookies don't disappear at one sitting!

Fruit Cake

PREPARATION TIME: 20 minutes

MICROWAVE COOKING TIME: 16 minutes

MAKES: 1 large cake

1½ cups dried mixed fruit
1¼ cups apple juice
½ cup butter or margarine
2 cups whole-wheat flour
2 eggs, beaten
2 tsps baking powder
1 tsp mixed spice

TOPPING
Assorted candied fruit
Apricot jam

Combine the fruit and the apple juice and allow to soak for at least 1 hour. Mix together the dry ingredients and rub in the butter or margarine until the mixture resembles fine breadcrumbs. Beat in the eggs and mix in the fruit and juice. Line the bottom of a deep 6 inch round dish with wax paper. Pour in the cake mixture and smooth the top. Let the mixture stand for a few minutes, then bake for 3 minutes on HIGH, followed by 13 minutes on MEDIUM, or until the center is just dry. Allow to cool slightly, then turn out onto a rack to finish cooling. You will be amazed at the rich sweet flavor of this cake, made with no sugar at all! Serve it whenever a fruitcake is called for.

This page: Sunflower Carob Cookies. Facing page: Apple Spice Ring (top) and Fruit Cake (bottom).

Peanut Butter Bran Cookies

PREPARATION TIME: 20 minutes

MICROWAVE COOKING TIME:
2 minutes per batch

MAKES: approximately 5 dozen

½ cup brown sugar
½ cup margarine
1 egg
1 cup peanut butter
1 cup bran
1 cup whole-wheat flour
½ tsp salt
½ tsp soda
½ tsp vanilla extract

Cream together the margarine, sugar, egg and peanut butter. Mix in the baking soda, salt and vanilla, then add the bran and flour. The dough should be very stiff; add extra flour if necessary. Drop by rounded teaspoonful around the edge of a plate which has been covered with wax paper. Flatten each cookie with the tines of a fork and microwave, 6-8 at a time, for 2 minutes on HIGH. Remove to a rack to cool. These rich and crumbly cookies are just the thing with a glass of milk. In the unlikely event of leftovers, they freeze well.

Carob Fruit Cake

PREPARATION TIME: 20 minutes

MICROWAVE COOKING TIME:
16 minutes

MAKES: 1 large cake

1½ cups raisins
1 cup apple juice
¾ cup butter or margarine
3 eggs
2¼ cups whole-wheat flour
¾ cup carob powder
2 tsps baking powder

Combine the raisins and the apple juice and allow to soak for at least 1 hour. Mix together the dry ingredients and rub in the butter or margarine until the mixture resembles fine breadcrumbs. Beat in the eggs and mix in the raisins and juice. Line the bottom of an 8 inch deep round dish with wax paper. Pour the mixture into the dish, smooth the top and allow to stand for a few minutes before baking for 3 minutes on HIGH, followed by 13 minutes on MEDIUM, or until the center is just dry. Allow to cool for a few minutes in the dish before turning out onto a rack to complete cooling. This is a really rich and spicy sugarless fruit cake which you will be proud to serve to guests and family alike.

Citrus Scones

PREPARATION TIME: 20 minutes

MICROWAVE COOKING TIME:
3 minutes per batch

MAKES: 12 scones

¼ cup butter
2 tbsps raw sugar
1 cup bran
1 cup whole-wheat flour
1 tsp baking powder
½ tsp cinnamon
Pinch salt
½ cup milk
¼ cup preserved mixed citrus peel

Combine all the dry ingredients and rub in the margarine until the mixture has the texture of breadcrumbs. Gradually add the milk to form a stiff dough, adding extra flour if necessary. Finally, mix in the peel. Roll out the dough on a floured surface to approximately ½ inch thick. Use a 2 inch round cutter to produce 12 scones. Place them around the edge of a dinner plate which has been covered with wax paper and microwave on HIGH for 3 minutes. Remove to a rack to cool. Served warm or cold, these scones are delicious for tea, and make a very nice breakfast bread as well.

Cornbread

PREPARATION TIME: 15 minutes

MICROWAVE COOKING TIME:
13 minutes

MAKES: 1 large round loaf

1 cup polenta or cornmeal
½ cup whole-wheat flour
1 tsp baking soda
½ tsp salt
1 egg
2 tbsps honey
1 cup yogurt

Combine the dry ingredients, then stir in the egg, honey, and yogurt. Spread into a loaf dish, the bottom of which has been lined with wax paper, and bake for 3 minutes on HIGH, followed by 10 minutes on MEDIUM. Turn out onto a rack to cool. This versatile and quickly made bread is the perfect accompaniment to a spicy dish like Barbecued Beans. It is equally delicious toasted and spread with butter and strawberry jam.

Facing page: Citrus Scones (top) and Cornbread (bottom).

then cut into 16 squares. Remove from the dish when fully cool. These moist, cake-like brownies are an irresistible treat, and so easily made.

Carob Brownies

PREPARATION TIME: 15 minutes

MICROWAVE COOKING TIME:
7 minutes per batch

MAKES: 16 brownies

½ cup margarine, cut into pieces
1 cup unsweetened carob drops
4 eggs
1¼ cups raw sugar
1 cup whole-wheat flour
1 cup walnuts, chopped
Pinch baking powder

Place the margarine and the carob drops in a bowl and melt on HIGH for 1-2 minutes. Allow to cool slightly, then beat in the eggs and salt. Stir in the baking powder, sugar and flour until they are just mixed. Bake in two 8 inch shallow round dishes, the bottoms of which have been lined with wax paper, for 5 minutes on HIGH, or until just set. Cut each brownie into 8 wedges while still warm. These rich and heavenly brownies are sure to become a firm favorite.

Hazelnut Brownies

PREPARATION TIME: 15 minutes

MICROWAVE COOKING TIME:
6-7 minutes

MAKES: 16 brownies

¾ cup brown sugar
½ cup butter or margarine
2 eggs
½ tsp vanilla extract
¾ cup whole-wheat flour
½ tsp baking powder
Pinch salt
½ cup hazelnuts, chopped

Cut the margarine or butter into small pieces, place it in a bowl and melt it in the microwave for 1-2 minutes on HIGH. Stir in the sugar and allow to cool slightly, then beat in the eggs. Add the vanilla extract and the dry ingredients, and finally mix in the hazelnuts. Line the bottom of an 8 inch square dish with wax paper and cover the corners with aluminum foil. Pour in the brownie mixture and smooth the top. Bake on a rack or on top of an inverted saucer for 5 minutes on HIGH, followed by 1 minute on MEDIUM. Allow to cool slightly,

This page: Carob Fruit Cake. Facing page: Hazelnut Brownies (top) and Carob Brownies (bottom).

DESSERTS

Carob Blancmange

PREPARATION TIME: 5 minutes

MICROWAVE COOKING TIME:
5 minutes

SERVES: 4 people

½ cup finely milled whole-wheat flour
¼ cup raw sugar
1 cup milk
2 tbsps carob powder
Slivered almonds, to garnish

Beat together all the ingredients in a
large bowl; the mixture will be lumpy.
Cook for 5 minutes on MEDIUM,
whisking very well after 2 minutes in
order to dissolve the carob powder.
Stir again at the end of the cooking
time and divide the mixture into four
small bowls. Decorate with slivered
almonds and leave to cool. Carob
gives this blancmange a rich and
spicy flavor. This dessert is nicest
when served chilled.

Maple Raisin Custard

PREPARATION TIME: 5 minutes

MICROWAVE COOKING TIME:
14 minutes

SERVES: 4 people

2 eggs
2 cups milk
3 tbsps maple syrup

**This page: Carob Blancmange (left)
and Maple Raisin Custard (right).
Facing page: Muesli Baked Apples
(top) and Baked Carrot Custard
(bottom).**

¼ cup raisins
Large pinch nutmeg

Beat the eggs well and whisk in the milk and maple syrup. Add the raisins and sprinkle on the nutmeg. Cook, uncovered, for 14 minutes on MEDIUM. Leave to stand for at least 20 minutes before serving. The custard will become firmer on cooling. The custard is very attractive when cooked in a clear glass bowl. For special occasions substitute cream for part of the milk. For a less rich custard, you can make this with skimmed milk.

Baked Carrot Custard

PREPARATION TIME: 20 minutes

MICROWAVE COOKING TIME: 22 minutes

SERVES: 4 people

2 cups carrots, finely chopped
4 tbsps water
½ cup unsugared dates, chopped
4 tbsps water
3 large eggs, beaten
1½ cups milk
1 tsp cinnamon
½ tsp nutmeg
¼ tsp ginger
¼ tsp ground cloves
½ cup chopped pistachios

Cook the carrots in a covered casserole with 4 tbsps water for 5 minutes on HIGH. Liquidize or rub them through a sieve without draining to make a purée. Cook the dates in 4 tbsps water for 2 minutes on HIGH and mash them without draining. Combine the puréed carrots, mashed dates, spices, beaten eggs and milk, then mix in the chopped pistachios. Cook, uncovered, in a shallow dish for 15 minutes on MEDIUM, or until the center is just set. Let stand for at least 10 minutes before serving. The carrots and dates provide the

sweetness in this sugarless, spicy custard. It can be served warm or cold, but for the strongest flavor, serve lightly chilled.

Muesli Baked Apples

PREPARATION TIME: 10 minutes

MICROWAVE COOKING TIME: 3-4 minutes

SERVES: 4 people

4 large red apples
4 tbsps sugar-free muesli
1½ tbsps brown sugar
2 tbsps butter
½ cup water

Wash and core the apples. Prick the skins in several places, but do not peel. Fill the cavities with a mixture of the muesli and the sugar. Place the apples in a casserole dish so that they are touching, dot the filling with butter and pour over the water. Bake, uncovered, for 3-4 minutes on HIGH, or until the apples are soft. Spoon over juices to serve. The microwave really excels at baked apples. These are delicious on their own or can be served with sweetened cream, yogurt or fromage frais.

Fruit and Bran Whip

PREPARATION TIME: 10 minutes

MICROWAVE COOKING TIME: 3 minutes

SERVES: 4 people

1lb blackcurrants or plums
4 tbsps water
Raw sugar to taste
½ cup bran
2 egg whites
Flaked almonds

Wash the fruit and, if using plums,

remove stones and roughly chop the fruit. Cook, covered, in the water for 3 minutes on HIGH. Liquidize or rub through a sieve without draining to make a purée. Add raw sugar to taste and mix in the bran. Whip the egg whites until they are stiff, but not dry. Fold them into the fruit and bran mixture. Do not overfold. Divide the whip into four dishes and chill before serving. Sprinkle with flaked almonds. For special occasions, this dessert looks very elegant when served in stemmed glasses.

Fresh and Dried Fruit Salad

PREPARATION TIME: 10 minutes

MICROWAVE COOKING TIME: 8 minutes

SERVES: 4 people

1½ cups mixed dried fruit
1 cup apple juice
2 dessert apples
1 orange

Combine the dried fruit and the apple juice in a bowl and microwave on MEDIUM for 8 minutes. Allow to cool. Wash the orange and cut four slices to use as a garnish, then peel and roughly chop the flesh. Wash and chop the apples, leaving the skins on. Combine the chopped apples and orange with the dried fruit and apple juice and chill. To serve, divide into 4 dishes and garnish each with an orange slice. This salad makes a refreshing end to a substantial meal. You can vary the fresh fruit as you wish.

Facing page: Fruit and Bran Whip.

Marmalade Bread Pudding

PREPARATION TIME: 10 minutes

MICROWAVE COOKING TIME: 14 minutes

SERVES: 4 people

6 slices whole-wheat bread
½ cup marmalade

2 large eggs, beaten
2 cups milk

Spread the bread thickly with the marmalade and cut it into 1 inch squares. Arrange the squares in a dish. Mix together the beaten eggs and milk and pour over the squares, making sure the bread is well soaked. Microwave for 14 minutes on MEDIUM, or until the milk and egg mixture is just set in the center. Let stand for at least 10 minutes before serving. Marmalade adds both sweetness and flavor to this simple version of bread pudding. Serve it warm or cold.

This page: Fresh and Dried Fruit Salad. Facing page: Marmalade Bread Pudding (top) and Apple Tapioca (bottom).

Apple Tapioca

PREPARATION TIME: 5 minutes

MICROWAVE COOKING TIME:
8 minutes

SERVES: 4 people

¾ cup tapioca
2 cups apple juice
½ tsp cinnamon

Combine all ingredients in a bowl
and stir well. Cook for 8 minutes on
HIGH, stirring well halfway through
cooking time. Spoon into individual
dishes, if desired, and leave to stand
for at least 5 minutes before serving.
Apple Tapioca can be served warm
or chilled and is very tasty topped
with apple sauce or cream. This is a
simple way to prepare tapioca
without using any sugar.

Apple Gingerbread Pudding

PREPARATION TIME: 20 minutes

MICROWAVE COOKING TIME:
7 minutes

SERVES: 4 people

¼ cup butter or margarine
1 large egg, beaten
½ cup molasses
1½ cups whole-wheat flour
1½ cups chopped apples
¼ cup raisins
½ cup yogurt
½ tsp baking soda
1 tsp baking powder
1 tsp ginger
1 tsp cinnamon
1 tsp cardamom

Cream together the butter and
molasses, beat in the egg, baking
powder, baking soda and spices. Stir
in the yogurt and add the flour. Fold
in the chopped apples and raisins.
Cook, covered, in a lightly-greased
bowl, which is large enough to allow
for rising, for 7 minutes on HIGH.

Uncover and let stand for at least
10 minutes before turning out. Apple
Gingerbread Pudding is a sugarless
treat best served warm with a little
bit of milk or cream to pour over.
Should you have any left over, it is
also delicious sliced and buttered as a
moist teabread.

**This page: Apple Gingerbread
Pudding (top) and Apple Sauce
Streusel Pudding (bottom). Facing
page: Sugarless Baked Apples with
Dates.**

Apple Sauce Streusel Pudding

PREPARATION TIME: 20 minutes

MICROWAVE COOKING TIME:
6 minutes

SERVES: 4 people

1lb apples, chopped or 2 cups
    unsweetened apple sauce
1½ cups brown breadcrumbs
1½ cups rolled oats
½ cup brown sugar
½ cup butter or margarine
2 large eggs, beaten
1 tsp baking powder
1½ tsps cinnamon
½ tsp cardamom

If using fresh chopped apples, cook them in a covered dish for 4 minutes on HIGH. Liquidize or rub them through a sieve to make a purée. Allow the purée to cool, then mix in the beaten eggs, spices and baking powder. Set aside. In a separate bowl combine the breadcrumbs, rolled oats and brown sugar. Rub in the butter or margarine until the mixture has the texture of fine breadcrumbs. Fold in the apple purée, making sure that the batter is fully mixed. Cook, covered, in a lightly greased bowl for 6 minutes on HIGH. Uncover and allow to cool for at least 10 minutes before turning out. Apple Sauce Struesel Pudding would normally be cooked by steaming. Instead, the microwave is used to produce a perfect result in a fraction of the time.

Sugarless Baked Apples with Dates

PREPARATION TIME: 10 minutes

MICROWAVE COOKING TIME:
3-4 minutes

SERVES: 4 people

4 large green apples

½ cup chopped, unsugared dates
4 tbsps sugar-free muesli
2 tbsps butter
½ cup apple juice

Core the apples. Prick the skins in several places, but do not peel. Fill the cavities with a mixture of the muesli and dates and place the apples in a casserole so that they are touching. Dot the filling with the butter and pour over the apple juice. Bake for 3-4 minutes on HIGH, or until the apples are soft. Although this recipe contains no sugar, the apples are delightfully sweet-tasting. They can be eaten on their own or served with cream.

Brown Bread Crumble

PREPARATION TIME: 15 minutes

MICROWAVE COOKING TIME:
5 minutes

SERVES: 4 people

½ lb apples
½ lb raspberries
Raw sugar to taste

TOPPING
¾ cup whole-wheat breadcrumbs
¾ cup rolled oats
¼ cup brown sugar
¼ cup butter or margarine
1 tsp cinnamon
½ tsp cardamom

Wash and slice the apples, but do not peel them. Place them in a small, deep dish and sprinkle on raw sugar to taste. Scatter over raspberries. To prepare the topping, combine the breadcrumbs, oats, muscovado sugar and spices. Rub in the butter or margarine until the mixture has the texture of fine breadcrumbs. Spread evenly on top of the apples and microwave for 5 minutes on HIGH, or until the apples are tender. Let stand for 5 minutes before serving. This crumble can be served either warm or chilled, and is delicious on its own. Even so, you may prefer to serve it topped with cream or whipped cream. For a real treat, try it hot with a scoop of vanilla ice cream.

Molasses Rice Pudding

PREPARATION TIME: 10 minutes

MICROWAVE COOKING TIME:
25 minutes

SERVES: 4 people

½ cup plus 2 tbsps brown rice, cooked
1 tbsp molasses
1 cup milk
2 eggs, beaten
¼ cup raisins
1 tsp cinnamon

To cook rice in the microwave, place it in a bowl and rinse several times in cold water. Cook in 1 cup water for 25 minutes on HIGH. Drain any excess liquid. Mix together the eggs, milk, molasses and cinnamon and add to the cooked rice. Stir in the raisins and bake, uncovered, on LOW for 25 minutes, or until the center is just set. Leave to stand for at least 5 minutes before serving. This nutty and distinctive rice pudding is made without any sugar. It is good served either warm or cold.

Facing page: Tapioca with Golden Raisins (top) and Molasses Rice Pudding (bottom).

Tapioca with Golden Raisins

PREPARATION TIME: 5 minutes

MICROWAVE COOKING TIME: 8 minutes

SERVES: 4 people

¾ cup tapioca
2 cups milk
½ cup golden raisins
2 tbsps brown sugar
Pinch cinnamon

Pistachio nuts, chopped

Combine all ingredients except the nuts in a bowl and stir well. Cook in the microwave for 8 minutes on HIGH, stirring well halfway through the cooking time. Spoon into 4 small dishes, if desired, and leave to stand at least 5 minutes before serving. Sprinkle with the nuts. The brown sugar gives this milk pudding a delicious distinctive taste. It can be served either warm, or chilled.

Peach Cobbler Cake

PREPARATION TIME: 15 minutes

MICROWAVE COOKING TIME: 12 minutes

SERVES: 4 people

14oz can peaches, drained
2 tbsps brown sugar
1 tbsp butter or margarine
Large pinch nutmeg

COBBLER
¼ cup butter or margarine
2 tbsps raw sugar
1 cup bran
½ cup whole-wheat flour
1 tsp baking powder
½ tsp cinnamon
Pinch salt
½ cup milk

Melt 1 tbsp butter or margarine in a 7 inch square or round dish for 1 minute on HIGH. Stir in the brown sugar and spread evenly over the bottom of the dish. Arrange the peaches on top. In a separate bowl mix together the dry ingredients and rub in the butter. Stir in the milk to form a soft dough. Spread the mixture on top of the peaches as evenly as possible and bake, uncovered, for 12 minutes on HIGH, or until the center is just cooked. Allow to cool for 15 minutes, then carefully invert onto a plate. Serve with yogurt. Other canned or cooked fresh fruit can be substituted for the topping in this attractive and quickly prepared dessert. It is best when served warm.

**This page: Peach Cobbler Cake.
Facing page: Brown Bread Crumble.**

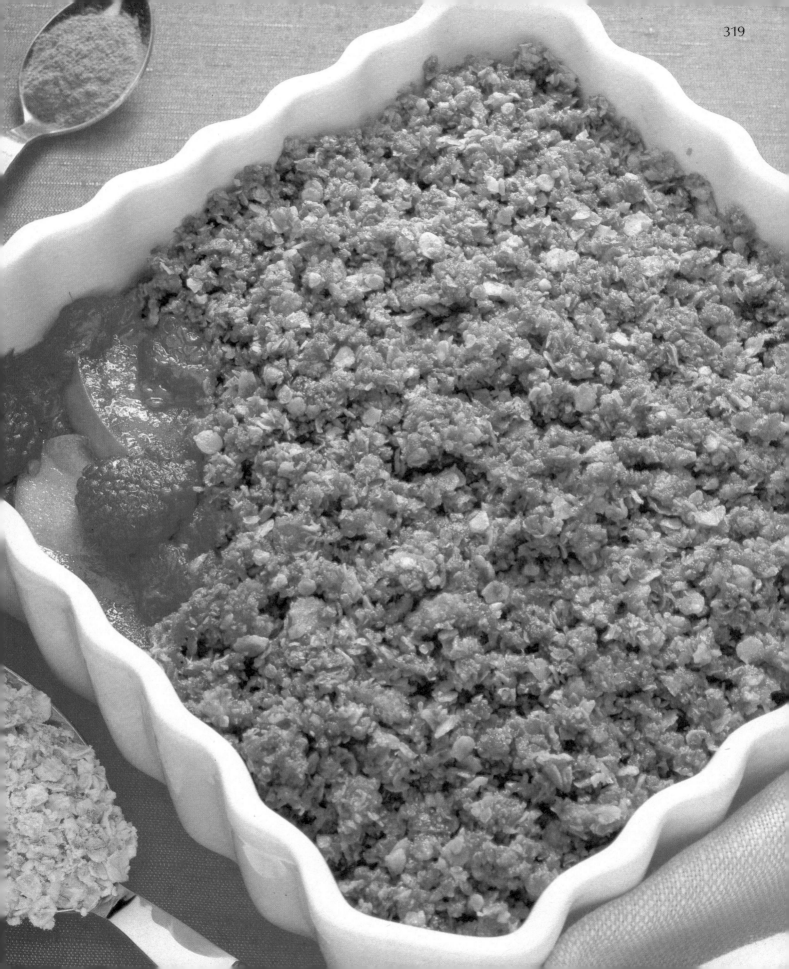

Microwave CHINESE COOKING

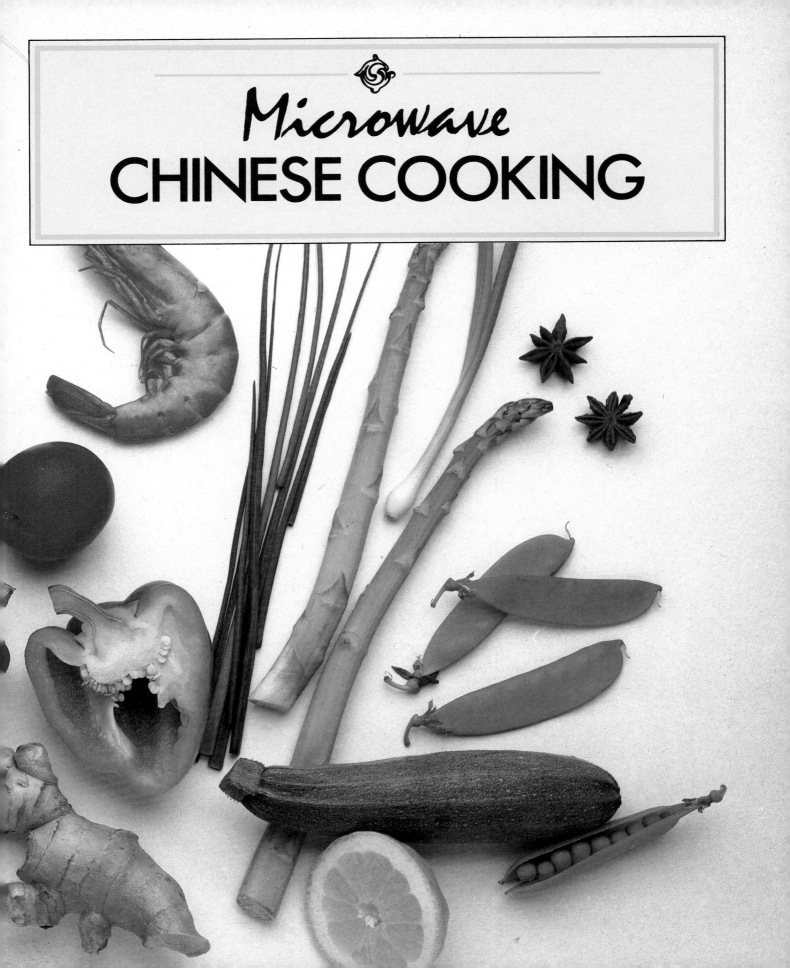

Microwave
CHINESE COOKING

INTRODUCTION

Chinese cooking means fast cooking. Microwave cooking does, too, so why not combine them. Many classic Chinese specialties are possible with a microwave oven. The usual cornstarch-based Chinese sauces need more thickening because liquids evaporate less in microwave cooking, but otherwise they are easy to do. Stir-frying transfers successfully from the wok to the browning dish, and you can even achieve a stir-fried effect without one.

Garnishes for Chinese dishes tend to be very simple. These two are easy to do and can be prepared in advance:

Chili flowers: Choose small red or green chili peppers. Cut in thin strips, lengthwise, to within ½-1 inch of the stem. Keep the stem end intact and carefully remove seeds and core. Place in ice water for several hours or overnight until the "petals" open up. Eat at your own risk!

Green onion brushes: Trim the onions into 3-4 inch lengths. Cut the greener end into thin strips and leave white "bulb" end intact. Alternatively, cut both ends into thin strips, leaving ½ inch of the middle intact. Soak as for chili flowers.

For a taste of China from your microwave oven, look for these ingredients:

Bamboo shoots – First growth of the bamboo plant, cut just as it emerges from the ground. Crisp, ivory-colored and slightly sweet, usually sold canned, sliced or in whole pieces which can be cut to various shapes.

Baby corn – Miniature variety of corn. Sold in cans and often available fresh. Needs very brief cooking.

Black beans – Used often in Cantonese cooking. Available in pre-prepared sauce or salted to preserve them. Salted beans should be soaked.

Chili peppers – Available dried or fresh. Usually red, they are often used in Szechuan cooking. Seeds are the hottest part, so remove for less heat.

Chili sauce – Available hot or sweet and made from fresh, red chili peppers.

Chinese cabbage – Usually refers to Chinese celery cabbage. Some varieties have thicker, whiter spines. Readily available in greengrocers or supermarkets. Smaller, stronger-tasting bok choy is rarely seen outside Chinese markets.

Chinese parsley – Also coriander leaves or cilantro. A pungent green herb with a leaf similar to flat parsley.

Five-spice powder – A combination of star anise, anise pepper, fennel, cloves and cinnamon. Use sparingly.

Ginger – Knobbly root that must be peeled before use. Use grated or thinly sliced in small amounts. Powdered variety available, and preserved pieces in sugar syrup.

Hoisin sauce – Used often in Chinese barbecue cooking. A thick vegetable-based sauce. Useful for stir-fried dishes and a dipping sauce as well.

Lotus – Root is available canned or fresh from Chinese groceries. Cut in thin rounds, it has a flower-like shape. Obtained from waterlilies. Seeds are available preserved or fresh at the Chinese New Year and reputedly bring good luck. Leaves are available from Chinese groceries to cook in or on. Should be soaked first.

Mushrooms, dried Chinese – Brown-black in color, must be soaked 15-30 minutes before use. Stronger in taste than fresh mushrooms, they also have a chewier texture.

Red bean paste – Made from boiled red beans or bean flour mixed with water and lard. Usually sweetened and used in desserts.

Red wine – Available from Chinese groceries, it has a flavor ranging from dry sherry to sweet white wine, depending on the variety brought. Substitute either sherry or white wine.

Rice vinegar – Made from rice and quite pale in color. Substitute white wine vinegar.

Sesame oil – Pressed from sesame seeds, it is golden in color with a nutty flavor. Expensive, so use as a flavoring at the end of cooking.

Sesame paste – Also called tahini and used in Middle-Eastern cooking as well. Thick, whitish paste, about the consistency of peanut butter and tasing of sesame seeds.

Soy sauce – Made from fermented soy beans. There are various strengths which will effect the color and flavor of the finished dish.

Star anise – Star shaped seed pod with a liquorice taste. Used in meat, poultry and sweet dishes.

Szechuan peppercorns – Also called wild pepper. Not readily available, so substitute black peppercorns.

Water chestnuts – Fresh variety is very difficult to obtain. Usually found canned, peeled, sliced or whole. Creamy white in color and crisp in texture.

White radish or Mooli – Very large. Delicious crisp texture and white translucent appearance. Barely needs cooking.

Wonton skins or wrappers – Thin sheets of egg noodle dough in large or small squares. The traditional wrapping for spring or egg rolls and dumplings with various stuffings. Can be steamed or cooked in liquid.

Wood or tree ears – Greyish black tree fungus. Sold dried and must be soaked before use.

Yellow beans – Whole in brine, paste or sauce form. They are golden brown in color and very salty.

NOTE: Recipes were tested in a 650 watt maximum oven. HIGH = Full or 100%, MEDIUM = 50%, LOW/DEFROST = 25%.

SAUCES, RICE AND NOODLES

Hot Mustard Sauce

PREPARATION TIME: 10 minutes

MICROWAVE COOKING TIME:
4 minutes

MAKES: About 3-4 cups

4 tbsps dry mustard
4 tbsps rice wine vinegar
1½ tsps cornstarch
½ cup water
3 tbsps honey
Salt

Mix the mustard and cornstarch together. Beat in the water, vinegar and honey gradually until smooth. Add a small pinch of salt and cook, uncovered, in a small, deep bowl for 4 minutes on HIGH. Stir every 30 seconds until thickened. Serve with appetizers or seafood.

Pineapple Sauce

PREPARATION TIME: 10-15 minutes

MICROWAVE COOKING TIME:
4 minutes

MAKES: About 2 cups

8oz can crushed pineapple, or 1 fresh
*   pineapple, peeled and cored*
1½ tsp cornstarch dissolved in 1 tbsp water
1 tbsp light soy sauce
1½ tsp sugar
1 tbsp white wine
1 piece ginger root, grated
Pinch salt

If using fresh pineapple, work in a

food processor until finely chopped. Add remaining ingredients and mix well in a small, deep bowl. Cook 4 minutes on HIGH until the sauce thickens and clears. Serve with duck or shrimp.

This page: Pineapple Sauce (top) and Plum Sauce (bottom). Facing page: Hot Mustard Sauce (top) and Sweet and Sour Sauce (bottom).

Plum Sauce

PREPARATION TIME: 10-15 minutes

MICROWAVE COOKING TIME: 10 minutes

MAKES: About 2 cups

8oz canned plums, stoned, or fresh plums, halved and stoned
1 cup apricot jam
¼ cup rice wine vinegar
2 tsp cornstarch
½ tsp five-spice powder

Combine all the ingredients in a large bowl or casserole. If using canned plums, include the juice, and cook 5 minutes on HIGH until the sauce thickens and clears. Purée until smooth in a food processor, if desired. If using fresh plums, add ¼ cup water to the ingredients and reserve the cornstarch until later. Cook the plums, covered, for 5 minutes on HIGH until soft. Mix the cornstarch and vinegar, add to the plums and proceed as for canned plums. Serve with pork or duck.

Shanghai Noodle Snack

PREPARATION TIME: 15 minutes

MICROWAVE COOKING TIME: 5-6 minutes plus 5 minutes standing time

SERVES: 6 people

1lb Chinese egg noodles
4 cups boiling water

SAUCE
2 tbsps cornstarch dissolved in ¼ cup water
2 tbsps rice wine
1 tbsp light soy sauce
1 cup light stock
1 small piece ginger root, thinly sliced
4 green onions, thinly sliced diagonally
Meat from one large crab or 1 6oz package frozen or canned crabmeat

Cook the noodles in the boiling water for 3 minutes on HIGH. Leave to stand 5 minutes, covered, while preparing the sauce. Combine the first 5 ingredients in a deep bowl, stirring well to mix the cornstarch. Cook 2-3 minutes until the sauce thickens and clears. Add the crab and onion and cook 30 seconds on HIGH. Drain the noodles well and toss with the sauce to serve.

Velvet Noodles

PREPARATION TIME: 20 minutes

MICROWAVE COOKING TIME: 8-12 minutes plus 5 minutes standing time

SERVES: 6 people

1½ tbsps light soy sauce
1 tbsp cornstarch
Dash sesame oil
3oz lean pork cut in small, thin slices
½ cup mushrooms, sliced
2 cups chicken stock
Salt
4 cups boiling water
2 packages medium Chinese noodles
½ head Chinese cabbage, shredded

Mix soy sauce, cornstarch and sesame oil together in a large bowl. Stir in the stock gradually and add the pork and mushrooms. Cover and cook for 5-8 minutes on HIGH or until pork is cooked. Add the Chinese cabbage and leave to stand, covered, while cooking the noodles. Put the noodles and water into a large, deep bowl. Cook for 3 minutes on HIGH, stirring occasionally. Leave to stand 5 minutes before serving. Add salt to the mushrooms and pork if desired. Drain the noodles and arrange on a serving dish. Pour over the sauce and toss before serving.

Tossed Noodles

PREPARATION TIME: 20 minutes

MICROWAVE COOKING TIME: 10 minutes plus 5 minutes standing time

SERVES: 6 people

1lb Chinese egg noodles
4 cups boiling water

½ cup soy sauce mixed with 2 tbsps cornstarch
3oz lean steak, cut in short, thin strips
1 tbsp oil
½ cup brown stock
4 green onions, sliced
½ cucumber, sliced
1 small piece white radish, diced
Fresh coriander leaves (Chinese parsley)

Cook noodles as for Velvet Noodles. Heat a browning dish 5 minutes on HIGH. Pour in the oil and add the steak. Cook 2 minutes on HIGH. Stir in the soy sauce, cornstarch and the stock. Cover and cook 3 minutes on HIGH. Add more stock if the sauce is too thick. Add the onions, cucumber and radish to the sauce, and leave to stand 5 minutes before serving. Pour over noodles and toss before serving. Garnish with whole coriander leaves.

Ham and Bean Fried Rice

PREPARATION TIME: 15 minutes

MICROWAVE COOKING TIME: 9 minutes plus 2 minutes standing time

SERVES: 4 people

3 tbsps oil
2 eggs, beaten
Salt and pepper
½ cup ham, chopped
4oz green beans, cut in thin, diagonal slices
3 cups cooked rice
1 tbsp soy sauce
4 green onions, chopped

Heat a browning dish 5 minutes on HIGH. Pour in half the oil and half the beaten egg and cook for

Facing page: Shanghai Noodle Snack.

30 seconds on HIGH on one side. Turn over and cook for 30 seconds on the second side. Repeat with remaining egg. Keep the egg warm and add the remaining oil to the dish. Heat for 1 minute on HIGH and add the ham. Cover the dish and cook for 1 minute on HIGH. Add the rice and cook, covered, for 5 minutes on HIGH. Add the beans, soy sauce and onions. Cook 1 minute on HIGH and toss the ingredients to mix well. Slice the eggs into thin strips and scatter over the top of the rice. Cover the dish and leave to stand for 2 minutes before serving.

Eight Precious Rice

PREPARATION TIME: 20 minutes

MICROWAVE COOKING TIME: 10 minutes plus 2 minutes standing time

SERVES: 4 people

3 tbsps oil
4oz chicken, cut in ½ inch cubes
4oz frozen peas
2oz shrimp
¼ cup diced bamboo shoots
8 water chestnuts, sliced thinly
½ cup mushrooms, sliced thinly
4 green onions, chopped
3 cups cooked rice
2 eggs, beaten
2 tbsps soy sauce
Salt and pepper

Heat oil in a large bowl 1 minute on HIGH. Add the chicken and cook, stirring frequently, for 3 minutes on HIGH. Cover the bowl loosely. Add the rice and cook 5 minutes on HIGH to heat through. Add the remaining ingredients and cook 1 minute on HIGH. Leave to stand, covered, 2 minutes before serving.

Subgum Fried Rice

PREPARATION TIME: 15 minutes

MICROWAVE COOKING TIME: 7 minutes plus 2 minutes standing time

SERVES: 4 people

3 tbsps oil
3 cups cooked rice
2 sticks celery, cut into small dice
½ cup mushrooms, roughly chopped
½ red pepper, diced
3 eggs, beaten
1 tbsp light soy sauce
Dash sesame oil
Salt and pepper

GARNISH
2 green onions, sliced diagonally

Heat oil in a large bowl for 1 minute on HIGH. Add the rice and cook

5 minutes on HIGH, covered. Stir in the eggs, soy sauce and vegetables and cook 2 minutes on HIGH. Add the sesame oil, salt and pepper and leave to stand 2 minutes before serving. Garnish with onions.

This page: Eight Precious Rice (top) and Ham and Bean Fried Rice (bottom). Facing page: Tossed Noodles (top) and Velvet Noodles (bottom).

Sweet and Sour Sauce

PREPARATION TIME: 10 minutes

MICROWAVE COOKING TIME:
4 minutes

MAKES: 1 cup

1 cup pineapple or orange juice
1 tbsp brown sugar
1 tbsp cornstarch
1 clove garlic, minced
1 tbsp vinegar
1 tbsp soy sauce
2 tsps ketchup
Salt and pepper

Combine all the ingredients in a deep
bowl or glass measure. Cook 4
minutes on HIGH, stirring often after
1 minute, until the sauce thickens and
clears. Serve with appetizers, seafood,
pork or chicken.

Fried Rice with Egg

PREPARATION TIME: 15 minutes

MICROWAVE COOKING TIME:
8-10 minutes plus standing time

SERVES: 4 people

3 tbsps oil
2 green onions, finely chopped
3 cups cooked rice
3 eggs, beaten
2 tsps white wine
Salt and pepper
Dash sesame oil

GARNISH
2 green onions, shredded

Put the oil and the finely chopped
onions into a large bowl and heat for
1 minute on HIGH. Add the rice and
cook for 5-7 minutes on HIGH, until
very hot. Stir in the eggs, wine, salt,
pepper and sesame oil and cook for
2 minutes on HIGH. Stir carefully
and leave to stand, covered, several
minutes before serving. Garnish with
the shredded onions. Serve with soy
sauce, or as an accompaniment to
other dishes.

**Fried Rice with Egg (top) and
Subgum Rice (bottom).**

Microwave
CHINESE COOKING

SOUPS AND APPETIZERS

Corn and Crabmeat Soup

PREPARATION TIME: 10 minutes

MICROWAVE COOKING TIME:
4 minutes plus 5 minutes
standing time

SERVES: 4 people

2 8oz cans creamed corn
1 onion
4 cups chicken stock
1 small piece ginger root, peeled and
    grated
1 tsp sherry
2 tbsps cornstarch
8oz crabmeat
2 green onions
Salt

Combine the onion and corn in a
deep bowl. Cover and cook 1 minute
on HIGH to soften onion slightly.
Add the ginger, sherry, stock and
cornstarch mixed with 2 tbsps water.
Cook for 2-3 minutes until
thickened, stirring halfway through
cooking. Stir in the crabmeat,
reserving about 2 tbsps for garnish.
Leave to stand, covered, for
3 minutes before serving. Sprinkle
reserved crabmeat and green onion
on top of each serving.

**This page: Chinese Noodle Soup
with Pork Dumplings (top) and
Corn and Crabmeat Soup
(bottom). Facing page: Chicken
Corn Chowder with Almonds
(top) and Soup of Mushrooms and
Peas (bottom).**

Wonton Soup

PREPARATION TIME: 20 minutes

MICROWAVE COOKING TIME: 17-18 minutes

SERVES: 4 people

12 wonton skins
3oz ground pork
2 green onions, finely chopped
1 tsp garlic, finely chopped
Pinch five-spice powder
1 egg, beaten
4 cups chicken stock
2 tbsps light soy sauce
½ head Chinese cabbage

Heat the chicken stock 10 minutes on HIGH. Mix pork, onions, garlic, spice powder and stuff the wonton skins. Brush the edges with beaten egg. Fold wontons in triangles and seal well. Combine the water and soy sauce in a large, deep bowl and add the stuffed wontons. Partially cover the bowl and cook 5-6 minutes on HIGH, or until wontons are tender. Add the shredded Chinese cabbage and cook a further 2-3 minutes on HIGH.

Chinese Noodle Soup with Pork Dumplings

PREPARATION TIME: 20 minutes

MICROWAVE COOKING TIME: 10 minutes plus 1 minute standing time

SERVES: 4 people

8oz ground pork
½ tsp ground ginger
1 tbsp cornstarch
2 tbsps light soy sauce
4 cups stock
¼ package thin Chinese noodles
1 tbsp rice wine
4 green onions, sliced

Mix the cornstarch with the soy sauce. Combine with the pork and ginger. Shape into small balls. Heat the stock 5 minutes on HIGH in a large, deep bowl. Add the pork balls and cook 2 minutes on HIGH. Add the noodles and wine and cook a further 3 minutes on HIGH. Add the green onions and leave to stand 1 minute before serving.

Chicken Corn Chowder with Almonds

PREPARATION TIME: 15 minutes

MICROWAVE COOKING TIME: 5-8 minutes

SERVES: 4 people

2 8oz cans creamed corn
4 cups chicken stock
2 chicken breasts, finely chopped
2 tbsps cornstarch
2 tbsps rice wine
½ cup toasted almonds
Salt and pepper

Combine corn, stock and chicken in a large, deep bowl. Partially cover and cook 3-5 minutes or until chicken is nearly cooked. Combine rice wine, cornstarch and stir into the soup. Cook 2-3 minutes to allow cornstarch to thicken and clear. Sprinkle with toasted almonds and serve.

Shrimp and Lettuce Soup

PREPARATION TIME: 10 minutes

MICROWAVE COOKING TIME: 12 minutes plus 5 minutes standing time

SERVES: 4 people

12oz peeled shrimp
1 cup rice
4 cups hot chicken stock
1 piece fresh ginger root, grated
1 small head lettuce, shredded
Salt

Put the rice, stock and ginger into a large, deep bowl. Partially cover and cook 12 minutes on HIGH, stirring often. Cook until the rice softens completely. Add the shrimp, lettuce and salt. Leave the soup to stand, covered, for 5 minutes. Shrimp should heat through in the stock.

Soup of Mushrooms and Peas

PREPARATION TIME: 15 minutes

MICROWAVE COOKING TIME: 10 minutes

SERVES: 4 people

12 dried Chinese mushrooms, soaked 30 minutes
4oz ham, shredded
4 cups light stock
1 tbsp light soy sauce
2 cups fresh peas
Salt and pepper

Remove the stems and slice the mushrooms finely. Combine with the remaining ingredients and cook 10 minutes on HIGH or until peas are just tender.

Facing page: Shrimp and Lettuce Soup (top) and Wonton Soup (bottom).

Steamed Crabmeat and Egg Custard

PREPARATION TIME: 30 minutes

MICROWAVE COOKING TIME:
8-9 minutes

SERVES: 4 people

2 eggs, beaten
½ cup chicken stock
1 tbsp sherry
6oz cooked crabmeat
4 chopped green onions
3 chopped water chestnuts
2 finely chopped Chinese mushrooms,
*   pre-cooked 30 minutes*
1 tsp grated fresh ginger root
Salt

Mix the eggs, stock, sherry and add
the remaining ingredients. Spoon
into lightly oiled custard cups. Cover
loosely and arrange in a circle on the

**Above: Barbecued Spare Ribs.
Right: Steamed Crabmeat and Egg
Custard.**

turntable and cook 1 minute on
HIGH. Reduce to LOW/DEFROST
and cook for 7-8 minutes or until
softly set. Unmold onto plates and
serve with soy sauce. Surround with
shredded Chinese cabbage if desired.

Barbecued Spare Ribs

PREPARATION TIME: 10 minutes

MICROWAVE COOKING TIME:
20 minutes

SERVES: 4-6 people

3lbs pork spare ribs, cut up

MARINADE
¼ cup dark soy sauce
3 tbsps hoisin sauce
1 tsp grated fresh ginger root
1 tbsp honey

Mix all the marinade ingredients in a large bowl and cook on HIGH for 1 minute. Add the ribs and mix to coat well. Cover and refrigerate for several hours, turning the ribs occasionally. Transfer the ribs to a shallow dish. Baste well with sauce and cover the dish with plastic wrap and cook on HIGH for 10 minutes, basting the ribs several times. Turn the ribs over and cook an additional 10 minutes on HIGH. Brush with any remaining marinade before serving. Garnish with cucumber twists if desired.

Stuffed Mushrooms with Pork and Water Chestnuts

PREPARATION TIME: 30 minutes

MICROWAVE COOKING TIME: 4 minutes per batch

SERVES: 4 people

12 dried Chinese mushrooms
4oz ground pork
2 water chestnuts, finely chopped
1 stick celery, finely chopped
2 tsps soy sauce
1 tsp oyster sauce
Salt and pepper

GARNISH
4 green onions, sliced

Soak the mushrooms in hot water for 30 minutes. Mix all the remaining ingredients. Drain the mushrooms and reserve ½ cup of the soaking water. Pat the mushrooms dry on paper towels and cut off the stems. Combine remaining ingredients and fill the mushrooms with the pork mixture, smoothing out with a knife. Place the mushrooms in 1 layer in a shallow dish, stuffing-side up. Pour

This page: Stuffed Mushrooms with Pork and Water Chestnuts. Facing page: Garlic Shrimp with Salt and Pepper (top) and Chili Shrimp (bottom).

around the soaking water and cover the dish with pierced plastic wrap. Cook on HIGH for 4 minutes. Baste occasionally with the mushroom liquid. Transfer the mushrooms to a serving dish and sprinkle with the onions. Serve hot.

Garlic Shrimp with Salt and Pepper

PREPARATION TIME: 10-15 minutes

MICROWAVE COOKING TIME: 4½-5½ minutes

SERVES: 4 people

1lb jumbo shrimp
2 tbsps oil
2 cloves garlic, minced
3 tbsps oyster sauce
2 tbsps soy sauce
1 tbsp lemon juice

2 tsp coarsely ground black pepper
Salt

GARNISH
Green onion brushes

Prepare the shrimp as for Chili Shrimp. Put the oil and garlic into a bowl. Cover and cook 1 minute on HIGH. Add the oyster sauce, soy sauce, lemon juice and cook 30 seconds on HIGH. Stir in the shrimp and cook for 3-4 minutes on MEDIUM. Sprinkle with salt and pepper before serving. Garnish with green onion brushes (see introduction).

Steamed Chicken Wontons

PREPARATION TIME: 20 minutes
MICROWAVE COOKING TIME:
10 minutes per batch
SERVES: 4 people

10oz ground chicken
2 chopped green onions
2 chopped water chestnuts
Small piece ginger root, peeled and grated
2 tbsps light soy sauce
1 tbsp rice wine
1 tbsp sesame oil
1 egg, beaten
Pinch sugar
Salt and pepper
30 fresh wonton skins

Grind raw chicken in a food processor and combine with the remaining ingredients except the wonton skins. Place a teaspoonful of the mixture in the center of each wonton and twist the ends together to seal. Brush lightly with water if the ends won't stick together. Place wontons in one layer in a casserole dish and barely cover with water. Cover with plastic wrap. Cook in 2 batches for 2 minutes on HIGH and 8 minutes on LOW/ DEFROST. Remove with a draining spoon. Serve with Sweet and Sour and Hot Mustard sauces.

Chili Shrimp

PREPARATION TIME: 10-15 minutes
MICROWAVE COOKING TIME:
4½-5½ minutes
SERVES: 4 people

1lb jumbo shrimp
2 tbsps oil
2 cloves garlic, crushed
2 tbsps chili sauce (hot or sweet)
1 tbsp rice wine
1 tbsp lemon juice
Salt

GARNISH
Chili pepper flowers

Remove the heads and shells of the shrimp, but leave on the very ends of the tails. Wash, de-vein and pat dry. Put the oil and garlic into a bowl and cover with plastic wrap. Cook on HIGH 1 minute. Stir in the chili sauce, wine, lemon juice and salt. Cook 30 seconds on HIGH. Add the shrimp and cook for 3-4 minutes on MEDIUM. Serve hot or cold. Garnish with chili pepper flowers (see introduction).

Steamed Barbecued Pork Dumplings

PREPARATION TIME: 20 minutes
MICROWAVE COOKING TIME:
17-18 minutes per batch
SERVES: 4 people

2 tsps oil
10oz ground pork
1 clove garlic, minced
Pinch sugar
2 tbsps soy sauce
2 tbsps cornstarch mixed with 3 tbsps stock
½ cup hoisin sauce
30 wonton skins

Combine oil, pork and garlic in a casserole dish. Cover and cook on HIGH 5 minutes, breaking up the pork frequently with a fork as it cooks. Mix the sugar, soy sauce, cornstarch and stock. Add to the pork and cook a further 2-3 minutes until sauce thickens and clears. Stir in the hoisin sauce. Fill the wonton skins and pinch the edges together, but leave some of the filling exposed. Place in one layer in a shallow dish, and barely cover with water. Cover the dish with plastic wrap and cook 2 minutes on HIGH and 8 minutes on LOW/ DEFROST. Serve hot.

Facing page: Steamed Chicken Wontons (top) and Steamed Barbecued Pork Dumplings (bottom) – served with Sweet and Sour and Hot Mustard Sauces.

POULTRY

Singapore Chicken

PREPARATION TIME: 20 minutes

MICROWAVE COOKING TIME:
11 minutes plus 2 minutes
standing time

SERVES: 4 people

2 tbsps oil
2 tsps curry powder
1lb chicken, skinned, boned and cut into
bite-sized pieces
1 large onion, cut in large pieces
1 8oz can pineapple pieces, juice reserved
1 10oz can mandarin orange segments,
juice reserved
1 tbsp cornstarch
1 cup bean sprouts
Dash soy sauce
Salt and pepper

Heat the oil in a large casserole dish
for 30 seconds on HIGH. Add the
curry powder, and cook 30 seconds
on HIGH. Add the chicken, cover
the dish and cook 5 minutes on
HIGH. Add the onion, mix the
cornstarch with the reserved
pineapple and orange juice and add
to the chicken. Cover and cook
5 minutes on HIGH, stirring
occasionally after 1 minute. When
the sauce thickens, add the
pineapple, orange segments and bean
sprouts. Leave to stand 2 minutes
before serving. Serve with fried or
plain boiled rice.

**This page: Sesame Chicken with
Garlic Sauce (top) and Lemon
Chicken (bottom). Facing page:
Singapore Chicken.**

Lemon Chicken

PREPARATION TIME: 30 minutes

MICROWAVE COOKING TIME:
7-9 minutes plus 2 minutes
standing time

SERVES: 4 people

4 chicken breasts, skinned, boned and cut
  into thin strips
4 tbsps soy sauce
2 tsps dry sherry or shao-hsing wine
Salt and pepper

SAUCE
3 tbsps salted black beans
2 tbsps water
6 tbsps lemon juice
1 cup chicken stock
4 tbsps sugar
1 tsp sesame oil
3 tbsps cornstarch
2 cloves garlic, finely minced
¼ tsp red pepper flakes

GARNISH
Lemon slices

Mix chicken with marinade
ingredients, cover and refrigerate
30 minutes. Crush the black beans,
combine with the water and leave to
stand until ready to use. Combine
remaining sauce ingredients in a
shallow dish. Add the chicken,
marinade and black beans, cover and
cook on HIGH for 7-9 minutes,
stirring halfway through the cooking
time. Once the cornstarch has
cleared, leave the chicken to stand,
covered for 2 minutes before serving.
Garnish with lemon slices and serve
with rice.

Sesame Chicken with Garlic Sauce

PREPARATION TIME: 30 minutes

MICROWAVE COOKING TIME:
7-9 minutes plus 2 minutes
standing time

SERVES: 4 people

6 chicken thighs, skinned
1 tbsp sesame oil

4 cloves garlic, finely minced
1 tsp finely chopped ginger root
1½ tsp brown sugar
2 tbsps dark soy sauce
½ cup chicken stock
½ tsp black pepper
2 tsps cornstarch
6 green onions, sliced
4 tbsps sesame seeds
Salt

Bone the chicken thighs and cut the
meat into thin strips or small pieces.
Combine the garlic, sesame oil,
ginger root, sugar, soy sauce and
pepper and pour over the chicken in
a shallow dish. Cover and refrigerate
for 30 minutes. Mix the cornstarch
and stock, add to the chicken and
marinade and stir well. Cover the
dish and cook on HIGH for 4-9
minutes, stirring halfway through the
cooking time. Add the sesame seeds
and onions and leave to stand,
covered, 2 minutes before serving.
Serve with rice or Chinese noodles.

Chicken with Pea Pods

PREPARATION TIME: 20 minutes

MICROWAVE COOKING TIME:
8½-9½ minutes plus 2 minutes
standing time

SERVES: 4 people

2 tbsps oil
1lb chicken breasts, skinned, boned and
  cut into thin slivers
2 tsps cornstarch
3 tbsps rice wine
3 tbsps light soy sauce
2 tbsps oyster sauce
4 tbsps chicken stock
4oz pea pods
Dash sesame oil
Salt and pepper

Heat the oil 30 seconds on HIGH in
a large casserole dish. Mix the
remaining ingredients except the pea
pods and pour over the chicken.
Cover and cook 7-9 minutes on
HIGH, stirring halfway through the
cooking time. Add the pea pods,
re-cover the dish and cook 30

seconds on HIGH. Leave to stand
for 2 minutes before serving. Serve
with rice.

Chicken with Hoisin Sauce and Cashews

PREPARATION TIME: 20 minutes

MICROWAVE COOKING TIME:
7-9 minutes plus 2 minutes
standing time

SERVES: 4 people

1lb chicken, skinned, boned and cut into
  bite-sized pieces
1 tbsp cornstarch
1 cup stock
1 tbsp light soy sauce
1 clove garlic, finely minced
1 tbsp white wine
4 tbsps hoisin sauce
½ cup roasted cashew nuts
4 green onions, diagonally sliced

Combine the chicken with all the
ingredients except the nuts and
onions. Put into a casserole dish,
cover and cook on HIGH for 7-9
minutes, stirring halfway through the
cooking time. Once the sauce has
thickened and the cornstarch has
cleared, add the nuts and the green
onions. Re-cover the dish and leave
to stand 2 minutes before serving.
Serve with rice.

**Facing page: Chicken with Pea
Pods (top) and Chicken with
Hoisin Sauce and Cashews
(bottom).**

HIGH, add bamboo shoots and leave to stand, covered, 2 minutes before serving. Serve with fried or plain boiled rice.

Lacquered Duck with Plum Sauce

PREPARATION TIME: 25 minutes

MICROWAVE COOKING TIME: 43-48 minutes plus 10 minutes standing time

SERVES: 4 people

SAUCE
See Plum Sauce recipe

GLAZE
¼ cup honey
4 tbsps soy sauce

5lb duckling

GARNISH
¼ cup toasted, chopped almonds
Green onion brushes (see Introduction)

Brush the duckling with the honey and soy sauce glaze. Cook on rack on HIGH for 10 minutes. Turn over, brush with the glaze and cook 10 minutes on HIGH. Turn again and brush with some of the plum sauce. Lower the setting to MEDIUM and cook 15-30 minutes or until tender. Cover and leave to stand 10 minutes before cutting into 8 pieces with a cleaver or poultry shears. Pour over remaining plum sauce and sprinkle over the almonds. Garnish with onion brushes and serve with rice.

Diced Chicken and Peppers

PREPARATION TIME: 20 minutes

MICROWAVE COOKING TIME: 8½-10½ minutes plus 2 minutes standing time

SERVES: 4 people

2 tbsps oil
1 clove garlic, minced
1lb chicken, skinned, boned and diced
2 green peppers, diced
1 small red chili pepper, diced
½ small can bamboo shoots, diced
1 tsp cornstarch

2 tbsps white wine
2 tbsp soy sauce
4 tbsps chicken stock
Pinch sugar (optional)
Salt

Heat oil 30 seconds on HIGH in a large casserole dish. Add the garlic and cook 30 seconds on HIGH. Add the chicken and stir to coat with oil. Add the chili pepper, cornstarch, wine, soy sauce and stock. Stir well and cover the dish. Cook 7-9 minutes on HIGH, stirring halfway through the cooking time. Add the green pepper, sugar (if using) and salt if needed. Cook 30 seconds on

This page: Diced Chicken and Peppers. Facing page: Lacquered Duck with Plum Sauce.

Empress Chicken

PREPARATION TIME: 30 minutes

MICROWAVE COOKING TIME:
15 minutes plus 3 minutes
standing time

SERVES: 4 people

4 chicken wings
4 chicken breasts, skinned
12 dried Chinese mushrooms
½ cup soy sauce
2 cups chicken stock mixed with 3 tbsps
*   cornstarch*
1 tbsp sugar
2 pieces star anise
2 slices ginger root
1 tbsp rice wine
½ tsp salt
2 cans bamboo shoots, drained and cut in
*   strips if thick*
4 green onions, sliced

With a heavy cleaver, chop the
chicken, through the bones, into
large chunks. Remove any splinters of
bone. Soak the mushrooms in hot
water for 30 minutes. Drain and trim
off the stems. Put the chicken,
mushrooms and remaining
ingredients, except the onions and
bamboo shoots, into a deep
casserole. Cover well and cook
15 minutes on HIGH or until the
chicken is completely cooked. Add
the bamboo shoots and sliced
onions. Leave to stand 3 minutes and
remove star anise before serving.

Golden Chicken with Walnuts

PREPARATION TIME: 20 minutes

MICROWAVE COOKING TIME:
7-9 minutes plus 2 minutes
standing time

SERVES: 4 people

1lb chicken, skinned, boned and cut into
*   bite-sized pieces*
1 tbsp cornstarch
1 tbsp light soy sauce
1 tbsp sherry
1 cup stock

1 small can salted yellow beans
¾ cup walnuts, roughly chopped
½ small can sliced bamboo shoots

Combine chicken, cornstarch, soy
sauce, sherry, stock, and yellow beans
in a casserole dish. Cover and cook
on HIGH for 7-9 minutes, stirring
halfway through the cooking time.
Once the sauce has thickened, add
the walnuts and bamboo shoots.
Leave to stand 2 minutes before
serving.

Duck with Pineapple

PREPARATION TIME: 20 minutes

MICROWAVE COOKING TIME:
9-10 minutes

SERVES: 4 people

SAUCE
See Pineapple Sauce recipe

5lb duckling
2 tbsps oil
2 tbsps soy sauce

GARNISH
4 chives, shredded

Skin the duck and remove the leg
and breast meat. Cut into thin
slivers. Heat a browning dish
5 minutes on HIGH. Toss the oil and
duck together, and add to the
browning dish. Cook, uncovered,
4 minutes on HIGH. Add the soy
sauce, cover the dish and reduce the
setting to MEDIUM. Cook a further
3 minutes or until duck is tender.
Remove duck to a serving dish and
keep warm. Coat with the pineapple
sauce and sprinkle on the chives.
Serve with rice.

Duck with Five Spices

PREPARATION TIME: 20 minutes

MICROWAVE COOKING TIME:
30 minutes

SERVES: 4 people

5lb duckling
½ cup rice wine
½ cup light soy sauce
2 tbsps honey
1 clove garlic, finely minced
1 tbsp five-spice powder
4 tbsps chicken stock
2 tbsps cornstarch, dissolved in 3 tbsps
*   water*

Remove the meat from the legs and
breast of the duck. Take off the skin
and cut the meat into bite-sized
pieces. Combine with the remaining
ingredients, except the cornstarch
and water, in a casserole. Cover the
dish and cook on HIGH for 10
minutes. Reduce the setting and cook
an additional 20 minutes on
MEDIUM. Check the level of liquid
from time to time and add more
stock or water if necessary. When the
duck is cooked, add a few spoonfuls
of the cooking liquid to the
cornstarch and water. Return the
mixture to the casserole and cook on
HIGH for 2-3 minutes to thicken the
sauce. Serve with rice or stir-fried
vegetables. Garnish with Chinese
parsley if desired.

Duck with Onions

PREPARATION TIME: 20 minutes

MICROWAVE COOKING TIME:
42-58 minutes plus 10 minutes
standing time

SERVES: 4 people

5lb duck
⅓ cup soy sauce
2 pieces fresh ginger root, peeled and
*   grated*
3 tbsps white wine

**Facing page: Empress Chicken
(top) and Golden Chicken with
Walnuts (bottom).**

1 tbsp sugar
2 tbsps cornstarch dissolved in 2 tbsps
*   water*
10 green onions
1 small can sliced bamboo shoots
4 Chinese mushrooms, soaked and sliced
Salt

Combine the soy sauce and grated ginger and brush over the breast side of the duck. Place the duck on a rack and cook for 10 minutes on HIGH. Turn over, brush with the soy sauce and cook 10 minutes on HIGH. Place in a very large casserole or bowl. Add 3 green onions, wine and 1 cup water. Cover the bowl or casserole and cook 15-30 minutes or until tender. Remove the duck and keep warm. Discard the cooked onions. Skim off fat from the cooking liquid and mix a spoonful of the liquid with the cornstarch and water and the sugar. Add the bamboo shoots, mushrooms and remaining onions, sliced, to the sauce. Cook for 2-3 minutes on HIGH until thick and clear. Cut the duck into 8 pieces and pour over the sauce to serve.

This page: Duck with Pineapple. Facing page: Duck with Five Spices (top) and Duck with Onions (bottom).

MEAT DISHES

Szechuan Beef

PREPARATION TIME: 20 minutes

MICROWAVE COOKING TIME:
6-18 minutes

SERVES: 4 people

1lb rump steak, shredded
2 tbsp oil
½ dried chili pepper, crushed
4 tbsps soy sauce
½ cup stock
2 tbsps cornstarch
3 sticks celery, shredded
1 sweet red pepper, shredded

Heat a browning dish for 5 minutes on HIGH. Combine meat and oil and add to the dish. Cook 2 minutes on HIGH in 2 or 3 batches. Re-heat browning dish 2 minutes after each batch. Add the crushed chili pepper. Mix the soy sauce and stock and gradually stir into the cornstarch. Pour over the steak and cook 2-3 minutes. Add the celery and red pepper and mix together with the meat and sauce. Cook a further 1 minute on HIGH until the sauce has thickened but the vegetables are still crisp.

Beef with Broccoli

PREPARATION TIME: 20 minutes

MICROWAVE COOKING TIME:
7-8 minutes

SERVES: 4 people

1lb rump steak, cut in thin strips
3 tbsps oil
¼ cup soy sauce
1 tbsp cornstarch

1 tbsp sherry
1 tsp sugar
⅓ cup stock
½ bunch broccoli
2 tsps grated ginger root
Salt and pepper

Heat a browning dish 5 minutes on HIGH. Mix the beef and oil and add to the dish. Cook 2 minutes on HIGH in 2 or 3 batches. Slice the stalks of the broccoli thinly on the diagonal. Separate the flowerets into small pieces. Toss in the oil with the

**This page: Beef with Broccoli.
Facing page: Peking Sweet Lamb
(top) and Szechuan Beef (bottom).**

meat and cook for 1 minute on HIGH. Leave to stand covered while preparing the sauce. Mix the soy sauce, cornstarch, sherry, sugar and ginger root in a small bowl. Cook 2-3 minutes on HIGH, until thickened.

Stir several times after 1 minute's cooking. Pour over the beef and broccoli. Cook a further 1 minute on HIGH. Adjust the seasoning and serve immediately with rice or noodles.

Beef with Tree Ears

PREPARATION TIME: 30 minutes

MICROWAVE COOKING TIME: 7-8 minutes

SERVES: 4 people

8 pieces dried black fungi (tree or wood ears)
1lb rump steak, cut in thin strips
3 tbsps oil
4 tbsps soy sauce
1 tbsp rice wine
2 tsps chili sauce (sweet or hot)
⅓ cup stock
1 tbsp cornstarch
1 small bunch chives, chopped

Soak the tree ears for 20 minutes in hot water. Heat a browning dish for 5 minutes on HIGH. Combine oil and meat and add to the dish. Cook 2 minutes on HIGH in 2 or 3 batches. Re-heat dish 2 minutes after each batch. Drain the tree ears well and add whole to the steak in the browning dish. Cook 1 minute on HIGH, turning once. Mix the remaining ingredients, except the chives, together and pour over the meat and tree ears. Cook 2-3 minutes on HIGH, until the sauce thickens and clears. Sprinkle over the chopped chives before serving.

Peking Sweet Lamb

PREPARATION TIME: 1 hour

MICROWAVE COOKING TIME: 8-9 minutes plus 2 minutes standing time

SERVES: 4 people

1lb lamb fillet or meat from the leg, thinly sliced
2 tbsps hoisin sauce
1 tbsp rice wine
1 tbsp sesame oil
2 tbsps sugar
2 tbsps light soy sauce
2 tbsps vinegar
1 tbsp rice wine
1 tbsp cornstarch
½ cup plus 1 tbsp brown stock
1 tsp grated fresh ginger root

GARNISH
4 green onions, diagonally sliced

Mix the lamb, hoisin sauce and 1 tbsp rice wine. Set aside for 1 hour. Combine the sesame oil and sugar in a casserole dish. Heat for 1 minute on HIGH and stir. Add the lamb to the casserole, cover and cook 2 minutes on HIGH. Lower the setting to MEDIUM. Mix the remaining ingredients together, except for the garnish, and pour over the lamb. Cook for 5-7 minutes more, or until lamb is tender. Leave to stand for 2 minutes before serving, garnished with the sliced green onions.

Steamed Beef Balls with Two Different Mushrooms

PREPARATION TIME: 30 minutes

MICROWAVE COOKING TIME: 11-14 minutes

SERVES: 4-6 people

20 dried Chinese mushrooms
12oz ground beef
3 tbsps light soy sauce
2 tsps dry sherry
2 tsps grated fresh ginger root
Salt and pepper
24 fresh or frozen shelled peas
12-14oz Chinese straw mushrooms or small button mushrooms
2 tbsps cornstarch dissolved in 3 tbsps water

Soak the dried mushrooms for 30 minutes in hot water. Combine the ground beef, half the soy sauce, sherry, ginger, salt and pepper and shape into 24 small balls. Press one pea into the top of each beef ball. Arrange in a glass dish with space between each ball if possible. Combine the remaining soy sauce

with 1 cup water. Pour over the beef balls and cover loosely with plastic wrap film. Cook on HIGH for 8-10 minutes. Turn the beef balls over and rearrange them once or twice during cooking. Make sure that those in the center are brought to the outside of the dish. When the beef balls are cooked, remove to a serving dish and keep warm. Arrange in rows or in a circle, pea-side up. Skim the fat from the top of the cooking liquid. Combine the cornstarch with a spoonful of liquid. Stir into the remaining liquid in the dish and mix well. Cook for 2-3 minutes on HIGH, stirring after 1 minute. Add the two different mushrooms and cook until the sauce thickens. Arrange the mushrooms on the serving dish, keeping the two different kinds separate. Pour over the sauce to serve.

Pink and Silver Pork

PREPARATION TIME: 15 minutes

MICROWAVE COOKING TIME: 11-16 minutes

SERVES: 4 people

8oz pork tenderloin, cut into thin shreds
8oz ham, cut into thin strips
1 cup light stock
4 tbsps rice wine
2 tbsps light soy sauce
1 clove garlic, finely minced
1 small piece fresh ginger root, grated
1 tbsp cornstarch mixed with 2 tbsps water
4oz bean sprouts

Combine all the ingredients, except the bean sprouts, in a large casserole dish and cover. Cook for 10-15 minutes on MEDIUM, stirring

Facing page: Steamed Beef Balls with Two Different Mushrooms (top) and Beef with Tree Ears (bottom).

halfway through the cooking time. Add the bean sprouts and cook a further 1 minute on HIGH. Leave to stand 2 minutes before serving.

Pork Chops, Shanghai Style

PREPARATION TIME: 15 minutes

MICROWAVE COOKING TIME: 14 minutes

SERVES: 4 people

⅓ cup soy sauce
1 tbsp brown sugar
1 tbsp oil
8 thin pork chops
1 onion, thinly sliced
2 tsps cornstarch mixed with 2 tsps water

Mix the soy sauce and sugar with ½ cup water. Heat a browning dish 5 minutes on HIGH. Pour in the oil and brown the pork on both sides about 2 minutes on HIGH. Brown in two batches if necessary. Remove the pork and add the onions. Cook to brown and soften slightly. Remove the onions from the browning dish and set aside. Return the pork chops to the dish and pour over the soy sauce mixture. Cover and cook a further 5 minutes on HIGH, or until the pork is tender. Remove the pork and keep warm. Mix the cornstarch and water with the soy sauce mixture. Stir well and cook 1 minute on HIGH to thicken slightly. Add the onions and cook a further 1 minute on HIGH. Pour over the pork to serve. Serve with stir-fried vegetables. Garnish with Chinese parsley leaves if desired.

Kung-Pao Lamb

PREPARATION TIME: 20 minutes

MICROWAVE COOKING TIME: 10½-11½ minutes

SERVES: 4 people

1lb lamb fillet or meat from the leg, thinly sliced
2 tbsps oil
1 clove garlic, finely minced
1 small piece fresh ginger root, grated
½ red chili pepper, finely chopped
4 tbsps soy sauce
½ cup stock
2 tbsps white wine
1 tsp vinegar
1 tsp sugar
1 tbsp cornstarch
1 small red pepper, cut in small dice
1 small green pepper, cut in small dice
4 green onions, sliced
½ cup roasted peanuts
Dash sesame oil

Heat a browning dish for 5 minutes on HIGH. Combine oil and lamb and add to the dish. Cook for about 2 minutes, turning often. Cook in

This page: **Kung Pao Lamb.** Facing page: **Pork Chops, Shanghai Style (top) and Lion's Head (bottom).**

two batches if necessary. Add the garlic, ginger and chili pepper and cook a further 2 minutes on HIGH. Mix the soy sauce, stock, wine, vinegar, sugar and cornstarch together and add to the meat. Cover the browning dish or transfer the ingredients to a covered casserole dish. Cook on MEDIUM a further 4-6 minutes or until the lamb is tender. Add the diced peppers and cook a further 1 minute on HIGH. Stir in the sesame oil, peanuts and the green onions. Heat 30 seconds on HIGH. Serve with rice.

Pork in Plum Sauce with Almonds

PREPARATION TIME: 30 minutes

MICROWAVE COOKING TIME:
11-18 minutes

SERVES: 4 people

SAUCE
Plum Sauce recipe
1 purple or red plum, thinly sliced

1lb pork tenderloin, cut in thin slices
2 tbsps oil
2 tbsps soy sauce

GARNISH
½ cup toasted whole almonds

When the plum sauce is ready, add the thinly sliced plum, keep the bowl covered and set aside while preparing the pork. Heat a browning dish for 5 minutes on HIGH. Pour in the oil and add the pork. Cook for 2 minutes on HIGH, stirring often. Add the soy sauce, cover the dish and cook for 5-7 minutes more on MEDIUM. When the pork is tender, pour over the plum sauce and heat for 1 minute on HIGH. Serve sprinkled with the toasted almonds.

Lion's Head

PREPARATION TIME: 20 minutes

MICROWAVE COOKING TIME:
19-20 minutes

SERVES: 4-6 people

2lbs ground pork
⅓ cup soy sauce
2 tsps dry sherry
1 tsp brown sugar
¼ cup cornstarch
2 tbsps oil
1 tsp granulated sugar
1½ tbsps soy sauce
1 head Chinese cabbage
Salt (if necessary)

Mix pork, ⅓ cup soy sauce, sherry, brown sugar, 1 tbsp cornstarch and shape into 2 inch balls. Heat a

browning dish 5 minutes on HIGH. Add the oil and the pork balls. Brown the pork balls 3-5 minutes on HIGH, turning often. Cook in 2 batches, re-heating the dish in between each batch. If the browning dish has a cover, leave the pork balls in it or transfer to a large casserole. Add the granulated sugar, remaining soy sauce and 1 cup water. Cover and cook 9 minutes on HIGH. Turn the pork balls often and rearrange to bring those in the middle of the dish to the outside. Shred the Chinese cabbage finely and add it to the casserole with the pork balls. Cook 1 minute on HIGH. Remove the pork

This page: Pink and Silver Pork (top) and Pork in Plum Sauce with Almonds (bottom). Facing page: Jade and Ivory Pork.

and Chinese cabbage to a serving dish and keep warm. Mix the remaining cornstarch with 2 tbsps water and add to the cooking liquid from the pork balls. Cook 2-3 minutes, uncovered, on HIGH or until the sauce has thickened. Arrange the cabbage on a serving dish with the pork balls on top. Pour over the sauce to serve.

Jade and Ivory Pork

PREPARATION TIME: 30 minutes

MICROWAVE COOKING TIME: 10-12 minutes

SERVES: 4 people

1lb pork tenderloin, cut in very fine strips
3 tbsps oil
3 tbsps yellow beans
4 tbsps light soy sauce
2 tbsps rice wine
1 tbsp cornstarch
¾ cup chicken stock
8oz can bamboo shoots, cut in strips if necessary
1 large green pepper, cut in strips about the same size as bamboo shoots

Heat a browning dish for 5 minutes on HIGH. Mix meat and oil and add to the dish. Cook for 2 minutes on HIGH, stirring often. Combine the yellow beans, soy sauce, wine, cornstarch and stock. Mix very well and pour over the pork. Cover the dish or transfer to a covered casserole and cook for 5-7 minutes on MEDIUM, stirring halfway through the cooking time. Cook on HIGH for 2 minutes until thickened. Add the pepper and bamboo shoots and cook a further 1 minute on HIGH. Serve with rice or noodles.

Beef with Green Pepper, Tomato and Black Beans

PREPARATION TIME: 30 minutes

MICROWAVE COOKING TIME: 8-10 minutes

SERVES: 4 people

1lb rump steak, cut in thin slices
4 tbsps soy sauce
2 tsps dry sherry or rice wine

SAUCE
3 tbsps salted black beans
2 tbsps water
1 cup brown stock
1 tbsp sugar
3 tbsps cornstarch dissolved in the stock
1 clove garlic, finely minced
1 large green pepper, cut in 1 inch pieces
3 tomatoes, peeled and quartered
Salt and pepper

Mix the steak, soy sauce and wine and leave to marinate, covered, in the refrigerator for 30 minutes. Crush the black beans and mix with the water. Leave to stand until ready to use. Combine all the ingredients in a shallow dish, except for the pepper and tomatoes. Cover the dish and cook on HIGH for 7-9 minutes, stirring halfway through the cooking

This page: Beef with Green Pepper, Tomato and Black Beans. Facing page: Shrimp with Pea Pods and Corn.

time. Once the sauce has cleared, add the pepper and tomatoes and cook 1 minute further on HIGH. Serve with rice. Garnish with green onion brushes if desired.

FISH AND SEAFOOD

Shrimp with Pea Pods and Corn

PREPARATION TIME: 20 minutes

MICROWAVE COOKING TIME:
5-8 minutes

SERVES: 4 people

1½ lbs shelled jumbo shrimp, uncooked
3 tbsps oil
1 clove garlic, minced
1 small piece ginger root, minced
4 tbsps light stock
4 tbsps light soy sauce
4 tbsps rice wine
2 tsps cornstarch
2 tbsps Chinese parsley
2oz pea pods
4oz baby ears of corn
Salt

Heat a browning dish for 5 minutes on HIGH. Shell and de-vein the shrimp if necessary. Add the oil to the dish and the shrimp. Add the garlic and ginger and cook for 1-2 minutes on HIGH, stirring often. Combine the stock, soy sauce, wine and cornstarch. Pour over the shrimp and cook for 3-4 minutes on MEDIUM, stirring halfway through the cooking time. Cut the stalks off the pea pods and add with the ears of corn to the dish. Cut the corn in half lengthwise if the ears are large. Cook for 1-2 minutes on MEDIUM, until the sauce thickens and clears. If the shrimp are cooked after 3-4 minutes, remove them before adding the vegetables. Serve with rice or noodles.

Sweet and Sour Shrimp

PREPARATION TIME: 20 minutes

MICROWAVE COOKING TIME:
4-5 minutes plus 2 minutes
standing time

SERVES: 4 people

SAUCE
Double recipe Sweet and Sour Sauce.
Use reserved pineapple juice made up to
2 cups with more canned juice.

1 large green pepper, cut in 1 inch pieces
4 tomatoes, peeled and quartered
4 green onions, cut in 1 inch pieces
8oz can pineapple pieces, juice reserved
1½ lbs shelled shrimp, de-veined

Prepare the Sweet and Sour Sauce.
Add the green pepper to the hot
sauce and cook 1 minute on HIGH.
Add the pineapple, tomatoes, onions,
shrimp and cover tightly. Leave to
stand 3 minutes before serving. Serve
with rice.

Embroidered Crabmeat Balls

PREPARATION TIME: 25 minutes

MICROWAVE COOKING TIME:
5-6 minutes

SERVES: 4-6 people

1lb crabmeat
2-3 egg whites
1 tsp salt
Pinch pepper
1 tbsp sherry
1 tbsp cornstarch
½ green pepper, finely chopped
¼ red pepper, finely chopped
2 tbsps finely chopped ham
2 green onions, finely chopped
3 large leaves Chinese cabbage, chopped
½ tsp ground ginger
1 cup hot chicken stock
2 tbsps cornstarch
2 tbsps light soy sauce
Dash sesame oil

Mix the first 11 ingredients, adding
only 2 egg whites. If the mixture is
dry and crumbly, add some of the
remaining white until the mixture
will hold together. Shape into 1 inch
balls. The balls should not be
smooth. Place in a single layer in a
large, shallow dish. Pour around the
hot stock and cover the dish. Cook
3 minutes on HIGH, rearranging the
balls once during cooking to bring
the ones in the center of the dish to
the outside. Remove the balls and
keep warm. Mix the remaining
cornstarch with the soy sauce in a
glass measure and gradually add the
stock. Stir well and cook 2-3 minutes
on HIGH, until thickened. Add the
sesame oil and pour over the
crabmeat balls to serve.

Scallops in Pepper Sauce

PREPARATION TIME: 20 minutes

MICROWAVE COOKING TIME:
13-15 minutes

SERVES: 4 people

1lb scallops, shelled and cleaned, roe
attached if possible
½ clove garlic, finely chopped
3 tbsps rice wine
3 tbsps light soy sauce
1 tbsp cornstarch dissolved in ⅓ cup light
stock
4 tbsps sweet chili sauce
1 small piece fresh ginger root, peeled and
chopped
1 green pepper, thinly sliced
4 green onions, sliced or shredded
Pinch sugar
Salt and pepper

If the scallops are large, cut in half,
horizontally. Place in a casserole dish
with the garlic, wine, soy sauce, sugar
and salt and pepper. Cover the dish
and cook for 10 minutes on
MEDIUM. Remove the scallops
and keep warm. Add the cornstarch
and stock to the hot cooking liquid
and stir well. Add the chili sauce and
ginger root and cook 2-3 minutes, or
until thickened. Add the green
pepper and onions to the sauce and
return the scallops to the dish. Cook
1-2 minutes on HIGH, until the
scallops are cooked and the
vegetables are still crisp. Serve with
rice.

Pineapple Shrimp with Peppers

PREPARATION TIME: 20 minutes

MICROWAVE COOKING TIME:
6-7 minutes

SERVES: 4 people

SAUCE
Pineapple Sauce recipe with
2 tbsps rice wine
2 tbsps light soy sauce
1 large green pepper, cut in thin strips

1½ lbs shelled jumbo shrimp, de-veined
3 tbsps oil

Add the rice wine and soy sauce to
the Pineapple Sauce recipe. If the
sauce is still too thick, thin with a
spoonful of water. Heat a browning
dish 5 minutes on HIGH. Pour in the
oil and add the shrimp. Cook 1
minute on HIGH. Pour over the
sauce, add the strips of pepper and
cook 3 minutes on MEDIUM. Do
not overcook or shrimp will toughen.
Serve with rice.

Facing page: Sweet and Sour
Shrimp (top) and Scallops in
Pepper Sauce (bottom).

2 tbsps cornstarch
3 fl oz vinegar
2 tbsps light soy sauce
2 carrots, thinly sliced
1 clove garlic, minced
2 green onions, sliced
Salt and pepper

Place the trout in a shallow dish with the sherry, ginger and enough water to just cover the fish. Cover the dish with pierced plastic wrap and cook 8-9 minutes on HIGH. Remove the fish to a serving dish and peel off the skin from one side. Cover and keep warm. Reserve the cooking liquid from the fish. Combine the remaining ingredients except the green onions and carrots in a deep bowl. Cook for 2-3 minutes on HIGH or until the sauce thickens and clears. Thin down the sauce with some of the fish cooking liquid until of thick coating consistency. Add the carrots and onions and cook 1 minute on HIGH. Pour over some of the sauce to serve with the fish and serve the rest of the sauce separately.

Shrimp with Peas

PREPARATION TIME: 15 minutes

MICROWAVE COOKING TIME:
3 minutes plus 2 minutes standing time

SERVES: 4 people

1½ lbs shelled jumbo shrimp
1 tbsp cornstarch
2 tbsps rice wine
⅓ cup light stock
2 tbsps light soy sauce
Dash sesame oil
½ cup frozen peas

Shell and de-vein the shrimp and set aside. Combine the remaining ingredients, except the peas, in a deep bowl. Cook for 2-3 minutes on HIGH, or until the sauce thickens, stirring after 1 minute. Add the shrimp, lower the setting to MEDIUM and cook for about 3 minutes. Check the shrimp after 2 minutes. They must not overcook or they will toughen. Add the frozen peas during the last 1 minute of cooking. Add salt if necessary and serve with rice or noodles.

Sweet and Sour Fish

PREPARATION TIME: 15 minutes

MICROWAVE COOKING TIME:
11-13 minutes

SERVES: 4 people

4 trout, cleaned and trimmed
2 tbsps sherry
1 small piece ginger root, peeled and sliced
½ cup brown sugar

Squid with Shrimp and Tomatoes

PREPARATION TIME: 25 minutes

MICROWAVE COOKING TIME:
4-5 minutes

SERVES: 4 people

8oz squid, cleaned
8oz shrimp, peeled
2 tbsps oil

This page: Sweet and Sour Fish. Facing page: Pineapple Shrimp with Peppers (top) and Shrimp with Peas (bottom).

SAUCE
¾ cup stock
2 tbsps rice wine
1 tbsp soy sauce
2 tbsps tomato paste
1 tbsp cornstarch
¼ tsp ground ginger
Salt and pepper
4 tomatoes, peeled and sliced

Heat the oil in a casserole dish for 30 seconds on HIGH. Cut the squid into rings and add to the oil with the shrimp. Stir to coat and cook, covered, on MEDIUM for 2 minutes. Set aside. If using cooked shrimp, add to the squid after 2 minutes. Combine all the sauce ingredients, except the tomatoes. Cook for 2-3 minutes on HIGH or until sauce has thickened. Add the tomatoes and pour over the squid. Leave to stand a few minutes to reheat the seafood. Serve with rice.

Crystal Steamed Sea Bass

PREPARATION TIME: 30 minutes

MICROWAVE COOKING TIME: 16-18 minutes

SERVES: 4 people

2¼ lb sea bass, cleaned and trimmed
1 small piece fresh ginger root, thinly sliced
1 cup white wine
1 cup water
2 tbsps vegetable oil and sesame oil mixed
1-2 carrots, cut in very fine shreds
6 green onions, cut in very fine shreds
1 tsp cornstarch
2 tbsps light soy sauce
Salt

Sprinkle the fish lightly with salt and place in a large, shallow dish or into a cooking bag. Cover head and tail with foil. Put the slices of ginger root into the cavity and pour over the wine and water. Cover the dish or seal the bag. Cook 14-16 minutes on MEDIUM, removing foil for the last 4-6 minutes. Leave to stand while preparing the vegetables. Heat a browning dish for 4 minutes on

This page: Crystal Steamed Sea Bass. Facing page: Squid with Shrimp and Tomatoes (top) and Embroidered Crabmeat Balls (bottom).

HIGH. Pour in the oil and add the carrots and onions. Cook, uncovered for 2 minutes on HIGH. Remove the fish to a serving dish. Strain the stock through cheesecloth to remove any sediment and add 1 tsp cornstarch and cook 2-3 minutes on HIGH. Pour over the fish. Sprinkle on the soy sauce and swirl through the clear stock. Sprinkle or arrange the vegetables before serving. Garnish with a sprig of Chinese parsley.

Fish Steamed on Lotus Leaves

PREPARATION TIME: 25 minutes

MICROWAVE COOKING TIME: 13-16 minutes

SERVES: 4 people

4 small fish such as red mullet or small trout
4 dried Chinese mushrooms, soaked 30 minutes in hot water
3 tbsps shrimp
2 tbsps oil
4 strips bacon, diced
1 small piece fresh ginger root, slivered
4 green onions, finely chopped
2 tbsps soy sauce
1 cup stock
2 tbsps cornstarch, dissolved in 4 tbsps of

Cantonese Lobster

PREPARATION TIME: 30 minutes

MICROWAVE COOKING TIME:
5-6 minutes plus 1 minute
standing time

SERVES: 4 people

1 1¼-1½ lb cooked lobster
2 tsps black beans soaked in 2 tbsps water
4-6 dried Chinese mushrooms, soaked
   30 minutes in hot water
2 tsps soy sauce
½ cup plus 2 tbsps light stock
4 tbsps rice wine
1 clove garlic, minced
1½ tbsps cornstarch dissolved in 4 tbsps
   mushroom soaking liquid
3 tbsps chives
1oz pea pods
4 leaves Chinese cabbage, cut into 1 inch
   strips
1½ oz bean sprouts
5 water chestnuts, sliced
Salt and pepper

Combine the soy sauce, stock, wine
and cornstarch. Cook in a deep bowl
for 2-3 minutes on HIGH, or until
the sauce thickens. If it is too thick,
add more of the mushroom soaking
liquid. Drain and slice the Chinese
mushrooms and add to the sauce
with the black beans, slightly
crushed. Remove the tail and claw
meat from the lobster and as much of
the leg meat as possible. Cut the
meat into ½ inch pieces, leaving the
claws whole if desired. Add the
vegetables to the sauce and cook 2
minutes on HIGH. Stir in the lobster
and leave covered for 1 minute before
serving. Use the whole claws without
their shells as garnish if desired.

**This page: Fish Steamed on Lotus
Leaves. Facing page: Cantonese
Lobster.**

the mushroom liquid
Salt and pepper
Sliced lotus root or bamboo shoots, cut in
   thin strips
2-4 lotus leaves, depending on size

Trim off the fins of the fish and trim
the tails neatly. Set fish aside in the
refrigerator until ready to cook.
Heat a browning dish for 5 minutes
on HIGH. Pour in the oil and add the
bacon. Cook 1 minute until beginning
to brown. Drain the mushrooms and
the shrimp. Dice the mushrooms and
add to the bacon along with the
shrimp, onions and ginger. Cook a
further 1 minute on HIGH or until
bacon is crisp. Place 1 or 2 lotus
leaves in the bottom of a large,
shallow dish. Lay the fish on top and
scatter over the bacon mixture.
Cover the fish with the remaining
lotus leaves and pour over the soy
sauce and stock. Cover the dish and
cook the fish on HIGH for 9-11
minutes. When the fish are cooked,
remove them and the lotus leaves
from the dish and keep them warm.
Add the cornstarch to the fish
cooking liquid and stir well. Add salt
and pepper and cook for 2-3 minutes
on HIGH, or until the sauce has
thickened. Add the lotus root or
bamboo shoots. Remove the top
layer of lotus leaves and serve the
fish on the bottom leaves with the
sauce.

Sesame Crab in Asparagus Ring

PREPARATION TIME: 20 minutes

MICROWAVE COOKING TIME:
9-10 minutes

SERVES: 4 people

3 tbsps sesame paste (tahini)
2 tbsps light soy sauce
½ cup light stock
2 tbsps sherry
1 tbsp cornstarch
2 tbsps Szechwan peppercorns
2 tbsps oil
1lb asparagus, fresh or frozen, cut on the
   diagonal into 2 inch pieces
2 tbsps Chinese parsley leaves, left whole
4 green onions, thinly sliced or shredded
Salt
Pinch sugar (optional)
1lb crabmeat (including some pink claw
   meat)

Sesame seeds

Combine the first 6 ingredients in
a deep bowl. Cook for 2-3 minutes
on HIGH, until thick, and set aside.
Heat a browning dish 5 minutes on
HIGH. Pour in the oil and add the
asparagus. Stir-fry on HIGH for
4 minutes. If further cooking is
needed, cover the dish and cook 1
minute on HIGH. Add the Chinese
parsley, green onions and crabmeat to
the reserved sauce. Reheat 1 minute
on HIGH. Add salt and sugar if
desired. Arrange the asparagus pieces

**This page: Sesame Crab in
Asparagus Ring. Facing page:
Kung Pao Shrimp (top) and
Crabmeat Egg Foo Yung,
Cantonese (bottom).**

in a ring on a serving dish and pile
the crabmeat mixture into the center.
Sprinkle with sesame seeds to serve.

2 heaped tbsps of the egg mixture at a time. Cook 2-4 patties at a time for 2-3 minutes on MEDIUM on the first side, turn over and cook 1-2 minutes on the other. Re-heat browning dish after each batch. Keep warm while making the sauce. Combine all the sauce ingredients in a deep bowl. Cook, uncovered, 2-3 minutes on HIGH or until the sauce thickens and clears. Pour over the Egg Foo Yung to serve.

Kung Pao Shrimp

PREPARATION TIME: 20 minutes

MICROWAVE COOKING TIME: 5 minutes plus 2 minutes standing time

SERVES: 4 people

1lb shelled jumbo shrimp, de-veined
1 tsp chopped fresh ginger root
1 tsp chopped garlic
Salt and pepper
¼ tsp sugar
1 small onion, coarsely chopped
1 zucchini cut into ½ inch cubes
½ cup roasted cashew nuts

SAUCE
1 tbsp cornstarch
½ cup stock
4 tbsps soy sauce
1 tsp red bean paste (optional)
1 tsp sesame oil
1 tbsp shao-hsing wine or rice wine

Combine the shrimp, ginger, garlic, sugar, salt and pepper in a casserole dish. Cover and refrigerate for 20 minutes. Combine all the sauce ingredients and pour over the shrimp. Cover and cook for 3 minutes on MEDIUM. Stir often and do not allow the shrimp to overcook. Add the remaining ingredients and cook 2 minutes on HIGH. Leave to stand 2 minutes before serving. Serve with rice.

Crabmeat Egg Foo Yung, Cantonese

PREPARATION TIME: 20 minutes

MICROWAVE COOKING TIME: 10-13 minutes

SERVES: 4 people

6 eggs
1 cup crabmeat
2 sticks celery, thinly sliced
6 large mushrooms, thinly sliced
1 cup bean sprouts
½ onion, thinly sliced
1 tsp sherry
Salt and pepper

2 tbsps oil

SAUCE
1 tbsp cornstarch
1 tsp sugar
1 cup chicken stock
2 tsp soy sauce
1 tsp sherry
1 tsp sesame oil
½ tsp ketchup
Salt

Heat a browning dish 5 minutes on HIGH. Beat the eggs and mix in the remaining ingredients except the oil and those for the sauce. Add oil to the browning dish and spoon in

VEGETABLES

Spinach, Chinese Style

PREPARATION TIME: 15 minutes

MICROWAVE COOKING TIME:
2 minutes plus 1 minute
standing time

SERVES: 4 people

1½ lbs fresh spinach, stalks removed
2 tbsps oil
Salt
Sugar
Soy sauce
2 green onions, white part only, finely
    sliced

Wash the spinach well and pat the
leaves dry. Heat a browning dish for
4 minutes on HIGH. Pour in the oil
and add the spinach. Add a pinch of
salt and sugar and cook, uncovered,
for 2 minutes on HIGH, stirring
frequently. Add the green onions and
a dash of soy sauce. Leave to stand
1 minute before serving.

Sweet-Sour Cabbage

PREPARATION TIME: 20 minutes

MICROWAVE COOKING TIME:
11-13 minutes

SERVES: 4 people

**This page: Spinach, Chinese Style
(top) and Spicy Cucumbers
(bottom). Facing page: Sweet-Sour
Cabbage.**

1 medium head white cabbage,
 about 2lbs
1 small red chili pepper (use less if desired)
½ cup light brown sugar
⅓ cup rice vinegar
2 tbsps light soy sauce
Salt
3 tbsps oil

Cut the cabbage into ½ inch slices, discarding the core. Cut the chili pepper into thin, short strips, discarding the seeds. Mix all the ingredients together except the oil. Pour the oil into a large bowl and heat for 2 minutes on HIGH. Add the cabbage and the liquid and cover the bowl with pierced plastic wrap. Cook on HIGH for 9-11 minutes. Allow to cool in the bowl, stirring frequently. When cold, refrigerate. Keeps several days.

Ten Varieties of Beauty

PREPARATION TIME: 20 minutes

MICROWAVE COOKING TIME:
6-8 minutes

SERVES: 4-6 people

4 tbsps oil
3 sticks celery, diagonally sliced
2 carrots, peeled and cut into ribbons with
 a vegetable peeler
3oz pea pods
1 red pepper, thickly sliced
4 green onions, diagonally sliced
8 ears of baby corn
2oz bean sprouts
10 water chestnuts, sliced
½ small can sliced bamboo shoots
10 Chinese dried mushrooms, soaked in
 hot water, stalks removed
1 cup chicken stock
2 tbsps cornstarch
3 tbsps light soy sauce
Sesame oil

Heat a browning dish for 5 minutes on HIGH. Pour in the oil and add the celery and carrots. Cook for 1 minute on HIGH. Remove from the dish and add the pea pods, red pepper and corn. Cook for 1 minute on HIGH and place with the celery and carrots.

Add the onions, bean sprouts, water chestnuts and bamboo shoots to the dish. Cook for 1 minute on HIGH, adding the mushrooms after 30 seconds. Place with the rest of vegetables. Combine the rest of the ingredients in a glass measure. Cook 2-3 minutes on HIGH until thickened. Taste and add salt if necessary. Pour over the vegetables and stir carefully. Reheat for 1-2 minutes on HIGH before serving.

Spicy Cucumbers

PREPARATION TIME: 30 minutes

MICROWAVE COOKING TIME:
2 minutes

SERVES: 4 people

1 large cucumber
Salt
3 tbsps light soy sauce
Pinch five-spice powder
¼ tsp crushed red pepper
2 tsp sesame oil
1 tbsp rice vinegar
3 tbsps Chinese parsley leaves

Peel thin strips off the cucumber for a white and green stripe effect. Cut in half lengthwise, or in quarters if the cucumber is thick. Cut the lengths into 2 inch pieces. Sprinkle with salt and leave to stand 30 minutes. Wash and dry well. Combine the cucumber with all the remaining ingredients except the parsley in a deep bowl. Partially cover and cook for 2 minutes on HIGH. Add the parsley and leave in the bowl to cool. When cold, refrigerate. Serve on the same day.

Beans with Tree Ears and Bamboo Shoots

PREPARATION TIME: 30 minutes

MICROWAVE COOKING TIME:
4 minutes

SERVES: 4 people

6 pieces Chinese black fungi (tree or
 wood ears), soaked 30 minutes
8oz green beans, cut into 2 inch diagonal
 pieces
2 whole pieces canned bamboo shoots,
 cut into thin triangular pieces
2 tbsps oil
2 tbsps soy sauce
2 tsps cornstarch
4 tbsps light stock and wine mixed
Dash sesame oil
Salt and pepper

Heat a browning dish for 5 minutes on HIGH. Pour in the oil and add the beans and bamboo shoots. Cook, uncovered, for 2 minutes on HIGH. Add the tree ears, cover the dish and leave to stand while preparing the sauce. Mix the remaining ingredients except the sesame oil in a glass measure. Cook for 2 minutes on HIGH, stirring once until thickened. Combine with the vegetables and stir in the sesame oil to serve.

Pea Pods with Water Chestnuts

PREPARATION TIME: 15 minutes

MICROWAVE COOKING TIME:
4 minutes

SERVES: 4 people

8oz pea pods, stems trimmed off
2 tbsps oil
Pinch sugar
Pinch salt
1 small can water chestnuts, sliced in
 rounds

Facing page: Ten Varieties of Beauty.

4 tbsps light stock
1½ tsps cornstarch
Dash sesame oil

Heat a browning dish for 5 minutes on HIGH. Pour in the oil and add the pea pods. Add the salt and sugar and cook 2 minutes on HIGH, stirring frequently. Add the water chestnuts, cover, and set aside while preparing the sauce. Combine the stock and cornstarch in a glass measure. Cook for 2 minutes on HIGH, stirring

This page: Pea Pods with Water Chestnuts. Facing page: Beans with Tree Ears and Bamboo Shoots.

once, until thickened. Add the sesame oil and mix with the vegetables to serve.

Asparagus Salad

PREPARATION TIME: 15 minutes

MICROWAVE COOKING TIME: 5-6 minutes

SERVES: 4 people

1lb fresh asparagus
3 tbsps soy sauce
2 tsps sesame oil
1 tbsp sesame seeds

Trim the ends of the asparagus

the broccoli stems. Cut the flowerets from the stems in small clusters. Peel the stems with a vegetable peeler and cut them into thin diagonal slices. Pour the oil into the browning dish and add the broccoli stem slices. Add the ginger and cook, uncovered, for 2 minutes on HIGH, stirring frequently. Add the flowerets, cover and set aside while preparing the sauce. Combine the remaining ingredients in a glass measure. Cook, uncovered, for 5-6 minutes on HIGH until thickened. Pour over the broccoli and stir together to serve.

Steamed Eggplant

PREPARATION TIME: 30 minutes

MICROWAVE COOKING TIME: 6-8 minutes

SERVES: 4 people

1 large or 2 small eggplants
1 tbsp sesame oil
3 tbsps rice vinegar or white wine vinegar
3 tbsps light brown sugar
2 tbsps light soy sauce
1 tbsp fresh ginger root, grated
1 clove garlic, minced
Salt

Cut off the stems of the eggplants and then cut them in half, lengthwise. Lightly score the surface of each half and sprinkle with salt. Leave to stand for 30 minutes. Combine the remaining ingredients in a glass measure. Cook for 1 minute on HIGH to dissolve sugar. Stir well and set aside to allow flavors to blend. Wash the eggplants and dry well. Cut in quarters, lengthwise, and then into 1 inch wedges. Put into a casserole dish with ½ cup water. Cover and cook 5-7 minutes or until just tender. Stir several times during cooking. Drain well. Pour over the sauce and serve hot or cold.

This page: Ginger Broccoli. Facing page: Asparagus Salad (top) and Steamed Eggplant (bottom).

Ginger Broccoli

PREPARATION TIME: 20 minutes

MICROWAVE COOKING TIME: 7-8 minutes

SERVES: 4 people

1½ lbs broccoli
2 tbsps oil
3 inch piece fresh ginger root, peeled and very finely shredded
Pinch salt
Pinch sugar
1 tsp cornstarch
½ cup light stock
Dash light soy sauce

Heat a browning dish for 5 minutes on HIGH. Cut off the tough ends of

spears, wash and drain well. Cut on the diagonal into 1½ inch lengths, leaving the tips whole. Put into a casserole dish with ½ cup water. Cook, covered, for 5-6 minutes on HIGH. The asparagus should remain crisp. Mix the soy sauce and sesame oil. Drain the asparagus well and toss with the soy sauce mixture. Sprinkle over the sesame seeds and serve hot or cold.

DESSERTS

Velvet Cream

PREPARATION TIME: 10 minutes

MICROWAVE COOKING TIME:
8-9 minutes

SERVES: 4 people

2 cups milk
4 tbsps smooth peanut butter
¼ cup sugar
2 tbsps cornstarch
½ cup finely chopped, roasted peanuts
1 tbsp sesame seeds

Combine all but 4 tbsps of the milk with the peanut butter and sugar. Heat for 5 minutes on HIGH. Combine the remaining milk with the cornstarch and stir into the peanut butter mixture gradually. Return to the oven and cook on HIGH for 3-4 minutes, or until the consistency of thick cream. Cook until the cornstarch thickens completely. Serve warm or cold, topped with peanuts and sesame seeds.

Treasure Rice

PREPARATION TIME: 25 minutes

MICROWAVE COOKING TIME:
40-41 minutes

SERVES: 4-6 people

3 cups glutinous rice or short grain rice
3 cups water
1 tsp salt
1 cup sugar
1 cup sweetened red bean paste
1 tbsp candied lotus seeds (optional)
¼ cup blanched whole almonds

4 red candied cherries
4 green candied cherries
2 rings candied pineapple
2-3 dates, stoned
4 candied apricots

Combine rice, salt and water and cook on HIGH for 10 minutes. Add the sugar and lower the setting to LOW/DEFROST and cook for

20 minutes. Spoon half of the cooked rice into a microproof glass serving dish. Spread over the bean paste and cover with the remaining rice. Cut the fruit into pieces and arrange decoratively on top of the rice. Cover the bowl with pierced plastic wrap and cook on MEDIUM for 4-5 minutes. If desired, combine 1 cup water with ½ cup sugar and 1 tsp

cornstarch in a glass measure. Cook for 6 minutes on HIGH and add a few drops almond extract. Pour several spoonfuls of the sauce over the pudding and serve the rest separately.

Jade Pieces

PREPARATION TIME: 1 hour	
MICROWAVE COOKING TIME: 43-49 minutes	
MAKES: 24 pieces (approx.)	

1 lb green split peas, soaked overnight, or brought to the boil, cooked 10 minutes on HIGH and left to stand for 1 hour
½ cup sugar
3 cups water
4 tbsps cornstarch
1 piece preserved ginger, finely chopped
3 tbsps desiccated coconut
Few drops green food coloring

Drain the peas and return them to a large glass bowl. Add the water, loosely cover the bowl and cook on HIGH for 40-45 minutes, or until the peas are very soft. Purée the peas with the sugar and food coloring. Mix the cornstarch with a little water and add to the peas. Return to the bowl and cook, uncovered, 3-4 minutes until cornstarch thickens. Add the ginger and pour into a shallow dish to the depth of 1 inch. Sprinkle the coconut over the surface and chill until firm. Cut into diamond shapes to serve.

Facing page: Velvet Cream (top) and Treasure Rice (bottom). This page: Date and Red Bean Winter Pudding (top) and Jade Pieces (bottom).

Date and Red Bean Winter Pudding

PREPARATION TIME: 20 minutes	
MICROWAVE COOKING TIME: 17-22 minutes plus 3 minutes standing time	
SERVES: 4 people	

1lb dried, stoned dates
3 cups water
½ cups red bean paste
1 cup sugar
4 tbsps cornstarch
⅓ cup white vegetable shortening or margarine
Pinch salt
½ tsp almond extract
2 tbsps sliced almonds

Place the dates in a large bowl and add the water. Cover loosely and cook 12-16 minutes on HIGH, or until the water boils and the dates begin to soften. Leave to stand 3 minutes. Drain the water from the dates and reserve 2 cups of the liquid and mix with the cornstarch, and cook 3-4 minutes on HIGH to thicken. Combine the dates, sugar, bean paste, shortening or margarine, salt and almond extract in a food processor and purée until smooth. Mix into the thickened date liquid and cook for 2 minutes on HIGH, stirring frequently. Pour into a serving bowl and chill. Sprinkle with almonds. May be served with cream if desired.

Microwave
INDIAN COOKING

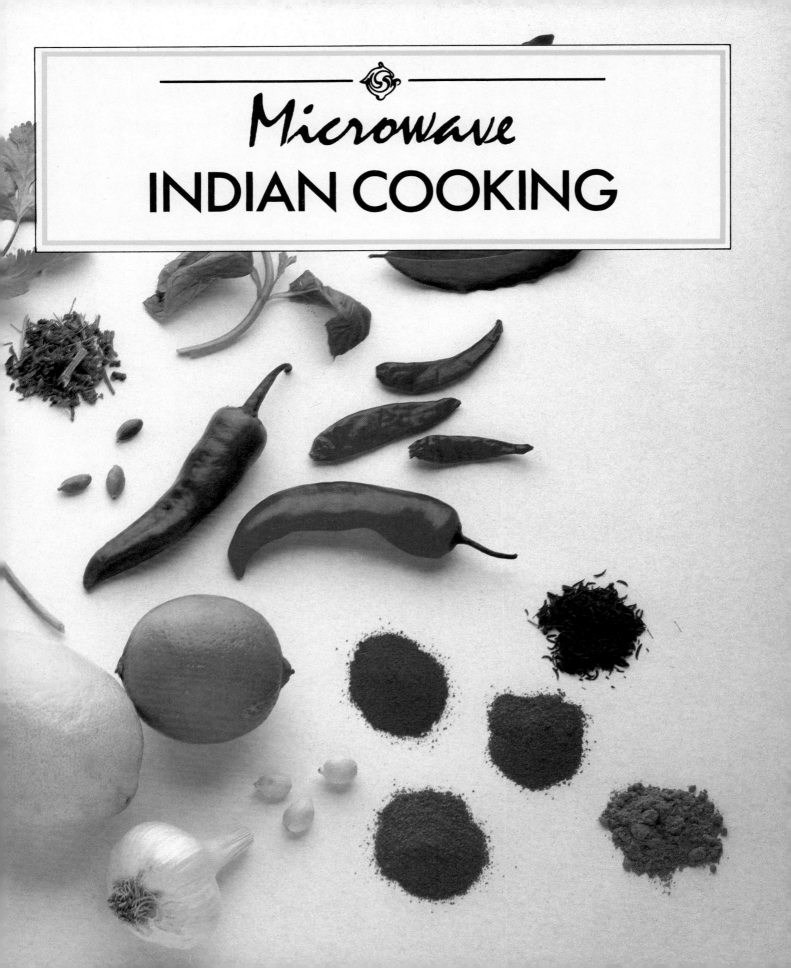

Microwave
INDIAN COOKING

As might be expected of a country as large and regionally diverse as India, the sub-continent's cuisine is far more varied and imaginative than the average restaurant menu could possibly reflect. Popular standby dishes such as Chicken Korma or Meat Bhoona are, of course, as popular around the world as they are in their native land, but there are also many recipes, such as Chicken and Almonds in Red Sauce or Malabari Fish, which fewer restaurants are likely to feature.

If the apparent complexity of preparation and long cooking times have put you off of trying to cook Indian meals in the past, then preparing them the microwave way will prove a real eye-opener. The recipes in this book form an authentic selection of Indian dishes, all specially adapted for quick and convenient microwave cooking.

Basically, an authentic Indian meal consists of a meat, poultry or fish dish, vegetable dish, bread and/or rice, pulse dish, yogurt relish, chutney or pickle and a relish salad. Fruit is usually offered as a dessert, but a sweet makes a meal a festive occasion. Vegetarians can substitute extra vegetable, rice or pulse dishes for meat, poultry or fish.

Aromatics are at the heart of Indian food, and while all Indian dishes are spicy, they are not necessarily hot. The "heat" comes from chilies, and their amount can be varied to suit personal taste. Of course, Vindaloo would not be Vindaloo without the fire! The following list is a guide to the spices used in these recipes. Many Indian spices are now readily available in supermarkets. Good Indian cooks buy whole spices in small quantities and grind them as needed to ensure freshness. A pepper grinder reserved for this purpose is a fast and easy way to do this. There are also small electric spice grinders you can buy and, of course, that old standby the mortar and pestle. If you do buy pre-ground spices, get the smallest container available and keep it airtight and away from bright light.

All the recipes were prepared and tested in an oven with a 700 watt maximum setting. If your oven is not 700w, convert timings in the following way:

500w oven – Add 40 seconds for each minute stated in the recipe.
600w oven – Add 20 seconds for each minute stated in the recipe.
650w oven – Only a slight increase in the overall time is necessary.

APPETIZERS

Hot and Spicy Mussels

PREPARATION TIME: 25 minutes

MICROWAVE COOKING TIME: 2-5 minutes plus standing time

SERVES: 4-6 people

4 dozen mussels in the shell
2 tbsps oil
1 piece ginger, grated
3 cloves garlic, crushed
1½ tbsps coriander seeds, slightly crushed
2 green chilies, seeded and shredded
Salt and pepper
Juice of 1 lemon
4 tbsps water
Grated fresh coconut or desiccated coconut

Scrub the mussels well and discard any that do not close when tapped or that have broken shells. Heat oil in a large bowl and add the ginger, garlic, coriander seeds, chilies and lemon juice with the water and mussels. Cover the bowl and cook 2-5 minutes on HIGH, stirring occasionally until the shells open. Discard any mussels that do not open. Sprinkle over the coconut and leave, covered, for 2 minutes before serving.

Tandoori Shrimp

PREPARATION TIME: 10 minutes

MICROWAVE COOKING TIME: 10-11 minutes

SERVES: 4 people

1lb jumbo shrimp
2 tbsps oil
1 small onion, finely chopped

2 tbsps coriander, chopped
1 clove garlic, crushed
1 tsp ground coriander
1 tsp ground turmeric
3 tomatoes, peeled, seeded and diced
1-2 tsps tomato paste
Salt and pepper
Juice of 1 lime or ½ lemon
2 tsps garam masala

This page: Hot and Spicy Mussels (top) and Tandoori Shrimp (bottom). Facing page: Chicken Tikka.

Shell the shrimp and de-vein them, but leave on the very ends of the tail shells. Put the oil, onion, garlic, chopped coriander, ground coriander

and turmeric into a bowl. Cover loosely and cook on HIGH for 2 minutes. Mix in the tomatoes, tomato paste, salt and garam masala. Cook on HIGH for 3-4 minutes, or until the tomatoes become thick and pulpy. Add the lime or lemon juice and the shrimp. Cook on HIGH for 3 minutes, stirring frequently, or until the shrimp curl slightly and become firmer. Serve with lime wedges on a bed of shredded lettuce.

Spicy Scrambled Eggs

PREPARATION TIME: 10 minutes

MICROWAVE COOKING TIME:
6-7 minutes plus 1-2 minutes standing time

SERVES: 4 people

2 tbsps butter or margarine
1 small onion, chopped
1 green chili pepper, seeded and chopped
1 tsp cumin
1 zucchini, cut in small dice
6 tbsps milk
5-6 eggs
Salt and pepper

GARNISH
Coriander leaves

Melt the butter in a deep bowl for 1 minute on HIGH and add the onion, chili, cumin and zucchini. Cook 2 minutes on HIGH, stirring once or twice. Beat the eggs with the milk and salt and pepper and pour into the bowl. Cook 3-4 minutes on HIGH, stirring occasionally. Leave to stand 1-2 minutes before serving.

Omelet

PREPARATION TIME: 10 minutes

MICROWAVE COOKING TIME:
5-6 minutes

SERVES: 1 person

2 eggs, separated
1 tsp water
1 tbsp butter or margarine
½ onion, finely chopped

1 small tomato, peeled, seeded and chopped
½ green chili, seeded and chopped
1 sprig coriander
Salt and pepper

Melt the butter in a shallow pie dish for 30 seconds on HIGH. Cook the onion 1-2 minutes to soften and add the tomato, chili and coriander. Beat yolks with the water. Beat the egg whites until stiff but not dry and fold into the yolks. Spoon the egg mixture into the pie dish, smoothing the top. Cook for 4 minutes on MEDIUM or until set. Fold over to serve, or turn out of the dish and cut into wedges.

Chicken Tikka

PREPARATION TIME: 10 minutes

MICROWAVE COOKING TIME:
5-6 minutes

SERVES: 4 people

1lb chicken, skinned, boned and cut into 2½ inch pieces

MARINADE
½ cup natural yogurt
1 clove garlic, crushed
1 small piece ginger, grated
1 tsp chili powder
2 tsps paprika
2 tsps garam masala
Juice of 1 lime
Salt and pepper
¼ tsp red food coloring (optional)
60ml/4 tbsps oil

GARNISH
Lemon wedges
Cucumber slices

Place the chicken in a large, deep bowl and mix in all the marinade ingredients except the oil. Leave to stand for 2 hours. Thread onto wooden skewers and place 2 kebabs at a time on a rack. Brush lightly with oil and cook for 5 minutes, turning frequently during cooking. Allow to stand, covered, while cooking the remaining kebabs. Serve garnished with lemon wedges and cucumber slices.

Kofta Kebabs

PREPARATION TIME: 20 minutes

MICROWAVE COOKING TIME:
5-6 minutes

SERVES: 4 people

8oz ground lamb or beef
¼ tsp ground ginger
¼ tsp chili powder
1 clove garlic, crushed
1 small egg, beaten
Salt and pepper

1 red pepper, seeded and cut into 1 inch pieces
4 tbsps oil

YOGURT SAUCE
¼ cucumber, grated
½ cup natural yogurt
1 tbsp chopped mint or coriander leaves
Pinch cayenne pepper

Mix the kofta ingredients together and shape into 1 inch balls. Thread onto wooden skewers, alternating with pepper pieces. Place on a rack and baste lightly with oil. Cook 2 kebabs at a time for 3 minutes on HIGH, turning frequently during cooking. Meanwhile, sprinkle cucumber with salt and leave to drain and pat dry. Mix with remaining sauce ingredients and serve with the kebabs.

Baked Kebab

PREPARATION TIME: 30 minutes

MICROWAVE COOKING TIME:
15 minutes

SERVES: 4-6 people

1 tbsp oil
1 small onion, chopped
1 red or green chili, chopped
1-2 cloves garlic, crushed
½ tsp ground ginger
¼ tsp ground coriander
¼ tsp garam masala
1lb ground lamb or beef

Facing page: Omelet (top) and Spicy Scrambled Eggs (bottom).

½ cup natural yogurt
2 eggs
Salt and pepper

GARNISH
Lemon or lime wedges

Heat oil and cook onion for 2 minutes on HIGH to soften. Mix in the remaining ingredients and press the mixture into a round, shallow dish. Cook on HIGH for 5 minutes. Reduce the setting to MEDIUM and cook a further 10-15 minutes or until the meat is no longer pink. Cut into small wedges or squares and serve with lemon or lime wedges.

Spiced Green Peas

PREPARATION TIME: 10 minutes
MICROWAVE COOKING TIME: 7-8½ minutes
SERVES: 4-6 people

2 tbsps butter or margarine
1 onion, thinly sliced
1 red chili, seeded and sliced
1 small piece ginger, grated
1lb frozen peas
2 sprigs coriander, chopped
Salt and pepper
Juice of 1 lime

This page: Spiced Green Peas.
Facing page: Baked Kebab (top) and Kofta Kebabs (bottom).

Melt the butter for 1 minute on HIGH. Add the onion and cook for 2 minutes on HIGH. Add chili and ginger and cook a further 1 minute on HIGH. Add the remaining ingredients and cook 3-4½ minutes on HIGH. Leave to stand 2 minutes before serving hot.

FISH AND SEAFOOD

Spiced Fish in Parchment

PREPARATION TIME: 20 minutes

MICROWAVE COOKING TIME:
22 minutes plus standing time

SERVES: 4 people

4 trout, cleaned and trimmed
1 tbsp coriander seeds, crushed
1 tsp cassia bark
2 tsps mustard seed
4 cardamoms, crushed
1 tsp cumin seeds
4 sprigs fresh coriander
Salt and pepper
Juice and zest of 1 lime

Place each trout on a circle of lightly oiled wax paper or baking parchment. Place coriander seeds, cassia bark, mustard seeds, cardamoms and cumin seeds on a plate and heat 2 minutes on HIGH. Sprinkle the spice mixture over each fish along with salt and pepper. Pour over the lime juice and add the zest. Place a sprig of coriander on each fish. Seal each paper package and place 2 at a time on a plate. Cook 10 minutes on HIGH. Leave to stand 3-5 minutes before serving and open each parcel at the table.

Jumbo Shrimp and Zucchini

PREPARATION TIME: 25 minutes

MICROWAVE COOKING TIME:
9 minutes plus standing time

SERVES: 4 people

1lb jumbo shrimp
2 tbsps oil
1 tsp paprika

½ tsp turmeric
1½ tsps ground cumin
Grated fresh ginger
1 clove garlic, crushed
1 red chili, seeded and shredded
2 zucchini, cut in matchsticks
7oz can tomatoes, crushed
1 bay leaf
2 tsps-1 tbsp cornstarch, mixed with

This page: Jumbo Shrimp and Zucchini. Facing page: Spiced Fish in Parchment.

3 tbsps lemon juice
Salt and pepper

Shell and de-vein the shrimp. Pour the oil into a casserole and add the spices, garlic and chili. Cook for 2 minutes on HIGH. Add the zucchini, tomatoes, bay leaf, cornstarch mixed with lemon juice, salt and pepper. Cook on HIGH for 5 minutes. Add the shrimp and cook 2 minutes on HIGH and leave to stand for 5 minutes to finish cooking. Remove the bay leaf. Serve with rice.

Sardine Fry

PREPARATION TIME: 20 minutes

MICROWAVE COOKING TIME: 13 minutes

SERVES: 4 people

½ tsp turmeric
2 tsps chili powder
½ tsp ground cumin
Salt
12 even-sized sardines, cleaned and trimmed
4 tbsps oil

Mix the spices together with the salt. Cut 2 slits in the side of each fish and rub with spice mixture. Heat a browning dish according to the manufacturer's directions and add 1 tbsp of oil. Cook 3 fish at a time for 3 minutes per side on HIGH. Continue with remaining oil and fish and reheat all the fish for 1 minute on HIGH before serving.

Steamed Fish with Cucumber

PREPARATION TIME: 20 minutes

MICROWAVE COOKING TIME: 8-11 minutes

SERVES: 6 people

2lbs whitefish, skinned and cut into even-sized serving pieces
2 tbsps coriander seeds, crushed
2 tbsps dill seed
1 small piece ginger, grated
Seeds of 6 cardamom pods, crushed
½ tsp saffron strands
1 tbsp chopped mint leaves
1 inch stick cinnamon

¾ cup unflavored yogurt
1 small cucumber, peeled, quartered and cut into 2 inch pieces
Salt and pepper

Place all the spices, seeds, saffron and mint on a plate and cook 2 minutes to roast. Mix the yogurt and salt and pepper. Pour over the fish and marinate for 2 hours. Place fish in a casserole, scraping off most of the marinade. Add the cucumber, cover and cook for 6-8 minutes on HIGH. Cook in two batches if necessary, arranging the fish with the thickest portion to the outside of the dish. Pour over the marinade and cook a further 2-3 minutes or until fish and cucumber are tender. Garnish with coriander leaves.

Shrimp and Tamarind

PREPARATION TIME: 20 minutes

MICROWAVE COOKING TIME: 5-6 minutes plus standing time

SERVES: 4 people

2lbs jumbo shrimp
2 tbsps butter or margarine
4 shallots, finely chopped
1 tbsp ground coriander
4 crushed cardamoms
2 tsps turmeric
Pinch nutmeg
1 green chili, seeded and shredded
1 pimento cap, cut into fine shreds
Juice of 1 lime
1 tbsp sugar
1 tbsp tamarind extract
¾ cup natural yogurt
Salt and pepper

Peel and de-vein the shrimp and set aside. Heat a browning dish according to the manufacturer's directions. Add the butter or margarine and shallot and cook 2 minutes on HIGH. Add the spices and shrimp and cook 1-2 minutes on HIGH. Pour into a casserole and add the chilies, pimento, lime juice, sugar and tamarind. Stir well and cook 2 minutes on HIGH. Stir in the yogurt, salt and pepper and leave to stand 3 minutes before serving.

Malabari Fish

PREPARATION TIME: 25 minutes

MICROWAVE COOKING TIME: 12-13 minutes plus standing time

SERVES: 4 people

4 tbsps desiccated coconut
½ cup water
4 tbsps oil
1 onion, finely chopped
½ tsp each of cinnamon, nutmeg, chili powder, cumin, coriander and turmeric
Pinch ground cloves
6 cardamoms
1 bay leaf
1 tsp fresh ginger, grated
1 clove garlic, crushed
Pinch salt and pepper
1lb whitefish, skinned, boned and cut into 2 inch pieces
8oz pineapple pieces and juice
1-2 green chilies, seeded and finely chopped
1 tbsp chopped coriander leaves
1 tbsp cornstarch
1 tbsp blanched almonds
1 tbsp raisins
½ cup unflavored yogurt

Place the coconut and water in a dish and heat for 30 seconds on HIGH. Leave to infuse. Place oil in a casserole and add the onion. Cover and cook for 2 minutes on HIGH. Add all spices, bay leaf, ginger and garlic and heat for 2 minutes on HIGH. Add the fish and strained juice from the pineapple. Add coriander, chilies, salt and pepper. Cover and cook for 6 minutes on HIGH. Strain the coconut and mix the liquid with cornstarch. Stir into the fish and cook a further 2-3 minutes, stirring carefully, or until the sauce thickens and clears. Add pineapple, almonds, raisins and yogurt. Cover and leave to stand 3-5 minutes before serving. Remove bay leaf.

Facing page: Steamed Fish with Cucumber (top) and Sardine Fry (bottom).

the whole spices and serve with rice. Garnish with desiccated coconut if desired.

Curried Shrimp with Bananas, Pineapple and Almonds

PREPARATION TIME: 20 minutes

MICROWAVE COOKING TIME: 12-13 minutes

SERVES: 4 people

2 tbsps oil
1 onion, finely chopped
1 clove garlic, crushed
2 tsps turmeric
2 tsps ground coriander
½ tsp ground cumin
¼ tsp each of ground cinnamon, nutmeg and ginger
2 tbsps flour
1½ cups fish or vegetable stock
1 tsp lime juice
2 tsps mango chutney
4oz canned pineapple pieces
1 large or 2 small bananas, peeled and cut into chunks
½ cup unblanched almonds, roughly chopped
12oz peeled, cooked shrimp

GARNISH
Desiccated coconut

Put the oil into a deep bowl and add the onion and garlic. Cover loosely and cook on HIGH for 3 minutes or until the onion softens. Stir in the spices and the flour and cook for a further 2 minutes on HIGH, stirring frequently. Gradually pour in the stock and add the lime and mango chutney. Cook for 6 minutes or until boiling, stirring frequently. Add the drained pineapple, bananas and almonds and stir well. Add the shrimp and cook on HIGH for 1-2

Shrimp Bhoona

PREPARATION TIME: 15 minutes

MICROWAVE COOKING TIME: 8-13 minutes plus standing time

SERVES: 4 people

2 tbsps oil
1 onion, sliced
2 tsps cumin
1 tsp coriander
½ tsp turmeric
2 cloves garlic, crushed
1 cinnamon stick
6 cardamom pods, crushed
2 bay leaves
1 tbsp flour

14oz canned tomatoes and juice
Pinch cayenne pepper
Salt and pepper
1lb shrimp
4 tbsps unflavored yogurt

Heat the oil for 30 seconds on HIGH in a large casserole. Cook the onion for 3 minutes on HIGH, add the garlic and spices and cook for 2 minutes on HIGH. Stir in the flour and add the tomatoes. Add cayenne pepper, salt and pepper and cook 3-5 minutes to thicken. Add shrimp and, if uncooked, cook a further 3 minutes on HIGH. Stir in the yogurt and leave to stand for 5 minutes before serving. Remove

This page: **Malabari Fish (top) and Shrimp and Tamarind (bottom).** Facing page: **Simple Fish Curry (top) and Shrimp Bhoona (bottom).**

minutes or until the shrimp and fruit are heated through. Sprinkle with desiccated coconut and serve with rice.

Simple Fish Curry

PREPARATION TIME: 20 minutes

MICROWAVE COOKING TIME: 10-13 minutes

SERVES: 4 people

2 tbsps butter or margarine
1 onion, chopped

½ tsp turmeric
1 tsp cumin
1 tbsp coriander
1 tsp paprika
Pinch mace
1 tsp fennel seed
1 tbsp flour
1 cup water
1 bay leaf
1 tbsp chopped parsley
1 tbsp desiccated coconut
1lb haddock or cod, cut in large pieces

Melt the butter in a shallow dish or casserole and add the onion, spices

This page: Curried Shrimp with Bananas, Pineapple and Almonds. Facing page: Marinated Leg of Lamb.

and fennel seed and cook 2 minutes on HIGH. Add the flour and water and blend well. Add the bay leaf and cook 5-6 minutes on HIGH to thicken. Add the parsley, coconut and fish and cook 3-5 minutes or until the fish is tender. Remove the bay leaf and serve with rice. Garnish with chopped coriander.

MEAT DISHES

Marinated Leg of Lamb

PREPARATION TIME: 20 minutes plus marinating

MICROWAVE COOKING TIME: 21 minutes plus standing time

SERVES: 6 people

2¼ lb leg of lamb, boned

MARINADE
1 cup natural yogurt
Juice of 1 lemon or lime
2 tsps chili powder
2 tsps turmeric
2 cloves garlic, crushed
1 small piece grated ginger
Pinch sugar
Pinch nutmeg
1 tbsp poppy seeds
1 tbsp chopped chives

Trim most of the fat from the outside of the lamb. Make four ½ inch cuts through the meat. Tie the meat with string to keep in shape. Combine the marinade ingredients in a large bowl and place in the lamb. Spread the marinade over, pressing it into the cuts. Cover and leave overnight in the refrigerator. Remove and place on a microwave roasting dish. Cook on HIGH for 15 minutes. Cover the thinner end of the lamb with foil (shiny side innermost) and cook a further 6 minutes. Baste with any remaining marinade every 2 minutes during cooking. Leave to stand 5-6 minutes before carving.

Meat Dupiaza

PREPARATION TIME: 25 minutes

MICROWAVE COOKING TIME: 28½ minutes plus standing time

SERVES: 4 people

3 tbsps oil
1 small onion, chopped
2 cloves garlic, crushed
1-2 red or green chilies, chopped
1 tsp ground coriander
2 tsps ground cumin
1 piece ginger, grated
3 whole cloves
6 cardamoms, slightly crushed
1lb lamb fillet or rump steak
Juice of 1 lime or small lemon
½ cup stock
2 medium onions, sliced in rings

Heat the oil for 30 seconds on HIGH in a casserole. Add the onion, garlic and chilies and cook for 2 minutes on HIGH. Add all the spices and cook a further 1 minute. Add meat and cook for 5 minutes on HIGH. Add stock and lemon or lime juice and cover the dish. Cook on HIGH for 20 minutes, stirring occasionally. Add the onion rings during the last 8 minutes of cooking. Stand for 5 minutes before serving with rice. Garnish with chopped coriander if desired.

Keema Peas

PREPARATION TIME: 15 minutes

MICROWAVE COOKING TIME:
13 minutes plus 5 minutes standing time

SERVES: 4-6 people

1lb ground lamb or beef
1 onion, chopped or sliced
1 clove garlic, crushed
½ a green or red chili, seeded and finely chopped
1 small piece ginger, grated
2 tsps cumin
2 tsps coriander
½ tsp turmeric
2 bay leaves
2 tsps crushed cardamom pods
½ cup frozen peas
4 tbsps stock
Salt and pepper
½ cup unflavored yogurt

Heat a browning dish according to the manufacturer's directions and, when hot, add meat, onion, garlic and chili. Cook on HIGH for 8 minutes, breaking up the meat with a fork during cooking. Add the ginger, cumin, coriander and turmeric during the last 2 minutes of cooking. Transfer the meat to a bowl or casserole, add bay leaves, cardamoms, peas and stock. Cover and cook 5 minutes on HIGH. Season with salt and pepper and stir in the yogurt. Leave to stand, covered, 5 minutes before serving.

Rogan Josh

PREPARATION TIME: 25 minutes

MICROWAVE COOKING TIME:
27½ minutes

SERVES: 4 people

4 tbsps oil
1 onion, sliced
2 cloves garlic, crushed
1 tsp cumin
2 tsps garam masala
2 tsps ground coriander
2 tsps paprika
1 tsp ground ginger
½ tsp cinnamon
1lb lamb fillet or rump steak, cut into 1 inch pieces
1 cup stock
2 bay leaves
2 tbsps blanched split almonds
2 tbsps golden raisins
Salt

Heat the oil for 30 seconds on HIGH in a large bowl or casserole. Add the

This page: Keema Peas. Facing page: Meat Dupiaza (top) and Rogan Josh (bottom).

onion and garlic and cook for 1 minute on HIGH. Add the spices and cook for 1 minute. Add the meat and stir to coat. Cover loosely and cook on HIGH for 5 minutes. Add the stock, bay leaves and salt, cover and cook 20 minutes on MEDIUM, stirring occasionally. Add the almonds and the golden raisins during the last 3 minutes of cooking. Allow to stand 5 minutes before serving. Garnish with bay leaves if desired.

Glazed Pork Chops

PREPARATION TIME: 25 minutes plus marinating

MICROWAVE COOKING TIME: 28-32 minutes

SERVES: 4-8 people

8 small pork chops
1 tsp oil

MARINADE
Juice of 2 lemons
¼ tsp ground cinnamon
½ tsp ground nutmeg
1 tsp paprika

SAUCE
⅓ cup plum or apricot jam
Juice and zest of 1 lime
Pinch cayenne pepper
1 tbsp grated ginger
1 tbsp grated onion
1½ tsps sesame seeds
Salt

Remove most of the fat from the chops and snip the edges to prevent curling. Combine marinade ingredients and pour over chops in a dish. Leave to stand for 1-2 hours. Combine all the sauce ingredients in a deep bowl and heat for 2 minutes on HIGH and set aside. Heat a browning dish according to the manufacturer's directions. Remove the chops from the marinade and pat dry on paper towels. Pour the oil into the hot browning dish and brown the chops, 2 at a time, for 2-5 minutes. Place the chops in a casserole, cover and cook on HIGH for 7 minutes. Pour off the meat juices and add with

any remaining marinade to the sauce and cook 5 minutes on HIGH to reduce. Pour over the chops and cook a further 10 minutes on HIGH or until tender and well glazed.

Vindaloo

PREPARATION TIME: 25 minutes

MICROWAVE COOKING TIME: 23-24 minutes

SERVES: 4-6 people

1 tbsp oil
3 cloves garlic, crushed
¼ tsp each of ground cumin, coriander, cinnamon, cloves, black pepper, ginger
1½ tsps turmeric
1 tsp mustard seed
3 bay leaves
1lb pork fillet, cut into cubes
4 tbsps tamarind extract
2 tsps tomato paste
2 tsps sugar
3 tbsps vinegar
1-2 green chilies, seeded and chopped
Water or stock to moisten
Salt

Heat oil and add garlic, spices and mustard seed. Cook 1 minute on HIGH. Allow to cool and pour over the pork cubes in a shallow dish. Stir to coat and add bay leaves. Leave to marinate overnight in the refrigerator, stirring occasionally. Mix the tamarind, tomato paste, sugar and vinegar and pour over the meat. Add water or stock to come a quarter of the way up the meat, and sprinkle over the chilies. Cover the dish and cook for 20 minutes on MEDIUM, adding more water or stock if drying out. When the meat is tender, leave the vindaloo to stand for 5 minutes before serving. If desired, the sauce may be thickened with 1 tbsp cornstarch mixed with 3 tbsps water or stock. Cook 2-3 minutes or until clear.

Facing page: Glazed Pork Chops.

Meat Bhoona

PREPARATION TIME: 25 minutes

MICROWAVE COOKING TIME:
27 minutes plus standing time

SERVES: 4-6 people

4 tbsps oil
1 onion, roughly chopped

3 cloves garlic, crushed
1 small piece ginger, grated
2 tsps ground coriander
1 tsp ground cumin
½ tsp ground cinnamon
¼ tsp ground cloves
¼ tsp turmeric
¼ tsp cayenne pepper
1 tsp chili powder
6 cardamoms, slightly crushed

This page: **Sweet and Sour Pork
with Spinach and Cucumber.**
Facing page: **Kofta Curry (top) and
Meat Bhoona (bottom).**

1 tsp fenugreek seeds (optional)
1½ lbs lamb fillet or rump steak, cut in
  1 inch pieces
¾ cup stock

2 tsps tomato paste
Salt
1 bay leaf
4 fresh tomatoes, quartered

Heat the oil for 30 seconds on HIGH in a large bowl or casserole. Add the onions and garlic and cook for 1 minute on HIGH. Stir in all the spices and cook 1 minute on HIGH. Add the meat and stir to coat thoroughly. Cover and cook for 5 minutes on HIGH. Add the remaining ingredients except the tomatoes and re-cover the dish. Cook 20 minutes on HIGH, stirring several times during cooking. Add the tomatoes during the last 3 minutes of cooking and leave to stand 5 minutes before serving.

Kofta Curry

PREPARATION TIME: 25 minutes

MICROWAVE COOKING TIME:
21-25 minutes plus standing time

SERVES: 4-6 people

SAUCE
2 tbsps oil
1 onion, roughly chopped
1 tbsp flour
¼ tsp cinnamon
¼ tsp ground cloves
1 tsp ground coriander
1 tsp ground cumin
1 tsp ground turmeric
Salt
1½ cups stock
4 tbsps natural yogurt
2 tbsps tomato paste

KOFTAS
1lb ground lamb or beef
1 small piece ginger, grated
1 clove garlic, crushed
2 tsps garam masala
¼ tsp cayenne pepper
Pinch salt

GARNISH
Coriander leaves or chopped chives

Heat the oil in a glass measure and add the onion. Cook for 3 minutes on HIGH, stirring occasionally. Add the flour and spices and cook 2

minutes on HIGH. Pour on the stock gradually and mix until smooth. Add salt to taste and the tomato paste. Cook 5 minutes on HIGH, stirring often after 1 minute. Set aside. To prepare the koftas, mix ingredients together and form into 1 inch balls. Arrange in 1 layer in a large, shallow casserole. Pour over the sauce and cover loosely. Cook for 4 minutes on HIGH. Rearrange the koftas and rearrange the dish. Cook on HIGH 4-6 minutes or until the koftas are firm. Add the yogurt to the sauce, stirring carefully. Cover the dish and allow to stand 3-5 minutes before serving. Serve garnished with chopped chives or coriander leaves.

Sweet and Sour Pork with Spinach and Cucumber

PREPARATION TIME: 25 minutes

MICROWAVE COOKING TIME:
24-35 minutes

SERVES: 4-6 people

2 tbsps oil
1lb pork fillet, cut into thin strips
1 tsp black pepper
½ tsp fennel or aniseed
¼ tsp nutmeg
¼ tsp turmeric
1 onion, finely chopped
1 clove garlic
2 whole cloves
2 cardamoms, crushed
Few pieces cassia bark
4 tbsps vinegar
4 tbsps dark brown sugar
¼ cup stock
1 tbsp cornstarch
4oz fresh spinach leaves, well washed and
   chopped
¼ cucumber, sliced
½ cup blanched almonds
Salt

Heat a browning dish according to the manufacturer's directions. Add the oil and fry the pork strips in 2 or 3 batches for 3-4 minutes per batch. Add onion and garlic together with pepper, fennel or aniseed, nutmeg and turmeric. Cook for 3 minutes on HIGH. Turn into a casserole dish and

add the vinegar, sugar, cloves, cardamoms and cassia bark and cover loosely. Cook 15-20 minutes on HIGH. Combine stock and cornstarch and pour over the meat. Stir well and add the spinach, cucumber and almonds. Cook 2-3 minutes or until the sauce clears and thickens. Allow to stand 2-3 minutes before serving.

Lamb Passanda

PREPARATION TIME: 20 minutes

MICROWAVE COOKING TIME:
22-29 minutes plus standing time

SERVES: 4-6 people

3 tbsps oil
1lb lamb fillet, thinly sliced
2 cloves garlic, crushed
1 tsp paprika
1 tsp turmeric
2 tsps ground coriander
1½ tsps garam masala
1 tbsp chopped mint
1 red chili, seeded and finely chopped
   (optional)
½ cup milk
½ cup ground almonds
½ cup natural yogurt
Salt and pepper

Heat a browning dish according to the manufacturer's directions. Add oil and lamb in 2 batches. Cook 3-4 minutes on HIGH per batch. Add the garlic and spices to the dish and cook 1 minute on HIGH. Transfer meat and spices to a casserole. Add the mint, chili pepper, milk and seasoning. Cook, covered, for 15-20 minutes on HIGH or until the lamb is tender. Stir in the almonds and yogurt and leave to stand, covered, for 5 minutes before serving.

Facing page: Lamb Passanda (top) and Vindaloo (bottom).

Microwave

INDIAN COOKING

CHICKEN DISHES

Chicken Dhansak

PREPARATION TIME: 1 hour

MICROWAVE COOKING TIME:
51-70 minutes

SERVES: 4-6 people

1 eggplant, sliced, scored and salted
1 cup red lentils, soaked overnight or
    rehydrated
1 slice onion
1 bay leaf
3 tbsps oil
2¼ lbs chicken, skinned, boned and cut
    into 2 inch pieces
2 cloves garlic, crushed
1 small piece ginger, grated
¼ tsp turmeric
½ tsp chili powder
1 tsp ground cumin
1 tsp ground coriander
1 inch piece cinnamon stick
2 sprigs fresh methi leaves (optional)
2 sprigs fresh coriander leaves, chopped
1 tbsp flour
½ cup chicken stock
1 tbsp dark brown sugar or jaggery
1 tbsp tamarind extract

GARNISH
Coriander leaves

Leave the eggplant to stand for
30 minutes. Rinse, pat dry and cut
into slices. To rehydrate lentils in the
microwave oven, place them in a
large bowl and cover with water.
Cover the bowl with plastic wrap
and heat for 8-10 minutes on HIGH.
Leave to stand for 1 hour. Drain and
cover the lentils with fresh water and
add the onion and bay leaf. Cook
30-45 minutes on HIGH, replacing
water as it evaporates. Cook until the
lentils are soft. Leave to stand while
preparing the chicken. Heat oil in a
casserole, add chicken, garlic and
spices and cook, covered, 5 minutes
on HIGH. Stir frequently while
cooking. Add methi, coriander, flour
and gradually stir in the stock. Add
jaggery or sugar, tamarind extract and
prepared eggplant. Cover and cook
on HIGH for 7-8 minutes. Drain the
lentils and discard onion slice and
bay leaf. Add the lentils to the
chicken and reheat 2 minutes on
HIGH before serving.

Goan Chicken

PREPARATION TIME: 25 minutes

MICROWAVE COOKING TIME:
27-30 minutes plus standing time

SERVES: 4-6 people

3 tbsps oil
1 tbsp ground coriander
1 tsp ground cumin
1 tsp ground cinnamon
1 tsp whole black mustard seeds (if
    available)
½ tsp ground cloves
½ tsp ground nutmeg
1 dried red chili (seeds removed if desired)
2¼ lbs chicken, skinned, boned and cut
    into 2 inch pieces
1 onion, finely chopped
2 cloves garlic, crushed
1 small piece ginger, grated
1 tbsp flour
1½ cups stock
½ a fresh coconut, grated
Salt

Heat a browning dish according to
the manufacturer's directions and
add the oil. Cook the spices, mustard
seeds and chili for 1 minute on
HIGH. Add onion, garlic and ginger
and cook a further 2 minutes on
HIGH. Scrape the mixture into a
large casserole. Re-heat the dish and
cook the chicken in 2 batches to
brown slightly. Place in the casserole
and stir in the flour. Gradually pour
over the stock, cover, and cook 20
minutes on HIGH. Add the coconut
and cook a further 2-5 minutes on
HIGH. Leave to stand 5 minutes
before serving.

Whole Spiced Chicken

PREPARATION TIME: 20 minutes
plus marinating

MICROWAVE COOKING TIME:
28-30 minutes

SERVES: 4-6 people

3½ lbs whole chicken

MARINADE
6 tbsps unflavored yogurt
1 clove garlic, crushed
1 small onion, grated
1 small piece ginger, grated
½ tsp ground turmeric
1 tbsp paprika
1 tsp garam masala
Salt and pepper
Juice of 1 lemon
1 tbsp cornstarch (optional)

Skin the chicken and lightly prick the
flesh all over. Mix the marinade
ingredients together and spread some

**Facing page: Chicken Dhansak
(top) and Goan Chicken (bottom).**

inside the chicken. Place the chicken in a roasting bag and spread with the remaining marinade. Set the chicken aside for 2 hours. Tie the roasting bag with string and place on a rack, breast side down. Cook on HIGH for 10 minutes. Turn over and cook a further 18-20 minutes more on MEDIUM, or until the legs move easily. Remove from the roasting bag to a serving plate and pour over the cooking juices. Thicken 2-3 minutes on HIGH with 1 tbsp cornstarch, if desired. Serve hot or cold, jointed or whole.

Tandoori Chicken

PREPARATION TIME: 20 minutes plus marinating time

MICROWAVE COOKING TIME: 15-20 minutes

SERVES: 4 people

This page: Whole Spiced Chicken. Facing page: Tandoori Chicken.

4 Rock Cornish hens, skinned and halved

MARINADE
2 cloves garlic, crushed
2 pieces ginger, grated
½ tsp ground black pepper
1 tsp chili powder

2 tsps paprika
1 tsp turmeric
Juice of 1 lime
1 cup unflavored yogurt

GARNISH
Lettuce
Tomato wedges
Lemon wedges

Prick the hens all over with a fork. Mix marinade and rub well into the hens and refrigerate overnight. Place the hens on a rack and cook 10-15 minutes on HIGH, basting frequently. Turn over halfway through the cooking time. Leave to stand, loosely covered, for 5 minutes before serving. Serve on a bed of shredded lettuce with tomato and lemon wedges.

Chicken Madras

PREPARATION TIME: 25 minutes

MICROWAVE COOKING TIME: 23 minutes plus standing time

SERVES: 4-6 people

3 tbsps oil
1 onion, chopped
2 cloves garlic, crushed
1 tsp chili powder
½ tsp ground coriander
½ tsp ground cumin
¼ tsp turmeric
¼ tsp fenugreek seeds, crushed
1 tbsp flour
1-2 chilies, finely chopped
2¼ lbs chicken, skinned, boned and cut into 2 inch pieces
1 bay leaf
2 curry leaves
4 tomatoes, skinned, seeded and roughly chopped
Salt
1 tbsp desiccated coconut
1 cup stock

Heat the oil for 1 minute on HIGH in a large bowl or casserole. Add the onion, garlic and spices and cook for 2 minutes on HIGH. Stir in the flour and add the chilies and chicken. Add the bay leaf, curry leaves, tomatoes, salt and coconut and gradually pour on the stock. Stir to mix well and

cover the dish. Cook on HIGH for 20 minutes or until the chicken is tender. Stir several times during cooking and leave to stand 3-5 minutes before serving. Remove the bay leaf and serve with rice.

Chicken Bombay

PREPARATION TIME: 25 minutes

MICROWAVE COOKING TIME: 23 minutes plus standing time

SERVES: 4-6 people

2 tbsps oil
1 onion, finely chopped
½ tsp turmeric
1 tsp ground coriander
1 tsp ground cumin
¼ tsp ground nutmeg
1 tbsp flour
2¼ lbs chicken, skinned and boned and cut into 2 inch pieces
¾ cup stock
Juice of ½ a lime
1 bay leaf
Salt and pepper
½ cup unflavored yogurt
½ cup split almonds
2 hard-boiled eggs, quartered

Heat the oil for 1 minute in a casserole. Add the onion, turmeric, coriander, cumin and nutmeg. Cook for 2 minutes on HIGH and stir in the flour. Add the chicken, pour over the stock and lime juice, add the bay leaf and stir well. Cover and cook for 20 minutes on HIGH or until the chicken is tender. Stir frequently during cooking. Stir in the yogurt, almonds and hard-boiled eggs and leave to stand 3-5 minutes before serving. Remove the bay leaf and serve with rice.

Chicken Korma

PREPARATION TIME: 25 minutes

MICROWAVE COOKING TIME: 23 minutes plus standing time

SERVES: 4-6 people

2 tbsps oil
1 onion, sliced
½ tsp turmeric

1 tsp coriander
¼ tsp cinnamon
1 tbsp flour
2¼ lbs chicken, shredded and boned
3 cardamoms
¾ cup stock
Juice of ½ a lemon
1 bay leaf
Salt and pepper
½ cup yogurt
½ cup cashews

Heat oil for 1 minute in a casserole. Add onion, turmeric, coriander and cinnamon and cook for 2 minutes on HIGH. Stir in the flour and add the chicken, cut into 2 inch pieces, and cardamoms. Pour over the stock and the lemon juice and stir well. Cover and cook for 20 minutes on HIGH or until the chicken is tender. Stir frequently during cooking. Remove the bay leaf and stir in the yogurt and the cashews. Leave to stand for 3-5 minutes before serving.

Butter Chicken

PREPARATION TIME: 25 minutes

MICROWAVE COOKING TIME: 23 minutes plus standing time

SERVES: 4-6 people

3 tbsps butter
1 onion, finely chopped
1 small piece ginger, grated
3 cloves garlic, crushed
½ tsp chili powder
½ tsp ground cumin
½ tsp ground coriander
¼ tsp ground cinnamon
3 whole cloves
1 bay leaf
3 cardamoms, crushed
1 tbsp flour
2¼ lbs chicken, skinned, boned and shredded
½ cup chicken stock
14oz canned tomatoes, crushed
Salt
½ cup unflavored yogurt

Facing page: Chicken Madras (top) and Chicken Bombay (bottom).

This page: **Chicken and Almonds in Red Sauce.** Facing page: **Butter Chicken (top)** and **Chicken Korma (bottom).**

GARNISH
Tomato wedges

Melt butter for 1 minute on HIGH and add the onion, ginger, garlic and spices. Cook 2 minutes on HIGH and stir in the flour. Add the bay leaf, cardamoms, cloves and chicken shreds. Gradually stir in the chicken stock and tomatoes. Cover and cook on HIGH for 20 minutes or until the chicken is tender. Stir occasionally while cooking. Add the yogurt and leave to stand 3-5 minutes. Remove the bay leaf and serve with tomato wedges.

Chicken and Almonds in Red Sauce

PREPARATION TIME: 25 minutes
MICROWAVE COOKING TIME: 19-22 minutes
SERVES: 4-6 people

1 large onion, chopped
1 small piece ginger, chopped
1-2 cloves garlic, crushed
2 tsps cumin seeds
1 tsp coriander seeds
¼ tsp turmeric
¼ tsp cayenne pepper
3 red peppers, seeded and roughly chopped
2 tbsps ground almonds
3 tbsps oil
1 cup water or stock

Juice of 1 lime
1-2 tsps sugar
2¼ lbs chicken, skinned and boned and cut into 2 inch pieces

GARNISH
Blanched almonds

Combine the first 8 ingredients in a blender or food processor and work to a paste. Add the ground almonds and process for 1 minute. Heat a browning dish according to the manufacturer's directions and add the oil. Pour in all the paste and cook for 1-2 minutes on HIGH. Place chicken pieces in a casserole and pour over the water or stock and lime juice. Add salt, pepper, sugar to taste and stir in the red pepper paste. Cover and cook on HIGH for 15 minutes or until the chicken is tender. Allow to stand 3-5 minutes and sprinkle with the blanched almonds before serving.

Chicken Biryani

PREPARATION TIME: 30 minutes
MICROWAVE COOKING TIME: 33-34 minutes plus standing time
SERVES: 4 people

½ cup basmati rice
1 tsp saffron
4 tbsps milk
4 tbsps butter or margarine
1 onion, thinly sliced
3 tbsps golden raisins
3 tbsps sliced almonds
1 tsp ground coriander
1 tsp ground ginger
¼ tsp ground cinnamon
4 chicken pieces, skinned and boned
1 bay leaf
2 cloves
1 cardamom, crushed
1½ cups hot chicken stock
½ cup frozen peas
¼ tsp rose water (optional)
Salt and pepper

Combine saffron and milk in a small bowl and heat for 30 seconds on HIGH. Leave to infuse. Wash the rice until the water runs clear and leave to drain. Heat a browning dish according to the manufacturer's

directions. When hot, melt the butter and brown the onions for 1 minute on HIGH. Add the golden raisins and almonds and brown 2 minutes on HIGH. Add the coriander, ginger and cinnamon and cook for 1 minute on HIGH. Combine rice with the onions, golden raisins and spices in a large casserole. Add chicken, cut into small pieces, bay leaf, cloves and cardamom pod. Pour over the chicken stock, cover and cook for 10 minutes on HIGH. Cook an additional 15 minutes on MEDIUM HIGH or 20 minutes on MEDIUM. Add the peas to the casserole and mix the saffron milk with the rose water, if using. Drizzle over the top of the rice and cook a further 4-5 minutes on HIGH. Leave to stand for 5 minutes before serving. Garnish with coriander leaves, if desired.

This page: Chicken Biryani. Facing page: Sweet and Sour Okra.

VEGETABLE, PULSE AND RICE DISHES

Sweet and Sour Okra

PREPARATION TIME: 15 minutes

MICROWAVE COOKING TIME:
4-5 minutes plus standing time

SERVES: 6 people

2 tbsps butter or margarine
1 tsp coriander seeds, crushed
2 tsps cumin seeds, crushed
½ tsp ground turmeric
3 cloves garlic, crushed
Juice of 1 lemon
1 tsp sugar
1lb okra, washed but left whole
6 tomatoes, peeled quartered and seeded

Melt the butter in a large casserole for 30 seconds on HIGH. Stir in the coriander, cumin, turmeric and garlic. Cook for 1-2 minutes on HIGH. Add the lemon juice, sugar and okra. Stir well and cover tightly. Cook on HIGH for 3 minutes. Add the tomatoes and leave to stand, covered, for 5 minutes before serving.

Vegetable Niramish

PREPARATION TIME: 15 minutes

MICROWAVE COOKING TIME:
10-15 minutes plus standing time

SERVES: 4-6 people

3 tbsps oil
1 onion, peeled and chopped
1 tsp cumin seeds
1 large potato, peeled and cut into chunks
4oz cauliflower flowerets, fresh or frozen

1 small eggplant
1 small green pepper, seeded and cut into
*   1 inch pieces*
2 small carrots, peeled and cut into
*   chunks*
Salt
1 tsp ground coriander
1 tsp chili powder
1 tsp turmeric
6 tbsps vegetable stock
Juice of 1 lime
2 sprigs fresh coriander leaves, chopped
1 green chili, seeded and finely chopped

Heat the oil for 30 seconds on HIGH
and add the onion and cumin seed.
Cook for 1 minute to slightly soften
the onion. Add the potato, cover and
cook 5 minutes on HIGH. Cut the
eggplant into chunks and add to the

potato with the cauliflower, green
pepper and carrot. Sprinkle on the
ground spices and pour over the
stock. Cook a further 5-10 minutes
on HIGH and add the coriander
leaves and the finely chopped chili.
Add the lime juice and salt to taste.
Stir and leave to stand, covered, for
5 minutes before serving.

Vegetable Curry

PREPARATION TIME: 15 minutes

MICROWAVE COOKING TIME:
10-15 minutes

SERVES: 4-6 people

2 tbsps oil
1 onion, finely chopped
1 large potato, cut into chunks
4oz green beans, cut into 2 inch pieces
2 carrots, peeled and cut into chunks
2oz okra, left whole
¼ cup frozen peas
1 clove garlic, crushed
1 tbsp curry paste
1 green chili, seeded and finely chopped
8oz canned tomatoes and juice
Salt and pepper
1 tbsp cornstarch mixed with 6 tbsps
*   water*
½ cup vegetable stock

Heat the oil for 30 seconds on HIGH
and stir in the onion. Cook on
HIGH for 1-2 minutes to soften. Add
the potato and cover the bowl. Cook
on HIGH for 10 minutes. Stir in the
remaining ingredients and re-cover
the dish. Cook on HIGH for a
further 5 minutes, or until the
vegetables are tender and the sauce is
thickened.

Kidney Bean Curry

PREPARATION TIME: 15 minutes

MICROWAVE COOKING TIME:
11-17 minutes plus standing time

SERVES: 6 people

2 tbsps oil
1 onion, peeled and thinly sliced
1 clove garlic, crushed
1 small piece ginger, grated
1 tsp chili powder
1 tsp ground coriander
1 tsp ground cumin
1 cinnamon stick
1 bay leaf
1 tsp garam masala
8oz canned red kidney beans, drained
15oz canned tomatoes and their juice
Salt
2 green chili peppers, seeded and thinly
*   sliced*
2 sprigs coriander leaves, chopped

Heat the oil for 30 seconds on HIGH
and stir in the onions, garlic, ginger,

**This page: Vegetable Curry. Facing
page: Vegetable Niramish (top) and
Kidney Bean Curry (bottom).**

chili powder, coriander, garam masala, cinnamon and cumin and cook for 1-2 minutes on HIGH. Add the remaining ingredients and cover tightly. Cook on HIGH for 10-15 minutes. Leave to stand 5 minutes before serving.

Spinach and Potato Bhaji

PREPARATION TIME: 20 minutes

MICROWAVE COOKING TIME: 11-16 minutes

SERVES: 6 people

2 tbsps butter or margarine
1 tsp chili powder
1 tsp cumin seed
1 tsp ground coriander
¼ tsp turmeric
1lb potatoes, peeled and cut into chunks
8oz fresh spinach, well washed and shredded, or chopped frozen spinach
Salt
1 tbsp lemon juice

Heat the butter or margarine in a large casserole and add the chili powder, cumin seed, ground coriander and turmeric. Heat for 1-2 minutes on HIGH. Add the potatoes and stir well. Cover and cook 10-14 minutes on HIGH. Add the spinach during the last 2 minutes of cooking. Add lemon juice and salt to taste.

Chickpeas with Spices

PREPARATION TIME: 15 minutes

MICROWAVE COOKING TIME: 5-6 minutes

SERVES: 4-6 people

2 tbsps oil
1 small onion, finely chopped
1 clove garlic, crushed
1 small piece ginger, grated
1 tsp ground coriander
1 tsp chili powder
¼ tsp turmeric
4oz canned tomatoes, roughly chopped

1 green chili, seeded and chopped
4 cardamoms, crushed
Salt
2 sprigs fresh coriander, chopped
1 bay leaf
15oz canned chickpeas
Juice of 1 lemon

Put the oil in a casserole and add the onion, garlic, ginger and ground spices. Cook 1 minute on HIGH. Add the tomatoes and juice, chilies, salt, coriander and bay leaf. Add the chickpeas and half of the liquid, salt, cardamoms and lemon juice and cover the casserole. Cook on HIGH 4-6 minutes or until completely heated through. Remove the bay leaf and serve as a side dish to other curries.

This page: Spinach and Potato Bhaji. Facing page: Chickpeas with Spices (top) and Dahl (bottom).

Dahl

PREPARATION TIME: 25 minutes

MICROWAVE COOKING TIME: 45 minutes plus 5-10 minutes standing time

SERVES: 4 people

8oz red lentils
4 tbsps butter or margarine
1 large onion, finely chopped
1 clove garlic, crushed
1 tsp cumin

¼ tsp garam masala
1 tsp sugar
1 tsp lemon or lime juice
1 bay leaf
1 small head white cabbage, cored and
   thinly sliced
¼ cup frozen peas
Salt

Heat the butter or margarine for 30 seconds on HIGH. Add the spices and chili pepper and cook for 1-2 minutes on HIGH. Add the sugar, lemon juice, salt and cabbage and stir well. Cover tightly and cook on HIGH for 6 minutes. Add the peas and cook a further 2-3 minutes on HIGH. Leave to stand 2-3 minutes before serving.

Saffron Leeks

PREPARATION TIME: 20 minutes plus chilling time

MICROWAVE COOKING TIME: 10 minutes

SERVES: 6 people

6 medium-sized leeks
3 cloves garlic, crushed
Grated nutmeg
Grated rind and juice of 1 lemon
1 small piece stick cinnamon
1 bay leaf
¼ tsp saffron
Cayenne pepper
4 tbsps vegetable oil
Salt

Trim the tops of the leeks neatly and cut them lengthwise almost in half. Rinse thoroughly and leave to drain. Place in a large, shallow dish with the garlic, nutmeg, lemon juice and rind, cinnamon, bay leaf and a pinch of cayenne pepper. Cover tightly and cook on HIGH for about 8 minutes. Drain the leeks, reserving the liquid and set the leeks aside to cool. Infuse the remaining liquid with the saffron for 2 minutes on HIGH. Combine the liquid with the oil and add salt to

1 tsp coriander
1 tsp turmeric
½ tsp cinnamon
½ tsp nutmeg
3 cups vegetable stock
Salt and pepper
1 bay leaf
5 tomatoes, peeled and seeded
1 tbsp tomato paste
Chopped coriander leaves
1 green chili pepper, finely shredded

Cover the lentils with water and soak overnight. Alternatively, microwave 10 minutes to boil the water and then allow the lentils to boil for 2 minutes. Leave to stand, covered, for 1 hour. Melt the butter or margarine for 1 minute on HIGH in a large casserole. Add the onion, garlic, and spices. Cook 4 minutes on MEDIUM. Drain the lentils and add

to the casserole with the vegetable stock. Cover and cook on HIGH for 45 minutes, or until the lentils are soft and tender. Add tomatoes and paste. Allow to stand, covered, 5-10 minutes before serving. Purée before serving and add the chopped coriander. Sprinkle the shredded chili on top before serving.

Spiced Cabbage and Peas

PREPARATION TIME: 15 minutes

MICROWAVE COOKING TIME: 9-11 minutes

SERVES: 6 people

3 tbsps butter or margarine
2 tsps cumin seed
1 green chili, seeded and finely chopped

This page: Saffron Leeks (top) and Spiced Cabbage and Peas (bottom). Facing page: Lamb Pilau.

taste. Lightly prick the leeks with a fork and place them in a shallow serving dish. Pour over the cooking liquid and oil mixture and chill 2-4 hours before serving.

Eggplant slices in Yogurt

PREPARATION TIME: 10 minutes

MICROWAVE COOKING TIME: 2-4 minutes

SERVES: 4-6 people

1 large eggplant, cut into ¼ inch thick
  rounds
Salt
3 tbsps oil
1 tsp chili powder
¼ tsp turmeric
1 tsp garam masala powder
1 green chili, seeded and thinly sliced
1 sprig methi or coriander leaves, chopped
½ cup natural yogurt
Paprika

Lightly score the eggplant on both sides and sprinkle with salt. Leave to stand for 30 minutes, drain and pat dry. Heat the oil in a casserole for 30 seconds on HIGH and stir in the chili powder, garam masala, chili and eggplant slices. Cover the dish and cook on HIGH for 2-3 minutes. Pour over the yogurt and leave to stand for 3-5 minutes. Sprinkle over the methi or coriander leaves and paprika and serve hot or cold.

Zucchini Curry

PREPARATION TIME: 20 minutes

MICROWAVE COOKING TIME: 4-5 minutes

SERVES: 4-6 people

1 tbsp oil
1 tsp cumin seed
1 tsp mustard seed
½ tsp chili powder
¼ tsp turmeric
8oz canned tomatoes and juice
1 green chili, seeded and finely chopped
8oz zucchini, cut into ¼ inch slices
Salt and pepper

Heat the oil for 30 seconds on HIGH and add the cumin seed, chili powder and turmeric. Cook for 1-2 minutes on HIGH. Add the tomatoes and juice, chili pepper and zucchini. Cover and cook on HIGH for 3 minutes. Add salt and leave to stand 1 minute before serving. If desired, thicken the liquid with 1 tbsp cornstarch mixed with 4 tbsps reserved tomato juice.

Brinjal Bartha

PREPARATION TIME: 30 minutes

MICROWAVE COOKING TIME: 12-20 minutes

SERVES: 6 people

2 eggplant
2 tbsps butter or margarine
1 small onion, finely chopped

This page: Zucchini Curry. Facing page: Eggplant Slices in Yogurt (top) and Brinjal Bartha (bottom).

1 tbsp coriander seed, crushed
2 tsps cumin seeds
1 clove garlic, crushed
2 tsps chopped parsley or coriander
Salt and pepper
Paprika

Cut the eggplant in half lengthwise, score the flesh lightly and sprinkle with salt. Leave to stand 30 minutes, rinse well and pat dry. Wrap the eggplant in plastic wrap and cook on HIGH for 5-7 minutes. Leave to stand, wrapped, for 5-10 minutes. Meanwhile, melt the butter on HIGH for 1 minute. Add the onions,

Cumin Rice

PREPARATION TIME: 5 minutes

MICROWAVE COOKING TIME: 12 minutes

SERVES: 4-6 people

2 tbsps butter or margarine
1 tsp cumin seed
¼ tsp turmeric
1 cup long grain rice
Salt and pepper
2 cups boiling water

Melt the butter in a large casserole or deep bowl for 30 seconds on HIGH. Add the cumin seed, turmeric and rice and stir well. Cook, uncovered, 3 minutes on HIGH. Add salt and pepper and pour on the water. Cover the bowl and cook on HIGH for 12 minutes, stirring once or twice. Leave the rice to stand for 5 minutes before serving.

Shrimp Pilau with Cashews

PREPARATION TIME: 6 minutes

MICROWAVE COOKING TIME: 12 minutes

SERVES: 4-6 people

4 tbsps butter or margarine
1 cup long grain rice
1 onion, peeled and finely chopped
6 cloves
6 cardamoms, crushed
1 tbsp crushed coriander seeds
1 small piece stick cinnamon
1 bay leaf
1 small piece ginger, grated
1 clove garlic, crushed
1 tsp garam masala
1 green chili, finely chopped
Salt and pepper
2 cups boiling water or fish stock
8oz peeled, cooked shrimp
Chopped coriander leaves or parsley
½ cup salted cashews

coriander seed, cumin seed and garlic and cook for 1-2 minutes on HIGH. Unwrap the eggplant and scoop out the pulp. Mix with the onions and spices by hand or in a food processor. Add the chopped parsley or coriander and adjust the seasoning. Sprinkle lightly with paprika to serve.

Lamb Pilau

PREPARATION TIME: 20 minutes

MICROWAVE COOKING TIME: 16 minutes plus standing time

SERVES: 4-6 people

4 tbsps butter or margarine
1 cup long grain rice
1 onion, finely chopped
1 clove garlic, crushed
1 small piece ginger, grated
4 tbsps cashew nuts
8oz cooked lamb, cubed
1 tsp black cumin seeds
1 tsp ground coriander
2 cups boiling stock
4 tbsps golden raisins
Salt and pepper
Chopped coriander leaves

Place the butter or margarine, rice, onion, garlic, ginger and cashew nuts in a deep casserole or bowl. Cook, uncovered, on HIGH for 3 minutes or until the onion is soft and the cashew nuts are lightly toasted. Add the spices and cook for 1 minute on HIGH. Stir in the lamb and the stock. Cover the bowl and cook on HIGH for 12 minutes. Add the golden raisins to the hot rice and leave to stand, covered, for 5 minutes before serving. Garnish with chopped coriander leaves.

This page: Braised Cauliflower. Facing page: Cumin Rice (top) and Spiced Pilau Rice with Peas (bottom).

Combine butter, onion, rice, spices, ginger, garlic, bay leaf and chilies in a large bowl or casserole. Cook 3 minutes to soften the onion and chilies. Pour in the boiling water or stock, cover the bowl and cook on HIGH for 12 minutes. When the rice has absorbed the water, add the shrimp and leave to stand, covered, for 5 minutes. To serve, chop the cashew nuts roughly and sprinkle on top with chopped coriander leaves.

Steamed Green Beans and Fennel

PREPARATION TIME: 20 minutes

MICROWAVE COOKING TIME: 10-12 minutes plus standing time

SERVES: 6 people

1lb green beans
1 small onion, finely sliced
1 small piece ginger, grated
1 tbsp butter or margarine
Salt
1 small bulb fennel, finely sliced

Slice the beans on the diagonal into ½ inch slivers. Mix all the ingredients together and cover well. Cook for 10-12 minutes and leave to stand 5 minutes, covered, before serving.

Vegetable Pilau

PREPARATION TIME: 15 minutes

MICROWAVE COOKING TIME: 15 minutes plus standing time

SERVES: 4-6 people

4 tbsps butter or margarine
1 cup long grain rice
1 onion, finely sliced
1 small piece cinnamon stick
1 bay leaf
4 cardamoms, crushed
4 cloves
½ tsp ground coriander
¼ tsp turmeric
¼ tsp garam masala
Salt and pepper
2 cups boiling vegetable stock or water
½ eggplant, cut into small cubes

2oz frozen cauliflower flowerets
4oz mixed frozen vegetables

Place the butter, rice, onion and spices in a large, deep bowl or casserole. Cook, uncovered, on HIGH for 3 minutes or until the onion is almost soft. Pour on the stock or water and add the eggplant. Cover and cook on HIGH for 10 minutes. Add the mixed vegetables and cauliflower and cook a further 1-2 minutes on HIGH. Allow to stand for 5 minutes before serving.

Braised Cauliflower

PREPARATION TIME: 10 minutes

MICROWAVE COOKING TIME: 6-8 minutes plus standing time

SERVES: 4-6 people

1 tbsp butter or margarine
2 tsps mustard seed
½ tsp turmeric
1 small piece ginger, grated
1 tsp cumin
¼ tsp paprika
¼ tsp coarsely ground black pepper
1 large cauliflower, cut into small flowerets
2 tbsps water
Salt
Lemon juice to taste

Melt the butter for 30 seconds on HIGH in a casserole and add the mustard seed, ginger, turmeric, cumin, paprika and pepper. Cook for 1-2 minutes on HIGH. Add the cauliflower and water and stir to mix well. Cover the casserole and cook

on HIGH 5-6 minutes. Add salt and lemon juice and stir again. Leave covered for 3-5 minutes before serving.

Lima Beans and Red Peppers

PREPARATION TIME: 10 minutes

MICROWAVE COOKING TIME: 10 minutes

SERVES: 4-6 people

1 tbsp butter or margarine
2 shallots, finely chopped
¼ tsp turmeric
½ tsp chili powder
1 tsp ground coriander
2-3 curry leaves, crushed
8oz lima beans, fresh or frozen
6 tbsps vegetable stock
1 green chili, chopped
1 large red pepper, seeded and cut in pieces equal in size to the beans
Salt and pepper

Heat the butter or margarine for 30 seconds on HIGH and add the shallots, turmeric, chili powder and coriander. Heat 1-2 minutes on HIGH to soften the shallots and cook the spices. Add the beans, vegetable stock, chili pepper and salt and pepper to taste. Cover and cook on HIGH for 8 minutes. Add the peppers and cook a further 2 minutes on HIGH. Leave to stand, covered, 1-2 minutes before serving.

Facing page: Steamed Green Beans and Fennel (top) and Lima Beans and Red Peppers (bottom). This page: Vegetable Pilau.

RELISHES AND ACCOMPANIMENTS

Mixed Fruit Chutney

PREPARATION TIME: 20 minutes

MICROWAVE COOKING TIME:
27-30 minutes

MAKES: 2 cups

½ tsp each of cumin seed, coriander seed,
    black sesame seeds and aniseed
4 tbsps chopped, unblanched almonds
2 apples, cored and chopped
4 plums, stoned and chopped
1 large mango, peeled, stoned and sliced
1 cup dates, pitted and chopped
4 tbsps raisins
1 small piece ginger, peeled and chopped
¾ cup brown sugar or jaggery
2-3 red chili peppers, finely sliced
¾ cup malt or cider vinegar
Salt
1 banana, peeled and sliced
1 small can pineapple pieces, drained and
    juice reserved

Combine all the spices and the
almonds in a large, deep bowl and
cook on HIGH for 5 minutes to roast
the spices and lightly brown the
almonds. Add the apples, plums,
mango, dates, raisins, ginger and
vinegar. Cover and cook on HIGH
for 2 minutes. Add all the remaining
ingredients and re-cover the bowl.
Cook a further 20 minutes on
HIGH, stirring occasionally. If the
chutney becomes too thick during
cooking add the reserved pineapple
juice. If at the end of 20 minutes the
chutney is not thick enough, uncover
the bowl and continue to cook
another 2-3 minutes. Allow the
chutney to cool and pour into

containers to keep in the refrigerator.

Poppadoms

PREPARATION TIME: 10 minutes

MICROWAVE COOKING TIME:
30 seconds per poppadom

SERVES: 8-10 people

1 package plain or spiced poppadoms
Oil

Brush each side of the poppadoms
lightly with a little oil and cook one
at a time on HIGH for 30 seconds, or
until crisp. To cook two together,
microwave for 1½-2 minutes on
HIGH. Serve as an accompaniment
to any of the main dishes, or as a
snack.

Mango Chutney

PREPARATION TIME: 15 minutes

MICROWAVE COOKING TIME:
30-35 minutes

MAKES: Approximately 4 cups

4 ripe mangoes
1 onion, finely chopped
1 clove garlic, finely chopped
1 tbsp grated fresh ginger root
1 tsp whole cloves
½ tsp turmeric
1 tsp ground coriander
¼ tsp Cayenne pepper

½ cup sugar
1 cup cider vinegar
Salt

Remove the stones from the
mangoes, scrape out the flesh and
chop roughly. Mix all the ingredients,
except the sugar and salt, together in
a large bowl and cover with pierced
plastic wrap. Cook for 15 minutes on
HIGH, stirring frequently. Remove
cloves and purée in a food processor.
Add the sugar and salt and cook,
uncovered, for 15 minutes on HIGH
or until thickened. Stir frequently.
Test by stirring with a wooden spoon;
if the spoon leaves a channel, setting
point has been reached. If not set,
cook for a further 5 minutes on
HIGH. Pour into hot sterilized jars,
seal and cover. Store in a cool place.

Chapatis

PREPARATION TIME: 6 minutes

MICROWAVE COOKING TIME:
16-20 minutes

SERVES: 8-10 people

1lb whole-wheat flour
Pinch salt
1 tbsp vegetable oil
½-¾ cup tepid water

Sift the flour and the salt into a
mixing bowl and return the bran to

**Facing page: Mixed Fruit Chutney
(top) and Mango Chutney (bottom).**

2 onions, thinly sliced
2 tsps ground coriander
¼ tsp paprika
Salt
Saffron
1 fresh coconut, grated and milk reserved
2 tbsps chopped coriander
1 tsp lemon or lime juice

Place the butter and onions in a large bowl and cook for 3 minutes on HIGH to soften the onions. Add the coriander, paprika and saffron and cook a further 1 minute on HIGH. Combine the coconut and its liquid and a pinch of salt. Cover and cook on HIGH for 2 minutes. Stir in the lemon juice and the chopped coriander and leave to cool. Keep in the refrigerator.
NOTE: May be served with finely chopped hard-boiled eggs sprinkled on top.

Marinated Mushrooms

PREPARATION TIME: 20 minutes
MICROWAVE COOKING TIME:
4-6 minutes
SERVES: 6 people

1 tbsp paprika
¼ tsp cayenne pepper
1½ tbsps ground coriander
1 tsp fennel seed
1 tsp dried basil
½ cup olive oil
3 cloves garlic, minced
Juice of 2 limes
2 bay leaves
Salt
1lb small mushrooms, left whole
1 tbsp tomato paste
2 pimentos, thinly sliced

Place the paprika, cayenne pepper, coriander and fennel in a large, deep bowl. Cook on HIGH for 1-2 minutes to roast the spices. Add the basil, salt and pepper, oil, lime juice, garlic and bay leaves. Clean the mushrooms and add with the tomato

the flour. Add the oil and enough water to mix to a soft, pliable dough. Cover and leave to stand for 5 minutes. Divide into 16-20 even-sized balls and roll out each ball on a lightly floured surface into 7 inch diameter circles. Meanwhile, heat a browning dish to the manufacturer's directions. Lightly grease the browning dish with oil and place 1 chapati on the browning dish, pressing down firmly with a spatula or palette knife. When small bubbles appear on the top of the chapati turn it over and place the chapati in the microwave oven for 1-1½ minutes on HIGH. Chapatis will be speckled brown on the side which was cooked

first and will puff up slightly as they cook. Continue with the remaining chapatis and brush each with a little melted butter. Keep the cooked chapatis well wrapped in a clean towel or foil. Serve warm.

Coconut Relish

PREPARATION TIME: 25 minutes
MICROWAVE COOKING TIME:
6 minutes
SERVES: 4-6 people

1½ tbsps butter or oil

This page: Chapatis (top) and Poppadoms (bottom). Facing page: Marinated Mushrooms (top) and Coconut Relish (bottom).

paste to the other ingredients. Stir well and cover loosely. Cook on HIGH for about 3-4 minutes. Add the pimento and allow to cool. Keep in the refrigerator.

Tomato Relish

PREPARATION TIME: 20 minutes

MICROWAVE COOKING TIME: 10 minutes

SERVES: 6 people

1lb tomatoes, peeled and roughly chopped
½ tsp basil
1 tbsp chopped mint leaves
Pinch saffron
Salt and pepper
Pinch sugar
1 tbsp chopped methi leaves or curry leaves
6 tbsps heavy cream

Combine the tomatoes, basil, mint, salt, pepper, saffron and sugar in a large, deep bowl. Cook on HIGH for 10 minutes or until the tomatoes are a thick purée. Allow to cool and combine the methi or curry leaves with the heavy cream. Spoon on top of the tomatoes and serve as a side dish.

Pineapple and Mint Chutney

PREPARATION TIME: 20 minutes

MICROWAVE COOKING TIME: 35 minutes

MAKES: Approximately 4 cups

3 cups fresh pineapple, chopped
2 cups distilled white vinegar
1½ cups golden raisins
1 small bunch fresh mint, chopped
¼ tsp ground nutmeg
1 small piece ginger, grated
Salt
1 cup sugar

Sprinkle the pineapple with a good pinch of salt and leave for 1 hour. Drain the pineapple and rinse in cold

water. Put all the ingredients except the sugar into a large bowl. Cover with pierced plastic wrap and cook for 15 minutes on HIGH, stirring frequently. Add the sugar and cook, uncovered, for a further 15 minutes on HIGH or until thickened. If necessary, add another pinch of salt and pour into hot sterilized jars. Seal, cover and keep in a cool place.

Spiced Pilau Rice with Peas

PREPARATION TIME: 10 minutes

MICROWAVE COOKING TIME: 12 minutes

SERVES: 4-6 people

4 tbsps butter or margarine
1 cup long grain rice
1 onion, finely chopped
1 tbsp cassia bark
3 cloves
3 cardamoms, slightly crushed
1 tsp black cumin seed
1 tsp red pepper flakes (optional)
2 cups boiling water
½-¾ cup frozen peas
1 tsp lemon juice
Salt

Place the butter or margarine, rice and onion in a large casserole or deep bowl. Cook, uncovered, on HIGH for 3 minutes until the onion is almost soft. Add the spices and pour on the water. Cover and cook on HIGH for 12 minutes. Two minutes before the end of cooking time add the frozen peas and the lemon juice and stir to mix. Cook for the remaining 2 minutes and leave to stand for 5 minutes before serving.

This page: Shrimp Pilau with Cashews. Facing page: Tomato Relish (left) and Pineapple and Mint Chutney (right).

DESSERTS

Carrot Halva

PREPARATION TIME: 15 minutes

MICROWAVE COOKING TIME:
15 minutes

SERVES: 4 people

2lbs carrots, peeled and grated
1 cup heavy cream
½ cup light brown sugar
1 tsp cinnamon
8 cardamoms, seeds crushed
½ tsp grated nutmeg
½ cup blanched almonds
½ cup pistachio nuts, chopped
4 tbsps desiccated coconut

Cook the grated carrots with the heavy cream and sugar on HIGH for 15 minutes. Add the cinnamon and nutmeg and leave to stand 15 minutes, stirring occasionally until the mixture is very thick. To serve, decorate with the chopped nuts and desiccated coconut.

Creamed Rice and Rose Water

PREPARATION TIME: 5 minutes

MICROWAVE COOKING TIME:
35 minutes

SERVES: 4 people

½-¾ cup rice
2 cups boiling water
Grated rind of 1 lemon
4 tbsps sugar
Pinch ground nutmeg
1½ cups evaporated milk
½ cup blanched sliced almonds
½ cup whipped cream
Few drops rose water

Silver dragees (balls)
Candied rose petals

Put the rice, water, lemon rind and nutmeg in a deep bowl or casserole and cook on HIGH for 10 minutes, stirring occasionally. Add the sugar and milk and cook on LOW or DEFROST for 20 minutes, stirring occasionally. Stir in the sliced almonds and continue to cook on LOW or DEFROST for a further 5 minutes. Allow to cool slightly and then fold in the whipped cream and rose water. Decorate with whole blanched almonds, silver dragees and candied rose petals. Serve warm or cold.

Sago Pudding

PREPARATION TIME: 10 minutes

MICROWAVE COOKING TIME:
22-23 minutes

SERVES: 4 people

2 cups milk
2 tbsps desiccated coconut
4 tbsps sago
2 tbsps sugar
2 tbsps golden raisins
8 small cardamoms, seeds removed and crushed
2 tbsps blanched sliced almonds
Pinch saffron
4 tbsps raisins
4 tbsps roughly chopped pistachio nuts

Place the milk, sago, coconut and sugar in a large bowl. Cook on HIGH for 5-6 minutes or until the milk boils. Stir well and add the golden raisins and cardamoms. Cover with

pierced plastic wrap and cook on HIGH for 2 minutes. Reduce the setting to LOW and cook for a further 15 minutes or until the sago is soft and clear. Stir every 5 minutes while cooking. Add the almonds and allow to stand for 5 minutes before serving. Spoon into serving dishes and sprinkle over the saffron, raisins and pistachio nuts.

Vermicelli Pudding

PREPARATION TIME: 5 minutes

MICROWAVE COOKING TIME:
12 minutes

SERVES: 4 people

4oz vermicelli, broken into small pieces
2 cups milk
1 bay leaf
2-4 tbsps sugar
2 tbsps blanched slivered almonds
1 tsp ground nutmeg
Grated rind of 2 limes

Combine the milk and vermicelli in a deep bowl. Partially cover and cook on HIGH for 10-12 minutes. Add the sugar during the last 2 minutes of cooking time. Stir in the nutmeg and the almonds and cover the bowl tightly. Leave to stand for 5-10 minutes. Remove the bay leaf and divide between 4 serving dishes. Grate ½ a lime over each serving and serve hot or cold.

Facing page: Carrot Halva.

Baked Mango and Rice

PREPARATION TIME: 20 minutes

MICROWAVE COOKING TIME:
30 minutes plus standing time

SERVES: 4 people

2 large ripe mangoes
Juice of 1 lime
½-¾ cup round grain or pudding rice
2 cups boiling water

Pinch cinnamon
Pinch nutmeg
2 tbsps sugar
6oz can evaporated milk

Slice both mangoes in half, reserving one half for garnish. Scoop the flesh from the other halves and purée in a food processor with the lime juice. Combine the rice, water, cinnamon and nutmeg in a large, deep bowl or

This page: Baked Mango and Rice. Facing page: Sago Pudding (top) and Vermicelli Pudding (bottom).

casserole and cook on HIGH for 10 minutes. Stir occasionally. Add the sugar and the evaporated milk and cook on LOW for 15 minutes, stirring occasionally. Allow to stand

for 5-10 minutes, covered. Put a layer of rice into a deep serving dish and spread over a layer of mango. Repeat until the rice and mango are used up, ending with a layer of rice. Sprinkle lightly with grated nutmeg and cook on LOW for a further 5 minutes. Slice the remaining mango thinly and decorate the top of the pudding before serving. Serve hot or cold.

Semolina Pudding

PREPARATION TIME: 5-6 minutes

MICROWAVE COOKING TIME: 17-20 minutes

SERVES: 4 people

2 cups milk
4 tbsps semolina
2 tbsps sugar
½ cup almonds and cashew nuts, mixed
½ cup raisins and golden raisins mixed
1 tsp crushed coriander seeds
½ tsp almond extract

Place the milk, semolina and sugar in a large bowl. Cook on HIGH for 5-6 minutes or until the milk boils. Stir well and add the remaining ingredients. Cover with pierced plastic wrap and cook on HIGH for 2 minutes. Reduce the power to LOW and then cook for 10-15 minutes or until thickened. Leave, stir every 5 minutes and allow to stand, covered, for 5 minutes before serving. The pudding should be quite thick.

Kulfi

PREPARATION TIME: 15 minutes

MICROWAVE COOKING TIME: 12 minutes

SERVES: 6-8 people

3 cups whipping cream
5 whole cardamom pods
4-6 tbsps sugar
Dash almond extract
½ cup chopped pistachio nuts

Place the cream and cardamoms in a

large, deep bowl. Cover loosely and cook on HIGH for 10 minutes or until the cream boils. Allow the cream to boil a further 2 minutes on HIGH and stir in the sugar. Remove the cardamom pods and allow the cream to cool completely. Place in a shallow container and put into the freezer. Stir occasionally as the cream freezes to break up the crystals. When the cream is completely frozen, break it into small pieces and work in a food processor until smooth. Pack into individual molds or a large freezer container and freeze until solid. To serve, place the molds briefly in warm water to loosen and turn out onto a plate. Sprinkle with the pistachio nuts. Alternatively, place the container in the microwave oven and heat for 10-20 seconds on

MEDIUM. Scoop into serving dishes and sprinkle the nuts on top.

Sweet Fruit Pilau

PREPARATION TIME: 25 minutes

MICROWAVE COOKING TIME: 15 minutes plus standing time

SERVES: 6 people

4 tbsps butter or margarine
1 cup long grain rice

This page: Kulfi (top) and Sesame Seed Meringue (bottom). Facing page: Sweet Fruit Pilau (top) and Semolina Pudding (bottom).

This page: **Banana Halva (left) and Creamed Rice and Rose Water (right).**

2 tbsps cashew nuts
2 tbsps almonds
2 cups hot milk
½ cup sugar
9 cardamom pods, slightly crushed
4 cloves
½ tsp grated nutmeg
Grated rind of 1 orange
Few drops orange flower water
4 tbsps black sesame seeds

GARNISH
1 small mango, sliced
2oz white grapes, peeled and seeded
1 orange, peeled and sliced
1 kiwi fruit, peeled and sliced

Combine the butter or margarine, rice, almonds and cashews in a large, deep bowl or casserole. Heat, uncovered, on HIGH for 3 minutes or until the nuts are lightly toasted. Pour on the hot milk and stir in the sugar. Add the cardamoms, cloves, nutmeg, orange flower water and orange rind. Reserve the orange for later use. Cover and cook on HIGH

for 12 minutes, stirring occasionally. Allow to stand for 5 minutes. Stir in the sesame seeds. Meanwhile, peel the orange and slice thinly into rounds. Arrange along with the mango, grapes and kiwi fruit on top of the rice to serve.

Banana Halva

PREPARATION TIME: 15 minutes
MICROWAVE COOKING TIME: 3-4 minutes
SERVES: 4-6 people

6 large ripe bananas, peeled and cut into 1 inch pieces
Juice of 1 orange
1 tsp light brown sugar or sugar to taste
Pinch nutmeg
Pinch ground coriander
Dash almond extract
½ cup whipped heavy cream
2 tbsps chopped blanched almonds, toasted

Place the bananas in a large bowl or casserole with the orange juice, sugar, nutmeg, coriander and almond

extract. Cover the bowl and cook on HIGH for 3-4 minutes, stirring occasionally. When the bananas are very soft, put in an electric mixer or food processor and process until smooth. Allow to cool completely and fold in the whipped cream. To serve, sprinkle with the chopped almonds.

Sesame Seed Meringue

PREPARATION TIME: 25 minutes
MICROWAVE COOKING TIME: 13-19 minutes
SERVES: 6 people

3 whole eggs
4 tbsps sugar
Dash orange flower water or almond extract
6 tbsps toasted sesame seeds
Dash lime juice
Pinch turmeric
1½ cups milk

MERINGUE
2 egg whites
½ tsp cornstarch
Pinch cream of tartar
½ cup sugar

Whisk the eggs with 4 tbsps sugar, orange flower water or almond extract, lime juice and turmeric until well mixed and frothy. Place the milk in a heatproof glass measure and cook on HIGH for 4 minutes. Gradually beat into the egg mixture, blending well, and stir in the sesame seeds. Pour into a shallow dish and place in a larger dish with enough hot water to come halfway up the sides of the dish. Cook on LOW for 10-13 minutes or until just set. Chill thoroughly. To prepare the meringue, place the egg whites, cornstarch and cream of tartar in a bowl. Beat until stiff peaks form. Add the sugar, a spoonful at a time, beating in-between each addition until the meringue is stiff and glossy. Spread over the custard completely to the edge of the dish. Microwave on MEDIUM for 3-6 minutes or until the meringue has risen and set. If desired, brown under a broiler before serving.

GLOSSARY

Allspice – Whole berries or ground, with the taste of nutmeg, cloves and cinnamon combined. Use in pickles, chutneys, curries, marinades for meat, poultry and fish and desserts.

Bay Leaves – Leaf of the sweet laurel tree. Use in curries, marinades for meat, poultry and fish and also poaching liquids for poultry and fish.

Cardamom – Whole pods or ground spice with a lemony taste. Native to India, Ceylon and Guatemala. Whole pods can be green, brown, black or white. White cardamom is bleached and does not have as much flavor. Crush pods slightly before using to release more flavor, or use only the seeds. Ground cardamom is usually expensive. Use in curries and lamb dishes, with rice and in desserts.

Cayenne Pepper – See chilies

Chilies – Fresh or dried, whole or crushed. Native to Central and South America, India and the Far East. Available fresh red or green. Mild red varieties are ground for paprika, hot for cayenne pepper. Use sparingly in meat dishes such as curries and chili con carne, chicken, fish, with eggs and cheese and rice and pasta. Always wash hands well after handling.

Cinnamon – Stick or ground spice with a strong, sweet taste. Use with meat and poultry and in curries. Most frequent use is in desserts. Use whole sticks in pickles and chutneys. Remove stick before serving. Rinsed and dried, sticks can be reused several times.

Cloves – Whole or ground spice. Very strong aromatic taste. Use with all meat, with chicken and fish, in curries, sauces and pilau rice. Most frequently used in sweet dishes and baked goods, pickles, preserves and chutneys.

Coriander – Spice is in seed or ground form and has a sweet, orange flavor. Leaves are used as a herb and look like flat parsley, but have a very strong taste. Use in stews and curries, rice pilaffs, with chicken and eggs in seed or ground form. Also used in sweet dishes. If using seeds, crush slightly to release more flavor. Use in leaf form like any herb, but especially in curries.

Cumin – Seed or ground spice. Very pungent and aromatic. Origin was Mediterranean, but also native to the Middle East, India and Turkey. Use in curries, marinades, chutneys, egg dishes and broiled meats, such as kebabs.

Curry Powder – Mixture of several ground spices such as turmeric, cumin, coriander, fenugreek, cayenne pepper and dehydrated ground garlic. Convenient, but not as flavorful as using individual spices. In addition to curries, use in chutneys and egg dishes. Curry paste, a combination of ground spices and oil, is available in various degrees of hotness.

Fennel – Seed or fresh tops of weed with a mild liquorice taste. Native to Europe and India. Green tops of the Florentine fennel bulb can be used as a herb. Seeds are usually pale green. Use in curries. Especially good with fish.

Fenugreek – Seed or ground spice. One of the ingredients in curry powder. Native to Europe, Morocco and India. Has a very strong, slightly bitter taste. Mostly used in curries.

Garlic – Fresh bulbs or dried powder, granules or salt. Pungent and highly aromatic. Native to countries with warm climates. Essential in curries. Use in chutneys, with eggs, rice and shellfish. Fresh garlic is the best form to use, however, 1/4 tsp garlic powder or granules is equal to 1 clove fresh garlic.

Ginger – Fresh root or ground. Native to Indonesia, India and Nigeria. Hot, peppery taste with slight sweetness. Peel and grate, chop or slice the fresh root. Use in curries, chutneys and desserts.

Mint – Fresh or dried herb. Very fragrant and sweet in its many varieties. Grown in most countries. Especially good with lamb. Fresh is preferable to dried.

Nutmeg – Whole berries or pre-grated spice. Sweet, aromatic and slightly nutty taste. Mace is the outer coating of the berry and is also available whole or ground. Use sparingly in stews and sauces. Good in curries, with pork, in rice puddings and other desserts.

Saffron – Strands or powder from the stigmas of crocus flowers. Strands are expensive and powder less so, however, not much is needed to give a golden yellow color to rice dishes.

Turmeric – Ground spice. Native to India, the Caribbean, Middle East, Africa and Ceylon. Gives curry powder its yellow color. Use in rice dishes and with seafood. Can be used as a saffron substitute.

Microwave
HERBS AND SPICES

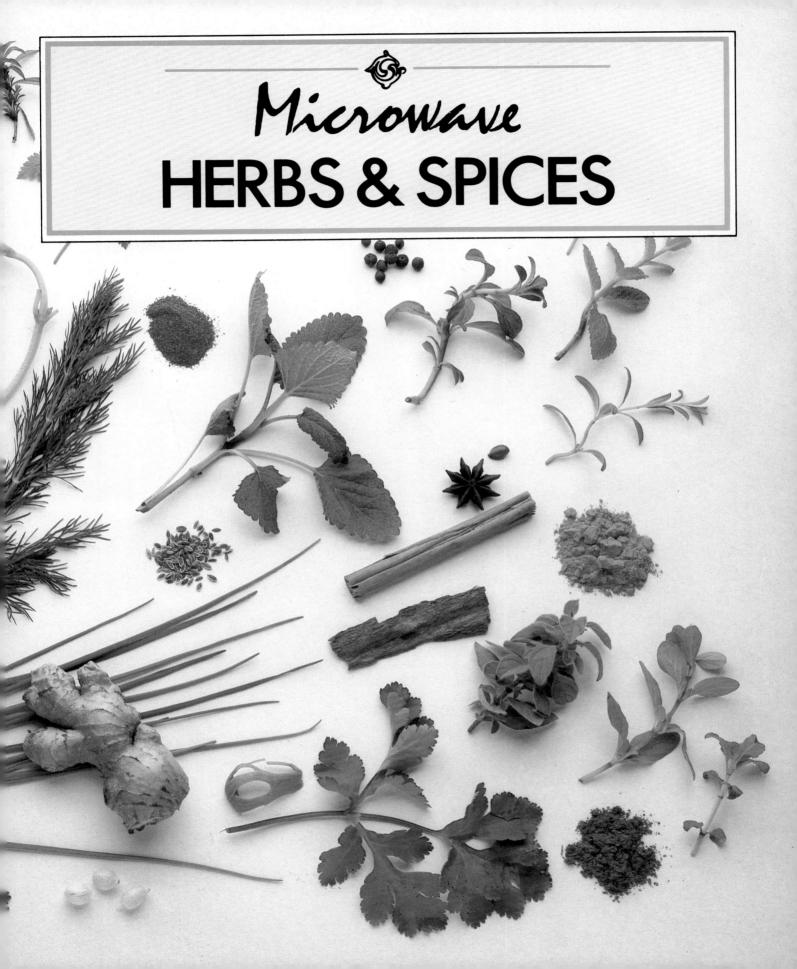

Microwave
HERBS & SPICES

INTRODUCTION

The use of herbs and spices to enhance the flavor of food is not a new idea. For centuries they have been used to make food more exciting and palatable. With the use of the microwave you can now make delicious, tasty dishes in double quick time.

Herb cookery is particularly suited to the microwave, as the quick cooking time does not impair the flavor of even the most delicate herbs. The recipes in this book have been tested using fresh herbs; if these are not available use dried, but remember that they have a more concentrated flavor so use only $^1/_3$-$^1/_2$ of the quantity stated. As well as cooking herbs, the microwave can be used to dry many herbs, with excellent results. Try parsley, chives, bergamot, the mints, lemon balm, marjoram, oregano, sage, tarragon, thyme and rosemary – they will have a much better color and flavor than when dried naturally. Dry herbs in small quantities, about $^1/_2$ oz at a time, on a double sheet of absorbent paper. Cook on HIGH for 2-4 minutes, turning and repositioning every minute; they are ready when they are just crisp. Store them crumbled or whole.

Spices have the best flavor when ground just before use, but if this is not convenient, make sure you buy good quality spices in small quantities. Both dried herbs and spices should be kept in airtight containers in a cool, dry place. If they have lost their aroma they will have lost their flavor, too, so discard and buy fresh.

The following glossary should help you to become familiar with the herbs and spices used in this book, but don't be afraid to experiment yourself – herb and spice cookery should be fun.

Allspice – Whole berries or in ground form, with the taste of nutmeg, cloves and cinnamon combined. Use in pâtés, pickles, stews and curries, marinades for meat, poultry and fish, with cheese, in baking and in desserts.

Aniseed – A native of the Middle East, now grown in south eastern Europe, North Africa, India and parts of Latin America. Spicy sweet licorice flavor, used in sweet and savory dishes. Use with all meats, especially curries, poultry, fish and fruit.

Basil – Fresh or dried leaves with a mild liquorice taste. The herb is native to Italy, France and Egypt, but grows easily elsewhere. Especially good with tomatoes and garlic. Use in all savory Italian dishes, as well as in stews and with chicken, fish, seafood, cheese, eggs and sauces, pasta and pizza. Use raw in salads.

Bay leaf – Leaf of the sweet laurel tree. Native to southern Europe, but can easily be grown as an evergreen in home gardens anywhere. One of the ingredients of the classic bouquet garni. Use in stews and curries, soups and sauces, marinades for meat, poultry and fish, and also in poaching liquids for poultry and fish. Gives interesting taste to pickles and preserves. Remove before serving.

Bergamot – Fresh herb native to North America and Europe. Use with meats, poultry and game. Plant has vivid red flowers that can be used as a tea.

Borage – Native to eastern Europe. Both the flower and leaves have a slight cucumber flavor. Add to salad, soups, cheese and eggs.

Cardamom – Whole pods or ground spice with a sweet, lemony taste. Native to India, Ceylon and Guatemala. Whole pods can be green, brown, black or white. White cardamom is bleached and does not have as much flavor. Crush pods slightly before use to release more flavor, or use only the seeds inside. Ground cardamom is usually expensive. Use in curries and lamb dishes, with rice and in desserts.

Caraway seed – Cultivated in parts of Europe, southern Mediterranean and the USA. Closely related to fennel and dill, can be used in both sweet and savory dishes. Add to salads, especially coleslaw, red cabbage, bread, cakes and cookies.

Cassia bark – Closely related to cinnamon; sold as quills, pieces or ground. Cassia is stronger and more bitter than cinnamon so is often reserved for savory foods. Use in curries, stews, casseroles and rice. Remove before serving.

Cayenne pepper – Made from the fruit and seed of the 'bird chili'. Very pungent, though not as hot as some chili powders. Use with fish, shellfish, chicken, cheese and eggs.

Celery seed – Small brown seeds that are sometimes ground and mixed with salt for celery salt. Native to India, Turkey and Egypt. Use in pickles, with eggs and cheese, with rice and pasta, with vegetables and in salad dressings.

Chervil – A fresh herb with delicate flavor and fragile leaves. Use in soups, salads and egg dishes.

Chilies – Fresh or dried, whole or crushed. Native to Central and South America, India and the Far East. Available fresh, red or green. Green chilies are the hotter of the two and the seeds are the hottest part. Mild red varieties are ground for paprika, hot for cayenne pepper. Use sparingly in meat dishes such as curries and chili con carne, and with chicken, fish, eggs, cheese, rice and pasta. Always wash hands well after handling.

Chinese five spice powder – Used in many authentic Chinese dishes. Available ready-made, it consists of ground anise, cassia bark, cloves, fennel and star anise.

Chives – Slender green herb with an onion taste. Originally from Denmark, but now grown in many countries. Good in any savory dish and in salads and dressings. Use as an attractive garnish.

Cinnamon – Stick or ground spice from Ceylon and the Seychelle Islands with a sweet, strong taste. Use with meat and poultry, with curries and stews. Most frequent use is in desserts and puddings. Use whole sticks in pickling and preserving, and with poached fruit. Remove stick before serving. Rinsed and dried, sticks can be reused several times.

Cloves – Whole or ground spice from Zanzibar and Madagascar, with very strong, aromatic taste. Use with all meat, especially ham and pork, with chicken and in fish dishes such as marinated herring, in curries, sauces and pilau rice. Most frequently used in sweet dishes and baked goods and in pickles and preserves.

Coriander – Spice is in seed or ground form and has a sweet, orange flavor. Leaves are used as a herb and look like flat Italian parsley, but have a very strong taste. Native to Central and South America, the Mediterranean, France, Morocco and Rumania. Also cultivated in India and Indonesia. Use in seed or ground form in stews and curries, rice, pilaffs, with chicken, cheese and eggs. Also used in sweet dishes. If using seeds, crush slightly to release more flavor. Use in leaf form like any herb, but especially in curries or Moroccan stews. Finely chopped leaves are the prominent flavor in Mexican salsas.

Cumin – Seed or ground spice. Very pungent and aromatic. Origin was Mediterranean, but also native to Middle East, India and Turkey. Use in curries, Mexican dishes, marinades, chutneys, with cheese and egg dishes and broiled meats, such as kebabs.

Curry powder – Mixture of several ground spices such as turmeric, cumin, coriander, fenugreek, cayenne pepper and dehydrated ground garlic. Convenient, but not as flavorful as using individual spices. In addition to curries, use in chutneys, salad dressings and egg and cheese dishes.

Dill – Seed or fresh and dried weed. Native to Europe and the United States. Seed has a flavor similar to caraway or anise. Especially good with fish, eggs and cheese. Also use in baking, in pickles, with vegetables and in salad dressings. Fresh dill weed makes an attractive garnish.

Fennel – Seed, or fresh tops or weed with a mild licorice taste. Native to Europe and India. Green tops of the Florentine fennel bulb can be used as a herb. Seeds are usually pale green. Use in Italian dishes, in curries and in sausage meat. Especially good with fish.

Fenugreek – Seed or ground spice. One of the ingredients in curry powder. Native to Europe, Morocco and India. Has a very strong, slightly bitter taste. Mostly used in curries.

Fines herbes – a mixture of herbs used in classic French cuisine. It consists of equal quantities of chervil, chives, tarragon and parsley.

Garam masala – Literally 'hot spices', this is an essential in Indian cookery. Use with meat, poultry, fish, rice, eggs, some vegetables and especially in curries.

Garlic – Fresh bulbs or dried powder, granules or salt. Pungent and highly aromatic. Native to southern Europe and countries with warm climates. Essential in curries and Mediterranean dishes. Use in chutneys, with eggs and cheese, rice, pasta and shellfish. Fresh garlic is the best form to use, however, $1/4$ tsp garlic powder or granules is equal to 1 clove fresh garlic.

Ginger – Fresh root or ground. Native to Indonesia, India, Nigeria. Hot, peppery taste with slight sweetness. Peel and grate, chop or slice the fresh root. Use in curries and Oriental dishes. Especially good with pork, ham and chicken. Use in preserves and desserts.

Herbes de Provence – Dried mixture of thyme, basil, savory, fennel and lavender flowers. Use with vegetables, all meats and fish, in sauces and stews with a Mediterranean influence.

Horseradish – Native to Europe and Asia. Use grated or as a sauce with fish, chicken, egg and vegetables.

Hyssop – A native herb of central and southern Europe. It is an ancient herb and is mentioned several times in the Bible. Slight minty taste, use in soups, salads, and stews – especially lamb. Traditionally added to cranberries, stewed peaches and apricots.

Juniper berries – Fruit of an evergreen, native to Europe. Use with meat, poultry, game and cabbage. Also add to pâtés.

Lemon balm – Native to the Mediterranean, the aromatic leaves have a strong lemon scent when crushed. Used chopped in stuffings, salads and desserts. Use whole to garnish fruit dishes.

Lemon grass – Native to Thailand and the Far East. Peel the outer layers and chop the core. Use in Indonesian and Oriental cooking.

Lemon thyme – Delicate lemon flavor, goes particularly well with chicken and fish.

Lovage – Native to the Mediterranean, but can be grown elsewhere. Robust flavor similar to celery. Use in stuffings, stews, soups and with fish.

Mace – Available as blades or ground. Tastes and smells similar to nutmeg, but is much stronger and should be used sparingly. Best kept for savory dishes, especially soups, sauces and casseroles. Can be used in milk puddings.

Marjoram – Fresh or dried herb. Asian and European origin. Similar taste to oregano. Use in all savory dishes. Young leaves can be used whole as a garnish or raw in salads.

Mint – Fresh or dried herb. Very fragrant and sweet in its many varieties. Grown in most countries. Especially good with lamb. Use with carrots, cucumbers, peas and new potatoes. Good in fruit desserts. Fresh is preferable to dried.

Mustard – There are three varieties of mustard: white, black and brown. English mustard is made from a blend of white and black mustard seeds with a little wheat flour and turmeric. Use whole seeds to flavor milk for sauces and for pickling, and in spice mixtures for meat and seafood.

Nutmeg – Whole berries or pre-grated spice. Native to Indonesia and West Indies. Sweet, aromatic and slightly nutty taste. Use sparingly in stews and sauces (especially cheese). Good in curries and with pork and veal. Generally reserved for desserts and baking.

Oregano – Fresh or dried (most common). Strong and pungent. Use in Italian and Spanish cooking. Good with all meats, rice, pasta and egg dishes. Essential on pizzas.

Paprika – Ground. Native to Hungary and Spain. Use with all meats and poultry. Add to cheese sauces and scrambled eggs. Essential in goulash and many eastern European dishes. Sprinkle onto casseroles, vegetables or fish as a garnish.

Parsley – Fresh or dried herb. Grown in all countries with a temperate climate. Use in stuffings, in all meat, poultry and fish dishes, sauces of all kinds and salad dressings. Use chopped or whole in salads and whole as a garnish. Flat-leafed variety has more flavor than curly-leafed. Fresh is easily available and much better than dried.

Peppercorns – Black, white, green and pink. Native to India, Brazil, Ceylon and Malaysia. Use black and white peppercorns ground as a basic seasoning. Crush the black or green peppercorns roughly for steak au poivre. Add whole to marinades or poaching liquids. Green peppercorns are fresh, unripe berries. Black are ripened and dried. White are ripened, soaked and skinned. Pink are usually preserved in vinegar. Use in all meat, poultry and fish dishes, with cheese and eggs, vegetables, rice and pasta.

Rosemary – Fragrant fresh or dried herb. Native to Europe. Grows to a large, evergreen shrub. Good with all meats, poultry and vegetables.

Saffron – Strands or powder from the stigmas of crocus flowers. Native to Italy, Spain and Portugal. Strands are expensive and powder less so, however, not much is needed to give a golden yellow color to rice dishes like risotto and paella. Also used in delicate seafood sauces and baked goods.

Sage – Fresh or dried herb. Native to Europe. Good with pork, poultry and game. Ingredient in stuffings. Also used with cheese and eggs. Flavor is very strong; use sparingly.

Salad burnet – Fresh herb which grows wild in many parts of Europe. Does not dry well and requires minimal cooking. Use in soups, salads and as a attractive garnish.

Savory – Fresh or dried herb. Native to Europe. Summer and winter varieties. Use with meats, poultry, fish, eggs and fruit. Good in soups and salads.

Star anise – Native to China and Japan, but also grown in the Philippines. It is a component of Chinese five spice powder. Use in Chinese cookery, with fish, shellfish, rice, pork and chicken.

Tansy – Quite bitter in flavor, so best used sparingly. Traditional herb at Easter added to puddings, custards and cakes. Also good with fish, eggs and cheese dishes.

Tarragon – Fresh or dried herb. French tarragon has a slight anise flavor. Russian tarragon looks the same but has less flavor. Was native to Siberia, but cultivated in France and Yugoslavia. Use with chicken, fish, eggs, game and vegetables. Classic ingredient in Bernaise sauce. Also use in vinegar and for salad dressings.

Thyme – Fresh or dried herb. Native to Europe and all temperate climates. Small, dark green leaves with pungent aroma. Use with all meat, poultry, game, fish dishes and vegetables. Add to rice and pasta, sauces, soups and stuffings.

Turmeric – Ground spice. Native to India, the Caribbean, Middle East, Africa, Ceylon. Gives curry powder its yellow color. Use in rice dishes and with seafood. Can be used as a saffron substitute.

All the recipes in this book were prepared in an oven with a 700 watt maximum output. For 500 watt ovens add 40 seconds for each minute stated in the recipe. For 600 watt ovens add 20 seconds for each minute stated in the recipe. If using a 650 watt oven only a slight increase in overall time is necessary.

SOUPS & APPETIZERS

Celery Cheese Dip with Chervil

PREPARATION TIME: 10 minutes

MICROWAVE COOKING TIME: 5-7 minutes

SERVES: 4-6 people

1 stick celery, finely chopped
1 tbsp butter
½ cup Port Salut or St. Paulin cheese, grated
½ cup natural yogurt
1 slice ham, finely chopped
1 tbsp chopped chervil

Put the celery and the butter in a small bowl and cook, uncovered, on HIGH for 3-4 minutes until tender but still slightly crunchy. Add the cheese and cook on HIGH for 2-4 minutes until melted, stirring frequently. Stir in the yogurt, chervil and ham. Chill thoroughly. Serve with sticks of raw vegetables or strips of pitta bread.

Swiss Cheese Layer

PREPARATION TIME: 5 minutes

MICROWAVE COOKING TIME: 3-5 minutes

SERVES: 4 people

1 cup grated Emmental cheese
1 tbsp chopped borage
4 eggs
Salt and pepper
1 cup grated Gruyère cheese
2 tsps savory
¼ cup cornchips, crushed

Mix the Emmental cheese and borage together and divide between 4 custard cups. Crack 1 egg into each dish and season to taste with salt and pepper. Mix the Gruyère cheese with the savory and top each dish with the cheese. Sprinkle with the crushed corn chips, arrange in a circle and cook on LOW for 3-5 minutes until the cheese melts and the eggs are cooked.

Celery Cheese Dip with Chervil (top) and Swiss Cheese Layer (bottom).

Zucchini Soup with Peppermint

PREPARATION TIME: 20 minutes

MICROWAVE COOKING TIME: 17-20 minutes

SERVES: 4 people

1 tbsp oil
1 medium onion, peeled and finely
    chopped
1 small clove garlic, peeled and crushed
2 medium potatoes, peeled and diced
1½ lbs zucchini, finely sliced
4 cups hot chicken stock
Salt
Freshly ground black pepper
2 eggs
1 tbsp grated Parmesan cheese
1 tbsp chopped peppermint
Pinch nutmeg

GARNISH
Fresh peppermint leaves
4 tbsps heavy cream (optional)

Put the oil, onion and garlic in a large bowl. Cook, uncovered, on HIGH for 2-3 minutes to soften, then add the potatoes and cook on HIGH for 2 minutes. Add the zucchini and cook on HIGH for 3-4 minutes. Stir in the stock, salt and pepper. Cover and cook for 5-15 minutes until the vegetables are soft. Purée in a blender or food processor and return to the bowl. Beat the eggs, cheese, peppermint and nutmeg together. Gradually add to the soup, whisking continuously. Cook, uncovered, on HIGH for 3-5 minutes or until hot, stirring once. Serve garnished with the peppermint leaves and/or a swirl of cream.

Hot Tomato Salad

PREPARATION TIME: 5 minutes

MICROWAVE COOKING TIME: 2-3 minutes

SERVES: 4 people

2 large beef tomatoes (total weight about
    1¼ lbs)
3 tbsps olive oil

1 tbsp cider vinegar
1 tsp chopped chives
1 tsp roughly chopped basil
½ tsp whole grain mustard

Slice the tomatoes and arrange on a micro-proof serving dish or on four individual dishes. Mix the oil, vinegar, chives, basil and mustard in a small jug and pour over the tomatoes. Cook, uncovered, on HIGH for 2-3 minutes until hot but not cooked. If using individual dishes, arrange these in a circle in the microwave. Serve immediately.

Cod and Mushroom Patty Shells

PREPARATION TIME: 10 minutes

MICROWAVE COOKING TIME: 6-9 minutes

MAKES: 18

6oz smoked cod

This page: Zucchini Soup with Peppermint. Facing page: Hot Tomato Salad (top) and Cod and Mushroom Patty Shells (bottom).

2 tbsps butter
2oz mushrooms, finely sliced
2 tbsps flour
½ cup milk
1 tsp chopped savory
2 tsps chopped chives
18 patty shells, cooked

Put the fish in a shallow dish, cover and cook on HIGH for 2 minutes and set aside. Put the butter in a small bowl with the mushrooms, cover and cook on HIGH for 1 minute until the mushrooms are soft. Gently stir in the flour and add the milk and the herbs. Cook on HIGH for 2-3 minutes until thickened, stirring frequently. Flake the fish into the sauce, divide the mixture between the pastry cases and arrange 6 at a time in a circle on paper towels. Cook on HIGH for 30 seconds-1 minute to reheat. Repeat with remaining patty shells.

Microwave
COOKING WITH HERBS

MEAT & FISH DISHES

Turkey Marsala

PREPARATION TIME: 15 minutes

MICROWAVE COOKING TIME:
22-29 minutes

SERVES: 4 people

4 4oz turkey breast fillets
1 small onion, peeled and finely chopped
1 red pepper, seeded and sliced
1 clove garlic, peeled and crushed
1 tbsp oil
8oz mushrooms, quartered
½ cup good hot chicken stock
4½ tbsps Marsala
2 tsps lemon verbena or lemon thyme
1 tbsp salad burnet
1 tbsp cornstarch
Salt
Freshly ground black pepper

Cut the turkey into thin slivers. Put the onion, pepper, garlic and the oil in a casserole and cook on HIGH for 3 minutes, until just beginning to soften. Add the turkey and cook on HIGH for 6 minutes, until almost cooked. Add the mushrooms and stir in the stock, marsala and herbs. Cover and cook on HIGH for 10-15 minutes until the meat is cooked and tender. Mix the cornstarch with 3 tbsps water and stir into the casserole. Cook, uncovered, on HIGH for 3-5 minutes until thickened, stirring twice. Season to taste with salt and pepper.

This page: Turkey Marsala (top) and Chicken and Lemon Parcels (bottom). Facing page: Chicken with Sausage Meat Stuffing.

Chicken with Sausage Meat Stuffing

PREPARATION TIME: 15 minutes

MICROWAVE COOKING TIME: 34 minutes

SERVES: 4 people

STUFFING
8oz pork sausage meat
½ cup crushed bran flakes
2 tbsps chopped mixed herbs
1 tbsp chopped parsley
2 tbsps grated fresh coconut or desiccated coconut
1 egg
Salt
Freshly ground black pepper
3lbs chicken
1 tsp soy sauce mixed with 1 tbsp water

Put all the stuffing ingredients into a bowl and mix well. Carefully lift the skin of the chicken away from the breast and body. Stuff the sausage meat between the skin and the chicken and spread out as evenly as possible. Place the chicken on a rack in a dish and brush with the soy sauce and water mixture. Cover with roasting film or a roasting bag which has been split open. Cook on HIGH for 10 minutes, then reduce setting and cook on MEDIUM for 24 minutes, or until the chicken is cooked. Shield the breast of the chicken with a small piece of foil for the last 10 minutes of cooking.

Chicken and Lemon Parcels

PREPARATION TIME: 20 minutes

MICROWAVE COOKING TIME: 10-15 minutes

SERVES: 4 people

4 4-6oz chicken breast fillets
1 tbsp oil
1 small onion, peeled and finely chopped
4oz mushrooms, finely chopped
2 tsps chopped tarragon
Salt
Freshly ground black pepper
4 tbsps unsalted butter
1 egg yolk
1 tbsp lemon juice
1 tbsp light cream

Flatten the chicken breasts between 2 sheets of wax paper using a rolling pin, taking care to keep the chicken in one piece. Set aside. Put the oil and onion together in a small bowl. Cover and cook on HIGH for 2 minutes to soften. Add the mushrooms and half of the chopped tarragon, cover and cook on HIGH for 1-2 minutes. Season to taste with salt and pepper. Divide the mixture between each chicken breast and fold up to form parcels. Arrange in a circle in a dish and cook, uncovered, on HIGH for 6-8 minutes. Transfer to a serving dish and keep warm. Meanwhile, put the butter in a small bowl and cook, uncovered, on HIGH for 1 minute or until melted. Mix the lemon juice, cream and egg yolk together and pour onto the butter; whisk. Cook on HIGH for 30 seconds-1 minute, whisking every 20 seconds until thickened. Pour the sauce over the chicken parcels to serve.

Veal and Garlic Cheese Rolls

PREPARATION TIME: 10 minutes

MICROWAVE COOKING TIME: 8-10 minutes

SERVES: 4 people

4 4-6oz veal escalopes
2 small cloves garlic, peeled and crushed
8oz low fat, soft cheese
Small bunch chives, chopped
Salt
Freshly ground black pepper
1 tsp paprika (optional)

Flatten the veal escalopes between 2 sheets of wax paper using a rolling pin and taking care to keep in one piece. Set aside. Combine the garlic, cheese and chives together and season with salt and pepper. Divide the mixture into 4, spread over each of the veal escalopes and roll up like a jelly roll. Sprinkle with paprika if desired. Arrange in a circle in a dish and cook, uncovered, on HIGH for 8-10 minutes. Serve immediately.

Liver Casserole

PREPARATION TIME: 15 minutes

MICROWAVE COOKING TIME: 15-20 minutes

SERVES: 4 people

2 tbsps butter
2 large onions, peeled and sliced
1 small clove garlic, peeled and crushed
1½ lbs lambs' liver, sliced
2 tbsps cornstarch
2 tbsps Cointreau
1 cup hot beef stock
1 tbsp chopped lovage
Salt
Pepper

GARNISH
Orange slices

Put the butter, onion and garlic in a casserole and cook on HIGH for 2 minutes, until soft. Toss the liver in the mixture until well coated. Cover and cook on MEDIUM for 10-15 minutes until just cooked. Blend the cornstarch with the Cointreau and add to the liver along with the beef stock; stir in the lovage. Season to taste. Cover and cook on HIGH for 3-4 minutes until the sauce is hot and thickened.

Facing page: Liver Casserole (top) and Veal and Garlic Cheese Rolls (bottom).

Beef Casserole with Herb Dumplings

PREPARATION TIME: 15 minutes

MICROWAVE COOKING TIME: 16-23 minutes

SERVES: 4 people

1 tsp oil
1 medium onion, peeled and finely chopped
12oz ground beef
2 tbsps all-purpose flour
½ cup beef stock
1 tbsp tomato paste
Salt
Freshly ground black pepper

HERB DUMPLINGS
1½ cups all-purpose flour
½ tsp baking powder
Pinch dry mustard
4 tbsps margarine
½ tsp chopped oregano
½ tsp chopped thyme
½ tsp chopped marjoram
Approx. 4½ tbsps milk

Put the oil and the onion in a casserole dish and cook on HIGH for 3 minutes until soft. Add the beef and cook on HIGH for 3-5 minutes, stirring occasionally. Stir in the flour, stock, tomato paste and seasoning. To make the dumplings: sift the flour, baking powder, mustard and a pinch of salt into a mixing bowl. Rub in the margarine until the mixture resembles fine breadcrumbs. Stir in the herbs. Add the milk gradually and mix to form a soft dough. Divide the dough into eight balls. Arrange around the edge of the casserole. Cover and cook on LOW for 10-15 minutes until dumplings are cooked.

Pork and Orange Casserole

PREPARATION TIME: 15 minutes

MICROWAVE COOKING TIME: 16-23 minutes

SERVES: 4 people

1 tbsp oil
1 medium onion, peeled and finely sliced
1lb pork – cut into ½ inch cubes
1 cup hot chicken stock
½ cup unsweetened orange juice
1 tsp oregano – roughly chopped
2 tsps basil – roughly chopped
1 orange, peeled and sliced
2 tbsps cornstarch
4 tbsps water

Put the oil and onion into a large casserole and cook on HIGH for 2 minutes to soften. Add the pork and cook on HIGH for 4-6 minutes, until almost cooked. Add the stock, orange juice, herbs and orange slices and stir. Mix the cornstarch with the water and add to the casserole. Cover and cook on MEDIUM for 10-15 minutes, until the meat is completely cooked and the liquid is thickened slightly, stirring occasionally. Serve with rice.

This page: Pork and Orange Casserole. Facing page: Beef Casserole with Herb Dumplings.

Casseroled Lamb

PREPARATION TIME: 15 minutes

MICROWAVE COOKING TIME: 35 minutes

SERVES: 4 people

1lb lamb fillet, cubed
1 tbsp oil
1 large onion, peeled and sliced
1 small clove garlic, peeled and crushed
2 tbsps flour
8oz zucchini, sliced
8oz carrots, peeled and sliced
1½ cups good hot beef stock
1 cup brown ale
2 tbsps chopped lemon thyme
1 tbsp chopped chervil
Salt
Freshly ground black pepper

Heat a large browning dish for the manufacturer's recommended time. Meanwhile, toss the lamb in the oil. When the dish is hot, add the meat and cook on HIGH for 2-3 minutes, stirring once. Add the onion and the garlic and cook on HIGH for 2 minutes, stir in the flour and add the remaining ingredients. Cover and cook on HIGH for 10 minutes then reduce setting and cook on MEDIUM for 20 minutes, stirring occasionally until the vegetables and meat are tender.

Stuffed Bacon Chops

PREPARATION TIME: 10 minutes

MICROWAVE COOKING TIME: 8-9 minutes

SERVES: 4 people

4 thick bacon chops
1 tbsp oil
1 small onion, peeled and finely chopped
1oz macadamia nuts, chopped
¾ cup cooked rice
¼ cup dried prunes, stones removed and chopped
1 tbsp chopped sage
Freshly ground black pepper
Salt
2 tbsps butter

Carefully cut a slit down the side of each bacon chop. Put the oil, onion and nuts in a small bowl and cook, uncovered, on HIGH for 2 minutes. Stir in the rice, prunes, sage, salt and pepper. Cover and cook on HIGH for 2-4 minutes until hot. Pack the stuffing into each chop. Heat a browning dish according to the manufacturer's instructions. Add the butter and quickly add the chops, press down slightly and turn browned side up. Cook, uncovered, on HIGH for 4 minutes or until cooked. Serve with a salad or green vegetables.

This page: Stuffed Bacon Chops. Facing page: Herb Lamb Noisettes (top) and Casseroled Lamb (bottom).

Herb Lamb Noisettes

PREPARATION TIME: 10 minutes

MICROWAVE COOKING TIME:
11 minutes

SERVES: 4 people

1 large onion, peeled and chopped
1 tbsp oil
1 7oz can chopped tomatoes
1 small clove garlic, peeled and crushed
1 tsp marjoram
1 tsp oregano
4oz button mushrooms
4 4oz noisettes of lamb
Knob butter

Put the onion and oil in a small bowl and cook on HIGH for 3 minutes, until soft. Add the tomatoes, garlic, herbs and mushrooms. Cook, uncovered, on HIGH for 3 minutes, stirring once. Set aside and keep warm. Heat a large browning dish for the manufacturer's recommended time. Add the butter and quickly place the noisettes in the dish and press each one down firmly, turn over and press down again. Cook on HIGH for 5 minutes. Transfer the noisettes to a warm serving dish and, if necessary, reheat the sauce for 1 minute on HIGH. Serve the sauce poured over the noisettes.

Smoky Haddock and Chive au Gratin

PREPARATION TIME: 10 minutes

MICROWAVE COOKING TIME:
5-8 minutes

SERVES: 4 people

12oz smoked haddock, skinned
½ cup white wine
Bay leaf
4oz mushrooms, sliced
2 tbsps butter
2 tbsps flour
½ cup milk
Small bunch chives, chopped
½ cup Cheddar cheese, grated
1 tbsp chopped parsley

4 tbsps brown breadcrumbs

Place the haddock in a shallow dish with the wine, bay leaf and mushrooms. Cover and cook on HIGH for 3 minutes until the fish is cooked. Set aside. Put the butter in a small bowl and cook on HIGH for 30 seconds. Stir in the flour and cook on HIGH for 30 seconds. Add the cooking liquor from the fish together with the milk and mix well. Cook on HIGH for 2-4 minutes, whisking every minute until thickened. Add the mushrooms, chives and fish, flaking the fish slightly as you do so, and mix well. Divide between four individual gratin dishes. Sprinkle over the cheese, parsley and breadcrumbs and cook on HIGH for 1-2 minutes or brown under the broiler.

Plaice with Herbed Mushrooms

PREPARATION TIME: 20 minutes

MICROWAVE COOKING TIME:
11-14 minutes

SERVES: 4 people

4 large plaice fillets
1 tbsp butter
Small clove garlic, peeled and crushed
1 small onion, peeled and finely chopped
8oz mushrooms, finely chopped
Salt
Ground white pepper
½ tsp chopped pennyroyal
1 tsp chopped parsley
1 tsp chopped dill
1 tbsp cornstarch
½ cup natural yogurt
1 egg yolk

GARNISH
Chopped parsley

Put the butter, garlic and onion in a small bowl and cook on HIGH for 2 minutes until beginning to soften. Add the mushrooms and herbs, cover and cook on HIGH for 2-4 minutes until the mushrooms are

soft. Season with salt and pepper. Cut the plaice fillets in half, lengthwise, and spread the stuffing over the fillets. Roll up the fillets and place in a circle, seamed side down, in a shallow dish. Cover and cook on HIGH for 6 minutes or until the fish is cooked. Transfer to a serving dish and keep warm. Mix the cornstarch with a little of the yogurt, add the remaining yogurt, egg yolk and any cooking liquor, season with salt and pepper, whisk and cook, uncovered, on HIGH for 1-2 minutes, whisking every 30 seconds until thickened slightly. Serve the fish rolls on a pool of sauce and sprinkle with chopped parsley.

Cheesy Fish Pie

PREPARATION TIME: 10 minutes

MICROWAVE COOKING TIME:
8-10 minutes

SERVES: 4 people

1lb smoked haddock fillets
3 tbsps milk
1 tbsp butter
Salt
Freshly ground black pepper
1 tbsp chopped basil
1 tbsp chopped sage
4oz mozzarella cheese, sliced
1½ lbs potatoes, cooked and mashed with
    2 tbsps milk and a pinch of nutmeg

Place the fish in an even layer in a shallow dish. Pour over the milk and dot with butter. Season to taste with salt and pepper. Sprinkle over the chopped herbs. Put the cheese slices on top of the fish and cover with the mashed potato. Cover and cook on HIGH for 8-10 minutes. Brown under the broiler if desired.

Facing page: Smoky Haddock and Chive au Gratin (top) and Cheesy Fish Pie (bottom).

Trout with Lovage and Yogurt Sauce

PREPARATION TIME: 10 minutes

MICROWAVE COOKING TIME:
12-18 minutes

SERVES: 4 people

1 tbsp butter
½ cup slivered almonds
1 tsp celery seeds
2 tbsps chopped lovage
4 medium trout, cleaned
Salt
Freshly ground black pepper

1 tbsp cornstarch
½ cup natural yogurt

Put the butter, almonds and celery seeds into a shallow dish and cook, uncovered, on HIGH for 4-8 minutes, stirring frequently, until the almonds begin to brown. Set aside. Divide about half the chopped lovage between the four trout, place inside each fish and season with salt and pepper. Arrange the fish head to tail in a shallow dish and cook on HIGH for 6-8 minutes until the fish is cooked, repositioning halfway through cooking. Set aside and keep warm. Mix the cornstarch with a little of the yogurt in a small bowl and then add the remaining yogurt. Cook on HIGH for 2-4 minutes, whisking frequently until thickened. Stir in remaining lovage. Serve the trout with the sauce and garnish with the browned almonds.

This page: Plaice with Herbed Mushrooms. Facing page: Trout with Lovage and Yogurt Sauce (top) and Orange Baked Fish (bottom).

Salmon Quiche

PREPARATION TIME: 10 minutes

MICROWAVE COOKING TIME:
14 minutes

SERVES: 4 people

1 cup whole-wheat flour
Pinch of salt
4 tbsps margarine
2-3 tbsps water
1 7oz can of red salmon
⅔ cup natural yogurt
1 tbsp chopped dill
1 tsp lemon juice
2 tsps tomato paste
1 tsp white wine vinegar
Salt
Pepper

GARNISH
Sprigs of dill

Put the flour and the salt in a mixing bowl. Rub in the margarine until the mixture resembles fine breadcrumbs. Add enough water to mix to form a wet dough. Put the pastry into a 6½ inch shallow flan dish and press out to form a pie shell. Prick the base with a fork and cook, uncovered, on HIGH for 3-4 minutes. Turn every minute. Drain the salmon and discard any bones and skin. Place the salmon in a mixing bowl with the yogurt, dill, lemon juice, tomato paste and vinegar and mix well. Season to taste and spread the mixture over the pie shell. Cook, uncovered, on LOW for 10 minutes until hot. Garnish with sprigs of dill.

Orange Baked Fish

PREPARATION TIME: 10 minutes

MICROWAVE COOKING TIME:
6-8 minutes

SERVES: 4 people

4 herrings
4 bay leaves
4 tbsps butter

Juice and grated zest of ½ orange
1 tbsp chopped dill

GARNISH
Orange slices

Rinse the fish and dry well. Place a bay leaf inside each fish. Place each fish on a sheet of non-stick baking parchment. Put the butter in a small bowl and cook on HIGH for 15-30 seconds to soften slightly. Beat in the orange juice, zest and dill. Divide the butter into four and spread some over each of the fish. Wrap each

This page: Salmon Quiche. Facing page: Mixed Vegetable Risotto (top) and Paella (bottom).

parcel separately, making sure the fish is totally enclosed. Cook on HIGH for 6-8 minutes, until the fish is cooked, repositioning the fish halfway through the cooking time. Serve in the paper, garnished with orange slices.

VEGETABLES, PASTA & GRAINS

Paella

PREPARATION TIME: 10 minutes

MICROWAVE COOKING TIME:
20-25 minutes plus 5 minutes
standing time

SERVES: 6 people

1lb monkfish, cut into cubes
1 tbsp oil
1 small onion, peeled and finely sliced
1 clove garlic, peeled and crushed
1 cup rice
2 cups hot fish stock or water
Few saffron strands, soaked in 2 tbsps
    water (optional)
8oz squid, cleaned and cut into rings
8oz shelled mussels
4oz shelled clams or cockles
2 tbsps chopped parsley
2 tbsps chopped coriander
Whole shrimp
Salt
Ground white pepper

Put the fish in a dish, cover and cook
on HIGH for 4 minutes then set
aside. Put the oil, onion and garlic in
a large casserole and cook on HIGH
for 2 minutes. Stir in the rice and
cook on HIGH for 1 minute. Stir in
the stock and saffron, if using. Add
the squid and cook, uncovered, on
HIGH for 10-15 minutes or until
most of the liquid has been absorbed
and the rice is almost cooked.
Carefully stir in the shellfish,
monkfish and herbs and cook on
HIGH for 2 minutes. Cover and
leave to stand for 5 minutes before
serving. Serve garnished with the
whole shrimp.

Mixed Vegetable Risotto

PREPARATION TIME: 15 minutes
MICROWAVE COOKING TIME:
25-30 minutes plus 5 minutes
standing time
SERVES: 4 people

1 tbsp oil
½ red pepper, seeded and diced
½ green pepper, seeded and diced
2 cups hot vegetable stock
1 cup brown rice
6oz button mushrooms, quartered
2 tsps chopped pennyroyal
2 tsps chopped hyssop
Salt
Freshly ground black pepper
4oz shrimp

Put the oil in a casserole and add the diced peppers. Cover and cook on HIGH for 3-4 minutes until the peppers are beginning to soften. Add the stock, rice, mushrooms, herbs and seasoning. Stir, cover and cook on HIGH for 25-30 minutes, or until most of the liquid has been absorbed. Stir in the shrimp and leave to stand for 5 minutes before serving.

Cheese and Tomato Pasta

PREPARATION TIME: 10 minutes
MICROWAVE COOKING TIME:
17-23 minutes
SERVES: 4 people

1 tbsp oil
1 medium onion, peeled and finely
    chopped
4oz mushrooms, finely sliced
1 tbsp tomato paste
1 10oz can tomatoes
2 tbsps fines herbes
3oz strong Cheddar cheese, grated
1 tbsp Parmesan cheese
8oz tagliatelle
3 cups boiling water

Put the oil in a medium bowl with the onion and cook on HIGH for 2 minutes until softened. Add the mushrooms, tomato paste and tomatoes and mix well, breaking up the tomatoes slightly. Cook, uncovered, on HIGH for 4-5 minutes or until boiling. Cook for a further 3-4 minutes until reduced slightly. Stir in the fines herbes, grated cheese and Parmesan. Cover and keep warm. Put the pasta and the water in a large bowl. Cover and cook on HIGH for 8-10 minutes or until the pasta is cooked. Drain and arrange on a serving dish. Reheat the sauce on HIGH for 1-2 minutes if necessary, and pour over the pasta to serve.

Leek and Potato with Lemon Thyme

PREPARATION TIME: 10 minutes
MICROWAVE COOKING TIME:
8-10 minutes
SERVES: 4 people

8oz leeks, trimmed, sliced and washed
8oz potatoes, peeled and sliced
Salt
Freshly ground black pepper
2 tbsps chopped lemon thyme
½ cup hot vegetable stock

Arrange the leeks and potatoes in layers in a micro-proof dish, sprinkling each layer with salt, pepper and lemon thyme. Pour over the stock. Cover loosely and cook on HIGH for 8-10 minutes until cooked.

Zucchini in Tomato-Bergamot Sauce

PREPARATION TIME: 10 minutes
MICROWAVE COOKING TIME:
10-15 minutes
SERVES: 4 people

1½ lbs zucchini
4 rashers bacon, rinds removed, chopped
1 large onion, peeled and finely chopped
1 clove garlic, peeled and crushed
14oz can tomatoes
2 tbsps bergamot
Salt
Freshly ground black pepper

Slice the zucchini diagonally and set aside. Put the bacon into a small bowl and cook, uncovered, on HIGH for 1-2 minutes until crisp. Stir in the onion and garlic and cook on HIGH for 2 minutes. Add the remaining ingredients and mix well. Cover and cook on HIGH for 10-15 minutes until the vegetables are tender.

Nut and Herb Bulgur

PREPARATION TIME: 10 minutes
MICROWAVE COOKING TIME:
13 minutes plus 5 minutes
standing time
SERVES: 4-6 people

1 small red pepper, seeded and sliced
1 small onion, peeled and chopped
½ cup hazelnuts, roughly chopped
¼ cup pinenuts
1 tbsp oil
4oz cucumber, diced
1 tbsp chopped coriander
1 tbsp chopped mint
2 tbsps chopped parsley
1½ cups hot chicken or vegetable stock
1¼ cups bulgur wheat

Put the pepper, onions, nuts and oil into a large bowl, cover and cook on HIGH for 3 minutes. Stir in the remaining ingredients. Cover and cook on HIGH for 10 minutes or until all the moisture has been absorbed. Leave to stand for 5 minutes and fluff up with a fork before serving. Serve hot or cold as an alternative to rice.

Facing page: Cheese and Tomato Pasta (top) and Nut and Herb Bulgur (bottom).

Potato Cakes

PREPARATION TIME: 10 minutes

MICROWAVE COOKING TIME:
4 minutes

SERVES: 4 people

1lb cooked potatoes
1 medium onion, peeled and finely
*   chopped*
2 tbsps fines herbes
1 tsp oil

Salt
Freshly ground black pepper

Mash the potato, add the onion and herbs; mix well. Divide the potato into four even portions and, using floured hands, form into four rounds about 1 inch thick. Preheat a large browning dish for the manufacturer's recommended time. Add the oil and quickly add the potato cakes, two at a time, and cook on HIGH for 2 minutes. Carefully turn over and cook on HIGH for a further 2 minutes until golden. Reheat the browning dish for a few minutes and repeat with the remaining potato cakes.

This page: Zucchini in Tomato-Bergamot Sauce. Facing page: Leek and Potato with Lemon Thyme (top) and Potato Cakes (bottom).

Rosemary Lyonnaise Potatoes

PREPARATION TIME: 10 minutes

MICROWAVE COOKING TIME:
12-15 minutes

SERVES: 4 people

1lb potatoes
2 tbsps butter
1 tbsp finely chopped rosemary
1 small clove garlic, peeled and crushed
1 small onion, peeled and finely chopped
2 tbsps milk
Salt
Pepper

Peel and thinly slice the potatoes. Put the butter, rosemary, garlic and onions in an 8 inch shallow dish and cook on HIGH for 3 minutes until soft. Stir in the milk, salt, pepper and potatoes and mix well. Spread out in the dish. Cover and cook on MEDIUM for 12-15 minutes until the potatoes are soft. Brown under a broiler if desired.

Braised Fennel

PREPARATION TIME: 5 minutes

MICROWAVE COOKING TIME:
5-7 minutes

SERVES: 4-6 people

2 8oz bulbs fennel, trimmed and shredded
2 tsps chopped lovage
4 tbsps hot vegetable or chicken stock
2 tbsps sherry
½ tsp celery seeds

Combine all the ingredients, except the celery seeds. Cover and cook on HIGH for 5-7 minutes until the fennel is just tender, stirring twice during cooking. Drain and transfer to a serving dish, sprinkle over the celery seeds and serve immediately.

Tarragon and Lemon Carrots

PREPARATION TIME: 5 minutes

MICROWAVE COOKING TIME:
10-12 minutes

SERVES: 4 people

1lb carrots, peeled and finely sliced
1 tbsp lemon juice
6 tbsps water
2 sprigs of fresh tarragon

GARNISH
Chopped tarragon
Grated lemon zest

Put the carrots in a casserole with the lemon juice, water and tarragon. Cover and cook on HIGH for 10-12 minutes. Drain and discard the tarragon sprigs. Garnish with chopped tarragon and lemon zest.

This page: Tarragon and Lemon Carrots (top) and Braised Fennel (bottom). Facing page: Rosemary Lyonnaise Potatoes.

Vegetable Pasta Salad

PREPARATION TIME: 5 minutes

MICROWAVE COOKING TIME:
8-10 minutes

SERVES: 4 people

8oz pasta bows
3 cups boiling water
1 7oz can tuna
⅔ cup corn kernels
⅔ cup cooked, sliced green beans
4 green onions, cut diagonally into ½ inch
 lengths
2 tbsps grated horseradish
1 tbsp lemon juice
4 tbsps mayonnaise
Salt
Freshly ground black pepper
1 tbsp chopped mint
1 tbsp chopped parsley

Put the pasta in a large bowl with the water. Cover and cook on HIGH for 8-10 minutes until tender. Drain and rinse with cold water, drain again and set aside. Break the tuna into large chunks, add the corn, green beans and onions, and mix well. Mix the horseradish with the lemon juice, mayonnaise and seasoning. Add to the pasta and toss to coat. Serve the pasta cold, sprinkled with the chopped mint and parsley.

DESSERTS

Poached Pears with Raspberry Coulis

PREPARATION TIME: 15-20 minutes

MICROWAVE COOKING TIME: 6-11 minutes

SERVES: 4 people

½ cup water
2 tbsps honey
2 tsps lemon juice
Few sprigs hyssop
4 pears
8oz fresh or frozen raspberries (thawed if frozen)
1 tsp chopped hyssop

GARNISH
Hyssop leaves

Put the water and honey in a large, shallow dish and cook, uncovered, for 1-2 minutes, stirring until the honey is dissolved. Add the lemon juice and hyssop sprigs. Peel the pears thinly and cut in half; carefully remove the core and stalk using a teaspoon. Place the pears in the syrup, cover and cook on HIGH for 5-10 minutes until the pears are tender. Meanwhile, purée the raspberries in a blender or food processor and then push the purée through a sieve to remove the pips. Sweeten the purée with a little of the cooking syrup if desired. Stir in the chopped hyssop. Carefully drain the pears and transfer to a serving dish. Chill thoroughly. Serve the pears

Facing page: Vegetable Pasta Salad. This page: Rhubarb Tansy (top) and Poached Pears with Raspberry Coulis (bottom).

with a little of the raspberry coulis poured over them, serve the remaining coulis separately. Decorate with hyssop leaves if desired.

Rhubarb Tansy

PREPARATION TIME: 10 minutes

MICROWAVE COOKING TIME: 10-12 minutes

SERVES: 4 people

1lb rhubarb, trimmed and cut into
   1 inch lengths
Pinch ground ginger
4 tbsps water
2 eggs, separated
Juice and zest of 1 lemon
⅓ cup sugar
1½ cups heavy cream
2 tsps chopped tansy

Put the rhubarb in a large bowl with the ginger and water. Cover and cook on HIGH for 10-12 minutes, stirring twice, until the rhubarb is mushy. Stir in the egg yolk, tansy, lemon juice and zest. Purée in a food processor or blender. Whisk the egg-whites to soft peaks, then whisk in the sugar, half at a time. Whip the cream to soft peaks and fold into the rhubarb mixture; fold in the egg whites and spoon the mixture into glasses. Chill thoroughly before serving with crisp cookies.

Grape and Bergamot Jellies

PREPARATION TIME: 10 minutes plus setting time

MICROWAVE COOKING TIME: 3-5 minutes

SERVES: 4 people

4oz green grapes
1½ cups unsweetened white grape juice
2 tbsps sugar

1 tbsp powdered gelatine
½ cup water
4 sprigs bergamot
Whipped cream to decorate (optional)

If the grapes are not seedless, cut in half and remove the pips. Skin the grapes if desired. Put the grape juice in a large bowl with the sugar and bergamot, and cook on HIGH for 2-4 minutes until the sugar is dissolved, stirring once. Allow to

cool slightly, then remove the bergamot. Mix the gelatine with ¼ cup of the water, cook on HIGH for 30 seconds, stir and cook for a further 30 seconds if necessary to dissolve the gelatine. Stir into the grape juice and add the remaining water. Divide the grapes between four glasses and pour in the jelly. Chill until set. Decorate with rosettes of cream if desired.

Pour into the bottom of the pudding basin. Put the remaining ingredients except the applemint into a mixing bowl and beat thoroughly until smooth; fold in the applemint. Carefully spoon the mixture on top of the apple. Cook, uncovered, on HIGH for 6-7 minutes until the mixture is just dry on top and beginning to come away from the sides. Cover and leave to stand for 5 minutes before turning out onto a serving dish. Serve hot or cold with cream or ice cream.

Orange with Lemon Balm

PREPARATION TIME: 10 minutes plus chilling

MICROWAVE COOKING TIME: 7 minutes

SERVES: 4 people

4 oranges
½ cup sweet white wine
1-2 tbsps honey
1 tbsp Grand Marnier
1 tsp chopped lemon balm

GARNISH
Whole lemon balm leaves (optional)

Peel the oranges, removing all the white pith. Cut the oranges into slices and arrange on a serving dish. Mix the wine, honey to taste and Grand Marnier together in a small bowl, stir in the lemon balm and cook on HIGH for 2 minutes. Stir to dissolve the honey and cook on MEDIUM for 5 minutes or until slightly reduced and syrupy. Pour over the oranges and chill thoroughly. Garnish with whole lemon balm leaves if desired.

Applemint Pudding

PREPARATION TIME: 10 minutes

MICROWAVE COOKING TIME: 9-12 minutes plus 5 minutes standing time

SERVES: 4-6 people

8oz cooking apple, peeled, cored and sliced
Small knob butter
2-4 tbsps granulated sugar
1 tsp chopped spearmint
½ cup margarine

½ cup dark brown sugar
1 cup all-purpose flour
1½ tsps baking powder
2 eggs
2 tsps golden syrup
2 tbsps milk
2 tsps chopped applemint
Oil to grease

Lightly grease a 4 cup pudding basin or bowl. Place the apples, butter and sugar to taste in a small bowl, cover and cook on HIGH for 3-5 minutes until soft and mushy, stirring occasionally. Stir in the spearmint.

Facing page: Grape and Bergamot Jellies (top) and Orange with Lemon Balm (bottom). This page: Applemint Pudding.

Microwave
COOKING WITH SPICES

SOUPS & APPETIZERS

Tomato Soup

PREPARATION TIME: 10 minutes

MICROWAVE COOKING TIME:
15-20 minutes

SERVES: 4 people

1 tbsp oil
2 carrots, peeled and finely chopped
1 onion, peeled and finely chopped
½ tsp ground allspice
¼ tsp ground ginger
2 rashers bacon, rind removed and
*   chopped*
2 14oz canned tomatoes
1 tbsp sugar
2 cups hot vegetable or chicken stock
Salt
Freshly ground black pepper
2 tbsps cornstarch
4 tbsps water
4 tomatoes, skinned and sliced

Put the oil, chopped vegetables,
spices and bacon in a large bowl.
Cover and cook on HIGH for 4-5
minutes. Add the canned tomatoes,
sugar and stock, cover and cook on
HIGH for 8-10 minutes or until
boiling. Reduce the setting to
MEDIUM and cook for 15 minutes.
Purée in a food processor or blender
if desired. Season to taste with salt
and pepper. Mix the cornstarch and
water together and add to the soup
along with the sliced tomatoes.
Cook, uncovered, on HIGH for 3-5
minutes, stirring once until the soup
is thickened slightly.

cook on HIGH for 15-20 minutes until all the vegetables are tender. Purée in a food processor or blender. Return to the rinsed out bowl, season to taste with salt and pepper and cook on HIGH for 5 minutes until boiling. Stir in the cream and cook on HIGH for 1-2 minutes to heat through. Sprinkle with chopped parsley to serve.

Spicy Hot Grapefruit

PREPARATION TIME: 10 minutes

MICROWAVE COOKING TIME: 3-4 minutes

SERVES: 4 people

2 pink grapefruit
1 tsp allspice

GARNISH
Lemon balm

Cut the grapefruit in half. Using a sharp knife or grapefruit knife, cut around the edges of the fruit between the flesh and the pith. Then cut down between each segment, removing the skin from the flesh. Take the core between finger and thumb and pull out, removing the skin. Remove any pips. Sprinkle the allspice over each grapefruit half. Arrange in a circle in the microwave oven and cook on HIGH for 3-4 minutes until hot. Garnish with lemon balm leaves.

Country Cream Soup

PREPARATION TIME: 10 minutes

MICROWAVE COOKING TIME: 26-32 minutes

SERVES: 4 people

1 tbsp oil
1 large onion, peeled and chopped
1 tsp ground coriander
3 sticks celery, chopped
1-2 turnips, depending on size, peeled and chopped
3 carrots, peeled and chopped
3 cups good hot vegetable stock
Salt
Freshly ground black pepper
½ cup heavy cream

GARNISH
Chopped parsley

Put the oil, onion and coriander in a large bowl, cover and cook on HIGH for 2 minutes. Add the other vegetables and cook on HIGH for 3 minutes. Pour in the stock, cover and

Facing page: Tomato Soup (top) and Country Cream Soup (bottom). This page: Spicy Hot Grapefruit.

Put the chicken livers and sherry together in a small bowl. Add the garlic and spices. Cover and cook on HIGH for 6-10 minutes, stirring twice. Place the mixture in a food processor and process until smooth. Add 1 cup of the butter and process again. Stir in the yogurt. Divide the mixture between 4 individual dishes or put in one large dish and chill slightly. Put the remaining butter in a jug and cook on HIGH for 1 minute or until bubbling. Leave to settle. Carefully pour a little of the clarified butter on top of the pâté, leaving behind the white sediment. Chill thoroughly before serving.

Spicy Chicken Liver Pâté

PREPARATION TIME: 15 minutes plus chilling time

MICROWAVE COOKING TIME: 7-11 minutes

SERVES: 8-10 people

1lb chicken livers, roughly chopped
3 tbsps sherry
1 small clove of garlic, peeled and crushed
Pinch ground bay leaves
Pinch ground cloves
¼ tsp ground mace
Salt
Pepper
1¼ cups butter
2 tbsps natural yogurt

Sardine Spreading Pâté

PREPARATION TIME: 10 minutes plus chilling time

MICROWAVE COOKING TIME: 2½-4 minutes

SERVES: 8 people

2 4oz cans sardines in oil
2 tbsps flour
½ tsp ground cumin
½ tsp ground fenugreek
1 tsp ground mild chili powder
½ cup milk
Salt
Freshly ground black pepper
½ cup natural yogurt
1 tbsp lemon juice

Drain the sardines, reserving 2 tbsps of the oil. Put the oil in a bowl, stir in the flour and spices, and cook on HIGH for 45 seconds. Add the milk and season with salt and pepper. Cook on HIGH for 1-2 minutes, whisking frequently until the sauce is thickened. Mash the fish with a fork and stir into the sauce. Stir in the yogurt and lemon juice. Pour into individual custard cups or one large dish and chill thoroughly before serving. Garnish with parsley.

MEAT & FISH DISHES

Pork with Spiced Apricot Sauce

PREPARATION TIME: 10 minutes

MICROWAVE COOKING TIME: 11-18 minutes

SERVES: 4 people

2 tbsps oil
1 small onion, peeled and chopped
1 small clove garlic, peeled and crushed
1 cup ready-to-eat dried apricots, chopped
2 tbsps sherry
½ cup water
½ tsp five spice powder
4 boneless pork loin chops

Put 1 tbsp of the oil in a small bowl and add the onion and garlic. Cover and cook on HIGH for 6-8 minutes to soften. Add the apricots, sherry, water and five spice powder. Cover and cook on HIGH until soft and pulpy. Set aside and keep warm. Heat a browning dish for the manufacturer's recommended time, add the remaining oil and quickly press the chops down onto the surface of the dish, then turn over and press down again. Cook on HIGH for 5-10 minutes until the chops are cooked. The apricot sauce can be thinned with a little of the juice from the chops if desired. Serve the chops with the apricot sauce.

Facing page: Sardine Spreading Pâté (top) and Spicy Chicken Liver Pâté (bottom). This page: Pork with Spiced Apricot Sauce.

Chicken in White Wine

PREPARATION TIME: 10 minutes

MICROWAVE COOKING TIME:
26 minutes

SERVES: 4 people

3lb chicken
1 tbsp oil
1 large onion, peeled and sliced
1 tsp ground coriander
2 tsps fennel seeds
½ tsp mace
½ head celery
1 bulb fennel
4 tbsps flour
1½ cups hot chicken stock
½ cup dry white wine
Salt
Freshly ground black pepper

Cut the chicken into eight pieces and remove the skin. Pre-seal the chicken in a browning dish or frying pan if desired. Put the oil and onion into a casserole with the spices. Cook, uncovered, on HIGH for 2 minutes. Cut the celery into 2 inch pieces, diagonally. Trim and shred the fennel. Add to the casserole and cook on HIGH for 4 minutes, stirring once. Stir in the flour, add the stock and wine and season to taste with salt and pepper. Add the chicken, cover and cook on HIGH for 20 minutes until the chicken is cooked and the vegetables are tender, stirring occasionally. If the chicken was pre-sealed, the final cooking time should be reduced by 5-10 minutes.

Sweet and Spicy Lamb

PREPARATION TIME: 10 minutes
plus standing time

MICROWAVE COOKING TIME:
35 minutes

SERVES: 4 people

1lb lamb fillet
¼ tsp ground ginger
¼ tsp ground cloves
¼ tsp ground mace

1 tbsp honey
1 tbsp Dijon mustard
1 clove garlic, peeled and crushed
2 tbsps white wine vinegar
1 red pepper, seeded and cut into 1 inch pieces
1 green pepper, seeded and cut into 1 inch pieces
6 green onions, cut into 1 inch lengths
1 8oz can pineapple cubes
4oz mushrooms, quartered if large
½ cup hot chicken stock
1 tbsp cornstarch
3 tbsps water

GARNISH
Green onion brushes

Cut the lamb into 1 inch cubes. Combine the spices, honey, mustard, garlic and vinegar. Stir in the lamb and leave to marinate for 1-2 hours. Put the peppers and onions in a casserole and cook on HIGH for 2 minutes. Stir in the lamb, marinade, pineapple and juice, mushrooms and stock. Cover and cook on HIGH for 10 minutes then reduce setting and cook on MEDIUM for 20 minutes until the lamb is tender. Mix the cornstarch and water and stir into the casserole. Cook, uncovered, on HIGH for 3-4 minutes, stirring once until the sauce is thickened. Garnish with green onion brushes.

Pork with Spiced Pears

PREPARATION TIME: 10 minutes

MICROWAVE COOKING TIME:
20-25 minutes

SERVES: 4 people

4 8oz pork chops
1 tbsp oil
1 medium onion, peeled and finely chopped
1 small clove garlic, peeled and crushed
Pinch ground cinnamon
Pinch ground cloves
Pinch ground cardamom
¼ tsp ground ginger
½ cup dry cider
2-3 firm pears, peeled, cored and sliced

1 tbsp cornstarch
3 tbsps water
Salt
White pepper

Put the oil in a small dish, add the onions and garlic, and cook on HIGH for 2 minutes. Stir in the spices and cook on HIGH for 1 minute. Add the cider and the pears, mix well, cover and cook on HIGH for 8-10 minutes until the pears are soft, stirring occasionally. Mix the cornstarch with the water and add to the pears. Cook on HIGH for 2 minutes, stirring once, until thickened. Season with salt and pepper and keep warm. Arrange the chops in a circle in a shallow dish, cover and cook on HIGH for 10 minutes or until cooked, turning over and re-arranging halfway through the cooking time. Arrange the chops on a serving dish and pour the sauce over. Cook on HIGH for 1-2 minutes to reheat the sauce, if necessary.

Saffron Chicken Avocados

PREPARATION TIME: 15 minutes

MICROWAVE COOKING TIME:
6-10 minutes

SERVES: 4 people

½ cup natural yogurt
Few strands saffron
2 chicken breast fillets, cut into slivers
2 tsps celery seeds
Salt
Ground white pepper

Facing page: Sweet and Spicy Lamb.

2 avocado pears
Lemon juice
2 sticks celery, chopped
½ cup brown breadcrumbs
½ cup grated Parmesan cheese

Mix the yogurt and saffron together and set aside. Put the chicken in a bowl with the celery seeds, salt and pepper. Cover and cook on HIGH for 3-5 minutes until the chicken is cooked, stirring once. Cut the avocados in half and remove the stones. Scoop out the flesh, leaving ¼ inch lining inside the shell; sprinkle the scooped-out shell with lemon juice. Chop the flesh and add to the chicken. Stir in the celery and yogurt, and pile back into the shells. Mix the breadcrumbs and the cheese together and sprinkle over the top. Arrange in a circle in the microwave and cook, uncovered, on HIGH for 3-5 minutes until hot. Brown under a broiler if desired. To serve as an appetizer, omit the breadcrumb topping and serve cold.

Spiced Stroganoff

PREPARATION TIME: 15 minutes

MICROWAVE COOKING TIME: 7-11 minutes

SERVES: 4 people

1lb fillet steak
1 tbsp oil
1 large onion, peeled and sliced
1 small clove garlic, peeled and crushed
8oz mushrooms, sliced
1 tsp brown mustard seeds
1 tsp ground cumin
1 tsp ground coriander
3 tbsps dry white wine
Salt
Pepper
½ cup sour cream
½ cup natural yogurt mixed with 2 tsps cornstarch

Cut the meat into very thin strips and toss in the oil. Heat a large browning dish for the manufacturer's recommended time. Add the meat and stir. Add the onion and garlic and cook, uncovered, on HIGH for 2-4 minutes until the onions are soft and the meat is almost cooked. Stir in the mushrooms, spices, wine, salt and pepper, and cook, covered, on HIGH for 4-5 minutes. Stir in the cream, yogurt and cornflour, and cook, uncovered, on HIGH for 1-2 minutes to heat through, stirring once. Take care not to let the mixture boil once the cream is added. Serve on a bed of rice.

This page: Saffron Chicken Avocados. Facing page: Chicken in White Wine (top) and Pork with Spiced Pears (bottom).

Duck Breasts with Spicy Apple

PREPARATION TIME: 15 minutes

MICROWAVE COOKING TIME:
12-17 minutes

SERVES: 4 people

4 8oz duck breast fillets
8 juniper berries, crushed
1 tsp ground cumin
½ tsp ground cardamom
2 tbsps butter
1-2 green eating apples

Cut a slit horizontally in each of the duck breasts and set aside. Place the juniper berries, cumin, cardamom and butter in a small dish and cook, uncovered, on HIGH for 1-2 minutes, stirring once. Core the apples and cut into ¼ inch thick slices. Toss in the butter mixture and cook on HIGH for 1-2 minutes until the apples are just beginning to soften, but still hold their shape. Divide the apple slices between the duck and place into each slit. Arrange the duck breasts in a circle in a shallow dish. Cover and cook on HIGH for 10-15 minutes until the duck is cooked, turning and repositioning halfway through the cooking time if necessary. Serve with green vegetables or salad.

Goulash

PREPARATION TIME: 10 minutes

MICROWAVE COOKING TIME:
34-35 minutes

SERVES: 4 people

1lb fillet steak, cut into 1 inch cubes
1 tbsp oil
2 large onions, peeled and sliced
2 carrots, peeled and sliced
1 clove garlic, peeled and crushed
2 tsps paprika
1 tsp caraway seeds
Pinch cayenne pepper
2 tbsps flour

1½ cups hot beef stock
3 tbsps tomato paste
3 tbsps natural yogurt

Heat a browning dish for the manufacturer's recommended time. Toss the meat in the oil and, when the dish is hot, quickly add the meat. Stir and cook on HIGH for 1 minute. Add the onions, carrots and the garlic. Cook on HIGH for 3-4 minutes until soft. Stir in the spices and the flour and cook on HIGH for 1 minute. Stir in the stock and tomato paste. Cover and cook on HIGH for 10 minutes then reduce the setting and cook on LOW for 20 minutes or until the meat is tender. Stir in the yogurt just before serving.

This page: Duck Breasts with Spicy Apple. Facing page: Goulash (top) and Spiced Stroganoff (bottom).

Spiced Meat Loaf

PREPARATION TIME: 5 minutes

MICROWAVE COOKING TIME:
25-30 minutes plus 5 minutes
standing time

SERVES: 6-8 people

8oz lean ground lamb
8oz lean ground pork
1 cup whole-wheat breadcrumbs
1 egg
½ cup desiccated coconut
4 tomatoes, skinned and chopped
½ cup walnuts, chopped
½ tsp ground ginger
½ tsp ground cardamom
½ tsp ground coriander
Salt
Freshly ground black pepper
4½ tbsps milk

Put all the ingredients into a large
mixing bowl and blend thoroughly.
Put the mixture into a micro-proof
loaf dish. Cover loosely and cook on
MEDIUM for 25-30 minutes,
repositioning three times during
cooking. Leave to stand 5 minutes
before turning out. Serve hot or cold.

Cheese and Nut Burgers

PREPARATION TIME: 15 minutes

MICROWAVE COOKING TIME:
6 minutes plus 1 minute
standing time

SERVES: 4 people

8oz ground beef
8oz ground pork
Salt
Pepper
Pinch cayenne pepper
2oz Cheddar cheese
1 tsp caraway seeds
¼ cup hazelnuts, chopped

Mix the beef and pork with the salt,
pepper and cayenne in a mixing bowl.
Shape into 8 flattened rounds, about
4 inches in diameter. Mix the cheese,
caraway seeds and nuts together and
place in the center of 4 of the rounds.
Top with the remaining rounds and
press the edges together well to seal-
in the filling. Arrange in a circle on a
dish lined with absorbent kitchen
paper and cook on HIGH for 4
minutes. Turn over and cook for a
further 2 minutes. Leave to stand for
1 minute before serving. Serve with a
green salad or in hamburger buns.
These burgers can be cooked in a
pre-heated browning dish, if desired,
for 4-5 minutes, turning once.

Cod and Shrimp Bake

PREPARATION TIME: 10 minutes

MICROWAVE COOKING TIME:
9-13 minutes

SERVES: 4 people

1lb cod
2 bay leaves
6 pink peppercorns
1 small piece fresh ginger, peeled and
    grated
½ tsp ground mace
4½ tbsps white wine
4½ tbsps fish stock or water
2 tbsps butter
2 tbsps flour
½ cup milk
6oz shrimp
½ cup salt and vinegar flavored potato
    chips, crushed

Cut the cod into 1 inch pieces and
place in a shallow dish. Add the bay
leaves, peppercorns, ginger, mace,
wine and stock/water. Cover and
cook on HIGH for 4 minutes until
the fish is almost cooked. Cover and
set aside. Put the butter in a small
bowl and cook on HIGH for 30
seconds to melt. Add the flour and
cook on HIGH for 30 seconds. Add
the fish cooking liquor and the milk,
and cook on HIGH for 2-4 minutes,
whisking every minute until
thickened. Add the shrimp, pour the
sauce over the cod and cook on
HIGH for 2-4 minutes until the
sauce is hot and the fish is fully
cooked. Sprinkle with the crushed
chips.

Salade au Fruits de Mer

PREPARATION TIME: 10 minutes
plus chilling

MICROWAVE COOKING TIME:
6-10 minutes

SERVES: 6 people

8 scallops with roes attached
4 tbsps water
Squeeze lemon juice
6oz monkfish, cubed
4oz shrimp
4oz mussels
4oz langoustines

DRESSING
4oz curd cheese
1-2 tbsps milk
4½ tbsps natural yogurt
Salt
Ground white pepper
Juice of ½ lemon
1 tsp Dijon mustard
1 tsp chili powder
Pinch cayenne pepper

Cut the scallops in half, horizontally,
and place with the monkfish, water
and lemon juice in a large bowl.
Cover and cook on MEDIUM for
5-8 minutes. Stir in the remaining
shellfish and cook on HIGH for 1-2
minutes. Leave to cool in the liquid,
then drain well. Blend the cheese,
milk and yogurt together in a food
processor or blender, add the lemon
juice, salt and pepper, and stir in the
mustard and spices. Toss the seafood
in the dressing to serve.

**Facing page: Cheese and Nut
Burgers (top) and Spiced Meat Loaf
(bottom).**

Creamy Shrimp Flan

PREPARATION TIME: 15 minutes

MICROWAVE COOKING TIME: 9-12 minutes

SERVES: 4 people

1 cup whole-wheat flour
Salt
4 tbsps margarine
2-3 tbsps water
2 tbsps butter
2 tbsps flour
½ cup milk
2 tbsps dry white wine
6 tbsps full fat cream cheese
8oz shrimp
½ tsp paprika
Pinch cayenne pepper
½ tsp curry powder
Freshly ground black pepper
2 tbsps Parmesan cheese

GARNISH
Chopped parsley

Put the flour, salt and margarine into a mixing bowl and rub in the fat until the mixture resembles fine breadcrumbs. Gradually add the water and mix to form a soft dough. Roll out the pastry and line an 8 inch flan dish. Prick the base with a fork and cook, uncovered, on HIGH for 2-4 minutes, turning during cooking. Put the butter in a small bowl and cook on HIGH for 45 seconds to melt. Add the flour, mix well and cook on HIGH for a further 1 minute. Add the milk, wine and cream cheese. Whisk, then cook on HIGH for 2-3 minutes until thickened, whisking occasionally. Add the remaining ingredients and mix well. Pour into the pastry case. Chill through to serve cold, or serve hot by cooking, uncovered, on HIGH for 3-4 minutes. Sprinkle with chopped parsley.

This page: Salade au Fruits de Mer. Facing page: Creamy Shrimp Flan (top) and Cod and Shrimp Bake (bottom).

Red Mullet en Papillote

PREPARATION TIME: 10 minutes

MICROWAVE COOKING TIME: 9-11 minutes

SERVES: 4 people

2 carrots, peeled and cut into matchsticks
Salt
3 tbsps water
¼ cup water chestnuts, cut into sticks
1 cup bean sprouts
Small piece lemon grass, peeled and chopped or 1 tsp grated lemon zest
2 tsps aniseed

1 tsp dill seeds
4 tbsps white wine
4 red mullet, cleaned
1 tbsp butter
Ground white pepper

Put the carrots, salt and water in a bowl and cook on HIGH for 2 minutes. Add the water chestnuts and cook on HIGH for 1 minute. Stir in the bean sprouts, lemon grass or lemon zest, aniseed, dill seeds and wine. Place each fish on a piece of non-stick baking parchment or wax paper. Divide the vegetables between the four fish and pour over the

liquid. Season with pepper, dot with the butter and wrap each parcel separately, ensuring that each fish is totally enclosed. Place in the microwave and cook on HIGH for 6-8 minutes until the fish is cooked, repositioning halfway through cooking time. Serve the fish in their parcels.

Mackerel with Ginger and Lime

PREPARATION TIME: 5 minutes

MICROWAVE COOKING TIME: 6-8 minutes

SERVES: 4 people

4 small mackerel, cleaned and trimmed
½ cup fish stock or water
2 tsps freshly grated ginger
Juice and grated zest of 1 lime

GARNISH
Lime slices
Parsley

Arrange the mackerel head to tail in a shallow dish. Mix the remaining ingredients together and pour over the fish. Cover and cook on HIGH for 6-8 minutes or until the fish is cooked. Carefully transfer the fish to a serving dish and serve garnished with lime slices and parsley.

Curried Fish

PREPARATION TIME: 15 minutes

MICROWAVE COOKING TIME: 11-15 minutes

SERVES: 4 people

1lb monkfish
1 tbsp oil
1 tbsp curry powder
2 tsps garam masala
½ tsp ground ginger
6 green onions, sliced

1-2 small turnips, peeled and diced
4 tomatoes, skinned and chopped
8oz sweet potato, peeled and cubed
½ cup natural yogurt
½ cup cashew nuts

Cut the fish into 1 inch cubes and set aside. Put the oil and the spices in a casserole and cook on HIGH for 1 minute. Stir in the onions, turnip, tomatoes and sweet potatoes. Cover and cook on HIGH for 5-7 minutes until just tender. Add the fish and continue cooking on HIGH for 5-6 minutes until the fish and vegetables are cooked. Stir in the yogurt and cashews, cook on HIGH for 1-2 minutes until heated through, stirring once.

This page: Curried Fish. Facing page: Mackerel with Ginger and Lime (top) and Red Mullet en Papillote (bottom).

VEGETABLES, PASTA & GRAINS

Carrots with Cumin

PREPARATION TIME: 5 minutes

MICROWAVE COOKING TIME: 10-12 minutes

SERVES: 4 people

1lb carrots, peeled
4½ tbsps hot vegetable stock or water
2 tsps cumin
Salt
Freshly ground black pepper
1 tbsp butter
2 tsps chopped parsley

Cut the carrots into thin strips about 2-3 inches long, and place them in a casserole with the vegetable stock, cumin, salt and pepper. Cover and cook on HIGH for 10-12 minutes, stirring once. Stir in the butter and toss well. Serve sprinkled with parsley.

Festive Brussels Sprouts

PREPARATION TIME: 5 minutes

MICROWAVE COOKING TIME: 10 minutes

SERVES: 4 people

1lb Brussels sprouts
1¼ cups fresh chestnuts, roughly chopped
4 tbsps water
Salt
2 tbsps butter
½ tsp aniseed
Freshly ground black pepper

Remove outer leaves from the sprouts, if necessary, and cut a cross

in the bottom of each. Put the chestnuts in a casserole with the water and salt. Cover and cook on HIGH for 2 minutes. Add the sprouts, cover and cook for 7-8 minutes until tender, stirring once. Drain well. Put the butter in a small bowl and cook on HIGH for 30 seconds until melted. Stir in the aniseed and pepper. Pour the melted butter over the sprouts and toss to serve.
NB: To remove the chestnut shells,

This page: Green Beans with Mustard Sauce. Facing page: Festive Brussels Sprouts (top) and Carrots with Cumin (bottom).

cut a slit in the base of each chestnut and cook, a few at a time, on HIGH for 2-3 minutes then remove shells.

Cabbage with Caraway

PREPARATION TIME: 5 minutes

MICROWAVE COOKING TIME: 7 minutes

SERVES: 4 people

1lb green cabbage
4 tbsps water
Salt
2 tbsps butter
2 tbsps caraway seeds
Freshly ground black pepper

Finely shred the cabbage and place in a roasting bag with the salt and water. Tie loosely and cook on HIGH for 5-6 minutes until cooked but still slightly crisp. Drain well. Place the butter in a large bowl and cook on HIGH for 1 minute or until melted. Add the caraway seeds and pepper and stir well. Add the cooked cabbage and toss. Serve garnished with extra caraway seeds if desired.

Green Beans with Mustard Sauce

PREPARATION TIME: 15 minutes

MICROWAVE COOKING TIME: 9-12 minutes

SERVES: 4 people

1lb green beans
½ cup hot vegetable stock or water
Salt
Approx. ½ cup milk
2 tbsps butter
2 tbsps flour
1 tbsp dry mustard
Ground white pepper

Trim the green beans and cut into 2 inch lengths. Put the beans in a casserole with the vegetable stock or

Gingered Rutabaga

PREPARATION TIME: 10 minutes

MICROWAVE COOKING TIME: 11-17 minutes

SERVES: 4 people

1lb rutabaga, peeled
4 tbsps water
Salt
Freshly ground white pepper
1 tbsp butter
2 tbsps fresh ginger, peeled and grated

GARNISH
Fresh ginger, peeled and cut into thin strips

Cut the rutabaga into small pieces and place in a bowl with the water, salt and pepper. Loosely cover and cook on HIGH for 10-15 minutes or until tender, stirring twice. Drain well and mash thoroughly or purée in a food processor with the butter. Stir in the ginger. Reheat on HIGH for 1-2 minutes if necessary. Serve hot. Garnish with fresh ginger if desired.

This page: Spiced Couscous with Chicken and Shrimp. Facing page: Cabbage with Caraway (top) and Gingered Rutabaga (bottom).

water and salt. Cover and cook on HIGH for 6-8 minutes until just tender, stirring once. Drain, reserving the cooking liquor. Set the beans aside and keep warm. Make the liquor up to 1 cup with the milk. Put the butter into a bowl and cook on HIGH for 30 seconds or until melted. Add the flour, mustard powder and pepper and mix well. Cook on HIGH for 45 seconds. Add the milk and cooking liquor and mix well. Cook, uncovered, on HIGH for 1 minute. Cook a further 1-2 minutes until thickened slightly, whisking every 30 seconds. Serve the sauce poured over the beans.

Spiced Couscous with Chicken and Shrimp

PREPARATION TIME: 5 minutes

MICROWAVE COOKING TIME: 9-14 minutes

SERVES: 4 people

1½ cups couscous
1½ cups water
Pinch salt
1 tbsp oil
2 tsps ground coriander
2 tsps ground fenugreek
1 tsp ground cardamom
2 chicken breast fillets, cubed
3 green onions, sliced diagonally
4oz shrimp

GARNISH
Whole shrimp

Put the couscous, water and salt into a large bowl and leave to stand while cooking the chicken. Put the oil and spices into a bowl and cook, uncovered, on HIGH for 1 minute. Toss the chicken in the oil and spice mixture, cover and cook on HIGH for 3-5 minutes until the chicken is cooked. Add the chicken and onions to the couscous (which will have absorbed much of the water) and mix well. Cover and cook on HIGH for 5-8 minutes, stirring in the shrimp after 3 minutes. Fluff up with a fork

before serving. Garnish with whole shrimp.

Lasagne Blanc

PREPARATION TIME: 10 minutes

MICROWAVE COOKING TIME: 30-40 minutes

SERVES: 4 people

1 onion peeled and studded with 6 cloves
1 bay leaf
Pinch nutmeg
1 tsp mustard seeds
1½ cups milk
4oz mushrooms, sliced
4½ tbsps white wine
3 tbsps butter
3 tbsps flour
Salt
Ground white pepper
8oz ham, diced
¾ cup peas
4 tbsps heavy cream
6oz ready-to-use dried lasagne noodles
1 cup Cheddar cheese, grated

Put the onion, bayleaf, nutmeg and mustard seeds in the milk, cover and cook on HIGH for 3-5 minutes until just boiling. Leave to stand for 10 minutes. Meanwhile, put the mushrooms in a small bowl with the wine, cover and cook on HIGH for 4-5 minutes until soft. Put the butter in a bowl and cook on HIGH for 30 seconds-1 minute until melted. Stir in the flour and cook on HIGH for 45 seconds. Strain the milk and add with the wine. Whisk well. Cook, uncovered, on HIGH for 3-4 minutes until the sauce begins to thicken, whisking frequently. Season with salt and pepper, stir in the ham, peas, cooked mushrooms, and the cream. Arrange layers of sauce and lasagne in a microproof serving dish. Sprinkle the top with cheese and cook on MEDIUM for 20-25 minutes until the lasagne is fully cooked and the dish is heated through. Brown under the broiler if desired.

Spaghetti alla Bolognese

PREPARATION TIME: 10 minutes

MICROWAVE COOKING TIME: 40-50 minutes

SERVES: 4 people

8oz spaghetti
1 clove garlic, peeled and crushed
1 large onion, peeled and finely chopped
1 stick celery, finely chopped
½ tsp ground allspice
¼ tsp ground cardamom
8oz ground beef
1 14oz can tomatoes
Worcestershire sauce
4½ tbsps beef stock
Freshly ground black pepper
Salt
1 tbsp cornstarch
3 tbsps sherry
4 cups boiling, salted water
1 tbsp oil
Grated Parmesan cheese to serve

Put the oil, garlic, onion, celery, and spices in a large bowl. Cover and cook on HIGH for 3-4 minutes until soft. Add the meat and cook on HIGH for 5-6 minutes until it has changed color, breaking up with a fork once or twice during cooking. Add the tomatoes, Worcestershire sauce and stock, and season to taste with the salt and pepper. Cover and cook on LOW for 20 minutes until the meat is tender and the flavors well blended. Mix the cornstarch and sherry together and stir into the sauce. Cook on HIGH for 2-3 minutes until thickened slightly, stirring once. Cover, set aside and keep warm. Put the spaghetti and water in a large bowl, cover and cook on HIGH for 8-10 minutes. Drain and mix with the sauce. Reheat for 1-2 minutes if necessary. Sprinkle with Parmesan cheese to serve.

Facing page: Lasagne Blanc (top) and Spaghetti alla Bolognese (bottom).

Red Hot Slaw

PREPARATION TIME: 10 minutes

MICROWAVE COOKING TIME:
4 minutes

SERVES: 8 people

1lb red cabbage, shredded
2 red onions, peeled and finely sliced
1 small white radish, peeled and grated
4 tbsps mayonnaise
4 tbsps natural yogurt
2 tsps grated horseradish
½ tsp aniseed
½ tsp chili powder

Mix the cabbage, onion and radish together in a large bowl. Cook, uncovered, on HIGH for 4 minutes until the vegetables are hot, but not beginning to cook. Mix together the mayonnaise, yogurt, horseradish, aniseed and chili powder and stir into the hot vegetables.

Wild Rice Pilau

PREPARATION TIME: 5 minutes

MICROWAVE COOKING TIME:
14-17 minutes plus 5 minutes standing time

SERVES: 4 people

1 tbsp oil
Piece cassia bark
4 black cardamom pods, crushed
8 cloves
4 black peppercorns
Piece star anise
⅔ cup long grain rice
¼ cup wild rice
2 cups hot vegetable stock
4 tbsps dry white wine
¼ cup slivered almonds
¼ cup raisins

Put the oil and the spices in a casserole and cook on HIGH for 1 minute. Stir in the rice and cook on HIGH for a further 1 minute. Add the stock, wine, nuts and raisins. Cook, uncovered, on HIGH for 12-15 minutes or until most of the liquid has been absorbed. Stir the rice and quickly cover with a lid and leave to stand for 5 minutes before serving.

Spicy Egg Fried Rice

PREPARATION TIME: 5 minutes

MICROWAVE COOKING TIME:
5-9 minutes

SERVES: 4 people

1 tbsp oil
1 small green chili, seeded and finely
*   chopped (optional)*
Small piece root ginger, peeled and grated
4½ cups cooked rice
2 tbsps light soy sauce
2 eggs
½ tsp five spice powder

Put the oil, chili and ginger in a medium bowl and cook on HIGH for 1-2 minutes until soft. Add the rice and cook, uncovered, on HIGH for 2-4 minutes until the rice is hot. In a small dish, beat the soy sauce with the eggs and five spice powder, then add to the rice. Cook, uncovered, on HIGH for 2-3 minutes, stirring regularly until the egg is cooked.

This page: Red Hot Slaw. Facing page: Wild Rice Pilau (top) and Spicy Egg Fried Rice (bottom).

INDEX